NOVEL RELATIONS

Novel Relations

VICTORIAN FICTION AND BRITISH
PSYCHOANALYSIS

ALICIA MIRELES CHRISTOFF

PRINCETON UNIVERSITY PRESS
PRINCETON & OXFORD

Copyright © 2019 by Princeton University Press

Published by Princeton University Press
41 William Street, Princeton, New Jersey 08540
6 Oxford Street, Woodstock, Oxfordshire OX20 1TR

press.princeton.edu

All Rights Reserved

Library of Congress Control Number: 2019937991
First paperback printing, 2022
Paperback ISBN 978-0-691-23459-5
Cloth ISBN 978-0-691-19310-6
eISBN 978-0-691-19420-2

British Library Cataloging-in-Publication Data is available

Editorial: Anne Savarese and Jenny Tan
Production Editorial: Jenny Wolkowicki
Production: Merli Guerra and Brigid Ackerman
Publicity: Alyssa Sanford and Katie Lewis
Copyeditor: Maia Vaswani

Cover art: Henry Joseph Redouté, "Star Glory, Morning Glory," 1827.

This book has been composed in Arno Pro

For my father,
Thomas Alan Christoff,
1952–2000

CONTENTS

Acknowledgments ix
Texts and Abbreviations xi

Introduction   1

1   Loneliness (*Tess of the D'Urbervilles*, Winnicott, Bollas)   22

2   Wishfulness (*The Mill on the Floss*, Bion, Phillips, Feminist and Queer of Color Critique)   46

3   Restlessness (*The Return of the Native*, Balint, "Colonial Object Relations")   108

4   Aliveness (*Middlemarch*, Joseph, Heimann, Ogden)   153

Coda   192

Notes 199
Bibliography 241
Index 261

ACKNOWLEDGMENTS

I DID NOT write this book alone. I am so grateful to all of the people, present and absent, who kept me company as I read and wrote, and who, by being with me, expanded exponentially what I was able to think and say. Enormous thanks to Marcelle Clements and Elaine Freedgood, who have been with me from the beginning, read every word, and taught me how to be a writer and teacher. Heartfelt thanks, too, to my dissertation advisors, Eduardo Cadava, Diana Fuss, Deborah Nord, and Michael Wood, who guided me through the earliest phases of this project and this career, and to the entire Princeton University English Department, especially Pat Guglielmi, Zahid Chaudhary, Meredith Martin, and Jeff Nunokawa. I am unbelievably lucky to have the institutional support of Amherst College, and so grateful to Julie Howland, Bette Kanner, and all of my colleagues in the English Department, who have believed in me and kept me learning. Thank you to the wonderful women in the Five College Victorianist writing group—Nellie Boucher, Suzanne Daly, Amy Martin, Cornelia Pearsall, and Lise Sanders—who have offered keen readings and steadfast support. Thanks to a yearlong fellowship with the American Psychoanalytic Association in 2010–11, I was able to take coursework, that year and many to follow, at the Berkshire Psychoanalytic Institute; I learned so much from Robin Renders and from the analysts and practitioners who took her courses with me, and offer them heartfelt thanks. Thank you to my wonderful research assistant Molly Pines, and to all of my students who, so generously, see the best in me. Sincere thanks to Anne Savarese, Jenny Tan, Maia Vaswani, Jenny Wolkowicki, Chris Ferrante, and the entire team at Princeton University Press who have done so much to make *Novel Relations* a real book. I am so grateful to the many beloved friends, family members, colleagues, mentors, readers, and advocates whose support has also helped bring this book into being: Scott Branson from the start, Jen Acker, Thomas Albrecht, Veronica Alfano, David Beckman, Naomi Beeman, Marissa Branson, Aviva Briefel, Adrienne Brown, Seb Caswell, Bill Cohen, Kara Dupuy, Renée Fox, Judy Frank, Rachel Galvin, Danny Hack, Anna Henchman, Jacob Hovind, Kelly Hurley, Anna Kornbluh, Grace Lavery, Wendy Ann Lee, Allen MacDuffie, Andrew Miller, Nasser Mufti, Sara Muller-Ravett, Ingrid Nelson, Andy Parker, Christina Parker, Zakir Paul, Adela Pinch, Pooja Rangan,

Lindsay Reckson, Curran Reynolds, Missy Roser and the entire Frost Library staff, Zach Samalin, Ellen Smith, Sonali Thakkar, Amy Whittier, Amanda Irwin Wilkins, Amelia Worsley, Danny Wright, and Geoff Sanborn, who made this project feel possible at crucial moments. I talked over every single one of these ideas, albeit in different form, with Jim Edmonstone, who made them sharper and more livable: thank you. I want to send special thanks as well to Lisa Brooks, Ronjaunee Chatterjee, Rhonda Cobham-Sander, Sergio Delgado Moya, Yomaira Figueroa, Leigh-Anne Francis, the late Manuel Matos, Luis Othoniel Rosa, Marisa Parham, Amy Wong, and my dear friends and utterly indispensable readers Sonya Posmentier and Anjuli Raza Kolb for helping me envision who I would most like to be as a Xicana scholar. I did not really know friendship until I met Jocelyn Peck Henin. She, Brook Frye, and Nina Griecci Woodsum hold me steady. I did know sisterhood: thanks to Diana Quinn Inlak'ech and Maria Christoff, and to our unbelievably strong mother, Judith Ann Mireles Christoff, for literally everything. Thanks to Adam Hinds, for the future.

A version of chapter 1 appeared in *NOVEL: A Forum on Fiction* 48, no. 1 (2015): 18–44, and it is reproduced here by permission of Duke University Press. Parts of chapter 4 are drawn, in modified form, from an earlier publication, "The Weariness of the Victorian Novel: *Middlemarch* and the Medium of Feeling," in "Genre and Affect," ed. Kelly Hurley, special issue, *English Language Notes* 48, no. 1 (2010): 139–54.

TEXTS AND ABBREVIATIONS

FREQUENTLY CITED TEXTS will be referenced parenthetically throughout, using the following abbreviations:

George Eliot

- DD *Daniel Deronda.* Edited with an introduction and notes by Terence Cave. New York: Penguin Books, 1995.
- M *Middlemarch.* Edited with an introduction and notes by Rosemary Ashton. Penguin Classics. London: Penguin Books, 2003.
- MF *The Mill on the Floss.* Penguin Classics. New York: Penguin Books, 2003.

Thomas Hardy

- J *Jude the Obscure.* Edited by Dennis Taylor. Penguin Classics. New York: Penguin Books, 1998.
- RN *The Return of the Native.* Edited by Tony Slade. Penguin Classics. London: Penguin Books, 1999.
- T *Tess of the D'Urbervilles.* Edited by Tim Dolin. Penguin Classics. New York: Penguin Books, 2003.

Michael Balint

- BF *The Basic Fault: Therapeutic Aspects of Regression.* New York: Tavistock, 1979.

W. R. Bion

A&I	*Attention and Interpretation.* New York: Karnac Books, 1984.
ARROGANCE	"On Arrogance." In *Second Thoughts: Selected Papers on Psychoanalysis*, 86–92. London: Routledge, 1984.
ATTACKS	"Attacks on Linking." In *Second Thoughts*, 93–109.
E	*Elements of Psychoanalysis.* New York: Karnac Books, 1984.
GROUPS	*Experiences in Groups and Other Papers.* London: Routledge, 1968.
TR	*Transformations.* New York: Karnac Books, 1984.
THINKING	"A Theory of Thinking." In *Second Thoughts*, 110–19.

NOVEL RELATIONS

Introduction

THE TWENTIETH-CENTURY psychoanalyst W. R. Bion argues that "the only true thought is one that has never found an individual to 'contain' it."[1] It cannot be contained by one person because, for Bion, thought is something that happens between two or more people—and so is feeling. In his strange, provocative, and often mystically inflected psychoanalytic writing, Bion uses the symbol "O" to designate the "truth" of any experience that transpires between two people: uncontainable and unknowable by either one of them alone, it resides somewhere between them, in the space where each person overflows into the other. In George Eliot's novel *The Mill on the Floss*, written one hundred years before, the O of such self-exceeding contact is marked by vibrations: chords struck on the piano, erotic energy that charges the air between Maggie Tulliver and Stephen Guest, the "low voice" that seems to emanate from the pages of Maggie's favorite book. Two things—two piano strings that sounded together make an octave, two voices harmonizing, two people in love, two people in dialogue in the psychoanalytic session, two writers speaking to each other across a century—resonate together in a way that brings out capacities of thought and feeling that neither could hold alone. *Novel Relations* begins from this insight to argue that we never read or write alone.

In Victorian studies, keeping pace with movements in contemporary critical thought, we say that we believe in relationality: in our profound interdependence with other people and their labor, in our inextricable connections to the natural world, in our merger with our technologies, and in our ongoing relations with our ancestors, who shape us and future generations. And yet I think these ideas are much easier to grasp intellectually than to really believe. Most of us continue to act, in our daily living and interacting and in our scholarship and daily institutional and pedagogical practice, from a place of deeply conditioned individualist assumption. We think we are reading and writing alone.[2]

Novel Relations tries for a deeper faith in relationality in the small but expansive sphere of novel reading. It shows how some aspects of our reading experience and critical practice might change if we actually believe in the forms of relationality that novels propose and effect. In Victorian novel studies (itself the matrix for some of the most important methodological and theoretical interventions in literary studies in the last few decades),[3] our work has to some extent resisted relationality—perhaps inevitably, and perhaps without our knowing. We have insisted on firm divides between characters, narrators, readers, and authors rather than theorizing their interrelation.[4] We have for the most part confined Victorian novels, geographically and temporally, to the single historical context of their scenes of production. We have insisted that Victorian novels should be read only with one another or their direct predecessors, and not with twentieth- or twenty-first-century narratives from across the globe.[5] And we have kept their impact to the printed page, not acknowledging how strongly novels—and novelistic form, in the particular argument of this book—shape both psyches and theories of the psyche, from the nineteenth century into the present day.

My book centers on four Victorian novels, two each by George Eliot and Thomas Hardy—two writers who have set the fundamental terms for contemporary critical conceptualizations of late nineteenth-century realism (Eliot and Hardy simultaneously insist on and problematize the notion of a steady reflection between representational and real worlds), domestic fiction (both writers at once emphasize and trouble the novel's reliance on the personal, the local, and romance, marriage, and family), and the psychological novel (both writers' works demonstrate an abiding interest in character and readerly interiority and in making overarching claims about social and psychic life).[6] I am particularly interested in the practices of narration and characterization deployed by Eliot and Hardy, which I think are more fruitfully uneven and unintegrated than retrospective accounts that place these writers in a realist tradition have tended to imagine.[7] *Novel Relations* reveals some of the ways in which the profound relationality of novel reading has been foreclosed and how we might open it back up for ourselves. My claim is that we have experienced this relationality even when we have not managed to reflect it in our literary criticism, scholarship, and novel theory. In an effort to draw out the relationality of these novels, I place them in conversation with a key theoretical discourse: British psychoanalysis, whose mid-twentieth-century theorists and practitioners developed "object relations" theory by building from the foundational writings of Sigmund Freud and Melanie Klein.[8]

Object Relations

The guiding insight of object relations psychoanalysis is that our psyches are built of internalized representations of other people—the objects of our love, need, desire, and affection, of our envy and our gratitude, of our hate, rage, resentment, and ambivalence, and, always, the objects of our active fantasy.[9] The world of social relations outside of us is reflected and mediated by a world of object relations within us, an "inner world" in which "every past or present relation either in thought or deed with any loved or hated person still exists and is still being carried on."[10] Joan Riviere's formulation is striking in its reach: every single relation to another, past or present, real or imaginary, in thought or deed, with every single person, loved or hated, still exists and is actively being conducted inside of us. It is like when the sustain pedal of a piano has been depressed: inside the body, the dampers are lifted and each string goes on vibrating long after the key is released. Except that in the inner world, those strings never stop vibrating and their sounds never die out.

In the imagination of Riviere and other post-Kleinian theorists, the inner world is densely populated, and is so from the start: beginning from the internalization of representations of our earliest caregivers, object relations do not simply infiltrate the psyche, they shape it. For these thinkers, the subject is a record of its object relations. A key intervention of *Novel Relations* is to add fictional characters to that population count. In *Tess of the D'Urbervilles* (1891), Hardy's title character reflects that she is not "an existence, an experience, a passion, a structure of sensations" to anyone but herself (*T* 91). But I think she becomes "an existence" and "an experience" to us too. Any one of us who has read *Tess* has a relation to her (and to Hardy's narrator) that is "still being carried on" in our psyches long after we have set aside the book.

Psychoanalysis has long been central to literary studies. And yet literary and cultural criticism has not kept pace with psychoanalysis itself, which displays a striking intellectual vitality in our present moment. While much existing psychoanalytic criticism relies exclusively on Freudian theory and its extensions in French thought (in the work of Jacques Lacan in particular, along with Julia Kristeva, Jean Laplanche, and André Green to a lesser extent), *Novel Relations* opens up an immensely generative archive for literary analysis by turning instead to post-Freudian British psychoanalysis. Specifically, I look to the generation of thinkers that came immediately after Melanie Klein and who developed, in several fascinating and sometimes conflicting directions, her abiding interest in object relations. Klein in turn reworked this strand of thought from Freud, drawing in particular from his work on mourning and melancholia and super-ego formations. The primary twentieth-century figures I engage are Donald W. Winnicott, Wilfred Bion, Michael Balint, Paula Heimann, Betty Joseph, and Masud Khan. And I look, too, to contemporary psychoanalysts and writers—especially Christopher Bollas, Thomas Ogden, Adam Phillips, Michael Eigen, Lucy LaFarge, and Edna O'Shaughnessy—who are bringing British object relations thought into the present day in eclectic and often surprisingly literary ways. Mid-century British theorists are beginning to gain visibility in both popular culture and academic scholarship.[11] In literary studies, Mary Jacobus and Eve Kosofsky Sedgwick, two scholars I greatly admire and engage with throughout this book, have written especially compelling work on British object relations thinkers, contributing to their popularity and the accessibility of their ideas.[12] And yet there has been no extended study of the connections between Victorian fiction and object relations thought.[13] *Novel Relations* sounds how deeply these connecting currents run. Object relations psychoanalysis allows us to read Victorian novels in new ways. And, just as crucially, it allows us to re-theorize how we read, in terms of both ordinary experience and literary critical practice. The intuition that founds this book includes a turn in the other direction as well: Victorian novels shape psyches and psychoanalytic theories in more interesting and thoroughgoing ways than we have previously understood.

The distinctive insights of British psychoanalysis, as they are taken up in this book, include the following:

A picture of subjectivity as always and essentially relational

The insight that it takes at least two people to think and to feel

Belief in, and reliance on, the seemingly supernatural fact of unconscious communication

Watching how group dynamics take on a (psychotic) life of their own

Trust in the natural unfurling of maturational processes and the environments that make those unfurlings possible

Respect for dependence and merger

An emphasis on first objects

Careful attention to the ongoing cycles of introjection and projection that make us who we are, and a focused elaboration of projective identification in particular

Noticing how readily and unconsciously we enter into one another's psychic dramas and fantasies, which never stay contained in the inner world alone

The understanding that interpersonal relations are enacted as much by atmosphere as by language

Listening for tone of voice, and tone of feeling, in the consulting room

Re-theorizing transference and countertransference dynamics

An emphasis on affect over instinct, health over symptom, quiet moments of going-on-being over spectacular demonstrations of drive, and the primacy of objects in shaping our needs and desires (rather than merely satisfying them)

A profound interest in describing the ineffable, the subtle, and the ordinary.

Relational Reading

A central claim of this book is that engaging with psychoanalytic theory beyond the usual suspects—Freud, Lacan, and Klein—engaged by literary and cultural criticism yields not only different readings of long-familiar novels, but also different *ways* of reading. Using the revisionary insights of British object relations thought means taking them seriously at the level of methodology as well as concept. Accordingly, *Novel Relations* is organized around "relational readings" that place Victorian novels and key works in object relations psychoanalysis side by side.[14] My goal is not to "apply" psychoanalytic ideas to novels nor to make a one-way historical argument that proves that the novels had a direct impact on later psychoanalytic theory. Instead, I want to allow the novels and the psychoanalytic texts to mutually illuminate one another. Relational reading allows me to attend to both the theory in Victorian fiction (psychological, relational, sociopolitical, and affective) and the literary in psychoanalytic theory without reducing one to the other. The analysts that I focus on are skilled and compelling writers in their own right. And perhaps unsurprisingly, several of the present-day practitioners I cite and think with in the book double as writers—literary essayists or prolific authors of psychoanalytic articles—and are frequently invested in literary analysis. (For example, Adam Phillips is a popular essayist, Christopher Bollas received his PhD in English and wrote a dissertation on Melville, and Thomas Ogden has written a series of papers that perform explicitly literary readings of foundational psychoanalytic texts.)[15] There is in fact a rich overlap between contemporary psychoanalytic writing and literary studies that merits further attention.

Relational reading requires deep immersion in both psychoanalytic and literary texts. And it requires a certain kind of belief or faith in relationality: that reading two texts together really does render something unprecedented and meaningful. To explain this, let me return to Bion's concept of O, the powerful but ineffable reality of the in-the-moment meeting of two (or more) people. W. R. Bion (1897–1979), a central thinker in the British school, was born in colonial India to English parents and educated in England. He was a tank officer in World War I and military psychologist in World War II. He was also, briefly, the therapist of Samuel Beckett.[16] Initially closely aligned with Klein, Bion later made major and far-reaching revisions to her theory. He is perhaps most famous for his work with groups and with psychotic patients. There, Bion argues that in any situation that includes two or more people, a "matrix of thought" evolves that is shared between the group members, but irreducible to any single subjectivity. *Novel Relations* argues that this picture of shared thought, affect, and psychic experience usefully illuminates the act of novel reading, with its own multiplicity of literary figures and subjectivities: reader, character, author, and narrator, and the space that "vibrates," as Eliot pictures it in *The Mill on the Floss*, around and between them.

The method of *Novel Relations* is to seek out something like the "O" of contact between Victorian novels and psychoanalytic texts. I argue that reading them together enlivens both, showing us what sings out for us in both the novel and the theory that we could not hear without bringing them into communication. My intention is to offer sustained literary readings, close and inquisitive, of both the fictional and theoretical texts I treat, and to experiment with methods for bringing the texts together. I hope my readings are both careful enough to stay faithful to the unique texture and specificity of each (rather than forcing the fictional and psychoanalytic texts to say or mean the same thing), and sensitive enough to capture the vibratory energy that, as Bion and Eliot insist, really does emanate from the striking together of two texts, like the prongs of a tuning fork set ringing.

Bion shares with the larger group of British psychoanalysts an abiding interest in reconceptualizing what takes place between two people in the psychoanalytic session and how it feels. Thinkers like Winnicott, Bion, Heimann, and Joseph form new ideas about the tasks of psychoanalysis and the mechanisms of psychic change. In particular, they update and refine standard conceptions of transference and countertransference dynamics, offering instead extended theories of projective identification, holding, containing, and moment-to-moment interpretation (all of which I explain in greater detail in this book's pages). *Novel Relations* shows how these feelings and phenomena of shared experience are reproduced at the site of reading—and, indeed, may have originated there.

The relational readings in this book take time to unfold. My chapters are fairly long, especially chapter 2, which describes psychic and novelistic overflow along with a river's flooding. And the order of the chapters is somewhat unconventional, in that the book does not move through the novels chronologically. Instead, I have arranged the chapters so that the book offers a systematic introduction (or, for readers already familiar with it, a deeper immersion) into British object relations thought, and into what I perceive to be its possibilities as and for literary theory, particularly studies of the novel. Each chapter introduces a new psychoanalytic thinker or concern, providing enough explication to make their ideas accessible to nonspecialists and enough quotation to make their particular writing styles come alive as well. Each chapter also treats a single novel with a similar degree of attention and granularity. Doing these things takes time and space but is essential to the project of this book. I am trying to evoke not only the content but also the *feel* of each side of the textual pairing: the author's style, the text's preoccupations, its form and textures. The chapters interweave psychoanalytic material and the novel in question, letting the texts read each other, as it were. I am as interested in the process of staging these relations as I am in the result. I want the chapters to read somewhat essayistically, and to say and do things that exceed what any introduction could preview or chapter summary could recapitulate. I want to create what Bion calls "the O of the experience of reading" these chapters (*A&I* 28).

I have devised the pairings and constellations of novels and psychoanalytic theory by following intuitions about special fit: about the shared concerns—thematic and formal, intersubjective and literary—of the texts I bring together. *Tess* and Winnicott (chapter 1) are both concerned with how we learn to feel alone—that is to say, alone and sustained, rather than alone and persecuted, lost, adrift, untethered. *The Mill on the Floss* and Bion (chapter 2) both care about sympathy and render it as at once paramystical and real: as a kind of unconscious communication. *The Return of the Native* and Balint (chapter 3) both investigate how spaces are never simply themselves but instead are repeatedly figured through metaphor and allusion and atmospherically charged—with feeling, with racial politics, and with overlapping imperial geographies. *Middlemarch* and Joseph and Heimann (chapter 4) are concerned with how we fend off feelings of weariness in order to make the world, our closest relationships, and our long novels feel ardent, energized, and alive.

Mosses, Lichens, Touchstones

Before saying more about the book's hoped-for contributions to Victorian, psychoanalytic, and novel studies, I want to offer a short example of the kind of relational reading that drives *Novel Relations*, highlighting from the start some of the book's interests and methodologies. D. W. Winnicott once famously and provocatively argued that there is no such thing as a baby: "If you show me a baby you certainly show me also someone caring for a baby."[17] First objects are preeminently important for British School psychoanalysts, who focused on the role of mothers and other primary caregivers in unprecedented ways. They highlighted what they saw as underrecognized realities of human existence, especially the fundamental facts of early dependence and merger. Winnicott (1896–1971) was a pediatrician, a child psychoanalyst, a hospital worker, and a group-home consultant. These experiences put him into contact with thousands of babies, mothers, and families. In his paradigm-shifting reconceptualization of infancy, he argues that babies are merged with their mothers not only in the womb, but for many months after birth. Physical and psychological independence is not an existential baseline, but is instead slowly gained over time, making separation not a primary fact but rather a maturational achievement.

Repurposing Winnicott's phrase, I want to say: There is no such thing as a book. If you show me a book you certainly show me also someone reading that book—and, specifically, someone actively dreaming up and creating the book alongside the writer.[18]

In what is probably his best-known essay, "Transitional Objects and Transitional Phenomena," originally presented in 1951 and expanded over the next decades, Winnicott makes an argument for the value of "creative living"—for experience infused with a sense of vitality, of reality rather than futility, because it inhabits a "transitional" area between the subjective life of fantasy and the objective life of external reality. In retrospect it seems surprising that it hadn't been addressed, but Winnicott was the first theorist to recognize and make something of the fact that many children have a special object they interact with in their infancy and early childhood: a blanket, a doll, a stuffed animal that they carry around with them and to which they grow extremely attached. Winnicott notices that these so-called transitional objects are animated with a special kind of life for the child, emanating from the glint of a marble eye or the warmth of cotton batting. This real physical object is dreamed into new vitality and animated existence by the child's capacity for fantasy. It provides comfort not only because it is soft and soothing, but because it gives the child a break from the growing need to separate out fantasy and reality, subjective and objective perception, "me" from "not-me." The transitional object sits somewhere just between these categories, and even adults agree not to throw this into question for the child: Winnicott writes that it is a "matter of agreement" between the parent and the child that the parent will never ask, "did you find this object in the external world, or did you dream it up yourself?"[19] Transitional objects are significant for Winnicott because they provide something that we will need throughout our lives: a space and mode to recur to when the "strain" of being firmly bordered is eased, a "resting-place for the individual engaged in the perpetual human task of keeping inner and outer reality separate yet interrelated."[20] Winnicott argues that transitional experience is the basis for all later cultural experience: from thumb-sucking and soft toys and singing oneself to sleep, the "resting-place" of transitional experience grows with the child, "spreading out" out and becoming "diffused" over "the whole cultural field," including "the intense experiencing that belongs to the arts and religion and to imaginative living, and to creative scientific work."[21]

Hardy too believes in the resting-place provided by aesthetic experience. In his essay "The Profitable Reading of Fiction" (1888), which predates Winnicott's paper by about sixty years, Hardy describes novel reading as itself a kind of transitional experience. Reading, Hardy writes, provides "relaxation and relief when the mind is overstrained or sick of itself." And yet, Hardy writes, reading requires creative labor too. Hardy's reader "wants to dream," and, indeed:

> The aim [of novel reading] should be the exercise of a generous imaginativeness, which shall find in a tale not only what was put there by the author, put he it never so awkwardly, but which shall find there what was never inserted by him, never foreseen, never contemplated. Sometimes these additions which are woven around a work of fiction by the intensive power of the reader's own imagination are the finest parts of the scenery.[22]

Hardy's reader is a maker: someone who shapes the text alongside the writer, someone who picks up the novel and adds to it, someone whose contributions just might form the most compelling part of the story.

In *The Return of the Native*, Charley, a young man long infatuated with the beautiful Eustacia Vye (and long resigned to the fact that she will never love him in return), looks after her devotedly when she returns to her uncle's house in despair following the breakup of her marriage to Clym Yeobright. Charley feeds her, soothes her, and locks away her uncle's pistols when he finds Eustacia gazing at them too long. And even more than this, Charley's gentle mode of caretaking comprehends her need for transitional experience. Assuming a "guardian's responsibility for her welfare,"

> he busily endeavored to provide her with pleasant distractions, bringing home curious objects which he found in the heath, such as white trumpet-shaped mosses, red-headed lichens, stone arrow-heads used by the old tribes of Egdon, and faceted crystals from the hollows of flints. These he deposited on the premises in such positions that she should see them as if by accident. (*RN* 330)

Charley, letting Eustacia stumble across these heath objects "as if by accident," does not ask, "Did I find that or did you?" "Did you find that, or did you create it?" And in this way, Charley's method of care could easily describe Hardy's own artistic practice: objects drawn from the natural world are left for readers to rediscover. Mosses and lichens, rocks and stones, the enticing objects in this list—half natural and half crafted, like the arrow-heads that lie just on the border of the organic and the man-made—are noticed and handled by Charley, noticed and handled by Eustacia, and in turn noticed and reimagined into their material shapes by the reader who comes across them deposited in the passage of a novel. For Eustacia, the curious objects found on the heath, the "white trumpet-shaped mosses" and "red-headed lichens" that are the rudiments of plant life as well as the rudiments of color and shape, are a place to rest her eyes and her mind, affording "relaxation and relief" to a mind "overstrained and sick of itself." And for the reader too, the objects are resting-places, in both Hardy's and Winnicott's senses of the term. Coming across them in the novel, we do not have to decide whether they belong to inner or outer reality, whether we found them or created them. The objects are indeed half perceived and half created, conjured up by our own "generous imaginativeness" wrapped around the words the author has left lying around.

Let these objects stand as touchstones: not only for reading as co-making, but also for the kinds of readings I am interested in pursuing in *Novel Relations*. I am less interested in the developmental claims of psychoanalytic thought than in their formal implications—that is to say, in the way British psychoanalysis imagines the structure of interpersonal relations, and in how this theory can in turn be used to reimagine the structure of literary relations. I am not interested in concrete applications or diagnostic readings, nor in tracing a character's development, in seeking out and assessing parent-infant relationships in novels, in saying who has a good-enough mother and who does not. I am wary, in other words, of psychoanalytic approaches that reduce, as Shoshana Felman has famously and importantly pointed out, the textuality of the text.[23] Symptom-finding and diagnosis-making approaches reduce two dimensions of textuality in which this book is particularly interested: the richness of fictionality (which, as I hope to show, spreads over the psychic as well as the literary realm) and the richness of our own reading experience—which this book attempts to render in all of its metaleptic discontinuity (chapter 1); its force of direct address, far-reaching resonance, and unwieldy futurity (chapter 2); its atmospheric power and microclimatological variability (chapter 3); and its narrative multivocality (chapter 4). *Novel Relations* wonders, and attempts to answer, in both the content and style of its writing: how do we keep this richness alive in our criticism and academic writing? Rather than attending to development as such, then, my readings focus on matters like the ones identified in the relational reading of *Return*'s lichens, mosses, and faceted crystals: on aesthetic experience, on the phenomenology of reading, on the capacities of the novel as a genre and their social and political implications, and, as I will go on to discuss, on the psychodynamics of our literary critical investments.[24]

The word "capacity" as the object relations thinkers deploy it (as in, for instance, Winnicott's essay on "The Capacity to Be Alone") has a double sense, pertaining both to ability, asking what a person is capable of, and to measure, asking what a person can contain, like a vase filled with water. Object relations theorists describe the unique capacities of psyches, highlighting what they can do and hold in health rather than focusing exclusively on their deficits and deficiencies in states of mental illness. Particular areas of interest for these analysts include the capacity for growth, the capacity to feel alive and real, the capacity to be creative, the capacity to hold others in mind in a way that sustains them and us, the capacity to experience unintegration, and the capacity to unconsciously dream more than can be directly interpreted and to feel beyond what can be conceptualized in language or in thought. And yet object relations theory is not some kind of positive psychology. British theorists are interested in less sunny or "friendly" (in Balint's phrase) capacities as well, including the capacity to feel empty, the capacity to hate reality, the capacity to attack links—the links between people, between ideas, or between words and their meanings—and one's own capacity to make links, and the capacity to feel what Winnicott names the "unthinkable anxieties" or "agonies" ("anxiety," he writes, "is not a strong enough word here"): falling to pieces, falling forever, having no orientation, feeling depersonalized or derealized, feeling unrelated to one's body, and feeling unable to relate to objects.[25] Building from these insights, *Novel Relations* looks to explore and describe the unique capacities of novels. What can they do? What can they hold? What can they create? What do they enable us to think and feel—and for that matter, what do they *disable* us from thinking and feeling?

The Geopolitics of British Psychoanalysis

Mid-twentieth-century London became a seedbed for psychoanalytic thought for geopolitical as well as intellectual reasons. Beginning in the 1930s, "Britain became home both to native psychoanalysts and to many Jewish refugees fleeing the Nazis and continental anti-Semitism," explains historian Michal Shapira. "Out of the once-flourishing psychoanalytic societies in Europe, only London remained as a real hub and a center for a unique intellectual diaspora."[26] Analysts from Vienna (home of the International Psychoanalytical Association, Freud, and his daughter Anna Freud), Berlin (where Karl Abraham had been a leading figure, and where Melanie Klein had trained but where her controversial ideas had garnered a mixed reception), and Budapest (home to Freud's influential contemporary Sándor Ferenczi and his trainees) converged in London at the British Psycho-Analytical Society (BPAS). The BPAS had been founded by Ernest Jones in 1913 and already comprised a thriving community, made up of psychoanalysts, medical practitioners, so-called "lay-analysts" (practitioners with psychoanalytic training but no previous medical experience), and Bloomsbury writers and intellectuals.[27] I want to take a moment to imagine how charged the atmosphere in London must have felt at that time: so many brilliant minds gathered together in a single place, pursuing psychoanalytic ideas with such a concentrated passion—and under the strain of such enormous fear and upheaval, and the pressure of so much hate and loss.

Relationships between the men and women now gathered together in the BPAS were hardly entirely pacific, especially following the death of Freud in 1939, when the society was ideologically split between the warring factions of the Viennese group (also known as the Anna Freudians) and the resident Kleinians (Klein had been living in London, where her ideas had been more enthusiastically received than in Berlin, since 1926). As debates rose to a heated pitch (and sometimes revolved around personality conflicts, private intrigues, and personal attacks) in the period 1941–45, giving rise to the so-called Controversial Discussions, bombs fell on London.[28] The blitzkrieg at "home" resounded in what was recognized as a "world" war of unprecedented scale and destructive force. Out of these discussions, and the settling dust of the conclusion of World War II in 1945, which brought with it efforts to redistribute imperial wealth and an upsurge of global decolonial struggle, grew not only a compromise in the BPAS (which developed three training and supervision tracks: Anna Freudian, Kleinian, and Independent), but a rich ferment of ideas, fundamentally transforming psychoanalytic theory and practice. In these years, and with the emergence of the "Independent" group in particular, psychoanalysis was given a distinctly "British" orientation and spin—distinct from classical Freudian technique, distinct from the ego psychology that became dominant (following the emigration of many German analysts) in the United States, and distinct from French theory.[29] The imbrication of psychoanalysis and modernist literature and culture, in England and on the Continent, is fascinating and has been well studied.[30] Equally significant, but less studied, is the impact of Victorian literature on psychoanalytic thought—and in particular, psychoanalytic thought as it developed and flourished in mid-twentieth-century Britain.

One of my aims is to show that this distinctive intellectual tradition is not located simply in England, but in the wider British Empire, even when this fact is not directly acknowledged. David Eng situates World War II, and the birth of psychoanalysis itself, within a longer history that includes the "string of colonial genocides in Africa, Asia, and the Americas" and "the Holocaust and its accelerated violence" to form the "racial century" of the years 1850–1950.[31] Part of what compels me to put Victorian novels (circa 1850) and object relations psychoanalysis (circa 1950) into conversation is the fact that they bookend this "racial century." It is not simply that British psychoanalysis and Victorian novels share concepts and areas of concern: subject formation, affect, interpersonal relations, the relationship between fantasy and reality, a focus on ordinary experience. More than this, these two moments and discourses are linked by the way they so clearly evoke the high-water marks of British colonization and decolonization—even in and through the ways both novels and psychoanalytic theory actively mute or avoid depicting that violence.

Indeed, I hope this can be one of the book's central interventions: to show that British psychoanalysis need not be only friendly, benign, and sealed off in the supposedly insular worlds of the nursery or the consulting room. Instead, object relations thought can have a very real purchase on the political sphere, even in and through these personalizing and interpersonalizing gestures and emphases—what we might call its insulating impulse. British psychoanalysis, with its emphasis on the infant, the self (including Winnicott's "True Self"), internalization, and diffuse states of being, can lend itself to being read and used apolitically. So can Victorian fiction, with its emphasis on the domestic (in both senses of the word: the home and national versus global politics), the local, the interpersonal, on romance, on marriage and the marriage plot, and on the psychological. And yet I want to insist that putting canonical nineteenth-century British domestic fiction and British object relations thought together can serve to amplify the geopolitical stakes of both. Relational reading can make more salient the fact that each of these discourses is located squarely—and indeed, actively participated—in the history of British Empire and the racially demarcating logic that subtended it, and that subtends global divisions of labor still.

The Hungarian British medical doctor and psychoanalyst Michael Balint (1896–1970) coined the term "the basic fault" to describe very early life disturbances in object relating and their subtle but significant aftereffects. In *Novel Relations*, I take up this term to describe the constitutive fault line in Victorian novel studies: the false disciplinary division that splits Victorian and postcolonial studies, and our tendency within the field of Victorian studies, narrowly drawn and construed, to ignore the colonial contexts in which Victorian fiction was produced and first received, and in which it continues to be received in the context of present-day neo-imperialism. In the context of a similar fault in psychoanalytic theory, I think of Anne McClintock's important clarification and call for scholarly reorientation in *Imperial Leather*, which bears repeating at length:

> All too often, psychoanalysis has been relegated to the (conventionally universal) realm of private, domestic space while politics and economics are relegated to the (conventionally historical) realm of the public market. I argue that the disciplinary quarantine of psychoanalysis from history was germane to imperial modernity itself. Instead of genuflecting to this separation and opting theoretically for one side or the other, I call for a renewed and transformed investigation into the disavowed relations between psychoanalysis and socio-economic history ... for it was precisely during the era of high imperialism that the disciplines of psychoanalysis and social history diverged.[32]

I hope that I answer to this call in these pages, following the "private, domestic" interests of British psychoanalysis—and of Victorian fiction—while also being attentive to the socioeconomic and imperial histories they inscribe *without explicitly formulating*.

The British psychoanalysts that I study in this book do not directly theorize empire, war, racial and ethnic difference, or racialized violence. And yet these matters touched many of their lives very deeply, in different colonial and expatriate contexts.[33] I think of Bion, born in colonial India, and well received in 1970s Brazil. I think of the Pakistani-British Masud Khan (1924–89), a student of Winnicott and an important figure in bridging the British and French psychoanalytic scenes, who was born in the Punjab, lived through Partition, and who theorized not imperial dislocation but rather the essential "privacy of the self."[34] I think of Balint himself, who was a World War I veteran of German Jewish descent who was forced to leave his native Hungary in 1939, and whose parents, still in Budapest, committed suicide to escape the concentration camps. I think of Paula Heimann (1899–1982), a German analyst of Russian Jewish descent who, threatened under Nazism, emigrated to England in 1933 with her daughter while her husband fled to Switzerland. I know of only one reference to her refugee status in all of her work, and it appears in the dream of one of her patients, who imagines that she is someone who has had a "rough passage" across the English Channel. Heimann's response is to resist the patient's fantasy that she is somehow damaged.[35]

So although these analysts and others in their circle were heavily impacted by the facts of British imperial practice and its aftermath, including especially its issue in struggles between European powers that led to World War II, their work almost never explicitly addresses these historical facts. However, what I want to argue here is that, despite immediate appearances, their theory embeds these facts in and as its very fabric: colonial and decolonial struggle form the material conditions of these texts' very production, reproduction, and reception. *Novel Relations* argues that British psychoanalytic theory, despite its elliptical treatment of these matters, contains ideas and methods that can be turned to productive account in the analysis of, one, the conditions of coloniality, postcoloniality, and racialization and, two, the effects of these conditions on the production of subjectivity and intersubjectivity as well as on *theories* of subjectivity and intersubjectivity. In my treatment of British psychoanalysis, I want, like McClintock, to refuse the "disciplinary quarantine of psychoanalysis from history" and instead to affirm the "disavowed relations" between British psychoanalysis and its "socio-economic history." And if "imperial modernity" (that is to say, modernity writ large) is made precisely by splitting metropole and periphery, the domestic and the political, the nation-state and the colony, psychoanalysis and social history, I want to show how central the Victorian novel is to the construction of this discursive split. The Victorian novel and British psychoanalysis have a special fit with each other, and this is not only due to their shared affective investments and views of a populated psyche, but also to their shared histories and complicities—avowed and disavowed alike. Indeed, the fact that both discourses treat British empire elliptically is part of what makes them such fitting interlocutors, bringing to life in each other something that has been eclipsed in each.

Linking

Reading object relations psychoanalysis well means addressing both its capacities and its incapacities. I believe that British psychoanalytic thought has the capacity to open many important questions (pertaining to literary form, reading experience, and political stakes alike) that have been foreclosed in mainstream critical responses to Victorian fiction. And yet I do not expect British psychoanalysis to be capable of all things. Bion argues that we attack the links between ideas when we cannot cognitively and emotionally bear the reality of their actual connection. Taking this insight seriously, *Novel Relations* offers an approach guided by object relations thought that ultimately takes British psychoanalysis beyond itself and looks to build wider relational networks for the Victorian novel. Theorizing issues like gender conscription and resistance, racialization, colonial and anticolonial engagements, and political futurity, I turn to thinkers and critics like Muriel Dimen, Jordy Rosenberg, José Esteban Muñoz, adrienne maree brown, Amador Fernández-Savater by way of Dora Zhang, Audre Lorde, bell hooks, Jodi A. Byrd, Lisa Stevenson, and others: thinkers who may not directly study or write about Victorian literature, but who show us how much can be gained by widening the typical critical conversations and drawing on knowledges in fields like critical race theory; gender, sexuality, and queer studies; feminist and queer of color theory; and settler colonial and Indigenous studies. I use relational thinking to reflect on the need to keep forging, rather than attacking, links between Victorian studies, with its traditionally British objects, and other continents, periods, fields, approaches, and political exigencies.[36]

Nor do I expect the Victorian novel to be capable of all things—to hold all of British psychoanalytic thought *avant la lettre* (although it does sometimes predict and help to form some of its key insights) or to stand outside of its historical moment. I treat the four novels at the center of each chapter both lovingly and critically, attending to their capacities and their incapacities alike. I want *Novel Relations* itself to be sensitive and capacious enough to mark a novel's profound powers, potentialities, and foresights, as well as its pronounced incapacities, failures, and oversights—including the ways in which novels can actively disempower people and even lead to enactments of discursive and real violence. One reason that I track critical responses to each novel as carefully as I do is that I am interested in what these novels have historically enabled and disabled in their readers and critics.

I want to clarify that even in and through its engagement with historical questions, *Novel Relations* remains at its base a work of literary theory and criticism. In offering new readings of four Victorian novels that may have come to seem overly familiar, my larger aim is to make British object relations psychoanalysis and its present-day incarnations available for novel theory and for novel criticism more generally. British psychoanalysis has much to teach us about our reading practices, both as ordinary readers and as, as some of us are, readers professionalized into academic literary study. There are several possible reasons why scholars of the Victorian novel have overlooked British psychoanalysis: the dominance of Freudian and Lacanian thought in literary theory, the dominance of historicist modes in Victorian studies that have turned attention to nineteenth-century physiology and psychology rather than to twentieth- and twenty-first-century psychoanalysis,[37] and, finally, the aspects of British psychoanalytic thought that make it seem unsophisticated and recalcitrant to use in literary studies, such as its attention to the maternal and to childhood development, its emphasis on affect and attachment rather than language, its popular-culture dissemination in the case of Winnicott, and its hyperspecialized technical vocabulary in the case of Bion. And yet it is for precisely these reasons that British psychoanalysis becomes compelling and renders surprising new readings. Object relations theory can make us better readers: more aware of the complexity of literary figures and their relations, more attuned to subtle workings of literary form, and more nuanced and more feeling in our responses to fiction and what it does to us.

Taking the interventions of object relations psychoanalysis seriously also means considering alternative pictures of temporality and historicity. Bion argues that psychoanalysis before Freud was a "thought without a thinker."[38] This insight helps us see how productive it can be to picture thoughts that are generated in the relation of two distinct historical moments. While there is a historical trajectory to be traced here, the heart of this book is not a concrete historicist claim tracking how Victorian novels informed later psychological theory. I do not set out to show what Winnicott read when, or which books were on the syllabus for Bion in his English public school or at Oxford, or on Khan's at the University of Punjab[39]—although we do know that many of these analysts read and studied Victorian fiction.[40] Nor is my interest in constructing a cultural history, although that too could be done: as I have mentioned, notable literary and cultural figures in Bloomsbury London (such as Lytton Strachey and Leonard and Virginia Woolf) had direct connections to Freud, Ernest Jones, and other thinkers in their circles and in the BPAS, including James and Alix Strachey.[41] Instead, *Novel Relations* is interested in the looser ways that the Victorian novel, as a dominant cultural form, has shaped the possibilities for thinking about human subjectivity. It is interested in how the forms of

Victorian fiction—the representational practices of narration, characterization, and depictions of conscious and unconscious thought and feeling—infiltrate theories of the psyche that were developed in the same geographic context and in a cultural milieu shaped by Victorian thought and cultural practices.[42] And finally, although this book shows that there is indeed a special fit between British fiction of the nineteenth century and British psychoanalysis of the twentieth, its larger objective is to make object relations thought available for novel studies more widely.[43]

Form and Feeling

Each of the four body chapters of *Novel Relations* is named for a particular "feeling of reading," to borrow Rachel Ablow's phrase. Loneliness, wishfulness, restlessness, and aliveness describe how and why we read.[44] They are feelings that are depicted in the novels and produced in the reader—as an emotional capacity that is generated, at least aspirationally, by novel reading. Theorizing these four particular structures of feeling in conjunction with British psychoanalysis, I want to show that feeling is not simply produced in and by individual subjectivity, but instead in and through literary form.[45] In keeping with this aim, each chapter that follows also offers a revisionary theorization, in conversation with existing literary critical accounts, of one of the basic formal elements of the novel: character, plot, setting, and narrative voice. My relational readings show that the unique emphases that distinguish British psychoanalysis from classical Freudian and Lacanian theory—discontinuity rather than self-consolidation, diffuse feeling-states rather than drives, the preverbal rather than our birth into language,[46] co-presence rather than dialogue, quiet states of "going-on-being" (Winnicott) or "lying fallow" (Khan) rather than dramatic demonstrations of need, having enough rather than being deprived—not only draw out underremarked phenomenologies of reading, but also offer a different formal imagination of Victorian fiction. I hope these chapters reveal sides of Eliot's and Hardy's fiction that we have experienced but have not previously had the terms to acknowledge.

Chapter 1, on loneliness and character in *Tess of the D'Urbervilles* (1891), speaks to the way we internalize novelistic structures and come to feel like literary characters. Like Tess, we imagine that others are with us, narrating and experiencing our lives alongside us, even when we are alone. Tess thinks that she is not "an existence, an experience, a passion, a structure of sensations" to anyone but herself. And yet Tess, a literary character, can *only* come into being in relation to others—not just to other characters in the book, but also to the novel's author, narrator, and readers. Alone with others, Tess introduces us to a notion of paradoxical solitude that D. W. Winnicott would explicitly theorize, more than half a century later, as a fact of psychic life in his essay "The Capacity to Be Alone" (1958). Winnicott describes the ability to be alone as a positive developmental achievement built on a paradoxical foundation: we learn to be alone by internalizing the presence of another. The chapter shows how Hardy anticipates Winnicott's theory of relational solitude by making and unmaking his character Tess, who becomes "an existence, an experience, a passion, a structure of sensations"—an internalized presence—to her readers as much as to herself, and who seems to likewise sense the presence of the narrator and the reader in the world of the story. Engaging with theories both of literary character (Gallagher, Lynch, Woloch) and of psychoanalytic reading (Silverman, D. A. Miller, Sedgwick, Bollas), I show how Hardy and Winnicott together help to solidify modern notions of personality and of solitude. And finally, I explore how this new take on character and personality formation through unintegration gives us new ways of thinking about novel reading and gender interpellation.

Chapter 2, on wishfulness and plot in *The Mill on the Floss* (1860), describes more than just Maggie Tulliver's perpetual states of dreaminess and longing. It points to fantasies of breaking novelistic, provincial, and subjective frames and reveals wishful thinking as the disavowed basis of George Eliot's theory of social realism. In *The Mill on the Floss*, books and subjectivities overflow like rivers. The key psychoanalytic interlocutor in this chapter is Wilfred Bion, whose unconventional ideas fundamentally altered modern psychoanalysis in the 1960s and 1970s, and yet remain opaque to nonspecialists—perhaps for the reason that Bion's prose, laden with Greek letters and mathematical symbols, is notoriously difficult to read. Concentrating on the novel's famously strange ending and on moments of unlikely, paramystical communion throughout the novel, I argue that *The Mill on the Floss* constructs an intersubjective model of mind that helps to shape Bion's later theories of unconscious communication. In turn, Bion's work (and its later explication by thinkers like Ogden and Jacobus) helps to uncover Eliot's deeper aim in the novel: not necessarily to strengthen social sympathies, but to animate psychic processes in generative, unpredictable ways. *The Mill on the Floss* teaches us to wish for other ways of being a woman, other ways of being gendered, other ways of being embodied, other forms of romance and family making, and other experiences of ethnic identity (briefly hinted at in the famous gypsy scene) than it can fully picture in its pages. The relational reading I frame between the novel and Bion also leads me to a critical redescription of plot: one that sees the future of this novel in feminist and queer of color theory (Lorde, brown, Muñoz, Ahmed) rather than in the flood that drowns Maggie in the novel's final scenes.

Chapter 3, on restlessness and setting in *The Return of the Native* (1878), turns from the ways reading Hardy's fiction can afford us opportunities for rest and unintegration to the "unrest" that undergirds Hardy's picture of life and, I show, the geographic restlessness of his figurative practice. As I describe in this introduction and in chapter 1, the long lyrical passages in Hardy's prose punctuate the feeling of doom that suffuses his fiction and offer us a respite from his shocking plots. And yet, Hardy's descriptions of place move us through allusions, historical references, and "similes and metaphors" at a breathless rate, taking us from Egdon Heath to India, from Hardyan Wessex to Byronic Judah, and from ancient Rome to the nineteenth-century Caribbean, in a few quick words. *The Return of the Native* has long been considered a hyperlocal novel with a striking, quasi-dramatic, unity of place. But by reading the novel in conversation with Balint, who makes the spatial metaphors of object relations explicit in his writings on medium, environment, and atmosphere, and with work in colonial history and postcolonial theory (McClintock, Stoler, Chatterjee, Wynter), I show how multiply worlded Hardy's hyperlocal setting really is, embedding on the spot the overlapping histories of the Roman, Ottoman, and British empires. The bright red and rusty brown hands and bodies that are blanched white at the end of the novel betray a "white mythology" that founds nineteenth-century English middle-class domestic life. Drawing on Balint's signal phrase, this chapter interrogates the complicities of the domestic Victorian novel and British psychoanalysis alike in obscuring colonial violence and exploitation as a basic fault at the center of these disciplines—but draws out too the capacities of relational reading to help articulate a more just and searching critical practice: what Balint calls a "new beginning."

Chapter 4, on aliveness and narrative voice in *Middlemarch* (1871–72), begins by highlighting the shift in the novel from the ardor of a Saint Teresa to the weariness of her modern counterparts. The novel uses weariness, most strikingly embodied in the aging scholar Casaubon, to describe the exhausting task of understanding others as well as the difficulty of reading the novel itself. While "weary experience" threatens to suffuse the entire novel, from syntax to structure, ardor and a second affective term, aliveness, describe the feelings created by the paired activities of metaphor-making and idealization in the novel. The narrative voice highlights both the capacity of life to feel empty, dull, deadened, and meaningless and its own power to reanimate it. This chapter synthesizes ideas introduced in earlier chapters: the rubric of deadness/aliveness, popular in current psychoanalytic thinking as a description of the feel of the analytic session, draws its theoretical grounding from a wide range of thinkers in the British tradition, including Klein, Riviere, Bion, and Winnicott. I highlight in particular the work of analysts Paula Heimann (1899–1982) and Betty Joseph (1917–2013), whose understandings of the multisubjectivity and the multi*vocality* of the analytic session allow us to see afresh the multiplicity of moods, tones, and rhetorical postures embedded in George Eliot's own narrative voice.

The chapter engages with literary critical accounts of omniscience (Jaffe, Freedgood) and of the neutrality of narrative voice (Barthes, Blanchot) to offer a defamiliarizing reading of Eliot in particular and of novelistic narration more generally. Finally, the paired terms of weary and ardent experience, of deadness and aliveness, can also be seen to illuminate which aspects of the novel have received attention in critical discourse (sympathy, marriage, even weariness itself) and which have been neglected (communitarian living, colonial space, and brown skin).

Generativity

Throughout its chapters, *Novel Relations* explores feelings of reading that are shaped, like the relational solitude I begin with, through the mediation of literary experience. The "novel" in my book's title therefore refers to both novelty and the novelistic. *Novel Relations* illuminates the way narrative and characterological structures make their way into modern theories of the psyche, shaping the ways we understand and experience our own subjectivity. The coda that closes the book gathers together threads from the chapters' relational readings, meditating in particular on the curious new conceptualization of presence and absence that object relations theory suggests and its stakes for politicized readings of Victorian fiction.

We might imagine loneliness, wishfulness, restlessness, and aliveness to be profoundly solitary emotions. But what my relational readings reveal is that we are never more intensely related to others than when we feel these ways. Although we might think of novel reading as a solitary activity as well, *Novel Relations* shows how intensely, if paradoxically, we are related to others while we read: to narrators, authors, characters, and other readers, and also to ourselves, in the new forms of self-relation evolved by Victorian novels and consolidated by British object relations psychoanalysis. Bringing these discourses together will, I hope, help us not only to feel but to understand our essential relationality more deeply.

The contemporary psychoanalyst Christopher Bollas has invented a new term to designate the opposite of trauma: "genera." Trauma, as Freud remarks, is an open wound. It draws in energy and psychic pain, pooling them "into an internal psychic area which is intended to bind and limit the damage to the self." But psychic genera, in Bollas's theory, sponsors a "very different kind of unconscious work." Rather than an open wound, it is a site of "psychic incubation," an inner place to gather resources so that one may turn outward, to "novel experiences" that bring the self "into renewing contact with [its] ideational and affective states, often within an enriching interpersonal environment." While trauma leads to repetition and acting out, genera lead to continual symbolic elaborations that "create intensified re-envisionings of reality."[47] This book views Victorian novels as sites for trauma and genera alike: for both the open internal wounds of repressed class-based and colonial violence and the possibility for opening up into new relations, resonances, and futures. In emphasizing the generative in Victorian fiction, *Novel Relations* looks for ways to renovate critical practice into pressing "re-envisionings of reality" even while taking historical trauma into account, and to take fuller measure of the wide relational possibilities—and realities—of novel reading.

1

Loneliness

TESS OF THE D'URBERVILLES, WINNICOTT, BOLLAS

> We ought to say a feeling of *and,* a feeling of *if,* a feeling of *but,* and a feeling of *by,* quite as readily as we say a feeling of *blue* or a feeling of *cold.* Yet we do not: so inveterate has our habit become of recognizing the existence of the substantive parts alone.
> —WILLIAM JAMES, PRINCIPLES OF PSYCHOLOGY, VOL. 1

CAN WE EVER truly be alone? This is a question that comes up everywhere in Thomas Hardy's writing, from his landscape descriptions laden with anthropomorphism to his characters' fantasies of social persecution. For Hardy, the sense of being alone is inflected by the many feelings and phenomena that resist it: memory, history, desire, habit, projection, paranoia, and the pull of the pathetic fallacy. Throughout his fiction and poetry, Hardy points to our tendency to people the world with other presences, even in moments of utmost solitude. But nowhere is this clearer than in *Tess of the D'Urbervilles.* Hardy's late novel, published in 1891, thematizes the problem of being alone and, I argue, takes it up as the novel's central formal concern. With *Tess of the D'Urbervilles,* Hardy asks what it means for both his characters and his readers to constantly sense or imagine the witnessing presence of another in a secular world—or, to put it more precisely, in a novelistic world.

The questions that suffuse the novel are condensed into a single enigmatic sentence describing Tess Durbeyfield. Hardy writes: "She was not an existence, an experience, a passion, a structure of sensations, to anybody but herself" (*T* 91). Read in one way, the sentence shows Tess overcoming a naive illusion regarding other people's concern for her and reaching an indisputable conclusion. She will never be an "experience" to anyone but herself because this is a plain fact of human existence. Even what is the most intense subjective experience to the individual will never be more than an idea to others. Solitude is a chilling and final fact. But read in another way, the notion that we are all fundamentally alone is undercut by the narrator's presence on the page, and the fact that Tess becomes "an existence [and] an experience" to the reader as well. At the very moment that Tess reflects on her solitude—on the inability of others to conceptualize her existence and understand her experience—the presence of a witness to her thoughts and sensations belies her insight. Even when we think we are alone, the novel seems to say, we are attended to and populated by others.[1]

In this chapter, I show that the novel's formal creation of this paradoxical and peopled solitude anticipates the concerns of D. W. Winnicott and other psychoanalytic thinkers in the British object relations tradition, who are concerned with the ways we take other people into our psyches and how these internal representations shape and structure us. In his 1958 essay "The Capacity to Be Alone," Winnicott makes the surprising argument that solitude is not distinct from interpersonal interaction, but is in fact founded upon it. "The capacity to be alone," he writes, "is a paradox; it is the experience of being alone while someone else is present."[2] This idea helps to illuminate not only Tess's musing on solitude, but also its connection to Hardy's experimentation in the novel with the making and unmaking of literary character.

And yet Hardy's work in turn poses an important question to Winnicott: What if the paradoxical nature of aloneness has as much to do with narrative as with psyche? Could our sense of observed interiority be structured by novelistic representation? This chapter, then, introduces a central methodological emphasis of this book: the importance of reading the Victorian novel and British post-Freudian psychoanalysis in a truly relational way, allowing for a bidirectional exchange of ideas between them. Moving in one direction, I want to show that Hardy's *Tess* both predicts and informs the work of mid-twentieth-century thinkers like Winnicott. Born in southwest England in 1896, Winnicott was himself a late Victorian. Educated in public boarding schools and later at Cambridge, Winnicott grew up reading nineteenth-century British novels, likely including Hardy's.[3] Winnicott's work is a continuous piece of a *longue durée* of thinking about character and psychology in the nineteenth and twentieth centuries,[4] in which the novel as a form plays a prominent role. But I want to move in the other direction as well, showing that Winnicott's insights help us to read the novel in new ways. My relational reading, then, reveals that even as Winnicottian theory illuminates *Tess*, Hardy's novel offers vital insights into and critiques of Winnicottian theory as well, ultimately helping to uncover the way the conventions of novel reading covertly make their way into theories of the psyche.

Specifically, my relational reading of Hardy and Winnicott explores the invention of a certain modern understanding of solitude. I take solitude to be not only a formal and thematic crux of *Tess of the D'Urbervilles*, but also a feeling created by reading that illuminates some of the underremarked ways nineteenth-century novels work on their readers. Critics have often assumed that we read novels in order to relieve our sense of solitude. As one of Hardy's contemporaries writes, "Books are our most steadfast friends; they are our resource in loneliness; ... they are our best company; they are a refuge in pain; ... they bring the whole world of men and things to our feet."[5] I want to complicate this view by arguing that novel reading may not be about the alleviation of loneliness, as we have long supposed, but rather about its creation—at least, in the new sense Hardy gives the term. We turn to novels like *Tess of the D'Urbervilles* in order to feel simultaneously alone and in the presence of someone else.

The analyst and essayist Adam Phillips argues that the distance between Freud's and Winnicott's respective understandings of solitude is a significant measure of their difference as thinkers: "For Freud solitude could be described only as an absence, for Winnicott only as a presence."[6] I point this out not simply to emphasize Hardy's affinity with Winnicott and the British object relations tradition, but also by way of a methodological intervention. By shifting psychoanalytic lenses—by thinking of *Tess of the D'Urbervilles* in terms that are not restricted to the Freudian and Lacanian vocabularies and concepts of the death drive, paranoia, voyeurism, and sadism—we can become aware of many things in Hardy's novel that we would otherwise overlook: other registers of feeling, a different phenomenology of reading, a different view of how the forms of Victorian fiction in turn form readers, and even, as I argue in the final section of this chapter, alternative views of how the novel imaginatively genders the reader.

The Plight of Being Alive

An early scene in *Tess of the D'Urbervilles* brings together the novel's two central concerns: what it means to be alone and what it means to be a literary character. Tess, avoiding prying eyes following her rape by Alec D'Urberville, goes on one of the many solitary walks that punctuate the novel:

> The only exercise Tess took at this time was after dark; and it was then, when out in the woods, that she seemed least solitary. She knew how to hit to a hair's-breadth that moment of evening when the light and the darkness are so evenly balanced that the constraint of day and the suspense of night neutralize each other, leaving absolute mental liberty. It is then that the plight of being alive becomes attenuated to its least possible dimensions. (*T* 85)

Completely alone in the woods, Tess feels "least solitary." The borderline time, precisely poised between day and night, is an index of Tess's own liminal being. When Hardy describes the attenuation of her existence, he is pointing not only to an "oceanic feeling" of disappearance in the face of nature but to something far more literal: Tess's uncertain ontological status as a literary character.[7] Hardy's propositions in this passage—"One feels least solitary when one is alone" and "One is most free when one is least"—are met by their logical complements in the rest of the book. To begin with the second, for Hardy and Tess alike, being is constraining. Tess believes that life is a cruel compulsion, and she wishes again and again that she had never been born. "I'd have my life unbe," runs the refrain of Hardy's poem "Tess's Lament."[8] As if in response, Hardy searches out ways to attenuate "the plight of being alive" in and through his fiction—for Tess and his readers alike. But the more pressing proposition is the first. If we feel least solitary when we are alone, the novel works to convince us that, inversely, we are never as alone as we think we are.

One reason that Tess cannot seem to be alone is that Hardy makes her particularly susceptible to the pathetic fallacy: the tendency to attribute the "characters of a living creature" to inanimate things, which John Ruskin had identified, half a century before Hardy wrote, as a "mistaken pleasure."[9] Although Tess spends a great deal of time alone in the novel, escaping watchful eyes to explore the landscape around her or following the path of seasonal farmwork, her solitude is mitigated by the way her natural surroundings melt into her mental landscape or seem to shape themselves to her mood. On one of her habitual night walks early in the novel, Tess, pregnant, imagines that the natural world is bemoaning her fall from grace:

> At times her whimsical fancy would intensify natural processes around her till they seemed a part of her own story.... The midnight airs and gusts, moaning amongst the tightly-wrapped buds and bark of the winter twigs, were formulae of bitter reproach. A wet day was the expression of irremediable grief at her weakness in the mind of some vague ethical being whom she could not class definitely as the God of her childhood, and could not comprehend as any other. (*T* 85)

The narrator is quick to point out Tess's error: the wind and the rain are not actually reproaching her, and the "phantoms and voices" Tess imagines opposing her are nothing but "sorry and mistaken creation[s]" of Tess's "whimsical fancy" (*T* 85). To think of "natural processes" like wind and rain as "a part of her own story" is, as Ruskin would put it, a fallacy indeed. It is an instance of mistaking the primrose in the "very plain and leafy fact of it" for the "associations and passions that crowd around it."[10] And yet the issue of impersonality is fundamentally confused by the novel's insistence on Tess's essential affinity with the natural world.[11] In the same passage, Hardy writes: "On these lonely hills and dales her quiescent glide was of a piece with the element she moved in. Her flexuous and stealthy figure became an integral part of the scene" (*T* 85). The equation is twofold: Tess's movement fits her to the land, while, at the same time, the undulating topography of the terrain, answering to the contours of Tess's curvy body, signals the pregnancy that Hardy cannot directly name. Tess cannot be alone: not because she has an overactive imagination, but because she is a literary character—an inhabitant of a world that is indeed "a part of her own story."

One of Hardy's greatest legacies might be both describing and creating paranoid-delusional thinking.[12] Tess's feeling, here and throughout the novel, that she is being watched places her in a long line of Hardyan protagonists, including most notably the lyrical speaker of "Hap" and Sue Bridehead of *Jude the Obscure*, who come to feel antagonized and persecuted by a cruel anthropomorphic force. But Tess is not, after all, merely imagining a witness to her shame, resolution, infatuation, joy, and disappointment. The God of Tess's childhood may not be watching her, but other "vague ethical being[s]" are: namely, the narrator and the reader. Paranoia becomes parabasis, a breaking of fiction's fourth wall: it is as if what Hardy's protagonists sense is not divine persecution, but rather the controlling contours of novelistic plot.

Among the many critical essays that focus on paranoia and its justification in Hardy's fiction, Kaja Silverman's "History, Figuration, and Female Subjectivity in *Tess of the D'Urbervilles*" is perhaps the most notable. In her remarkable reading of *Tess* through the lens of Lacanian psychoanalysis, Silverman argues that the novel offers a "nightmarish view of the symbolic order—a traumatic apprehension of the central role played in the constitution of the subject by the language and desire of the Other."[13] Silverman focuses in particular on the merciless pursuit of Tess by male desire and vision, pointing out that Tess is watched and hounded not only by the central male characters in the novel (Alec and Angel alike) but also by the cruel and punishing gaze of the authorial eye. The novel for Silverman is an eloquent if disconcerting testament to "the pressure exerted upon female interiority by female specularity" and the deformations it causes.[14] There is no question about the astuteness of Silverman's reading and the insight it offers into the production of gendered subjectivity. But it does risk missing at least half of the picture presented in the novel. To say that Tess is not alone even when she feels most solitary is not to say that she is necessarily pitilessly surveilled—as the novel puts it in relation to Alec d'Urberville, "doomed to be seen and marked and coveted" by the wrong man (*T* 43). Might it be possible instead that Tess is being watched by a benign rather than a persecutory presence? That she is inhabited by beneficent rather than punishing others?

My shift in emphasis here is double. I want to consider, spurred on by Winnicott and the psychoanalytic tradition he represents, alternative structures of surveillance and their internalization. And I also want to move away from Tess as person—and even from Tess as figure and figuration, as in Silverman's reading—to Tess as character, focusing on Hardy's emphasis on laying bare the narrative structures that comprise his fiction.[15] When Hardy has Tess feel watched, he is not revealing her personal psychology, but instead pointing to her status as a character, to his own role in engineering her demise, and, perhaps most importantly, to the literary conventions that dictate the ways readers gain access to her interiority.

After all, the reason the line concerning Tess's "existence" and "experience" emblematizes the problem of being alone so well has as much to do with its form as its content. Looking at the sentence in context only makes this clearer. Hardy writes:

> She might have seen that what had bowed her head so profoundly—the thought of the world's concern at her situation—was founded on an illusion. She was not an existence, an experience, a passion, a structure of sensations to anybody but herself. To all humankind besides Tess was a passing thought. Even to friends she was no more than a frequently passing thought. (*T* 91)

Located in the uneasy space between character and narrator in free indirect discourse (the next paragraph begins with the ambiguous "Whatever Tess's reasoning"), the passage makes it difficult to tell whose sentiment it voices. The problem is only heightened by the conjectural quality given to the passage by its opening clause: "She might have seen." Does the sentence report Tess's thought, translating it from the first to the third person? Or does the narrator instead highlight a missing insight and philosophical truth that would be a comfort to Tess if she only knew it? Either way, the impossibility of separating those thoughts from the narrative voice exposes the novel's strange structure of aloneness. Tess may not be "an existence, an experience, a passion, a structure of sensations to anybody but herself," but the form of that very sentence might be seen to give the lie to its content. The long extension of the list of states of being ("an existence, an experience, a passion, a structure of sensations"), in all of its symmetry and alliteration, marks the sentence as a composition. Another presence asserts itself on the page even while declaring that Tess is utterly and existentially alone.

The Capacity to Be Alone

The question of whether we can ever truly be alone has a special urgency for psychoanalytic thought concerned with object relations, and for Winnicott in particular. If our psyche is structured on a set of identifications—if we are composed of internalized images of others[16]—is there such a thing as a nonrelational existence? This is the question that undergirds "The Capacity to Be Alone." Winnicott begins his essay by pointing out that the problem of aloneness, while central to psychoanalytic theory, is remarkably underexamined in the field.[17] Winnicott argues that psychoanalytic theory lacks a way of thinking about solitude in its nonpathological forms:

> More has been written on the *fear* of being alone or the *wish* to be alone than on the *ability* to be alone; also a considerable amount of work has been done on the withdrawn state, a defensive organization implying an expectation of persecution. It would seem to me that a discussion on the *positive* aspects of the capacity to be alone is overdue.[18]

Winnicott's essay attempts to solve this problem by thinking about solitude in terms of health, making solitude not a material fact ("[a] person may be in solitary confinement," he writes, "and yet not be able to be alone") nor a deficit, but rather a positive psychic achievement.[19]

For Winnicott, the ability to be alone is based on a paradox, because we can only feel alone in an authentic way—without feeling constantly impinged upon by the outside world or hypervigilant to its dangers—once we have internalized experiences of being safely alone in the presence of another. In Winnicott's model, the capacity to be alone begins in the earliest experience of the infant, where the mother's (or a mother proxy's) protective half attention opens up a space for solitude and for play: the mother is "reliably present" even if she is "represented for the moment by a cot or a pram or the general atmosphere of the immediate environment."[20] Repeated experiences of being alone with the mother lead to the sophisticated form of the capacity to be alone, which for Winnicott is "nearly synonymous with emotional maturity."[21] Gradually, as Winnicott describes it, this "ego-supportive environment is introjected and built into the individual's personality, so that there comes about a capacity actually to be alone."[22] For the infant, being alone means being in the presence of someone else physically; for the adult, being alone means being in the presence of someone else psychically. Winnicott's solitude, then, is ultimately as relational as Hardy's: "Even [when actually alone], theoretically, there is always someone present, someone who is equated ultimately and unconsciously with the mother, the person who, in the early days and weeks, was temporarily identified with her infant, and for the time being was interested in nothing else but the care of her own infant."[23]

For Winnicott, there is simply no such thing as a one-body relationship, but only a two-body relationship stored as solitude. Indeed, we can only feel truly alone once the mother or the "holding environment" she provides has been internalized.[24] Without being in relation to someone else, we cannot feel the sensation of aloneness. And in fact, without the acquired capacity to be alone, we cannot feel any sensation of personal existence at all. This is what Winnicott emphasizes again and again in his essay. For the infant, "it is only when alone (that is to say, in the presence of someone) that the infant can discover his own personal life. The pathological alternative is a false life built on reactions to external stimuli."[25] The infant can only experience "sensation" and "impulse" as his or her own when paradoxically alone; and likewise it is only in this state that the adult can "have an experience which feels real":

> A large number of [these early] experiences [of being alone with someone else as an infant] form the basis for a life that has reality in it instead of futility. The individual who has developed the capacity to be alone is constantly able to rediscover the personal impulse, and the personal impulse is not wasted because the state of being alone is something which (though paradoxically) always implies that someone else is there.[26]

What is truly personal can be discovered only through the detour of interpersonal relations. Or to put it more radically, the personal is a set of interpersonal relations. Winnicott's essay points out something important about solitude, although it is also something that *Tess of the D'Urbervilles* has shown us long before psychoanalysis: that the "personal" is an inherently intersubjective construct.

Hardy's novel makes this clear to us through our relationship to Tess. The pivotal passage on Tess's "existence" to others around her does not draw our attention solely to the narrator and the author of the book; it numbers the reader too as one of the "friends" to whom Tess is, possibly, a "frequently passing thought." But in a novel intent on "viewing life" from "its inner side" (*T* 168), doesn't Tess become more to us than that? The passage compels us to ask not only what is Tess? but, more pointedly, what is Tess to us? "An experience, a passion, a structure of sensations"? How do we live what we read, and how do the passions and sensations of a literary character structure our own experience?

Throughout the novel, there is a notable urgency behind Hardy's efforts to make Tess real, to other characters, to readers, and perhaps even to herself. This insistence surfaces most overtly in the novel's engagement with the discourses of sympathy critics generally take to be dominant in the nineteenth-century novel: How do we gain access to the thoughts and feelings of others? How can we understand that other subjectivities are as deep and complex as our own? These questions are primarily framed and answered through Angel Clare and his evolving conception of Tess, over the course of the novel, as a real person rather than simply an epiphenomenon of his own desire. He initially perceives Tess as "the merest stray phenomenon," a "rosy warming apparition" that only gradually acquires the "attribute of persistence in his consciousness" (T 129). Even after he falls in love with Tess, he cannot conceive of her as a fully fleshed-out being. When Angel compares Tess to a morning glory, he uses the flower as both a term of endearment and a denial of the possibility of history (equivalent here to a sexual history) for Tess: "My Tess has, no doubt, almost as many experiences as that wild convolvulus out there on the garden hedge, that opened itself this morning for the first time" (T 177). The comparison is apt because it contains the seeds of its own undoing: the convolvulus, better known as the morning glory (see figure 1.1), opens freshly every day. Eventually, Angel has both to come to terms with Tess's past, and to apprehend its secondary importance to her thoughts and intentions: "The beauty or ugliness of a character lay not only in its achievements, but in its aims and impulses; its true history lay, not among things done, but among things willed" (T 340). Angel comes to understand that Tess's interiority is as real and as important as her outward history. (Although the persistence of aesthetic judgement in his remark, assessing the "beauty or ugliness" of her character, should still send up a warning flag for readers concerned with Tess's well-being in Angel's mind and hands.)

But the novel nuances the discourse of sympathy as it is traditionally understood as access to the thoughts and intentions of others.[27] If Hardy insists on making Tess real to us, one of his strongest ploys is an insistence on representing not merely her thoughts, but equally compelling moments of self-absence, nonthought, and attenuated consciousness. Rich descriptions of rapture, exaltation, reverie, dreams, drowsiness, and wonder suffuse Hardy's novel: Tess rocked to sleep by the rhythm of her horse's footsteps and the swaying of the wagon (T 32),[28] Tess lulled into a trance by the mechanical gestures of milking a cow (T 150), Tess adrift in a state of "percipience without volition" as she lies exhausted by demanding physical labor at Flintcomb-Ash Farm (T 293).[29] Paradoxically, Tess may seem most real to us in states where her personality is the most diffuse and dissolved.

Correspondingly, for many readers, the most memorable scenes of *Tess of the D'Urbervilles* are those in which nothing happens at all—scenes where action and event give way to description and to sensation. In her 1892 review of the novel, Clementina Black wrote: "The wholesome life of the dairy farm, and the wonderful pictures of changing aspects and seasons, the descriptions of three or four solitary walks remain with us like bits of personal

FIGURE 1.1. Morning Glory.

experience."[30] Modern readers are just as taken as their Victorian counterparts with the novel's lyrical moments and the shifts they stage. The critic Gillian Beer, for instance, points to the contradiction of "plot" and "writing" in Hardy's fiction, noting that the sense of doom that pervades his work subsides in moments of rich material description, where apprehension gives way to the "moment-by-moment" fullness of the text and to "sensation full of perceptual pleasure."[31] Scenes like these certainly "break the tense thread of the action," as another Victorian reviewer put it.[32] But they also stage interruptions of character and even the notion of personality as self-identity. Perhaps the most celebrated of these interludes takes place at Talbothays Dairy. Walking through an overgrown garden, Tess picks up traces of its vegetal and animal life:

> The garden . . . had been left uncultivated for some years, and was now damp and rank with juicy grass which sent up mists of pollen at a touch; and with

tall blooming weeds emitting offensive smells—weeds whose red and yellow and purple hues formed a polychrome as dazzling as that of cultivated flowers. She went stealthily as a cat through this profusion of growth, gathering cuckoo-spittle on her skirts, cracking snails that were underfoot, staining her hands with thistle-milk and slug-slime, and rubbing off upon her naked arms sticky blights which, though snow-white on the apple-tree trunks, made blood-red stains on her skin. (*T* 122–23)

Here, the experience of solitude as persecution gives way to an experience of solitude as expansive release. The passage, like others, works to overdetermine the equation of Tess and her surroundings. It is not only that Tess's "uncultivated" beauty and natural fecundity are reflected in the analogue of the garden, or even that Tess's own voluptuousness is met by sensuous, adjective-heavy description. Rather, Tess and the landscape almost literally merge as the garden's substances meet and mark her body. And what is more, Tess, caught up in a state of "exaltation" in which she is "conscious of neither time nor space" (*T* 123), does not simply dissolve into the landscape. She also dissolves into the passive observation or "registration" of the narrator, as Beer puts it, or alternately, into the reader's own feeling of pleasure in noting the sensual details of the material of the natural world.[33] As the past tense slides into the immediacy of gerund forms ("gathering," "cracking," "staining," "rubbing"), Tess's sensations and the reader's own are made to coincide. If passages like these "remain with us like bits of personal experience," as Black puts it,[34] perhaps that is because what Beer identifies as the "sense perceptions" that throng Hardy's writing come to belong as much to the reader as to Tess herself as their direct recipient.[35]

But this is precisely where we can see a final turn of logic behind Hardy's insistence that Tess is not "an existence [and] an experience" to anyone but herself. Tess, a literary character, has no self to speak of. The reader feels Tess's sensations not alongside her, but rather in her place. Catherine Gallagher's essay "The Rise of Fictionality" offers a theory of literary character that helps to articulate the stakes of Hardy's fiction. Gallagher argues that we enter represented subjectivity "subliminally understanding that we are, as readers, its actualizers, its conditions of being, the only minds who undergo these experiences."[36] While Gallagher's piece makes no direct reference to Hardy, this statement resonates with *Tess* in a striking way. It allows us to reread what I have identified as the novel's most pressing line in the following way: Tess is not the *only* person to whom she is "an existence, an experience, a passion, a structure of sensations," but rather the *only* person to whom she is *not* those things. Tess exists in relation to us, her "actualizers," but in no other way. What distinguishes Gallagher's theory is her insistence that we are not drawn to characters by a sense of identification, as we are accustomed to thinking, but rather by our attraction to ontological difference. Characters are not beings with "multiple levels of existence, a surface and recesses, an exterior and interior," but rather what Gallagher calls "nonbeings," or, after Jeremy Bentham, "imaginary nonentities." Their lack of existence and our consequent ability to see inside of them is the source of their affective appeal.[37]

Readers Victorian to modern have complained that Tess is an uneven and inconsistently drawn character. Her interiority seems to come in and out of focus. While at one moment she seems and feels like a fully realized sensual being, at the next, Hardy points to her status not as person but as literary construct. He calls Tess "the most living, intensest" (*T* 157) of all the women that surround her, and "deeper-passioned" (*T* 138) than them too, making her by extension the most vital of literary characters. But he also goes out of his way to play her name against the word "text," reducing her being to nothing but mere letters on a page. The critic John Bayley complains that Hardy "cannot hold [his protagonist] steadily either before himself or before us." Tess is "discontinuous," he writes.[38] At one moment, a clear excess of feeling is willed into her image; but at the next, her interiority seems completely emptied out as she mechanically fulfills her role in a melodramatic plot with a shocking ending. What exactly is Tess? An individual with psychological depth, or merely the "prototype of the wronged maiden" (*T* 94)? A physical presence or a representational significance?[39]

Gallagher's view helps us to read Hardy's supposed inconsistencies in depicting Tess as an inscribed theory of literary character, in which representations of consciousness and of physicality quickly turn over into exposures of their fictionality. When Hardy describes the sensation of staring into Tess's "large tender eyes," he uses them as a window into the deepest of souls and most unknowable of psyches (*T* 90). But his description is unmoored by Tess's physical indescribability. Her eyes are "neither black nor blue nor gray nor violet; rather all those shades together, and a hundred others, which could be seen if one looked into their irises—shade behind shade—tint beyond tint—round depths that had no bottom" (*T* 90). The vertiginous descent into Tess, "shade behind shade" and "tint beyond tint," trails off and comes up with nothing. If her eyes have no color and there is "no bottom" to their round depths, this is at least in part an admission that there is nothing there to describe, body or soul. This is the paradox of literary character as Gallagher phrases it: "Seemingly intimate revelations of the character's depths are also revelations of its textual nature."[40] Hardy at once endows Tess with unfathomable depths and exposes the trick of language that allows him to do so.

And yet I am not convinced that the story ends there. If Hardy's novel is illustrative of Gallagher's thinking, it simultaneously works to unsettle its fundamental terms. Tess may not be a person, but she's not exactly a "nonentity" either. Hardy is not content to dissolve the illusion of Tess's physicality altogether. Her sensuality reasserts itself in startling flashes, as when we catch a glimpse of the most intimate places of her body, like "the red interior of her mouth" as she yawns, open "as if it had been a snake's," or a flash of her white armpit, a piece of "satin delicacy above the sunburn," as she stretches her arms above her head, waking up from sleep as "warm as a sunned cat" (*T* 169). If existence is figured as a burden for Tess throughout the novel, in her wishes never to have been born or to "be saved from leading any life whatever" (*T* 244), Tess's protests are more than a generalized complaint about the horrors of being alive. They also say something more specific about Tess and her ontology as a literary character: that she exists in some way despite her fictionality, and that if she cannot fully be, she cannot fully "unbe" either.

Tess as text, Tess as type, Tess as "real vitality, real warmth, real incarnation" (*T* 150)—Hardy wants to have it all these ways at once. In his constant and disconcerting shuttling between representational codes, Hardy gets us to wonder whether we should think of Tess as a real person or as a literary character, and whether we can even maintain this distinction. While Hardy's tendency to move back and forth between contradictory characterological codes has largely been viewed as a failure of artistic control, or even as an unsettling reflection of the strange admixture of desire and sadism he feels for his creation, I am arguing that something else is at stake here.[41] The "discontinuity" of Tess—what I would like to describe as Hardy's constant and deliberate making and unmaking of his character—serves an important purpose: it places Tess within the population of a literary field that also includes readers and authors. Gallagher's "ontological difference" fades into a condition where readers cannot quite distinguish themselves from literary characters. Reading *Tess*, we begin to question our own status. To the people around us, isn't our interiority as fictional as a literary character's? And aren't we just as prone to thinking of our life stories in terms of narrative convention? Hardy's novel points to the way we internalize narrative structures and come to feel like literary characters. We imagine that others are with us, narrating and experiencing our lives alongside us, even when we are alone.

Metalepsis and Unintegration

To describe what is at stake here narratively and rhetorically, a phrase more apt than *parabasis*—Hardy speaking out from the book in order to lay bare the construction of his fiction and his protagonist—might be the term *metalepsis*, defined by Gérard Genette and paraphrased by Elaine Freedgood as a "breakdown of the boundary between levels of narration" where one figure—an author, narrator, or character—intrudes unexpectedly into another "frame."[42]

Freedgood tells us: "Genette has written that metalepsis is troubling because it seems to suggest that 'the extradiegetic is perhaps always diegetic and that the narrator and his narratees—you and I—perhaps belong to some narrative.'"[43] Hardy, taking pleasure in the breaking of narrative boundaries, makes characters, narrators, and readers belong to one and the same frame. Reading *Tess*, we get a powerful sense of the porousness of book and world—and more than that, of the fictiveness of both. In his excellent and influential study *The One vs. the Many*, Alex Woloch argues that character is as much a product of form as it is of reference. Literary character is established not only by the quality of its representation (by which we frequently mean the representation of a character's interiority), but also by quantitative and structural considerations: how much space the character occupies in the book, and the way a character comes into relief through a competition with other characters for narrative attention.[44] Hardy's novel widens the field for this claim in two directions. First, as my reading of *Tess* shows, characters are defined not only in relation to one another, but also in relation to narrators, readers, and authors. And second, Hardy's novel and his use of metalepsis within it show us that the same thing goes for readers, who are products of a similar kind of mutual constitution drawn from the way we relate to a field of other figures, ambiguously real and fictional.

To put it differently, if Winnicott shows us that our sense of personal existence is established by our relationship with others, Hardy intervenes by widening the cast of characters from whom we draw this sense of "personality." And personality, in Winnicott's sense, does not mean our defining traits and characteristics, but instead, as if borrowing Hardy's notion, a sense of our own existence, experience, passions, and structures of sensation. *Tess* shows us that we gather a sense of our "reality" rather than "futility" through our interactions not only with the people who surround us in the real world, but also with the "people" we encounter in reading fiction. Tess takes up residence in the reader's mind and shares that space with a host of other persons and characters, entering our psyches not as a consolidated entity or identity, but precisely as a set of discontinuous experiences and self-states from which we can draw.

Hardy's formal experimentation with literary character turns out to be a meditation on the way novel reading shapes and structures the subjectivity of the reader. Hardy insists not only that we think about characters in terms of the population of a wide literary field that also includes narrators, authors, and readers, but also that we think about the constitution of people within this wider field as well. If character is a product of form as much as reference, so too, Hardy shows us, is our own subjectivity. With this idea in mind, we find that a large part of what makes Winnicott's description of "the capacity to be alone" so remarkable is the fact that it can be read as a description of reading the nineteenth-century realist novel:

When alone in the sense that I am using the term, and only when alone, the infant is able to do the equivalent of what in an adult would be called relaxing. The infant is able to become unintegrated, to flounder, to be in a state in which there is no orientation, to be able to exist for a time without being either a reactor to an external impingement or an active person with a direction of interest or movement. The stage is set for an id experience. In the course of time there arrives a sensation or an impulse. In this setting the sensation or the impulse will feel real and be truly a personal experience.[45]

Reading *Tess*, we "become unintegrated," we move between subject positions and their diffusions and between ontologies, and we allow Tess's sensations to "feel real" and to become a "truly personal experience."

Like Winnicott, Hardy is interested in paradox and the suspension of binary oppositions. Hardy's fiction makes it impossible to tell the difference between perception and projection, between an incident and its narration, between experience and retrospective meaning-making, everyday life and narrative codes and plots, subjective and objective knowledge, and, finally, between being alone and being in the presence of others. But his work in turn poses an important question to Winnicott: What if our sense of observed interiority is not reinforced by novel reading, but shaped by it?

Tess of the D'Urbervilles trains us to understand and experience solitude in a particular way. The novel's moments of expansive solitude and its departures into rapture, reverie, and daydream are ultimately as prescriptive as they are descriptive. The novel's lyrical interludes in which Tess, alone, becomes little more than a "sheaf of susceptibilities" (*T* 176) picture for the reader an idealized version of his or her own experience with the book. Hardy wants us to be as lost in the words on the page as Tess is lost in the beauty and bounty of the natural world. This is what Hardy implies when he writes, in his 1892 preface to the fifth edition of *Tess*, that the novel is "an impression" and "not an argument" (*T* 463). Hardy blurs the boundaries between character, narrator, author, and reader—whose impression is the novel?—and renders the reader as "susceptible" as Tess.[46] Indeed, Tess's absorbed abstraction within the book becomes a stand-in for the desired aesthetic experience of the reader, and there are two important consequences of this substitution. First, it highlights Hardy's role in standardizing a certain modern (and culturally specific) view of the consumption of the novel, in which the act of reading is no longer understood as taking place among a community of readers but is instead pictured as a silent and solitary act.[47] And second, the blurring of Tess's experience and our own models the novel's relational structure of solitude. Reading the novel, we are alone with *Tess*—whether we designate that solitude as being alone with the character herself or alone with the book that bears her name. That is to say, we are at once completely alone and with someone or something else. We read in order to gain the feeling of aloneness that can only be produced in relation to other presences and the "holding" or "facilitating" environments they create. We read in order to find what Phillips, building on Winnicott, writes that we can find only in solitude: something that is beyond our own "omnipotent control but not, by virtue of being so, persecutory."[48]

To understand both Tess and the reader as backed by a nonpersecutory presence or a supportive environment is to challenge the accepted understanding of Hardy as a punishing author who is as bent on the suffering of his readers as on the misfortunes of his characters, and of *Tess* as an overwhelmingly dark and pessimistic novel. And it is also to challenge—or better, to complement—those readings of *Tess* that focus exclusively on paranoia and persecution in the novel and in its accompanying affects. Because even as *Tess of the D'Urbervilles* constructs a massive constellation of paranoid concerns, it also opens a different kind of interpretive possibility. As I have tried to show, for as many moments as there are in the novel where a solitary Tess feels persecuted, watched, and hunted, there are moments where she feels rapturously and peacefully alone. In this way, the novel's very real bipolarity seems to echo the split between what Eve Kosofsky Sedgwick calls, in her now well-known formulation, paranoid and reparative reading. Sedgwick draws her model of critical practice from the psychoanalytic thinker Melanie Klein, whose notions of the paranoid/schizoid and depressive positions form the basis, respectively, for paranoid reading (which Sedgwick identifies as the dominant critical practice) and reparative reading (the alternative critical relationship to literary texts for which Sedgwick advocates). While paranoid reading looks for a hidden meaning below the surface of the text, reparative reading focuses on the text itself, in all of its richness and detail.[49] For Sedgwick, paranoid reading is dangerous because it sweeps up and erases the local and contingent in favor of its own grand-scale epistemological narratives.[50] In paranoid reading, we lose sight of what we experience in order to emphasize what we know.

What is remarkable about *Tess of the D'Urbervilles* is that it offers incredibly concrete analogues of these styles of reading in its own pronounced oscillations—between doom and reprieve, between Tess's paranoia and her sense of well-being, and also between plot and description, the formation of character and its undoing, and the reader's experience oscillating between anxiety and joy, terror and release. In *Tess*, paranoid reading is not saved for later generations of critics (who would uncover Hardy's cruelty or his lust) because it is built—along with its alternative—into the fabric of the novel itself. The novel therefore collapses the difference not only between critical practice and the simple experience of reading, but also between the inside and the outside of the book—put most radically, it collapses the distinction between experience and its interpretation, and therefore also between character and reader.[51]

And yet Hardy's sense of what constitutes a "reparative" practice differs from Sedgwick's in an important way. Where "reparation" as Sedgwick frames it points to the consolidation of the self and others (from part-objects to whole-objects), Hardy points instead to the extreme diffusion of self and the pleasure we take (to recall his phrase) in the "attenuation" of our "being"—a line we might gloss more precisely as the attenuation of our sense of solidified identity. What reliably brings Tess a sense of reprieve from paranoia is not Sedgwick's reparation, which "assemble[s] and confer[s] plenitude on an object that will then have resources to offer to an inchoate self,"[52] but rather the dissolution of a rigidified version of her own subjectivity in "exaltation" (*T* 123) and in self-absent "reverie" (*T* 127). The distance between Sedgwick's and Hardy's notions of reparative practice reflects in turn the distance between their psychoanalytic models and parallels: between Klein (an originator of object relations thought and a vital influence on the later British tradition) and her one-time trainee Winnicott (who draws on Klein and her thinking of pre-Oedipal life in particular, but who breaks with her completely on the subject of drive theory).[53] While Klein's work centers on the aftermath of aggressive attacks and the ways in which we try to repair the damage our own sadism (real or imaginary) has done, Winnicott takes a step to the side of the drives altogether, both sexual and aggressive.[54] His focus is on the moments of experience that do not stage exaggerated thought or action but consist in a simple "going-on" of our own being—where we can discover our own bodies, minds, and impulses, and where they can "feel real." Rather than concentrating on how we put ourselves and others back together after we have taken them apart—by destroying or dismantling them with our aggression—Winnicott's work centers on the quiet joys of "unintegration," which he calls our true primary state of being, and the ways in which we can recover this unintegrated state in our adult lives.[55] Unintegration, he clarifies, is not the same as *dis*integration, a dissolution connected with early "unthinkable anxieties," including the fear of not being held, of being dropped, or of "falling forever."[56] (For Winnicott, the literal and the metaphoric are always deeply connected: holding is at once a fact of early life and, abstracted, our sense of feeling safe in the world in later life.) Instead, unintegration, like the ability to be alone, is a vital "capacity."[57] Our continued contact with unintegration in adult life gives us the possibility of feeling real and maintains personality in its truest, adjectival sense.

What I am arguing here is that novel reading is one place where we get to experience the unintegration that Winnicott describes. In *Tess*, the formal unintegration of the novel both echoes and helps to create this experience. And indeed, as a number of critics have noted, Hardy's larger body of work displays the same insistence on formal disunity and discontinuity. Marjorie Levinson, for instance, argues that Hardy's poetry disrupts the common lyrical tropes of "self-integration and self-recognition." His poetry, she writes, "breaks the contract of bourgeois subjectivity," in which an "interest in the world" returns an "enhanced, empowered" image of the self "organized by desire" and "purpose."[58] The same might be said for *Tess*, whose own internal "non-coherence" reflects not only that of Hardy's protagonist and the reading subject, but also that of what Levinson calls Hardy's larger "critico-aesthetic project."[59] Hardy is uninterested in bringing it all together—whether we mean by that the pieces of his literary oeuvre, his novel, or his character. Instead, he deliberately sets out to describe and facilitate the experience of unintegration.

The resonance between Hardy's novel and Winnicott's theorization, half a century later, of unintegration is not, I think, a matter of simple analogy. Nor does it mean that *Tess of the D'Urbervilles* simply illustrates what we might imagine to be the universal, ahistorical truths of subject formation garnered by psychoanalytic theory. Instead, I would argue that the model of mind presented in Winnicott's work is shaped by the Victorian novel, in direct and indirect ways. If this relationship has not always been clear, it is because we simply have not yet understood all that the Victorian novel places before us, in its themes, its forms, and in the experience of reading that it creates and promotes. In turn, bringing together Hardy's and Winnicott's work and their combined understanding of solitude helps us to revise and rethink our existing models of novel reading. Novels like *Tess* do not simply, as one long-standing view of the novel's ideological work would have it, indoctrinate, interpellate, or discipline us.[60] Nor do they exclusively offer models of identification founded on the "aggrandizement of the individual consciousness,"[61] or of reading as a mere "tool" for "the production and regulation of subjectivity."[62] They also offer us, if only intermittently, new ways to understand and to experience subjectivity as diffuse, discontinuous, and relational. In the unintegrated state of novel reading, we are at once released from ourselves and enabled to experience sensations at their most personal. And the feeling of being alone with Tess/*Tess* stays with us long after we close the book.

Gender and Maternity

I want to close by gesturing to one further stake of reading Hardy with Winnicott—a stake that also helps us draw out the questions of gender and maternity that centrally inform both texts and that have so far remained implicit in this chapter. *Tess of the D'Urbervilles* offers within its pages a very concrete, nonmetaphoric way of being paradoxically alone: pregnancy. Tess's sense of being at once alone and with someone else is not merely an imaginary construct when she is "with child"; while carrying her unborn baby, Tess is literally inhabited by another presence. And yet, for all of his interest in relational solitude, this is a subject that Hardy is strangely reluctant to treat. The months of Tess's pregnancy are eclipsed by the panic of supposed fallen womanhood that surrounds them. And indeed, the episode with her child once he is born is so brief, and the story's ending, with the murder of Alec and the execution of Tess, is so dramatic, that it is easy to forget that, within the novel's pages, a child is born and dies.[63] In the novel's representational economy, Tess's pregnancy serves the specific purpose of making sexual intercourse legible, and her child becomes little more than a fleeting emblem of her "fall."

A stunning eulogy to the "tender and puny" (*T* 92) newborn infant after its death—after only a handful of days and a handful of pages—reasserts in a newly haunting way the novel's questions of existence and experience: "So passed away ... a waif to whom eternal Time had been but a matter of days merely, who knew not that such things as years and centuries ever were; to whom the cottage interior was the universe, the week's weather climate, new-born babyhood human existence, and the instinct to suck human knowledge" (*T* 96). What evokes our sadness and tenderness is not just that this infant is deprived of a life on a grander scale—that he will not experience "years and centuries," that he will never know "the universe" beyond the cottage walls—but that the minuscule portion of life he does experience expands to fill the measure, as if it were all that could be. The increasing abbreviation of the sentence's appositional structure and the elimination of the copula ("was") in the final clauses of these lines—"the week's weather climate," "new-born babyhood human existence," "the instinct to suck human knowledge"—emphasize the radical interchangeability of these vastly different scales of experience, putting the part right on par with the whole. Is "human knowledge" ultimately anything more than "the instinct to suck"? Hardy's lines become less a eulogy to the child than an occasion to exercise his eloquence on the sorrow of a universal human predicament: that each of us occupies only a very limited perspective.[64] Hardy describes Tess's baby as "a child's child—so immature as scarce to seem a sufficient personality to endow its producer with the maternal title" (*T* 94). The baby is so little a child—so minimally an existence or "personality"—that Tess herself is barely a mother. As Hardy puts it, she hardly merits the "maternal title," and at any rate she bears it for only a few days, because her child dies almost immediately. Why doesn't Hardy let Tess be a mother?[65]

One way to understand this problem is to think of maternity not as eliminated from the story, but rather as suffusing the entire narrative structure of the novel. The model for understanding narrative structure in this way is, again, Winnicott, who also offers in his work a second, more concrete way of thinking about paradoxical aloneness: in the analytic situation itself, which Winnicott understands as both an outgrowth of and an analogue for the infant's experience of being alone in the presence of the mother. By making analysis a site where the "holding environment" of infancy is recreated, Winnicott radically reconceptualizes the role of the analyst and the mechanism of the analytic cure. Rather than imagining the analyst as a father figure, traditionally understood as a model for the remaking of the super-ego,[66] he makes the analyst a mother figure, one who holds, provides a space for unintegration, and facilitates the construction of a sense of "reality" and "personality." Winnicott's shift from Oedipal to pre-Oedipal dynamics and relationships offers a newly central position to a maternal element in the construction of the psyche (that is to say, to a pointedly benign maternal element, unlike in Melanie Klein's work and imagination), painting a picture in which we internalize not only prohibition but also protection and facilitation. And for his own part, Winnicott was not the least reluctant to adopt the maternal title. In a parallel to his work on the "good-enough mother," Winnicott describes his own role as that of the "good-enough analyst," writing that "there is nothing we [analysts] do that is unrelated to childcare or to infant-care."[67] In the same essay, Winnicott figures himself as a pregnant woman when he argues that the analyst's particular tools—his or her "personality, capacity for identifying with the patient, technical equipment, and so on"—relate not just to motherhood and to "the multifarious details of childcare" but "in a more specific way to the special state that a mother is in (perhaps father also, but he has less opportunity to show it) in the short time-space covering the later stages of pregnancy and the first months of the infant's life."[68] Like the pregnant Tess on her twilight walks, Winnicott is "showing."

Following Winnicott's lead in thinking about structures where a maternal presence is instrumental in forming and re-forming a sense of our own being allows us to rethink some of our most basic presuppositions concerning gender and narration in the nineteenth-century novel. To take the most direct line of thought first, Winnicott's work offers the possibility of radically repositioning *Tess of the D'Urbervilles*, moving it from the territory of the male gaze into the realm of maternal gaze or, rather, maternal presence. The history of the novel and its criticism has taught us to think of omniscient narration as male by default and to understand the reader, whether male or female, as coerced into identification with the narrator's masculine prerogatives. What Judith Fetterley famously writes of "classic American literature" could well be applied to British fiction as well: "To read the canon ... is perforce to identify as male." Our literature "insists on its universality at the same time that it defines that universality in specifically male terms."[69] This textual operation is particularly striking in *Tess*, where Alec's and Angel's desire for Tess inevitably bleeds outward. Several critics have explored the narrator's implication in Tess's rape and demise; as Penny Boumelha puts it, "The narrator's erotic fantasies of penetration and engulfment enact a pursuit, violation and persecution of Tess in parallel with those she suffers at the hands of her two lovers."[70] And the reader, a structural component of the narrator's long looks and admiring descriptions of Tess's voluptuous body and "mobile peony mouth" (*T* 14), cannot escape involvement in this violence. Our desire for Tess, whether an urge to penetrate into her thoughts or to feel the overgrown garden's saps and pollens on her skin,[71] implicates us in the violation of her body and her privacy. The reader becomes part of the damage done to Tess by a desire that the novel, in one way of reading it, insists on coding as essentially masculine and aggressive: the "trac[ing]" of "a coarse pattern" on "beautiful feminine tissue" (*T* 74).

But Winnicott's work has the potential to change our overdetermined understanding of these operations of reading and writing. By urging us to look at the quiet moments of experience that are dictated by more than just the drives, and by turning from id- to ego-sensation, Winnicott urges us to look at narrative lulls and the alternatives they enact.[72] And by focusing on the facilitation of personality rather than the impingement of others' desires from the outside, Winnicott's theories help us to ask if there are other ways to understand the work of narrators and readers and, indeed, if there are other ways to gender them. Can we separate out moments of narrative desire from those of narrative tenderness? Can we call those moments of respite within the novel—where plot gives way to description, where pursuit gives way to rest and paranoia to reparation—moments of maternal handling where, rather than being watched, Tess is being held? And if so, who exactly are we calling a mother figure? Is it Hardy, the narrator, or the reader? Or is it, by extension, the novel itself? If the novel is a space not simply for subjectification, but also for unintegration, is it possible to understand its operations in the terms of Winnicott's holding environment?

This understanding of the work of the novel is akin to what the modern psychoanalyst Christopher Bollas argues for in his own work, which extends Winnicott's theories of mother-infant experience into an aesthetic theory. Bollas argues that all aesthetic experience is essentially linked to the maternal: it is a literal reexperiencing of the earliest object relation between mother and child. Bollas builds on Winnicott's understanding of this relation by arguing that the mother not only "holds" the infant and "provides" for it "a continuity of being" but, more importantly, "transforms the subject's internal and external world."[73] In our earliest days, Bollas argues, the mother is experienced as a "transformational object" whose ordinary tasks of caretaking—feeding, soothing, holding, cleaning, dressing, changing diapers—completely alter both the infant's environment and its accompanying internal states. This experience happens before we understand it, and so it can never be directly represented (making it part of what Bollas calls "the unthought known")—but it can be existentially or affectively reexperienced. And, according to Bollas, this is something we very much desire. We go through our lives looking for traces of this early maternal experience in other places and seeking new "transformational objects" through which we can recreate it and refind what we experienced with the mother. Bollas, an analyst who earned a PhD in literary studies and is deeply interested in our experiences with art, argues that aesthetic objects most reliably offer us the experience of being transformed inside and out. Bollas describes aesthetic experience as the "moment" when a person feels "deep subjective rapport with an object—a painting, a poem, during an opera or symphony, before a landscape" and argues that this "psychosomatic" experience of "uncanny fusion" is "an event that recalls the kind of ego experience which constituted his earliest experiences."[74] We read for a sense of fusion and transformation that also puts us back in relation to the mother.

Though Bollas offers a compelling way to extend Winnicott's thought into aesthetics, he ultimately simplifies some of the most crucial contributions Winnicott's work can make to the study of the novel. Bollas's most striking claim is that the aesthetic and the maternal are ultimately synonymous because each term indicates a process through which "character" is shaped. He writes:

> The mother's idiom of care and the infant's experience of this handling is the first human aesthetic. It is the most profound occasion where the content of the self is formed and transformed by the environment. The uncanny pleasure of being held by a poem, a composition, a painting, or, for that matter, any object, rests on those moments (they are moment as the infant cannot link them with cognition) when the infant's internal world is given form by the mother.[75]

Directly comparing the mother holding the infant to the novel holding the reader, Bollas makes sure that we understand the formal operations of the aesthetic as an echo and extension of the mother's techniques of care. Moreover, these parallel operations, "where the content of the self is formed and transformed" (in other words, made form), are internalized and come to make up our deepest and most intimate relation to ourselves. Just as Winnicott's capacity to be alone depends on a maternal presence that structures the psyche not by imposition, but by receding into the background—not supervising or surveilling, but simply watching over—Bollas's aesthetic moment insists on a reimagination of the novel's operations as formal, constitutive of character and personality, interpersonal, and essentially maternal.[76]

Bollas is explicitly interested in flipping the paternal metaphors of psychoanalysis. In his essay "Psychic Genera," for example, he codes a neglected aspect of the unconscious—its receptive rather than repressive function—as "maternal."[77] Following Bollas's approach by taking *Tess* as a "maternal" novel raises two sets of questions: it leads us to ask how the novel handles Tess and also how the novel handles the reader, and where these two "aesthetics" coincide and where they diverge. Bollas's emphasis on the intermittent nature of aesthetic experience—it occurs only in certain moments of reading, listening, or viewing—gives us yet another way to account for the intermittencies and discontinuities of *Tess of the D'Urbervilles*, for Tess and the reader alike. Sometimes Tess is pursued, and sometimes, only sometimes, she is held. The quiet moments that punctuate this otherwise relentlessly plotted and driven novel could be seen to stage the aesthetic/maternal moment as Bollas understands it. In this reading, we can take these scenes as moments of maternal care in which Tess feels a sense of fusion with her world and the reader feels a sense of fusion not only with the book as aesthetic object, but also with Tess. But what becomes of unintegration in this model? In his emphasis on fusion, does Bollas cover over the experience of discontinuity so vital to Winnicott's theoretical formulations? Does his work foreclose some of the complexities of Winnicott's thought?

It is precisely the novel's quiet moments and the way in which they act on us that lead me to ask if there is a subtler way of understanding gender in Winnicott and in *Tess* as well as in the operations of the novel. Rather than use Winnicott's work simply to reverse the traditional values of the paternal and maternal metaphors of psychoanalysis, as Bollas does, or simply to reverse the traditional gender coding of narration and the kinds of subjectivity it enables, can we use Winnicott's work to trouble these distinctions themselves? For Winnicott, after all, being a mother has little to do with one's gender: it has to do instead with being a first object and, more specifically, with providing an environment that allows for solitude and for unintegration. "Mother" is merely the conventional name given to a specific kind of care. Winnicott makes himself a mother by suspending gender altogether. And we could say that *Tess* operates in a similar way. It is not simply that the novel shuttles readers between subject positions, identifications, classically masculine and feminine roles, and desires of all kinds—between being Tess and wanting her, between sympathy and lust, between the will to destroy and "the will to enjoy" (*T* 286) rising "automatically as the sap in the twigs" (*T* 100), between feeling pollen on our skin and wanting to feel it on Tess's. More importantly, the novel trains us to think of being a subject at all as limiting and constraining, and, formally and thematically, it poses an alternative to this constriction in unintegrated being. It teaches us to want to transcend the gender binary, to want to "attenuat[e]" the "plight of being" gendered "to its least possible dimensions" (*T* 85), to embrace those intermittent moments where gender feels "marginal and contingent," or "porous and insubstantial"—where we can be alone with our bodies without overwhelming cultural intrusion and we can feel their impulses as personal.[78] *Tess of the D'Urbervilles* shows us how we read ourselves into solitude. At the same time, it asks if we can read our way out of the constrictions of identity that it figures most forcefully through the traditional categories of character and gender. For Tess, there is arguably no way out of the gender binary and its constraints. Occasional moments of respite and release are not enough to save her from the fate that Hardy has foreordained for her: destruction by the unrelenting forces of plot, genre, gender conscription, sexual violence, industrial capitalism, and insurmountable class difference. *Tess* is a tragedy. But for readers, who may feel Tess's experience as their own in certain moments or in certain states and yet are ultimately handled differently by the novel, perhaps the answer is different. Can we read our way out of gender? It may be just a fantasy, but it is one we live out, however intermittently, by reading *Tess*.

2

Wishfulness

THE MILL ON THE FLOSS, BION, PHILLIPS, FEMINIST AND QUEER OF COLOR CRITIQUE

Significantly, [Isaac Luria, the sixteenth-century Jewish mystic] left no writings, and, when questioned by a disciple about his reasons for not setting out his teaching in book form, he replied: "It is impossible because all things are interrelated. I can hardly open my mouth to speak without feeling as though the sea burst its dams and overflowed. How then shall I express what my soul has received, and how can I put it down in a book?"

—BION, *ATTENTION AND INTERPRETATION*[1]

I can imagine there may be ideas which cannot be more powerfully expressed because they are buried in the future which has not happened, or buried in the past which is forgotten, and which can hardly be said to belong to what we call "thought."

—BION, "CAESURA"

Our work is to make the unimaginable feel tangible, become a longing.

—ADRIENNE MAREE BROWN, TRANSFORMATIVE JUSTICE ACTIVIST, WRITER, AND COEDITOR OF *OCTAVIA'S BROOD*, IN AN INTERVIEW IN THE *NEW INQUIRY*, APRIL 2017

IN *THE MILL ON THE FLOSS* (1860), the character Philip Wakem animatedly declares that "we can never give up wishing and longing while we are thoroughly alive" (*MF* 314). Philip is speaking to the novel's heroine, Maggie Tulliver, whose perpetual states of yearning make up so much of George Eliot's early novel. Maggie is constantly wishing for more: for more attention from her brother, for more adoration from the people she loves, for more books, for a better education, for more opportunities than her provincial life can afford, for more music and "more instruments playing together" (*MF* 341), for more love, for more substantial contact with others, for things to be different than they are. Philip, protesting Maggie's brief attempt to give them up, makes "wishing and longing" the very essence of life and its feeling of aliveness. Gillian Beer extends this claim, making "wishing and longing" the very shape of the novel: Beer argues that George Eliot allows "the unassuageable longings of her heroine" to shape the novel's plot, which overflows like a flooding river, "glid[ing] out of the channeled sequence of social growth and mak[ing] literal the expansion of desire."[2]

The unconventional and highly influential British psychoanalyst Wilfred Bion (1897–1979)[3] authors a model of the psyche that is founded on overflowing. His most enduring contribution is the notion of the container/contained: the idea that we use other people's psyches as containers for thoughts and feelings that cannot be fully contained within our own. Overwhelming and inassimilable thoughts and feelings are sent out, via the mechanism of projective identification, into another's psyche, where they can be "contained" (processed, metabolized, thought, or as Bion puts it, "dreamed") before being returned in a more manageable form.[4]

Bion's theories have a special pertinence to the Eliot of *The Mill on the Floss*—an early Eliot; a pre-*Middlemarch* Eliot; the Eliot, one could argue, of dreaming, reverie, fantasy, wish-fulfillment, and the bizarre ambience of mobile feelings. *The Mill on the Floss* resonates with Bion's key concept of the container/contained in its clear concern with what can and cannot be contained—with rivers that overflow their banks and flooding that far surpasses previous high-water marks, with sexual desire that flows out of significant looks and the ends of brushed fingertips, with vital energy transferred back and forth between people, with subjectivity that overflows the bounds of a single character or consciousness, with feelings that cannot be contained within the covers of a book and voices that speak out beyond the page, and with "wishing and longing" to exceed one's own subjective and cultural bounds. Indeed, the novel makes flooding and feeling nearly synonymous terms. *The Mill on the Floss* is organized around moments when, as Eliot puts it, "feeling, rising high above its average depth, leaves flood-marks which are never reached again" (*MF* 349). It is organized, in other words, around moments when feeling overflows its container. And just as flooding and feeling become paired terms, "wishing and longing" become synonyms to living, as Philip's impassioned declaration makes clear. Bion and the novel together teach us that we can never be fully contained within ourselves, and that "alive"-ness itself means feeling our own excessiveness to the bodies, lives, and narrative modes that so imperfectly contain us.

Despite the fact that Bion's radical revisions of Freudian and Kleinian theory have made him one of the most influential figures in contemporary psychoanalytic theory and practice, his work remains a largely untapped resource in the world of literary and critical theory.[5] One reason for this is that Bion's work is notoriously difficult to read, making it opaque to nonspecialists in and out of the psychoanalytic world. Bion's prose, punctuated with Greek letters and mathematical symbols, can feel forbidding and strange, and his major works—the book series that includes *Learning from Experience* (1962), *Elements of Psychoanalysis* (1963), *Transformations* (1965), and *Attention and Interpretation* (1970)—are appended with a difficult-to-decipher grid of his own creation (see figure 2.1). And yet we would not have modern psychoanalysis as we know it without his unconventional ideas, which have paved the way for both "contemporary Kleinian" and modern "relational" approaches. Bion's work, first on groups and group dynamics (in the 1940s and early 1950s) and later on the psychoanalytic situation (from the 1950s to his death in 1979), theorizes, in all of its strangeness, the process and experience of making contact with others—not necessarily through our social selves, fully formed egos, or conscious minds, but rather unconscious to unconscious. Given this emphasis, Bion's theories make for an illuminating, if defamiliarizing and sometimes discomfiting, pairing with George Eliot, as a novelist indisputably interested in thinking and its narrative correlatives (in psychologically minded omniscient narration and the development of free indirect discourse), and also in interpersonal feeling and shared emotional states—that is to say, in sympathy. Reading Eliot in conversation with Bion makes her theories of the direct transmission of feeling from book to reader appear as strange as they indeed are, and as we would indeed feel them to be if they were not by now so familiar, conventionalized, and routinized as *the* mode of moral/ethical reading.

By bringing Bion and Eliot into conversation with each other, I hope to advance the book's larger project of piecing together the unremarked intellectual history that spans from Victorian fiction to twentieth-century British psychoanalysis and its modern inheritors. Summarizing Bion's major contribution, Thomas Ogden writes, "[Bion] introduced the idea that in the beginning (of life and of analysis) it takes two people to think."[6] George Eliot would add that it takes two people to feel. While Bion's theories have effectively relocated the center of psychoanalytic theory and practice,[7] an attentive reading of *The Mill on the Floss* reveals that, a century before Bion, George Eliot was using her fiction to stage and think through similar problems of interpersonal thinking and feeling. This chapter explores how literary figures of feeling (wishing, longing, flooding, overflowing) and structures of narration (a destabilization of the chronology of plot; a flexible and changing narrative voice; and fluid models of interchange between narrator, character, reader, and author) in *The Mill on the Floss* help to shape later models of mind, outlining in particular the notion that

THE GRID

	Definitory Hypotheses 1	ψ 2	Notation 3	Attention 4	Inquiry 5	Action 6	...n
A β-elements	A1	A2				A6	
B α-elements	B1	B2	B3	B4	B5	B6	...Bn
C Dream thoughts dreams, myths	C1	C2	C3	C4	C5	C6	...Cn
D Pre-conception	D1	D2	D3	D4	D5	D6	...Dn
E Conception	E1	E2	E3	E4	E5	E6	...En
F Concept	F1	F2	F3	F4	F5	F6	...Fn
G Scientific deductive system		G2					
H Algebraic calculus							

FIGURE 2.1 Graph included with Wilfred Bion's major works.

it takes *at least* two people to think, to feel, to fantasize, and to dream. (Bion phrases this as a math equation: container/contained ≥ 2.) Eliot and Bion alike argue that uncanny and unlikely forms of contact are in fact ubiquitous, despite their seemingly fantastical or mystical nature, and in spite our attempts to deny or disown them. My relational reading of *The Mill on the Floss* and Bion's psychoanalytic writing reveals this kind of unconscious communication to be at once fictional and suprafictional: a matrix of thought attainable only where literary writing and psychological theory meet.

The Feminist Bildungsroman

When Gillian Beer argues that *The Mill on the Floss* loses its form in a flood of desire, she is referencing the novel's famously perplexing ending: a flood that both kills its heroine and, as Beer's argument runs, causes the novel to lose its form too, gliding out of social realism and its concomitant plots of individual development and the strengthening of social sympathies (as George Eliot would have it in her own important imprint on nineteenth-century realism) into the realms of fantasy, regression, shapeless desire, disconnection, and, indeed, catastrophe and death.[8] Readers Victorian to modern have been distressed by the novel's ending. The flash flood that drowns Maggie Tulliver and her brother Tom in the novel's final pages seems also to drown out and dissolve the novel's most difficult moral and narratological problems. As the writer A. S. Byatt puts it, "it can, and I think must, be argued that the Flood is no resolution to the whole complex novel we have—to the problems of custom, development, sexuality, intellectual stunting, real and imaginary duty which we have been made to see and live."[9] A striking departure from the realist fabric of Eliot's novel, perhaps what is most distressing about the ending is its clear recourse to wish-fulfillment: just as Maggie is praying for an escape from the difficulties of her life, floodwaters sweep in to carry her away to a death that is framed not as "agony" but as a perpetual reunion with her beloved brother, Tom. Critics have tended to condemn the novel's ending as escapist departure or authorial failure, as an inadequately prepared tragedy or a mark of "the presence of the author's own personal need" cropping up in the text.[10]

Feminist critics, beginning with Virginia Woolf, have looked to both recuperate the novel's ending and to identify Maggie's "wishing and longing" with the condition of feminine subjectivity itself. If the novel overflows with desire, they argue, this is not owing to any mistake or failure on Eliot's part. Hardly "melodramatic" or "implausible"—charges commonly levelled, Nancy K. Miller argues, against the plots of women's fiction—the ending reveals that a proper resolution of Maggie's difficulties simply is not possible within the confines of the conventional plots and forms of nineteenth-century fiction.[11] Wishing and longing, then, are central not only to the story and the form of *The Mill on the Floss*, but also to its critical reception. In 1919, Virginia Woolf wrote that George Eliot's heroines "do not find what they seek, and we cannot wonder. The ancient consciousness of woman, charged with suffering and sensibility, and for so many ages dumb, seems in them to have brimmed and overflowed and uttered a demand for something—they scarcely know what—for something that is perhaps incompatible with the facts of human existence."[12] In Woolf's description, women's "consciousness"—definitionally constrained, definitionally wishing for more—can and must flood its temporary container, whether that container takes the shape of a literary character (a Maggie, a Dorothea, a Dinah, a Hetty) or of a real living woman (a Mary Ann Evans, a Virginia Woolf, a Victorian or modern femme-identified reader), demanding "something" that Woolf herself cannot quite name. *The Mill on the Floss* concretizes this overflowing in its ending, giving us a natural disaster that seems to emanate from a woman's demand "for something" not yet nameable: as George Eliot writes of Maggie, "words rose that could find no utterance but in a sob" (*MF* 536)—or rather, no utterance but in a flood. A flood that, in the novel, both has very real material effects and stands in for the social disaster of gender inequality and its own irreparable psychic and material "ravages" (*MF* 543).

Writing in 1979, sixty years after Woolf, Gillian Beer argues that *The Mill on the Floss* raises the important question, "Can the female self be expressed through plot or must it be conceived in resistance to plot?"[13] Indeed, much feminist criticism of the novel in the 1970s and 1980s (by writers including Sandra Gilbert and Susan Gubar, Elaine Showalter, Marianne Hirsch, and Elizabeth Abel) dedicated itself to debating whether or not *The Mill on the Floss* is usefully considered under the rubric of the Bildungsroman, and whether distinctly female versions of the genre's masculinist plots of development and ambition might be extrapolated from women's fiction and become useful as critical tools for understanding the novel.[14] For Beer, the determinism (which she argues is a distinctly nineteenth-century invention) of novelistic plot is so forceful that it threatens to do away with other insights, temporalities, and modes of experience. So strong is this determinism, too, that it makes women's attempts in their fiction to sidestep it "take the aspect," as Beer puts it in her unmarked quotation of *Middlemarch*, of "error" and "illusion":

The all-inclusiveness which is essential to deterministic organisation of experience means that any method of seeking escape from its omnivorous powers will be cast as wish-fulfillment, impossibility, something freakish and fitful, something delusory. Feelings take the aspect of error and faith the aspect of illusion. So all such assertion of apparently other perceptions—the indeterminate, the reversible, the reality of that which might have been, the multiplicity of the future, the moment broken away from sequence ... fear without object, lack without object—is seen as second-order experience, doomed and negative.[15]

Beer lists alternate perceptions that come to the fore when "deterministic organizations of experience" are placed in abeyance. A new value can be placed on "the indeterminate, the reversible, the reality of that which might have been, the multiplicity of the future, [and] the moment broken away from sequence."

And Mary Jacobus, writing in 1981 and building on the work of Woolf, Beer, and, most centrally, the feminist psychoanalytic critic Luce Irigaray, works to redeem just these qualities and alternate perceptions as the very marker of a feminist criticism.[16] Asking what distinguishes feminist criticism, despite the fact that it necessarily "remains imbricated within the [masculinist] forms of intelligibility ... against which it pushes," Jacobus answers: "Surely, the direction from which that criticism comes—the elsewhere that it invokes, the putting in question of our social organization of gender; its wishfulness, even, in imagining alternatives."[17] In this answer, Jacobus describes a genealogy of wishfulness that begins with Eliot's *The Mill on the Floss* and extends into the "necessary utopianism of [modern] feminist criticism,"[18] which, by definition, longs for something beyond the current "social organization of gender" and seeks alternatives to the determinisms of gender inequality and the gender binary.

Psychoanalytic thinking is central to these feminist trajectories. Beer argues that Freudian psychoanalysis plays a key role in solidifying the ideology of determinism born in the nineteenth century.[19] She is referring most directly to the extension of determined thought into formulations of the unconscious and unconscious thinking. But we might also think of the role of psychoanalysis in reifying plots of individual development in and as plots of sexual difference and sexual desire. Freud's Oedipal plot famously provides a fixed path for psychic subject formation: "Anatomy is destiny." *The Mill on the Floss* offers another version of this oracular statement by way of a quotation of Novalis that connects literary and "real" personhood: "Character is destiny." But Eliot's narrator offers this statement only to undercut it and its parallel notion of predetermined stories and selves: "Character is destiny. But not the whole of our destiny." The narrator tells us that, no matter how well we know Maggie, we cannot guess what will happen to her next, because "tragedy" comes from without as well as from within. "Maggie's destiny, then, is at present hidden, and we must wait for it to reveal itself like the course of an unmapped river"—a river, the narrator notes, that is "full and rapid" (*MF* 418), ready to overflow its banks.

Taking wishfulness seriously, this chapter is interested in uncovering modes of psychoanalytic thought that can, like Eliot's novel, give us ways to explore and reprioritize so-called "second-order experience," finding alternatives to the "deterministic organizations of experience" central to both Oedipal narratives and the genre of the Bildungsroman—two plots of subject formation that are often linked in novels and literary criticism alike. Doing so gives us ways of seeing aspects of *The Mill on the Floss* that we have overlooked in our critical emphasis on plot, character formation, and the novel's jarring ending, and of opening up for investigation some of the formal features of the novel that have not received sufficient attention. These features include its overflowing plot, its surprisingly changeable narrative voice, and the remarkably fluid relations it stages between its various literary figures, including writer, narrator, character, and reader. These are all ways that the novel has of making us wish for, in Beer's phrases, "the reality of what might have been" and the "multiplicity of the future."

And so the overflowing plot points, too, to the novel's many unpredicted and unpredictable futures, in places as wide-ranging as Bion's psychoanalytic theories, postcolonial studies, African American literature, woman of color feminism, and contemporary queer and queer of color theory. This chapter concludes by exploring (and creating) some of these new plot points. Here, I'll give the reader just a few quick indications of the future relations, sketched well beyond its own ending, that *The Mill on the Floss* has already created. When I think of such futures of the novel, I think of Daniel Hack's compelling claim that Charles W. Chesnutt's *The House Behind the Cedars* (1900) invokes and reworks *The Mill on the Floss*, both inscribing some of the novel's racial prejudice (Maggie's racialization "literalized and sustained," her plot becomes the plot of the "tragic mulatta") and sowing, crucially, "the seeds of its counternarratives."[20] I think of Simone de Beauvoir's adoration-filled childhood reading of the novel, which she recounts in her *Memoirs of a Dutiful Daughter* (1959). George Eliot, "an iconic female intellectual figure of the nineteenth century," was profoundly shaping of de Beauvoir, whom Toril Moi calls "the emblematic intellectual woman of the twentieth."[21] De Beauvoir's autobiography, Laura Green argues, attempts, "with mixed success, to reimagine the fatal identifications in *The Mill on the Floss* [such as Maggie's readerly identification with de Staël's heroine Corrine] as relations of acknowledged and productive same-sex desire."[22] And I think, finally, of the philosopher and feminist cultural studies scholar Sara Ahmed's adoption of Maggie Tulliver as a figure for feminist thought, action, and being, whose girlhood "willfulness" (her disobedience, desire, and willingness to speak out against injustice) persists not only into her womanhood but also long after her death.[23] How could we imagine a novel with such a future ahead of it to be contained within its own covers, its own plot, or in any singular subject's *bildung* or tragedy?

Relational Oedipus

Bion's revised reading of the Oedipus myth offers both an interruption of a particularly forceful determinist plot and a model of interpretation that I want to deploy in my own relational readings. Bion argues that Freud's overstress on the sexual elements of the Oedipus myth drowned out other important elements of the story. In *Elements of Psychoanalysis*, Bion writes:

> Freud's use of the Oedipus myth illuminated more than the nature of the sexual facets of the human personality. Thanks to his discoveries it is possible by reviewing the myth to see that it contains elements that were not stressed in the early investigations because they were overshadowed by the sexual component in the drama. The developments make it possible to give more weight to other features. (*E* 45)

Bion argues that it is not only important to stress these other elements, but, crucially, to read them in concert with one another:

> No element, such as the sexual element, can be comprehended save in its relationship with other elements; for example the determination with which Oedipus pursues his enquiry into the crime despite the warning of Tiresias. It is consequently not possible to isolate the sexual component, or any other, without distortion. Sex, in the Oedipal situation, has a quality that can only be described by the implications conferred on it by its inclusion in the story. (*E* 45)

Bion argues, then, not only for a renewed exploration of the myth, but for a new method of reading it: one that deprioritizes the "train of causation" in order to focus instead on "the function of linking all elements to confer upon them a particular psychic quality"—to focus, in other words, on relation (*E* 46). Bion's list of the "elements" of the Oedipus myth, "ignoring the narrative chain of the story except for its contribution to linking the components with each other," reads as follows:

1. The pronouncement of the Delphic Oracle.
2. The warning of Tiresias, blinded for his attack on the serpents whose coupling he had observed.
3. The riddle of the Sphinx.
4. The misconduct of Oedipus in arrogantly pursuing his inquiry and thus being guilty of hybris [*sic*].

Added to these are a series of disasters:

5. The plague inflicted on the population of Thebes.

6. The suicides of the Sphinx and Jocasta.
7. The blinding and exile of Oedipus.
8. The murder of the King.

It is noteworthy that:

9. The original question is posed by a monster, that is, by an object composed of a number of features inappropriate to each other. (E 46–47)

Bion emphasizes elements of the myth resonant with his own interests at this stage in his career: curiosity, arrogance, knowledge, disaster, catastrophe, and his notions of linking and "attacks on linking."[24] For Bion, it is "inadequate to regard the Oedipus situation as a part of the *content* of the mind" alone (its drives, sexual desires, fantasied scenarios, and familial configurations), since the Oedipus situation also usefully illuminates its very process (E 49). The myth pictures both the ability to think and to be curious, and the violent destruction of these abilities in stupidity, arrogance, or stupor. Bion repurposes the Oedipus myth from an exploration of sexuality to an exploration of "the psychomechanics of thinking" (E 94). This shift also makes the Oedipus myth (not, Bion pointedly remarks, the Oedipus theory) useful for rethinking the psychoanalytic process itself.[25] Bion writes: "The riddle traditionally attributed to the Sphinx is an expression of man's curiosity turned upon himself. Self-consciousness or curiosity in the personality about the personality is an essential feature of the story: psychoanalytic investigation thus has origins of respectable antiquity" (E 46). Psychoanalysis, Bion argues, exists when and wherever man turns his curiosity back on his own mind and its capacities. (Throughout his work, Bion will be interested in both the fundamental "functions" of the mind and their active negations: identifying these functions as knowledge, love, and hate, Bion designates them, throughout his work, with the paramathematical symbols K, L, H, or, in their negative form, as the mind's own attack or destruction on these capacities in the self or in the other, –K, –L, and –H, spelled out as minus K, minus L, etc.)

Bion's theories can help us to articulate a new method of psychoanalytic reading for novel studies: rather than "reading for the plot," as in Peter Brooks's dominant and drive-centered model, Bion helps us to flesh out, as in his defamiliarization of the Oedipus myth, a way of "reading for relation," deprioritizing plot to focus on overlooked "elements" of form and figuration. Economic and compelling (puns intended) as it is, there is little wonder why Brooks's model has gained such traction in literary studies. Brooks uses Freud's *Beyond the Pleasure Principle* to outline a "master-plot" of nineteenth-century literature and its reading, arguing that reading is driven, like the Freudian subject, by dialectical desire: by the desire to make meaning (the life-instincts, libido, sexuality, or Eros) and the desire to get to the end of the story, marked as it is by death and the extinction of meaning (the death drive or Thanatos). Plot, Brooks argues, is thus an active force rather than an inert form, and the reading of narrative is a driven and compelled activity that insists on forward motion and is frequently figured, in the story itself, in the rubric of the central character's ambition.[26] There is no doubt about the utility of this model, and in particular its protest against structuralism's lack of dynamism. But the emphasis on plot-as-drive can occlude other elements of narrative and form, as well as other ways of reading and of being in relation to the text. Following Brooks, it has been taken for granted in novel studies that drive and plot are analogous to each other. But what happens if we disrupt this assumption? British psychoanalytic theory, with its own decentering of the drive, allows us to articulate some of the alternatives, raising the question of what novels, plots, characters, and reading look like in the abeyance (if not the absence) of the clothesline of individual desire, development, and drive.[27]

Bion's theories, I will suggest, give us three main ways to read for relation rather than plot. The first is to redirect our attention from the singular protagonist and the individual reader (avatars for each other in Brooks's model) to the shifting and multiform relations between literary figures of all kinds: characters, narrators, authors, and readers, implied and otherwise, in all of their various degrees of fictionality and embodiment. The second is to focus on ways of describing the experience of reading (what Bion will describe, in a phrase akin to "the O of psycho-analysis," as "the O of the experience of reading") in fuller phenomenological detail, including cognitive and affective experiences not limited to desire-as-drive. Wishfulness itself describes a mode of desiring related to, but more diffusive than, drive—a mode of desiring that is less directed than nebulous, less subject centered than shared. Third and finally, this method of reading opens up a space for less deterministic—and more feminist—plots: for novels, for subject formation, and for critical interpretation alike.

It is important to note that Bion does not by any means entirely dispense with the drives, nor even challenge the prominence of the death drive, as some of his contemporaries in the British school did. A follower of Klein rather than part of the Independent or Middle group, Bion simply prioritizes other concepts and experiences in his work. A Bionic reading, then, does not in any sense ignore or downplay aggressive or sexual drives, motives, and experiences. But it does offer other vocabularies—sometimes complementary, sometimes challenging—in which to conceive of them. Indeed, Bion's work is notable for offering not a distinct split in approaches, but rather a "drive-and-relationship coordinated view."[28]

Indeed, one of Bion's favorite tropes is that of "reversible perspective," and he gives us concrete ways of picturing it. In *Elements of Psychoanalysis*, Bion points to an image most readers will be familiar with: the famous black-and-white line drawing that can be seen, by mentally reversing figure and ground, as either a vase or two faces (*E* 50). In his earlier work *Experiences in Groups*, Bion is explicit about what such images illustrate: "the need for employing a [clinical] technique of constantly changing points of view." Every psychoanalyst "must see the reverse as well as the obverse of every situation, if he can," Bion writes, and offers a second reversible image to illustrate this:

[The analyst] must employ a kind of psychological shift best illustrated by the analogy of this well-known diagram.

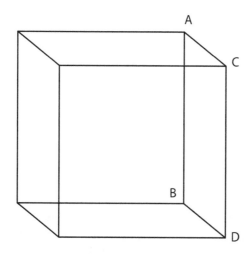

The observer can look at it so that he sees it as a box with the corner A B nearest to him; or he can view it as a box with the corner C D nearest to him. The total number of lines observed remains the same, but a quite different view of the box is obtained. (*Groups* 87)

Bion's contemporary Hannah Segal argues for something similar to reversible perspective in a remarkable verbal case history that Bion loves to paraphrase: we have to be able to understand, in the case of a performance by a great classical violinist, that we can equally call what we are seeing high art or simply someone masturbating in public.

In the case of the ending of *The Mill on the Floss*, this notion of reversible perspective might mean understanding that the book is not only death driven, but also future oriented; that it is not only a death wish, but also a wish to be with others in real ways—that, in Sedgwick's terms, it encapsulates possibilities for reparative reading and not just its paranoid alternative. Bion's plots, then—plural, in contradistinction to what Brooks calls "Freud's masterplot"—include the stories of both linking and attacks on linking, stories of both development and regression, and, in addition, noncausal plots of unexpected relation and unforeseen futures. (I work to spell out some of those futures for *The Mill on the Floss* in this chapter's conclusion.) Bionic plots and relational reading help to open up, then, some of the alternative modes and temporalities Beer highlights: "the indeterminate, the reversible, the reality of that which might have been, the multiplicity of the future, the moment broken away from sequence," reclaiming elements of wish-fulfillment in the novel rather than writing them off.

"Wishing and longing," while modalities of desire and not without their own determinations, open up a future—the possibility of new plots—in a way that drive cannot. These futures may not be immediately actionable or politically efficacious, but "longing" makes them begin to "feel tangible"—a first step, as the activist adrienne maree brown argues in this chapter's final epigraph, toward political change. *The Mill on the Floss* encodes, in the story of Maggie Tulliver's development and premature death, worries about the limitations of existing social forms. But it also encodes, not simply in its plot, but in the various levels of textual relations it posits, a deep yearning for more capacious ones—and in doing so it intimates something about the richer forms of relation that lie beyond what is immediately available, or that indeed already exist within it and are merely denied by conventional modes of understanding. Maggie is hemmed in by what both her provincial world and the novel form have to offer her. But the limitations Maggie experiences teach readers to wish for more: for other ways of being a woman, other ways of being gendered, other ways of being embodied, other forms of romance and family making, other experiences of ethnic identity, and other ways of writing novels. These wishes are at once contained in the novel and by definition exceed its bounds.

Dreaming and Reverie

The Mill on the Floss begins with a dream and arguably ends with one too, especially if we follow Freud's classic definition of dreams as staging in the present the fulfillment of a wish. The novel opens by introducing us to the river, Maggie, and Dorlcote Mill through a series of reveries. These overlapping scenes of being lost in thought, or in what Eliot calls "waking dream," begin and end in the novel's first-person narrator, and, indeed, reveal the strangeness of the narrator's positioning at once inside and outside of the story. The narrator reports, in the present tense, wandering along the banks of the Floss, entranced by watching its "dark, changing wavelets" of flowing water and "listen[ing] to its low, placid voice" (*MF* 9). Eliot urges us to participate in this reverie by making the act of reading symmetrical to the raptness the narrator describes: "The rush of the water and the booming of the mill bring a dreamy deafness which seems to heighten the peacefulness of the scene. They are like a great curtain of sound, shutting one out from the world beyond" (*MF* 11). The narrator becomes symmetrical with little Maggie too, as the two figures stand across the water from each other equally transfixed by the motion of the water and of the mill, its "unresting wheel sending out its diamond jets of water" (*MF* 10). Staring at the same thing, the reveries of Maggie and the narrator merge, and merge, ideally, with the reader's reverie as well, the noise of the novel "shutting [us] out from the world beyond," just like the rush of the water does.[29]

For a number of modern Freud scholars, Freud's "dream-work" is better understood as a verb rather than a noun. The dream-work is a process of making, whose result, as Samuel Weber points out, is not a work in the aesthetic sense—the dream as a work of art—but instead "a working-through."[30] And indeed, as Adam Phillips specifies in his biography *Becoming Freud*, "dream-work" as a verb refers to more than the making of a dream. Far more expansively, it refers to "the [very] way we digest and metabolize our experience."[31] The Freudian notion that experience needs to be worked over and worked through in order to become usable comes most fully alive in the hands of Bion, who dedicated much of his career (particularly his early career) to writing about the ways that we "digest and metabolize our experience" or instead refuse to do so, destroying our own capacity for thinking, for making links, for "learning from experience," and for dreaming—which is indeed a term Bion uses at times to describe any psychic working-through of the raw sensory data. In Bion's iconoclastic and counterintuitive formulation, dreaming takes place both during sleep and during waking life, and it is what transforms bare "sense-impressions" into true "elements of experience," ready to make and carry meaning.[32]

Bion writes in his notebooks in 1959: "*Freud* says Aristotle states that a dream is the way the mind works in sleep: *I* say it is the way it works when awake."[33] Bion sets himself apart from Freud by arguing that dreaming takes place in waking as well as sleeping life, and also in his insistence that work has to be done on sensory experience to render it accessible to the unconscious, and not just the other way around. Bion writes:

> [The] psychoanalytic use of the dream as a method by which the unconscious is made conscious is an employment in reverse of what is in nature the machinery that is employed in the transformation of the conscious into material suitable for storage in the unconscious. In other words, the dream work we know is only a small aspect of dreaming proper—dreaming *proper* being a continuous process belonging to the *waking* life and in action all

through the waking hours, but not usually observable then except with the psychotic patient. . . . *Freud* meant by dream work that unconscious material, which would otherwise be perfectly comprehensible, was transformed into a dream, and that the dream work needed to be undone to make the now incomprehensible dream comprehensible. *I* mean that the conscious material has to be subjected to a dream work to render it fit for storing, selection, and suitable for transformation from paranoid-schizoid to depressive position, and that unconscious pre-verbal material has to be subjected to reciprocal work for the same purpose.[34]

The dream-work, then, is not simply the process of decoding dreams, of making the unconscious conscious, but also of making conscious material available for the crucial work of unconscious processing in the first place. "Sense-impressions" have to be dreamed in order to become true "elements of experience," ready to make and carry meaning, ready to be learned from. Experience has to be dreamed before it can be used, before it can become experience proper.

Crucially, Bion conceptualizes dreaming, in a way distinct from Freud, as a social process. The more common and technical term Bion uses for dreaming, in his curious and paramathematical language, is "alpha-function" (a-function). Alpha-function names for Bion the most basic and fundamental operation of the psyche, one that transforms beta-elements (β-elements)—the "undigested or non-dreamed facts" of sensory life—into alpha-elements (a-elements) that can be further thought, felt, linked, dreamed, and remembered.[35] Vitally, alpha-function at first takes two: the infant relies on the mother's alpha-function and her ability to contain and transform beta-elements into alpha-elements for her, before developing alpha-function of her own. Bion puts it like this: "the failure to establish, between infant and mother, a relationship in which normal projective identification is possible precludes the development of an alpha-function and therefore of a differentiation of elements into conscious and unconscious" (Thinking 115). Bion's theories describe how, from the moment of our birth, we use others to digest and metabolize our experience with and for us, to take on our own feelings and return them to us in a more processed form. The baseline assumption for Bion, then, is that feeling is something that is simply too much to bear on one's own. This is not only a surprising and counterintuitive notion, but also one that stages a dramatic shift in psychoanalytic theory. As Ogden argues, it "expands the focus of attention in the psychoanalytic setting beyond the exploration of conflict" between opposing impulses (love and hate, libido and aggression) or even "between sets of thoughts and feelings" (Ogden gives the example of "the wish and need to become a separate subject" and "the fear of the isolation and loneliness that would involve") to look instead at our very capacity to think and feel and to *tolerate* what it is that we think and feel. Ogden writes:

> In Bion's hands, the central concern of psychoanalysis is the dynamic interaction between, on the one hand, thoughts and feelings derived from lived emotional experience (the contained) and, on the other, the capacity for dreaming and thinking those thoughts (the container). The aim of psychoanalysis from this perspective is not primarily that of facilitating the resolution of unconscious conflict, but facilitating the growth of the container-contained.[36]

I hope you hear in this notion some resonance with George Eliot: with her preoccupation, as Gillian Beer notes, with hyperesthesia, or feeling too much, and the terrible pressure it exerts on our bodies and minds, and with her famous lines on the subject that argue that if we were able to register the full range of sentient experience, "our frames could hardly bear much of it" (*MF* 194).[37] But perhaps we can hear even more strongly, in Bion's emphasis on dreaming and on reverie (the primary mode in which we receive the projective identifications of others), the Eliot of *The Mill on the Floss*.

In the novel's opening, the narrator dreams of standing across the flowing water from Maggie at Dorlcote Mill. And then the narrator wakes up. But, as if true to Bion's theory—"I say [the dream] is the way [the mind] works when awake"—the narrator wakes into dreaming. In these early pages of *The Mill on the Floss*, we learn that the narrator's experience of being with Maggie at the river was only a dream, and that the elbows "benumbed" by resting on the stone bridge staring into the water are in fact elbows benumbed by being pressed against the arms of the chair in which our narrator "dozed off," remembering Dorlcote Mill as it was many years ago. This scene of narration (and narration as dreaming) is revealed in a few quick sentences at the end of the novel's first chapter:

> It is time [. . .] for me to leave off resting my arms on the cold stone of this bridge. . . .
> Ah, my arms are really benumbed. I have been pressing my elbows on the arms of my chair and dreaming that I was standing on the bridge in front of Dorlcote Mill as it looked one February afternoon many years ago. Before I dozed off, I was going to tell you what Mr and Mrs Tulliver were talking about as they sat by the bright fire in the left-hand parlor on that very afternoon I have been dreaming of. (*MF* 11)[38]

Reverie encases dream encases reverie, in a cycle that points to the fluid relations between processing experience in dream and waking, consciously and unconsciously, and that points too to the fluid relations between the imagined psyches of narrator, character, and reader that Eliot frames from the start. It is the narrator who at once grounds and ungrounds these fluid relations and shared reverie, strangely positioned here and throughout the novel as neither fully personified nor fully omniscient, neither fully inside nor outside of the action, but rather shuttling between first-person and third-person narration, between gendered embodiment and the free-floating consciousness we have come to associate with Eliot's famously magisterial narrative voice. After this brief moment of direct address, the narrator's first-person identity and present-tense pronouncements fade into the background as we are immersed instead in third-person, past-tense narration of scenes in Maggie's childhood life mainly in the voice we are more accustomed to identifying as that of George Eliot's narrator. But the novel's narration never fully stabilizes, staging occasional returns to first-person remembrance, and occasional moments of personification. These shifts in the narrator's position and voice have proved disconcerting to modern readers and critics working to uphold a certain image of Eliot's writing or of nineteenth-century realism. But rather than glossing over or critiquing this uneven narration, we might use it to explore what the novel has to teach us about dreaming, feeling, fantasy, and reverie, and the new forms of subjectivity and relationality they create.

Adding to the strangeness of the novel's opening is the fact that the book never closes its frame narrative: we never return to the opening scene of armchair remembrance. But the story arguably does come full circle with its self-proclaimed "dreamlike" (*MF* 538) ending that has long perplexed the novel's readers with its clear recourse to wish-fulfillment. Maggie's wishes to be closer to others and for more opportunity for variety and vivacity in her life are continually thwarted—until they are not, with the arrival of the prayed-for catastrophe that takes her back in time to childhood closeness with her brother in precisely the kind of fantasied ending that, Debra Gettelman points out, Eliot was otherwise well known for rejecting.[39] Flooding and feeling overlap once again in this sudden ending: Eliot describes the "strong resurgent love" Maggie feels toward her brother as itself a watery current, one that "swe[eps] away all the later impressions of hard, cruel offence and misunderstanding, and [leaves] only the deep, underlying, unshakable memories of early union" (*MF* 539). The twin floods of natural disaster and "strong resurgent love" also sweep away any typical impediments to the novel's fantasied ending where Tom and Maggie drown locked in a loving embrace, "living through again in one supreme moment, the days when they had clasped their little hands in love, and roamed the daisied fields together" (*MF* 542). These impediments include the prescriptions of social convention, the teleology of the Bildungsroman, Eliot's typical mode of realist representation, and the dictates of heteronormative sexuality that would push Maggie into the arms of one of her potential lovers, Stephen or

Philip, rather than into her brother's. Readers and critics have long been "puzzled" (a phrase Maggie's father repeatedly uses to describe the modern world that defies his comprehension) by this ending. As Byatt puts it: "there is an incoherence" in *The Mill on the Floss* "which puzzles each reader, each reading."[40] Bion's theories may not eliminate what is puzzling in the novel, but they may help us to tolerate it.[41]

A central tenet of Bion's theory of thinking is that frustration must be tolerated rather than evaded, for the sake of reality, certainly, but also for the sake of development itself. Bion writes, "Inability to tolerate frustration can obstruct the development of thoughts and a capacity to think, though a capacity to think would diminish the sense of frustration intrinsic to appreciation of the gap between a wish and its fulfillment" (Thinking 113). Since we will never immediately get everything we wish for, and since we may never get what we wish for at all, frustration is a fact of our existence, and the question for Bion is whether we can allow this frustration to be part of our actual experience (in his specialized understanding of the term, as in the expression "learning from experience," as that which can be dreamed, processed, or worked over unconsciously). Thinking "modifies" frustration and makes it bearable, but frustration is what makes thinking available in the first place. If wishes immediately came true— as Freud postulates we feel they do in our earliest experience, when "whatever was thought of (wished for) was simply presented in a hallucinatory manner, just as still happens with our dream-thoughts" and when we therefore believed in our own omnipotence—we would have no need nor occasion for thinking. But neither would we have any contact with reality, and therefore no real satisfaction either.[42] As Adam Phillips glosses Bion, "unwillingness to bear with frustration" is nothing other than a "failure of imagination," and one that results in turn in a failure to picture what real satisfaction would look and feel like (although that satisfaction, being real, will necessarily be shot through with frustration). "To take Bion seriously," Phillips writes, "if we can't think our frustrations—figure them out, think them through, phrase them—we can't seek our satisfactions. We will have, as they say, no idea what they are."[43]

What would satisfaction look like, for Maggie and for the readers continually disappointed in the novel's ending? Even Eliot registered dissatisfaction with the novel's ending, regretting that "the '*epische Breite*' [epic breadth] into which I was beguiled by love of my subject in the first two volumes, caused a want of proportionate fullness in the treatment of the third."[44] But she protests too against the "artificial necessities of dénouement" in general,[45] arguing that that "endings are inevitably the least satisfactory part of any work in which there is any merit of development."[46] Putting the conventional reading of the novel's ending in Freudian-Bionic terms, we might say that it looks more like hallucinatory wish-fulfillment than actual satisfaction. What Maggie prays for is in fact an end to her experience of long suffering, and what arrives is just that, although that end comes, perhaps as it only can, in death. To return to Adam Phillips's terms, it may well look like a "failure of imagination" not to be able to imagine a life for Maggie beyond young adulthood and beyond life in St. Ogg's, a satisfaction that is realistic and mixed rather than ecstatic. The flood is wished for: it will reunite Maggie and Tom and return them to their childhood love, it will give George Eliot a way to end her long, front-loaded novel, it will save Maggie from having to lead a difficult life, and it will save the reader from an even more tragic ending than the novel's ecstatic death. Crucially, though, it is unclear to whom this wish belongs: Maggie, George Eliot, the narrator, or the reader. In this view, what the ending registers is not simply the determination of a wish and its fulfillment, but, for readers at least, the sublimation of wishfulness: an affective comportment that at once bears with frustration and longs for its realistic and satisfactory solution, even where given social circumstances do not permit its realization. The ending does not offer possibilities for Maggie, but it does invite the reader to enter into reverie and to "dream" them.

The term "reverie," which Eliot uses throughout the novel (*MF* 192, 237, 300, 384, 398, 400), has a special place in Bion's theory too. It is an essential component of his reworking of Melanie Klein's concept of projective identification in the container/contained concept. Transforming projective identification from a pathological process into an essential mode of communication, Bion argues that projective identification is not merely a fantasy, but instead a genuine way of transmitting and sharing private experience by psychically recreating it in the mind of another. And "reverie" is that psyche's mode of reception. In Klein's theory, projective identification is a process in which unwanted thoughts, feelings, and parts of the self are projected "into" another person, as a means both of ridding oneself of them and of remotely controlling the other.[47] Importantly, these transformations take place for Klein in unconscious fantasy, which she denotes with the spelling "phantasy." Projective identification therefore denotes a wish, an imaginary arrangement of affairs that makes it easier to deal with self-other relations by redistributing affects, traits, and abilities. Bion's intervention in moving from projective identification to his concept of the container/contained is to transform what Klein views mainly as a pathological and fantastic process into something that can be useful and realistic—albeit uncannily so. Bion argues that projective identification is a direct way to reach others in fact, not merely in phantasy: it is a "primitive form of communication," one that "provides a foundation on which, ultimately verbal communication depends" (Arrogance 92). Projective identification is "primitive" in the sense that it is our earliest mode of communication, one that we employ long before we have words at our disposal. "In its origin communication is effected by realistic projective identification," Bion writes (Thinking 118). It is also primitive in the sense that we fall back into using it in situations in later life when words fail us. Describing the roots of projective identification in the mother-infant relationship, Bion writes:

> Ordinarily the personality of the infant, like other elements in the environment, is managed by the mother. If the mother and child are adjusted to each other, projective identification plays a major role in [this] management . . . ; usually an omnipotent phantasy, [projective identification in this context] is a realistic phenomenon. This, I am inclined to believe, is its normal condition.

For Bion, the idea of sharing feelings, personalities, and self-states, as fantastic as it sounds, is above all else a "realistic" phenomenon. He continues:

> When Klein speaks of "excessive" projective identification I think the term "excessive" should be understood to apply not to the frequency only with which projective identification is employed but to excess of belief in omnipotence. As a realistic activity it shows itself as behavior reasonably calculated to arouse in the mother feelings of which the infant wishes to be rid. If the infant feels it is dying it can arouse fears that it is dying in the mother. A well-balanced mother can accept these and respond therapeutically: that is to say in a manner that makes the infant feel it is receiving its frightened personality back again, but in a form that it can tolerate—the fears are manageable by the infant personality. (Thinking 114–15)

Projective identification's recourse to fantasy does not disqualify its real effects, but in fact enables them—perhaps in the same way that beginning in reverie allows Eliot to open her novel.[48] Crucially, Bion argues that what makes a mother capable of receiving the infant's projective identifications is a "capacity for reverie." When the infant "feels it is dying," the mother daydreams that the infant is dying. Unlike the infant, however, the mother has the ability to transform this fear, in fact and in fantasy alike: she can comfort the infant and change its state, and she can ease her own fear and psychically reassure herself. The mother's reverie answers the call of the infant's projective identification, and becomes a communication in turn.[49] As Bion puts it, "The mother's capacity for reverie is the receptor organ for the infant's harvest of self-sensation gained by its consciousness" (Thinking 116). The mother's capacity to dream her infant's self-sensation—to encase it in her own reverie, to contain it, to "digest and metabolize" it through her own alpha-function—is what makes it possible for it to be returned to the infant as accessible self-sensation at all.[50] Reverie creates an interpersonal circuit, the "interplay through projective identification between the rudimentary consciousness and maternal reverie" (Thinking 116), that is vital to the development of the infant and later internalized as its own container/contained system, making it possible for the infant to "dream" its own experience and self-sensation.

The mother-infant scenario of containing feelings for others extends into both the analytic situation and everyday interpersonal interaction.[51] In "Attacks on Linking," Bion describes this work as one of the analyst's central tasks, essentially rewriting, in a short case history, the mother-infant scenario in the analytic one: "When the patient strove to rid himself of fears of death which were felt to be too powerful for his personality to contain he split off his fears and put them into me, the idea apparently being that if they were allowed to repose there long enough they would undergo modification by my psyche and could then be safely reintrojected" (Attacks 103). In his essay "On Arrogance," Bion affirms that this is indeed the analyst's role: "the implicit aim of psychoanalysis to pursue the truth at no matter what cost" is all but synonymous, he argues, with the "capacity for containing the discarded, split-off aspects of other personalities while retaining a balanced outlook" (Arrogance 88–89).

As Bion makes clear, containing another's feelings is no easy task. They are taken in not as theories, but as actual powerful feelings, whose object and recipient are confused: the analyst doesn't simply feel the patient's fear, but feels it as a fear of his own. The analyst must be able to "tolerate the stresses associated with the introjection of another person's projective identifications" (Arrogance 88), and to channel them into reverie. Reverie, then, becomes not simply a way of turning in, but also an opening out to sociality, since, in a surprising move, Bion makes our own imaginings, memories, and self-preoccupations the avenue through which we "realistically" gain access to others—as strange as such an experience might feel, or as painful. Reverie for Bion is not private, but rather radically intersubjective. George Eliot's *The Mill on the Floss* argues this point as well, not only in its multiple depictions of reverie, but also in its narrative form, in which the relations between character, reader, author, and narrator are remarkably fluid.

Thoughts without a Thinker

At the start of *The Mill on the Floss*, who is dreaming whose experience? Does the narrator dream his/her/their/its own experience ("I remember . . . I remember . . .")? Does the narrator dream Maggie's, as she stares at the water and watches her father return home? Or is it the reader who dreams all of this? Nicholas Dames, describing both the experience of reading and the way it was conceptualized by the nineteenth-century thinkers E. S. Dallas and George Henry Lewes, writes: "Caught in the dream of her novel, the reader is not far from dreaming itself."[52] If the reader is not far from dreaming, whose experience is it that the reader dreams? The narrator's, Maggie's, or her own? Or, we could ask, is it the novel, with its extended reveries on childhood and the power of first attachments, that in fact dreams the reader's experience? The undecidability of this question may be precisely the point. To return to Ogden's summary of Bion's larger project, what is at stake is our ability to contain and feel our own feelings, and the ability to contain and think our own thoughts. For, according to Bion, the development of thoughts (and, analogously, feelings) comes first, and the ability to think them second: "they require an apparatus to cope with them." Thinking is a *secondary* development and only demanded because thoughts themselves are so hard to bear. "I repeat—thinking has to be called into existence to cope with thoughts" (Thinking 111).

And so we might also extend the question "who is dreaming whose experience?" to the relation between Eliot's and Bion's work: Does Bion dream Eliot's thoughts—ones that her fiction can suggest but not quite articulate? Or does Eliot dream Bion's—ones that his theory gathered, even beyond his knowledge, from the forms of Eliot's fiction? Either way, what we have is indeed a disruption of deterministic plot. In his gloss of Bion's ideas, Ogden evokes a number of literary texts, making an implicit argument for the power of literature to explicate psychoanalytic ideas more clearly and suggestively than psychoanalysis itself. Defining beta-elements, Ogden writes: "I have found no better words to describe these nascent thoughts than those used in a poem by Edgar Alan Poe: β-elements might be thought of as 'Unthought-like thoughts that are the souls of thought.'"[53] (The reference is to Poe's 1848 poem "To Marie Louise.") A page earlier, Ogden argues, citing *Attention and Interpretation*, that, "for Bion, psychoanalysis before Freud was a thought without a thinker, a thought awaiting a thinker to conceive it as a thought."[54] In keeping with his understanding of thought developing in advance of an apparatus to think those thoughts, Bion maintains that psychoanalysis existed before Freud "discovered" it. This notion, too, Ogden glosses by way of literature, musing in a footnote:

> I am reminded here of a comment made by Borges regarding proprietorship and chronology of ideas. In a preface to a volume of his poems, Borges wrote, "If in the following pages there is some successful verse or other, may the reader forgive me the audacity of having written it before him. We are all one; our inconsequential minds are much alike, and circumstances so influence us that it is something of an accident that you are the reader and I the writer— the unsure, ardent writer—of my verses."[55]

Borges speaks to the sense of discovery and recognition that occurs so often in reading—the readers' sense that they have found their own thoughts and feelings in the words someone else has written—and audaciously takes it to the next level, apologizing to his own readers for writing their ideas before them. The "accident" of being positioned as reader or writer is merely that. The opening of *The Mill on the Floss*, and indeed the novel as a whole, stages this kind of shared reverie between reader and writer, and between narrator and character too, giving us thoughts with several possible thinkers, dreams with several possible dreamers. And the relation between Eliot and Bion stages the altered temporality of such reverie as well: Bionic thought before Bion was a thought without a thinker, but was starting to be thought in Eliot's novel; an aspect of Eliot's thought could not arrive until Bion appeared to think her thoughts.

Wishful Realism

If Bion's theories describe how, from the moment of our birth, we use others to contain and transform overwhelming and inassimilable thoughts and feelings, ones that are "too powerful" for a single personality alone (Attacks 103), *The Mill on the Floss* makes wishing itself the signal instance of such powerful, uncontainable feeling. The tendency of wishfulness to overflow its container, to diffuse and spread to other "personalities" and subjectivities, to overspill the container of literary forms themselves, is clear in the novel's opening and closing. And, indeed, wishes resonate beyond Maggie's desires and beyond George Eliot's desires in this particular novel to suffuse her larger literary project. As Debra Gettelman argues, "the relation between thought and deed, and wishes and their realization, preoccupies George Eliot's fiction."[56] While Bion reshapes projective identification into a more visceral and telegraphic mode of communication than words themselves, Eliot likewise has her own dreams of the direct transmission of feeling. In one early letter, she writes: "When a sort of haziness comes over the mind making one feel weary of articulated or written signs of ideas does not the notion of a less laborious mode of communication, of a perception approaching more nearly to intuition seem attractive?"[57] And indeed, imaginings of a "less laborious mode of communication" appear throughout *The Mill on the Floss*: in Maggie's reading of Thomas à Kempis, in Maggie and Stephen's mutual reverberations to music and to desire, in Maggie and Dr. Kenn's instant connection, and finally in the "gift of transferred life" (*MF* 523) that Philip Wakem says that Maggie has given to him in the letter he writes to her near the end of the novel. (Perhaps this fantasy, too, is precisely what is at the heart of the novel's technique of free indirect discourse.) In what follows, I will look at each of these scenes of uncanny communication in more detail. But I want first to think about the wish at the heart of Eliot's aesthetic philosophy: the hope that feelings might be directly transmitted to others is clear in her extensive formulations of sympathy as the cornerstone of her larger literary project. As she puts it in a letter written in 1859, "those who read [my books] should be better able to *imagine* and to *feel* the pains and joys of those who differ from themselves in everything but the broad fact of being struggling erring human creatures."[58] Eliot hopes that feelings created by words on the page can spill over not only into our hearts and minds, but also into our real-world social interactions. If (and only if, Eliot believes) we can learn to feel with literary characters, we can also learn to feel with our living and breathing neighbors. Reading becomes, as Thomas Albrecht puts it, a training ground for "an extension beyond the limitations of the self," a way of spilling out beyond the confines of our own limiting subjectivity.[59]

But there are no guarantees that Eliot's project—what J. Hillis Miller calls her "affective-performative theory of realism"—will work. Eliot dreams of being an author who has the power to transmit just the right feelings to the reader, and she fantasizes that these feelings will produce just the right social effects. And yet she also betrays deep anxieties about the efficacy of her literary project. Eliot's sympathetic performative is, like all performatives, "unpredictable and unmeasurable." Miller writes: "It is impossible to know whether anything really happens as a result of [a performative's] force.... A performative can never be controlled, defined, or have a decisive line put around its effects."[60] Like a river overspilling its banks, performatives refuse to stay the course, exposing the wishful basis of Eliot's theories of literary realism. But what if, picking up on Bion's terms, we were to view Eliot's wish for the creation of sympathy in her readers not as an "omnipotent phantasy" but rather a "realistic phenomenon"? From Bion's perspective, the transmission of feeling between psychic and literary containers that Eliot envisions may not be so fantastic, but instead a fact of social and emotional life.[61] Bion writes: "An emotional experience cannot be conceived of in isolation from a relationship."[62] The question I want to raise in turn is to what extent Bion's theories of subjectivity-as-intersubjectivity are shaped by literary relations.

Quiet Hand, Talking Book

If *Tess* is concerned with relational solitude—with aloneness sustained by earlier experience with others, with psyches that are never singular but are always densely populated—*The Mill on the Floss* is concerned with relationality in more concrete terms: with the possibility of actual togetherness with another person. How do we make and sustain connections with other people? This is the question that the novel presses on Maggie Tulliver, with her story's fluctuating rhythms of intense attachment and devastating separation, of finding and losing objects of love. The question becomes especially acute for Maggie in the following forms: How do we give others access to the parts of ourselves that feel most real—namely, the seemingly nonsocial or (to use a Winnicottian term) noncommunicating parts of ourselves? Is doing so really possible, or is that just wishful thinking? Throughout the novel, Maggie longs to be with others in meaningful ways, and struggles when her attempts to do so are continually restricted: by gender norms that distance her from her brother; by limited access to education and books that keeps her from feeling connected to other minds; by family tragedy and an economic position that restricts her to domestic space and to unfulfilling work; by her "brown skin," which acts in the novel as a kind of double barrier separating her from others in her provincial world; by social rules that take any relationship between a man and woman to be romantic or sexual; and, indeed, by a limited imagination of what forms familial and social relationships more generally might take, both in the world of the novel's setting and in the world of domestic fiction, with its limited repertoire of available plots, settings, and narrative forms. While *Tess* speaks to the fact that we can be physically alone (walking, daydreaming, reading) and still be with others, *Mill* speaks to the fact that we can be physically with someone else without actually being in contact with that person.

But *The Mill on the Floss* speaks to something else too: to the fact that connections and relations can open up in surprising directions, that communication can take place in uncanny and unbidden ways, and also that early ways of relating and the closeness they bring can sometimes be restored, as if by magic, in later life. If, as adults, Maggie and Tom speak to each other without ever really hearing one another, it's also possible for Maggie and Dr. Kenn to understand something important about each other without speaking at all. And if Maggie cannot read as many books as she might wish, the ones she does have speak to her with a kind of preternatural force. While Klein and Winnicott write about a sense of companionship in terms of internal object worlds, within the British tradition, it takes Bion's distinctive approach to address the questions of togetherness, contact, and presence in a concrete way: in the world of real physical social relations. The theory of unconscious, nonverbal communication that undergirds Bion's picture of the container/contained also directly informs his view of psychoanalytic practice. There, two people share in the "truth" of an emotional experience (what Bion will designate O) that involves thoughts and feelings contained not in any one person, but rather generated between them.

If this sounds mystical, that is not out of keeping with Bion's intentions, nor with the concerns of *The Mill on the Floss*. Bion directly argues that there is something fundamentally inexplicable about how psychoanalysis (and the principles of ordinary intersubjective interaction that it deploys in exaggerated form) works, and cites several mystical writers to describe it: Saint John of the Cross, Meister Eckhart, Issac Luria, and the Blessed John Ruysbroeck. Meanwhile, in her novel, George Eliot seems to argue that there is something mystical about reading itself. We see this most clearly in Maggie's reading of the medieval religious mystic Thomas à Kempis, an experience accompanied by both the "quiet hand" of an earlier reader, who has marked the text with underlined sentences and arrows in the margins, and a "low voice" that seems to spring from the book's pages and sound out its words (*MF* 302–4).

Bion writes that "there is a matrix of thought which lies within the confines of the . . . group, but not within the confines of the individual" (*Groups* 91). Freud understood this, Bion argues, and it is a key insight of psychoanalysis, which doesn't actually look at individual psychology, but examines instead "the relationship between two people" in its dedicated "study of the transference" (*Groups* 104). Bion's earliest work extends the "depth and width" of Freud's investigation by looking at small groups. What both the pair- and group-therapy situations attest to is the existence of a "matrix of thought" created interpersonally: to thoughts held by the collective but not necessarily by any of its individual members. There are, in other words, things that can be thought and felt only by two or more people. *The Mill on the Floss* argues that such a matrix of thought applies to the relations between book and reader as well. What Maggie manages to think and feel while reading à Kempis emanates not only from the author, not only from her own heart and mind, but from a "matrix of thought" that develops between them, like a charged field of sonic vibrations. Moreover, this matrix draws in more than a pair: in addition to including Maggie and the book's author, it includes the book's earlier reader, the one who has annotated the text, and, by logical extension, the reader of *The Mill on the Floss*, the one who reads alongside Maggie the long passages of à Kempis that Eliot incorporates into the novel. Drawing on this scene of reading, Eliot invites us to think of reading her own novel as a similarly animated and vibratory relational experience.

Maggie's reading of Thomas à Kempis, uncanny from the start, models a relationality between literary figures that Eliot would like her own book to take up and effect. At this point in the novel, Maggie is thirteen years old and home from school taking care of her sick father. Sunk deep in wishfulness, the book arrives to her as if by the force of her own yearning:

> She thought it was part of the hardship of her life that there was laid upon her the burthen of larger wants than others seemed to feel, that she had to endure this wide hopeless yearning for that something, whatever it was, that was greatest and best on this earth. She wished she could be like Bob [her childhood friend], with his easily satisfied ignorance, or like Tom, who had something to do on which he could fix his mind with a steady purpose and disregard everything else. (*MF* 300)

If Maggie's very essence seems to be "wide hopeless yearning," the narrator is quick to clarify that this is not a unique condition, nor precisely a universal one (as in Nancy Armstrong's argument that this sense of wanting more than one's social conditions can provide is precisely what defines a novelistic protagonist).[63] Instead, it is a condition of being a woman in this particular time and place. The narrator's better understanding of this situation than Maggie's creates a somewhat ironic commentary on Maggie's sense of her own uniqueness, and is signaled by one of Eliot's characteristic narratorial interjections: "Poor ____!" The paragraph concludes in a single lengthy sentence that laments the ways that young women are deprived of both true education and true guidance:

> Poor child! as she leaned her head against the window-frame with her hands clasped tighter and tighter and her foot beating the ground, she was as lonely in her trouble as if she had been the only girl in the civilised world of that day, who had come out of her school-life with a soul untrained for inevitable struggles—with no other part of her inherited share in the hard-won treasures of thought, which generations of painful toil have laid up for the race of men than shreds and patches of feeble literature and false history—with much futile information about Saxon and other kings of doubtful example, but unhappily quite without that knowledge of the irreversible laws within and without her which, governing the habits, becomes morality, and, developing the feelings of submission and dependence, becomes religion:—as lonely in her trouble as if every other girl besides herself had been cherished and watched over by elder minds, not forgetful of their own early time when need was keen and impulse strong. (*MF* 300)

Maggie is not as lonely as she imagines herself to be because she's not the only girl in this situation, and she is not as lonely as she imagines herself to be because she is not, after all, thinking alone. Thinking with and alongside her is the narrator ("Poor child!"), the author (a woman and autodidact herself deprived, thirty years before, in the time the novel is set, of the education she describes as being desirable), and the reader. And what is more, none of these figures are singular. The narrative voice contains at once character and narrator, feeling and commentary, youth and age, sentiment and its analysis, closeness and distance, and also positions that are coded as girl and boy. The narrator intones all of these things at once: a certain closeness to Maggie's feeling of lonely girlhood, a masculine posture of armchair historian, the male essayist George Eliot's most ardent opinions (the sense of "irreversible laws within and without"), and what we cannot help but feel is Mary Ann Evans's own remembered (and remaining) ardent wish to be "cherished and watched over by elder minds."

And, indeed, this wish is reiterated later in the novel when Maggie meets Dr. Kenn: she sees in his "plain, middle-aged face" a "grave, penetrating kindness ... seeming to tell of a human being who had reached a firm, safe strand, but was looking with helpful pity towards the strugglers still tossed by the waves," and which seems to hold for Maggie a promise of help (although he will not, in the end, be able to save her from drowning). The narrator then generalizes:

> The middle-aged, who have lived through their strongest emotions, but are yet in a time when memory is still half passionate and not merely contemplative, should surely be a sort of natural priesthood whom life has disciplined and consecrated to be the refuge and rescue of early stumblers and victims of self-despair: most of us at some moment in our young lives, would have welcomed a priest of that natural order in any sort of canonicals or uncanonicals, but had to scramble upwards into all of the difficulties of nineteen entirely without such aid, as Maggie did. (*MF* 453)

The narrator is at once young and aged: at once in Maggie's position and in the position of "most of us" who are now middle-aged, at once a priest of the natural order and in need of one him- or herself. Middle-agedness in fact identifies precisely this in-between-ness or shuttling between positions, "passionate" and "contemplative" alike. Mary Ann Evans, or, as she now signed herself, Marian Evans Lewes, was forty-one years old when she published *The Mill on the Floss* under the name of an ostensibly middle-aged man.[64]

The book thus arrives to Maggie, in the chapter entitled "A Voice from the Past," as a girl full of yearning and one seeking a guide—and, as it turns out, a personified book will do. Maggie has filled her young years with an "eager life in the triple world of reality, books, and waking dreams" (*MF* 287), but this chapter finds her sick of everything she has to read, schoolbooks and "shreds and patches of feeble literature" alike:

> Sometimes Maggie thought she could have been contented with absorbing fancies: if she could have had all Scott's novels and all Byron's poems!—then perhaps she might have found happiness enough to dull her sensibility to her actual daily life. And yet . . . they were hardly what she wanted. She could make dream-worlds enough of her own—but no dream-world would satisfy her now. She wanted some explanation of this hard, real life: the unhappy-looking father seated at the dull breakfast-table; the childish bewildered mother; the little sordid tasks that filled the hours, or the more oppressive emptiness of weary, joyless leisure; the need of some tender, demonstrative love; the cruel sense that Tom didn't mind what she thought or felt, and that they were no longer playfellows together; the privation of all pleasant things that had come to her more than to others: she wanted some key that would enable her to understand, and, in understanding, endure, the heavy weight that had fallen on her young heart. (*MF* 298)

The "absorbing fancies" of poems and novels merely "dull" the "sensibility." Maggie wants "some key" that will help her understand dullness itself: the "hard, real life" of the too-solid breakfast table and the "heavy weight" of weariness, boredom, routine, and lack of possibility. And then Bob delivers a stack of books that includes the one that seems to be the answer to her unformulated prayers, an "explanation" that indeed seems to arrive like a friend: "*Thomas à Kempis?*—the name had come across her in her reading, and she felt the satisfaction every one knows, of getting some ideas to attach to a name that strays solitary in the memory" (*MF* 301). The reading comes across her as much as she comes across it, in Eliot's interesting reversal of agency, which invites us to partake of the excited feeling of familiarity—"the satisfaction every one knows"—as much as Maggie does. "She took up the little, old, clumsy book with some curiosity: it had the corners turned down in many places, and some hand, now for ever quiet, had made at certain passages strong pen and ink marks, long since browned by time. Maggie turned from leaf to leaf and read where the quiet hand pointed . . ." (*MF* 301). The rest of Eliot's page is text, over 250 words, drawn from à Kempis's *The Imitation of Christ*. These selections, connected by ellipses, are apparently those pointed out by the "quiet hand":

> Know that the love of theyself doth hurt thee more than anything in the world. . . . If thou seekest this or that, and wouldst be here or there, to enjoy thy own will and pleasure thou shalt never be quiet or free from care: for in everything somewhat will be wanting [. . .] . . . . Blessed are those ears that receive the whispers of the divine voice, and listen not to the whisperings of the world. Blessed are those ears which hearken not unto the voice which soundeth outwardly, but unto the Truth which teacheth inwardly . . . (*MF* 301)

Maggie thrills to this message of renunciation: to the possibility of living without wishes, and to the possibility of hearing "the whispers of the divine voice" so clearly that they will muffle out, like the "rush of water" and "booming of the mill" at the start of the novel, the "whisperings of the world":

> A strange thrill of awe passed though Maggie while she read, as if she had been wakened in the night by a strain of solemn music, telling of beings whose souls had been astir while hers was in stupor. She went on from one brown mark to another, where the quiet hand seemed to point, hardly conscious that she was reading—seeming rather to listen while a low voice said . . . (*MF* 302)

Another long passage of à Kempis is incorporated here, so that the reader of *The Mill on the Floss* is carried along with Maggie's reading of *The Imitation of Christ*, both pointed on by the "quiet hand" of an unknown earlier reader and by the quiet hand, too, of George Eliot's own curation of the text. *The Imitation of Christ* is figured as more than just a written text: "this voice out of the far-off middle ages, was the direct communication of a human soul's belief and experience." The book is not self-contained, but rather the "outpourings" of a soul that can't help but touch on and enter into the "belief and experience" of others' souls. "I suppose that is the reason why," the narrator muses, this "small old-fashioned book . . . works miracles to this day, turning bitter waters into sweetness" (MF 303). Perhaps it even works miracles through a secondhand reading, by way of passages contained in *The Mill on the Floss*. And perhaps *The Mill on the Floss* is capable of working miracles too?

Bion had a notion that psychoanalysis and art alike might affect miracles of a kind, and at times he gives these miracles quite simple names: "transformations," which then becomes another of his technical terms with its corresponding sign, T. Bion writes: "The patient is coming to me for help and one reason for his distress is that his formulation does not afford scope for the solution of his problem" (*Tr* 123). The analyst's task is to restate or redescribe the problem in terms that *will* afford a solution. Bion writes of the patient: "he is stating *his* experience inadequately for *my* purpose which is to know what he is talking about and to meditate upon it. (What he is talking about = O.) I therefore transform his statement" (*Tr* 123)—in this case, by formulating it in different words: by offering an interpretation. Making transformations, T, from O (psychic reality, "what the patient is talking about," the "truth" of an emotional experience) is one of the primary tasks of psychoanalysis. It is also, Bion argues, something that art, literature, and music do for us: if psychoanalytic interpretation "affords a link between unsophisticated emotional problems, their unsophisticated solutions, and the possibility of their restatement in sophisticated terms admitting of sophisticated solutions, then it may be that musical and other artistic methods afford a similar link" (*Tr* 125). Bion continues: "In the poem [the material of transformations] may be found in the long-short of the rhythm; in painting it may be found, not as Vitruvius sought to find it, in a golden section or other geometric plan as the method of construction, but in the matter from which the construct is formed" (*Tr* 125–26). As he puts it elsewhere, the very "patterns of pigment on canvas" (*Tr* 33) have the power to work miracles. Transformations can change, in Bion's powerful opening image, "a path through a field sown with poppies" (*Tr* 1) by way of painting into a work of art, and likewise the emotional experience between analyst and patient, by way of analysis, into "psycho-analytic description" (*Tr* 4). What is miraculous is that in these transformations, something inherently ineffable and unknowable, "like Kant's thing-in-itself" (*Tr* 12)—O—has become available to representation, to knowing, to working-over and working-through, to the possibility of a "sophisticated solution." (It is unclear exactly what O directly stands for in Bion's work, since his usual translation of it is "truth" or "ultimately reality"—but perhaps O is for Eliot's "outpourings"?)

Bion's O, introduced in *Transformations* (1965) and discussed in more detail in *Attention and Interpretation* (1970), supposes what current-day psychoanalyst and psychoanalytic scholar Michael Eigen calls an "area of faith" in psychoanalysis.[65] Bion demands that we accept the reality of something that we cannot directly know or directly describe, but that we can only be or become. His chief analogy for O in *Transformations* is the analytic session, and indeed, Bion's entire corpus is dedicated to articulating the "ineffable" experience of analysis, even though and even precisely because it is impossible to fully describe—it is a thing that can be experienced but never fully known: "no one can ever know what happens in the analytic session, the thing-in-itself, O; we can only speak of what the analyst or patient *feels* happens, his emotional experience, that which I denote by T" (*Tr* 33). And yet what happens is indisputably real. Bion describes this by way of one of his favorite heuristics, the notion of "reversible perspective" I earlier described. Bion writes: "It is as if in one view man can never know the thing-in-itself, but only secondary and primary qualities; whereas in the other view he can never 'know' anything *but* the thing-in-itself" (*Tr* 40). An act of faith, F, is required to accept the existence of O, to accept that a large part of our experience is somehow beyond us, to accept that, just as there is a "matrix of thought" shared by the group but not held by any of its individual thinkers, something happens between the analyst and the patient that they both "know" but of which neither of them is in full possession. And faith is required, too, in the act of reading Bion's own inscrutable texts: because clinical experience "concerns the communication of material from an experience that is ineffable," to understand Bion's writing about it "the reader will need to be indulgent if he is to grasp the meaning I wish to convey" (*Tr* 51).

George Eliot has no such faith in the "indulgence" of her own readers to grasp her meaning. The inclusion of a mystical text in the fabric of the social realist novel seems to demand a series of complicated rhetorical moves for the narrator, as the novel works at once to avow the power of the book and disavow any too-simple belief in it. The narrator first works to create distance between Maggie's instant and ardent faith and a more seasoned skepticism by pointing out Maggie's misreading of the text. Maggie sees in the book "a secret of life" (*MF* 302), the "suddenly apprehended solution of a problem" (*MF* 303). "With all the hurry of an imagination that could never rest in the present," Maggie eagerly forms "plans of self-humiliation and entire devotedness," and the narrator just as eagerly critiques these plans: "in the ardour of first discovery, renunciation seemed to her the entrance into that satisfaction which she had so long been craving in vain." But this is wishful thinking too: "She had not perceived—how could she until she had lived longer?—the inmost truth of the old monk's outpourings, that renunciation remains sorrow, though sorrow borne willingly. Maggie was still panting for happiness, and was in ecstasy because she had found the key to it" (*MF* 303). While seasoned readers of George Eliot know to be suspicious of any "key," whether a key to living or a Key to All Mythologies, Maggie does not, partly because she has not "lived longer" and partly because she has not had Eliot to read. It is indeed a distinctive part of Maggie's tragedy as the novel frames it that she does not have the imaginative and realist literature she would need to help her both understand her real-life situation (the "dull breakfast-table") and imagine possibilities for her adult life. Maggie believes she has found the key to happiness in self-renunciation, taking the quoted words of à Kempis directly to heart: "Forsake thyself, resign thyself, and then shalt thou enjoy inner peace. . . . then shall immoderate fear leave thee and inordinate love shall die" (*MF* 302). But, as Bion would put it, Maggie's "formulation" of the problem "does not" yet "afford scope" for its solution. The narrator points this out too, but not without the perceived need of defending the book and its capacities in turn: "[Maggie] knew nothing of doctrines and systems—of mysticism or quietism: but this voice out of the far-off middle ages, was the direct communication of a human soul's belief and experience, and came to Maggie as an unquestioned message" (*MF* 303). In a move quite typical to Eliot's fiction, the narrator first teaches us to deem Maggie's acceptance of the message as too "unquestioning," and too youthful, and then challenges "our" judgment of it as such, returning to the first-person voice in order to do so. The book is indeed a "direct communication," even if Maggie reads its message incorrectly:

> It was written down by a hand that waited for the heart's prompting, it is the chronicle of a solitary, hidden anguish, struggle, trust, and triumph—not written on velvet cushions to teach endurance to those who are treading with bleeding feet on the stones. And so it remains to all time, a lasting record of human needs and human consolations, the voice of a brother who, ages ago, felt and suffered and renounced . . . under the same silent far-off heavens, and with the same passionate desires, the same strivings, the same failures, the same weariness. (*MF* 303)

A "lasting record of human needs and human consolations," "the voice of a brother" speaking directly from the past: the narrator affirms Maggie's own mystical experience, her sense of hearing and feeling the book rather than reading it in a more traditional sense. The book is not self-contained, but rather the "outpourings" of a "human soul's belief and experience" that irresistibly flow into the beliefs and experiences of others, resonating with "the same passionate desires, the same strivings, the same failures, the same weariness" that define their needs and consolations, under the "same silent far-off heavens." Reading the book is a way to socially dream those inherently social feelings.

And yet just as the narrator seems to feel compelled first to critique and then to defend Maggie's reading, this ardent avowal of the book's power seems to require another justification in turn, and indeed one of the novel's most interesting. This turn shows the narrator/implied writer reflecting on his/her/their/its own "tone" of voice. Immediately following the passage above ("I suppose . . ."), a new paragraph begins:

> In writing the history of unfashionable families, one is apt to fall into a tone of emphasis which is very far off from the being the tone of good society, where principles and beliefs are not only of an extremely moderate kind, but are always presupposed, no subjects being eligible but such as can be touched with a light and graceful irony. (*MF* 303)

The reflection on the class-based difference between tones of "emphasis" and "irony" in fact performs such a change in tone, moving from an emphatic belief in miracles to ironic commentary. "Good society," the narrator declares, "has its claret and its velvet carpets, its dinner-engagements six weeks deep," its "opera" and its "thoroughbred horses" and its "lounges" and "clubs": "how should it," then, the narrator asks, "have time or need for belief and emphasis?" (*MF* 303–4). But irony, it turns out, is dependent on emphasis for its very existence.

> But good society, floated on gossamer wings of light irony, is of very expensive production; requiring nothing less than a wide and arduous national life condensed in unfragrant deafening factories, cramping itself in mines, sweating at furnaces, grinding, hammering, weaving under more or less oppression of carbonic acid—or else, spread over sheepwalks, and scattered in lonely houses and huts on the clayey or chalky corn-lands, where the rainy days look dreary. The wide national life is based entirely on emphasis—the emphasis of want, which urges it into all the activities necessary for the maintenance of good society and light irony: it spends its heavy years often in a chill, uncarpeted fashion amidst family discord unsoftened by long corridors. (*MF* 304)

The passage is remarkable in that it itself does the work of condensing wide sweeps of time and space in its brief sketches of "national life," taking us from scene to scene, from factories to mines to sheepwalks, through the linking principle of gerund forms: "cramping," "sweating," "grinding, hammering, weaving." The gerund forms of manual labor strangely evoke the gerund forms of dreaming in the novel's opening and in other punctual scenes—Maggie "sobbing," "grinding and beating" her wooden doll's head against the chimney's bricks in the attic (*MF* 31), "the meal forever pouring, pouring" in the mill that is "a little world apart from . . . outside everyday life" (*MF* 32).[66] Here though, gerund verbs form both a dream of being able to see and contain all of "arduous" and "wide" national life within a novel's pages and one of the novel's most trenchant critiques of class privilege and the alienated labor upon which it depends. Good society has irony and "velvet carpets," while the working class has "the emphasis of want" and short uncarpeted hallways that do nothing to muffle "family discord"—Eliot remarkably reinserts the Tulliver family in this acrobatic final phrase, continuing in a defense not only of Maggie's reading, but also the wide national life's need for religion. Alongside this, she defends the need for a literature depicting "the histories of unfashionable families," and the consequent need to strategically deploy something like religious "enthusiasm" in her own writing:

> Under such circumstances there are many among its myriads of souls who have absolutely needed an emphatic belief, life in this unpleasurable shape demanding some solution even to unspeculative minds; just as you inquire into the stuffing of your couch when anything galls you there, whereas eider-down and perfect French springs excite no question. Some have an emphatic belief in alcohol, and seek their *ekstasis* or outside standing-ground in gin, but the rest require something that good society calls enthusiasm, something that will present motives in an entire absence of high prizes, something that will give patience and feed human love when the limbs ache with weariness and human looks are hard upon us—something, clearly, that lies outside personal desires, that includes resignation for ourselves and active love for what is not ourselves. Now and then that sort of enthusiasm finds a far-echoing voice that comes from an experience springing out of deepest need. And it was by being brought within the long lingering vibrations of such a voice that Maggie, with her girl's face and unnoted sorrows, found an effort and a hope that helped her through two years of loneliness, making out a faith for herself without the aid of established authorities and appointed guides—for they were not at hand, and her need was pressing. (*MF* 304–5)

There are many things to note in the enthusiastic culmination of this long passage. Perhaps the first is the amazing flexibility of its own narrative voice, moving not only between emphasis and irony, not only between first and third person, but also between an "us" subject to "weariness" and "hard looks" and an "us" standing outside of such a position—the "us" of eider-down couches and of critical looks at the need for religion in the working classes, although perhaps after reading this passage and learning why such a need arises, our looks will be softened by transformative sympathy. A second is how much time the passage elapses in Maggie's own life, taking her through many long lonely years without a guide "at hand" except for the "far-echoing" and "long lingering vibrations" of the voice of à Kempis—and except for, of course, the "quiet hand" that is at hand too, showing that it takes two or more people to read (as in Bion's math equation: "♀♂ ≥ 2"). A third perhaps is its framing of life as being in need of "solution," which is also to say in need of reformulation, through the words and indeed the lives of others—the life of à Kempis ("an experience... of deepest need"), the life of Christ, and perhaps the life of Maggie, "with her girl's face and unnoted sorrows." And finally I want to point out that the passage, like Bion's formulations of O, also carves out space for an area of "faith"— although Maggie's self-made faith will not be the precise kind of faith the novel ultimately recommends, just as religion will not ultimately be its particular style of "emphasis"—at least, not this religion.

More Instruments Playing Together

The Imitation of Christ offers a kind of religious quietism, both in the sense of relying on "silent prayer" and quieting one's own desires. To quote again the quoted text, à Kempis writes that a man, "having left all," should "leave himself, and go wholly out of himself, and retain nothing of self-love"; then "superfluous cares" and "evil perturbations" will fly away; "then shall immoderate fear leave thee and inordinate love shall die" (*MF* 302). But Maggie and *The Mill on the Floss* are not on the side of quiet. They are on the side of music, they are on the side of emphasis, and they are on the side of inordinate love, even if that means inordinate love unto death. As Maggie puts it, "I [always] wanted more instruments playing together—I wanted voices to be fuller and deeper" (*MF* 341). Philip Wakem's critique of Maggie's reading, a few years down the line during their meetings in the Red Deeps, may stand in for a critique of Eliot's own (just as his letter to Maggie at the novel's close echoes her ethics of sympathy): he argues that Maggie's stylized quietism is nothing more than stupefaction, a way of deafening herself and stunting her senses:

> You are shutting yourself up in a narrow self-delusive fanaticism which is only a way of escaping pain by starving into dulness [*sic*] all the highest powers of your nature. Joy and peace are not resignation: resignation is the willing endurance of pain that is not allayed—that you don't expect to be allayed. Stupefaction is not resignation: and it is stupefaction to remain in ignorance—to shut up all the avenues by which the life of your fellow-men might become known to you. (*MF* 340)

The narrator is at pains to point out Philip's "double impulse" (*MF* 341) in this speech and its selfish motivation—to have Maggie as a lover—and Maggie knows it too. Nevertheless, Philip's words are such a direct echo of the narrator's earlier assessment of Maggie's use of à Kempis and her misunderstanding of resignation that we can't help but hear them in the vocal register of earnest truth. Philip's language of stupefaction, self-benumbing, and deadened feelings as opposed to the "keenness" of the "faculties" (*MF* 314) make his ideas consistent with the ones George Eliot's narrators return to again and again, in a desire for the heightened sensibilities offered, as in *Middlemarch*, by the telescope, the microscope, and extrasensory perception of the squirrel's heartbeat and in the paired insight that most of us walk about "well wadded with stupidity" (*M* 194). It is ironic that à Kempis's religious text is denounced by both Philip and the novel's more-knowing narrator when it arguably teaches some of the same lessons as George Eliot's own secular religion of sympathy. Maggie learns from the book—as Dorothea after her, emerging from the "moral stupidity" into which we are all born (*M* 211), learns from her own life—not to think of her own suffering alone while ignoring the suffering of others; she learns that her own desires, and indeed her own self, are in fact obstructions to a clearer and larger vision; she learns that problems arise from "fixing her heart on her own pleasure, as if that were the central necessity of the universe" (*MF* 302). But it is perhaps because the lesson à Kempis offers Maggie is so close to Eliot's own moral philosophy that it must at times be denounced so vigorously. It contains a spiritual truth, but one that can so easily be co-opted into religious fanaticism (not unlike the kind Mary Ann Evans experienced in her own young life) that Eliot's narrator and Philip alike must distance themselves from it, and, knowing more, work to coax Maggie out of it. But the dismissal of this particular area of faith does install another in its place: wishing. Wishing for more music, wishing for inordinate love, and wishing for "an intense and varied life" (*MF* 387).

Wishing, for Philip, becomes a marker of disability, of the lack of fit between what we can imagine and what we can do. In his speech to Maggie, he uses wishing to recognize both his physical disability (the early illness that has left him weak and "deformed" by a hunchback) and his perceived failure as an artist: "I delight in fine pictures—I long to be able to paint such. I strive and strive, but can't produce what I want. That is pain to me, and always *will* be pain, until my faculties lose their keenness, like aged eyes" (*MF* 314). The circuit between physical and artistic dis-ability, psychic and physical "pain," sensory and creative faculties, and between illness and its metaphors is dizzying in its reversals and recodings. But it also allows Philip to speak, fearfully, about his limited prospects for a romantic and sexual future: "Then, there are many other things I long for . . . things that other men have, and that will always be denied me" (*MF* 314). Wishing is a desire for contact of various kinds in contradistinction to shutting up the avenues of the senses to look inward (as in the instructions of Descartes's *Meditations*: "I shall now close my eyes, stop up my ears, turn away all my senses . . . and thus communing only with myself, and examining my inner self, I shall try to make myself, little by little, better known and more familiar to myself"[67]); it is a desire for relation in contradistinction to "shut[ting] up all the avenues by which the life of your fellow-men might become known to you" (*MF* 314).

Wishing, for Maggie, becomes a marker of disabling social conditions. It betrays a longing for greater access and greater purpose within a patriarchal England (and its empire) that limits the possibilities for women's lives and women's "consciousness"—a consciousness that nevertheless overspills its bounds and yearns for material conditions that will support it. This is what Virginia Woolf describes in her remarkable reading that translates the religious yearning shared by George Eliot's heroines into a secular and feminist wishfulness. A George Eliot heroine "cannot live without religion," Woolf writes, and yet "she no longer knows to whom to pray." Her prayer is "uttered" as a "demand for something," but she "scarcely know[s] what," and it is likely something "incompatible with the facts of human existence."[68] All of this is true of Maggie Tulliver, whose final prayer, at the end of the novel, is a kind of "demand" for possibility, but one posed in such a way that its fulfillment, in this story and in this setting, can only be manifest as regression—as a return to a time of "unsophisticated emotional problems." It is a prayer for "unsophisticated solutions" that are in fact "incompatible with the facts of human existence" (we cannot return to our childhood days, we cannot sexually partner off with our brothers, we cannot die in a perfect merger with anyone else). The flood is in fact a dissolution of Maggie's problems and the problems of the book rather than their "sophisticated solution." And indeed, this watery dissolve reveals that Maggie's prayer for an ending is perhaps more directly addressed to her secular author than to a conventional God, exchanging one "Unseen Pity that would be with her to the end" (*MF* 536) for another.

Wishing in the novel, then, irradiates two ideas that are central to both *The Mill on the Floss* and the connection between Eliot's and Bion's thinking. The first is the persistence of the container as a controlling metaphor in literary and psychological writing. The second is a kind of belief in wishing and acts like it—praying, longing, yearning, intense feeling, reading, hearing and making music, loving—to not only overspill containers of self, psyche, and given social position, but also, crucially, to make contact with something beyond them. Wishes do not always come true. To believe they did would be, as Bion puts it, an excessive reliance on omnipotent phantasy. But sometimes they do, and it would be just as active a hallucination not to see this. And more importantly, their projection of a space beyond the immediately realistic present carves out a space for possibility, for change, for what is not quite thinkable yet within existing social configurations and literary forms, and perhaps most importantly, for contact.

What is valuable about à Kempis, then, is less the message his book presents (and which the novel ultimately dismisses) than the experience Maggie has of reading it: her feeling of being in contact with both the writer and earlier readers; of being reassured that she is part of a wider network of hearts and minds, and always has been, even before she knew it; her sense that there are indeed teachers and guides in the world whose experience can be relied upon; her faith in the power of words to open experience up rather than close it down. If the novel ultimately steers Maggie and its own readers away from à Kempis, it is because it wants to define its own "area of faith" not in renunciation (à Kempis: "cleave not unto ['earthly things,' including other people], lest thou be entangled and perish" (*MF* 302)—Maggie drowns precisely by clinging to her brother), not in pulling inward (à Kempis: "Blessed are those ears that receive that receive the whispers of the divine voice, and listen not to the whisperings of the world. Blessed are those ears which hearken not unto the voice which soundeth outwardly, but unto the Truth with teacheth inwardly . . ." [*MF* 302]—Maggie wants to hear the world's music, wants to hear more voices singing together), but rather in the reality and power of interpersonal relations, as miraculous and ineffable as they are. Neil Hertz describes à Kempis's text as an "allegorical drama of internalization": Maggie's reading is "an incursion by means of which self-identity is breached and a new attachment secreted in that interior space."[69] But the more vital force of à Kempis's *The Imitation of Christ*, I would argue, is in its power of externalization. Maggie's recitation of its well-known words at the end of the novel bring the flood; the narrator's recitation of its words, earlier in the novel when they are incorporated wholesale, open the domestic story to the sights, sounds, and concerns of the "wide and arduous national life condensed in unfragrant deafening factories, cramping itself in mines, sweating at furnaces, grinding, hammering, weaving" (*MF* 304). This gesture to the larger national life is not sustained, but it provides a valuable glimpse and whisper of the other stories a novel might tell, of the other lives with which middle-class and upper-class readers are necessarily in contact, whether or not they know it.

Inadequate Containers

Characters, psyches, people, books, narrative forms, bodies, and nations are continuously imagined, within novels, literary criticism and theory, and psychological discourse alike, as containers of various kinds. Characters are containers for "qualities"; the modern Bildungsroman is a container for a story of growing up; psyches are containers, in British psychoanalysis, for internal objects; the nation is a container, in what remains a dominant theory for scholars of nineteenth-century literature, for cohesive imagined communities.[70] In both *The Mill on the Floss* and in Bion's writing, the use of the container metaphor runs rampant. Bion writes: "According to his background a patient will describe various objects as containers, such as his mind, the unconscious, the nation; others as contained, such as his money, his ideas" (*A&I* 122). Even casual references to "events that occur 'in analysis' or 'in the past' or 'inside' or 'outside'" (*A&I* 109) should resonate for the analyst, Bion instructs, as references to the container/contained and its system of relations. There is a mode of psychoanalytic listening—call it Kleinian—in which every dream, every utterance, every description of the world (and of literary forms) can be heard as referencing the internal object world. Everything can be heard, in other words, multiphonically, as revealing not only what is directly described but also the imagined state of one's inner contents.[71] We can certainly read *The Mill on the Floss*, with its many references to containers, vessels, vehicles, and receptacles, in this way. Take the following passage, in which a young Maggie sits vigil next to her sick father:

> Maggie in her brown frock with her eyes reddened and her heavy hair pushed back, looking from the bed where her father lay, to the dull walls of this sad chamber which was the centre of her world, was a creature full of eager, passionate longings for all that was beautiful and glad: thirsty for all knowledge: with an ear straining after dreamy music that died away and would not come near to her: with a blind, unconscious yearning for something that would link together the wonderful impressions of this mysterious life and give her soul a sense of home in it. (*MF* 247–48)

Maggie's eyes hold tears; she is contained within the "dull walls" of the "sad" bedroom "chamber," which is contained in turn by the walls of the "world"; she is a "creature full of eager, passionate longings" and "yearning"; she wants to take in "knowledge"; she wants to feel that "her soul" is contained "in this mysterious life." But if Bion and Eliot both engage the kind of Kleinian psychoanalytic speaking and listening I have described, it is in an effort to consider what *cannot* be contained, both "inside" the psyche and "within" the metaphor of containing itself. The form of the above sentence reflects this concern. With a series of colons, Eliot unconventionally breaks her sentence into individual, self-contained parts. Yet each part "strains" toward the next, the contents of one description spilling over into the needed explanation of the next. The passage continues:

> No wonder, when there is this contrast between the outward and the inward, that painful collisions come of it. A girl of no startling appearance, and who will never be a Sappho or a Madame Roland or anything else the world takes wide notice of, may still hold forces within her as the living plant-seed does, which will make a way for themselves, often in a shattering, violent manner. (*MF* 248)

Seeds burst open and inner "forces" will out. Tears spill from Maggie's eyes, books burst their bindings, minds meet somewhere outside themselves, and nations extend into empires. (Even the novel's pastoral vision of preindustrial England is not self-contained: the river Floss carries "merchant ships from beyond the village borders" into the "traditional yeoman world" of St. Oggs, bearing goods from the British Empire as well as the first signs of the "economic modernity" of global capitalism.)[72]

It is a marker of the complexity of Bion's and Eliot's thinking that they both deploy and critique the fantasy of being self-contained. Wishing, feeling, flooding (along with their cognates: desire, "thirst," "yearning," "longing," "straining after"), and the fluidity of character/narrator/reader/writer relations are all ways that *The Mill on the Floss* gets us to imagine the inadequacy of imaginary containers and their tendency to overflow. Bion's critique of the container as a stand-alone metaphor comes in his insistence on the container/contained as a set of interactive relations, in his running commentary on the limitations of language, including his own invented sign systems (such as his decision to use the symbols ♀♂ to represent the container/contained), to adequately describe psychoanalytic experience, and in his theory of O as a kind of experience that fully belongs to no individual person. He writes: "the only true thought is one that has never found an individual to 'contain' it" (*A&I* 117). Among the novel's inadequate containers—sites where a myth of self-containment fails to account for an underlying relational reality—are the nation, the gender binary, metaphor, "maxims," skin, ethnic categories, monogamy, compulsory heterosexuality, and any single literary figure (character, narrator, reader, author) taken out of connection with its others.

Catastrophic Development

Part of what makes some of these containers inadequate is the too-simple notion of plot—its determinism, its exclusively forward motion, its relentless drivenness—that helps to shape them. Development itself is problematized in the novel, both for its violent effects and its failure to capture how deeply regression, and not simply progress, shapes experience. As Jed Esty puts it, tracking the long critical debate about whether or not *The Mill on the Floss* qualifies as a Bildungsroman, "The process of maturation generates absolute losses for Maggie: There are moods, sensations, relationships, and experiences that cannot survive into adulthood."[73] Bion has equally useful ways for thinking about regression, which he begins to chart in his study of the Oedipus myth. He writes: "The common-sense view of mental development is that it consists in an increase of capacity to grasp reality and a decrease in the obstructive force of illusions." Concomitantly, the common-sense view of the psychoanalytic process is that it involves "the exposure of archaic phantasies to modification by a sophisticated capacity" to grasp reality. Such a "supposition," however, "cannot stand up to rigorous examination" (*E* 51). Instead, development is marked not only by a failure to grasp reality, but an outright "hatred" of it (and indeed, the "hatred of reality" is one of Bion's signal phrases).

In his earliest work, *Experiences in Groups*, Bion argues that his patients evince a fundamental distrust and "hatred of the process of development itself." He writes:

> There is a hatred of having to learn by experience at all, and a lack of faith in the worth of such a kind of learning. [And yet a] little experience of groups soon shows that this not simply a negative attitude; the process of development is really being compared with some other state, the nature of which is not immediately apparent.... [Eventually] in the group it becomes very clear that this longed-for alternative to the group procedure is really something like arriving fully equipped as an adult fitted by instinct to know without training or development exactly how to live and move and have his being in a group.... My experience of groups, indeed, indicates that man is hopelessly committed to both states of affairs. (*Groups* 89–90)

Man is "hopelessly committed" to two states of affairs, or to two contradictory wishes, at once: the wish, first, to grow up, to learn, to develop, and, second, the wish that such development were not necessary at all.[74] And perhaps not without good cause. For Bion argues that maturation is necessarily marked by catastrophe.[75]

In a stunning reworking of Freud's famous comparison of psychoanalysis to archaeological excavation, Bion writes, "the spectacle presented is one, to borrow Freud's analogy, similar to that of the archaeologist who discovers in his field-work the evidences, not so much of a primitive civilization, as that of a primitive catastrophe" (Arrogance 88). What the analyst uncovers in the unconscious is not evidence of growth, nor even of a refusal to grow, but rather outright destruction. Building on this reworked analogy in "Attacks on Linking," Bion stipulates that unlike the ruins of "a primitive civilization," those of the "primitive disaster" will not settle: "The value of the [archaeological] analogy is lessened because in the analysis we are confronted not so much with a static situation that permits leisurely study, but with a catastrophe that remains at one and the same moment actively vital and yet incapable of resolution into quiescence" (Attacks 101). Bion is most directly describing the hatred of reality and "destruction of a capacity for curiosity" that he identifies as the hallmark of psychotic illness (Attacks 101). But his theories also emphasize that there is a psychotic part of every personality. And so in psychotic and nonpsychotic personalities alike, what development means is that the catastrophe continues.

The Mill on the Floss too is interested in the ubiquity of "primitive disaster," including the loss of "first things." Maggie phrases her understanding of this movement in the language of hyperbole and destiny, calling it the "trial" she has to "bear in everything": "I may not keep anything I used to love when I was little.... I must part with everything I cared for when I was a child" (*MF* 313). She means more than anything her relationship to her brother Tom, which she imagines as an ideal closeness that, if it ever existed, we see only in its lapses. But Tom, and object loss in general, stand in for a more exacting developmental/catastrophic process to which the novel devotes a great deal of its attention: the process of becoming gendered and the way it not only divides Tom and Maggie, brother and sister, but also proves to be the site of "primitive catastrophe" within Maggie, her own personal ruins. The flood is not the novel's only "natural" disaster.

Boy and Girl, Arm and Arm

If *Tess* brings our attention to the experience of being gendered by offering moments of imaginary release from it, *The Mill on the Floss* instead describes this experience from the inside out, narrating the process of gender conscription and its costs. The novel narrates two significant consequences of this violent social process: sexual differentiation and sexual attraction—two movements that describe the push-and-pull toward and away from others of "the opposite sex" (as we naively refer to it in the language of gender binarism), as well as the curious bipolar magnetism of one's own assigned gender identity, at once attractive and repulsive. The dual story of Tom and Maggie Tulliver's "development" is also the story of their separation by way of normative gender conscription—by way of what Althusser, working from Lacan's theories of "sexuation," describes as "the long forced march which makes mammiferous larvae into human children, *masculine* or *feminine subjects*."[76] The novel narrates Maggie's and Tom's "long forced march" into humanity along the diverging paths of boyhood and girlhood. Indeed, Althusser's description could easily serve as a plot summary of *The Mill on the Floss* and the biological/evolutionary metaphors that inform it: the "small animal ... becomes human-sexual by crossing the infinite divide that separates life from humanity, the biological from the historical, 'nature' from 'culture.'"[77] Eliot is deeply interested in this crossover and its felt costs. As children, "Maggie and Tom were still very much like young animals," Eliot writes. They nuzzle each other—rubbing cheeks, noses, and foreheads—"with a humiliating resemblance to two friendly ponies" (*MF* 43). But as they grow, they have to learn more "human" or "human-sexual" behaviors. They have to learn distance from each other's bodies, and other equally severe forms of separation as well: different habits of mind; different behavioral standards; different notions of kinship and relationality; different sexualities; and, as literary characters, different treatments by the narrator, including differing amounts of narrative attention and distinct descriptive protocols.

(While narrative descriptions of Maggie's and Tom's internal experience are, early in the novel, closely interwoven, as the novel progresses and the two grow, Tom's experience drops out of the story, out of the reach of free indirect discourses and out of Maggie's view as well. As if to press this point, Maggie's realization in book 6 that Tom is in love with their cousin Lucy is posed as a dramatic reveal of his interior life, and one delivered to Maggie and to the reader at the same time.)[78]

Their "forced march" also includes compulsory heterosexuality and its key "cultural" outgrowth: monogamy. As if a natural consequence of becoming differentiated as a girl and a boy (that is to say, of undergoing the awful rigors of girl and boy training, which the novel describes in detail), the novel insists that they must find another boy or girl to pair off with. "Character is destiny" becomes "monogamy is destiny"—and a destiny to be avoided, for Maggie, only at the price of death. While the novel doesn't offer viable, livable alternatives to these pseudocompulsory arrangements of gender and sexuality, it does portray them as costly, painful, and limiting, entailing artificial and hyperbolically framed binary choices: boy or girl, Tom or Philip, Philip or Stephen, passion or duty, compulsion or "wayward choice" (*MF* 491).

It also portrays something that is perhaps even more disturbing: the enormous appeal of these normative categories, and the ways they get charged with libidinal power. This is, in part, what Bollas describes in his essay "Why Oedipus?": the way we are drawn to and comforted by regressive arrangements. Psycho-evolution is inevitably accompanied by psycho-devolution: "to go forward," Bollas writes, "we go back."[79] The Oedipal complex for Bollas means that we seek refuge from the ever-increasing complexity of experience by regressing into the simpler and more easily understood human relations of family and conventional romance, which save us from the group and from ourselves. He writes:

> Give the ordinary unbearableness of [the complexity born of having a mind to oneself], I think that the human individual partly regresses in order to survive, but this retreat has been so essential to human life that it has become an unanalyzed convention, part of the religion of everyday life. We call this regression "marriage" or "partnership," in which the person becomes part of a mutually interdependent couple that evokes and sustains the bodies of the mother and father, the warmth of the pre-Oedipal vision of life, before the solitary recognition of subjectivity grips the child.... To go forward in life, we go back, back to the places of the mother and the father, where we can

evoke these figures as inevitably comforting and practically as defensive alternatives to a madness always latent in groups: to the groups of social life, and more so to the group that is mental life.[80]

Indeed, this is one meaning of Bion's container/contained function, and especially the way the word is used in popular psychoanalytic (and pop-psychological) speech: it can be "containing" to return to the family, or to recreate a new one in the image of the family of origin. The novel supplements Bollas's insight, adding that it is not just the containers of "marriage" or "partnership" that are part of the "unanalyzed convention" of human regression, but also the (markedly inadequate) containers of the gender binary as well. Forced into these reductive categories, gender conformity becomes a regressive comfort, "boy" and "girl" becoming "defensive alternatives" to more malleable modes of gender expression and the wider range of our lived experience. In these terms, Maggie and Stephen's desire for each other is not simply illicit, but containing, and gathers part of its intense erotic charge from this function: for these two characters, each of whom is described in terms of some deviation from binary gender norms, pairing off affirms their respective femininity and masculinity as well as the sexual attraction between these terms.

The novel has a remarkably concise way of framing all of this. The entire drama—one that is not simply psycho-sexual, but also, drawing on Bion's rereading of the Oedipal myth as a psychodynamics of thinking, what we might call psycho-sexual-cognitive—is conveyed in the novel by talking about arms. Bill Cohen makes this clear when he describes the romance that makes up the final third of the novel as the "scandal plot" in which "Stephen Guest, admiring Maggie Tulliver's arms, persuades her to fall into his."[81] He is referring to one of the novel's most famous scenes, in which Stephen takes action on the sexual attraction that has been circulating between him and Maggie by grabbing her arm—the same "brown" (*MF* 108) or "large round" (*MF* 399) arm that has already received a great deal of narrative attention—and kissing it. Maggie refuses this advance, but Stephen's action becomes an impetus to discuss the mutual attraction that has to this point remained in the realm of "mute confession" (*MF* 460). In a much-cited narrative intrusion, Maggie's arm becomes a sign of her universal femininity, and Stephen's feeling for it a sign of his properly heteronormative masculinity:

> Who has not felt the beauty of a woman's arm?—the unspeakable suggestions of tenderness that lie in the dimpled elbow and all the varied gently lessening curves down to the delicate wrist with its tiniest, almost imperceptible nicks in the firm softness. A woman's arm touched the soul of a great sculptor two thousand years ago, so that he wrought an image of it for the Parthenon which moves us still as it clasps lovingly the time-worn marble

of a headless trunk. Maggie's was such an arm as that—and it had the warm tints of life. (*MF* 460)

Cohen points out that a number of sex scandals accrue to this passage and to its soft and tender arm: in addition to the illicit romance of Maggie and Stephen, the passage created a literary critical sex scandal as well,[82] when contemporary critics expressed shock and dismay at the impropriety of a female author (George Eliot's identity was known at this point) describing male sexual arousal.[83]

What strikes me about the passage is the way it seeks to stabilize not only Maggie's and Stephen's gender and sexual identities, but also those of the narrator and the reader: "Who has not felt the beauty of a woman's arm?" The question both offers refuge to the narrator and reader in male heterosexual desire and, of course, undercuts this stability through both the form of the sentence—a question—and the known facts of female authorship and female readership, which effectively introduce a much wider world of gender identities and sexual desires.

The passage has its complement in the narrator's earlier praise of Stephen's arm. When Stephen offers his arm to Maggie, the narrator reflects: "There is something strangely winning to most women in that offer of the firm arm: the help is not wanted physically at that moment, but the sense of help—the presence of strength that is outside them and yet theirs, meets a continual want of the imagination" (*MF* 425). I think this may be one of the sexiest passages in all of George Eliot's fiction (and *The Mill on the Floss* her sexiest novel). Like the passage above, it is coercively so. It directs readers in the physicality of heteronormative desire and its psychic and cognitive payoffs: the "tenderness" of a woman's touch, the "sense of help" and "strength" in a man's. Look, the novel says, at the security heteronormativity has to offer, and look at how the draw to it is powered by the excitement of sexual attraction. The physical sensations (more properly named psycho-cognitive-physical sensations, as reading these two writers together makes clear) of this kind of deeply heteronormative sexual desire are novel feelings to Maggie, as the narrator is at pains to make clear. Meeting Stephen for the first time, "Maggie felt herself, for the first time in her life, receiving the tribute of a very deep blush and a very deep bow from a person toward whom she herself was conscious of timidity. This new experience was very agreeable to her.... There was a new brightness in her eyes, and a very becoming flush on her cheek" (*MF* 391). And later, when Stephen catches Maggie as she trips stepping out of the boat after a rowing expedition: "It was very charming to be taken care of in that kind and graceful manner by some one taller and stronger than oneself. Maggie had never felt just in the same way before" (*MF* 398). New, new, new—this feeling is attributable not just to Maggie's attraction to Stephen, not just to her attraction to his particular kind of masculine physicality (which, however, needs confirmation too, in and through Maggie's femininity), but to her own newfound and pleasurable ability to inhabit and embody norms of feminine heterosexuality from which she has been excluded throughout her life (first as a tomboy, and later as overly sexual).

And yet the ending of the "firm arm" passage thematizes the problem I am describing in its emphasis on the "*continual want of imagination*" that creates desire for "a firm [masculine] arm." Read most concretely, the phrase is meant to tell us what women want: strength that is "outside them and yet theirs." But Eliot plays too on the notion of a "want of imagination" not as a desire but rather as an outright *failure* of imagination (as, for instance, Adam Phillips uses the phrase): conventional gender roles themselves demonstrate a "continual want of imagination," a failure to picture a fuller range of possibilities, a regressive falling back to "the places of the father and the mother," an attack on linking. Through this storyline—the complete or incomplete plots of "sexuation," of "socialization," of the sex scandal, of romance or the marriage plot, of the resolution/regression of the Oedipal complex—the novel expresses an incredibly complex set of feelings and desires. It communicates the violence, loss, and horror of the gender binary and heteronormativity—and it communicates too their persistent appeal, on the levels of both cognition and desire.

O Is for . . .

If the watchword for Eliot and Bion is relationality rather than self-containment, then the challenge that results is how to describe the strange things that happen between two (or more) people—especially in forms (the Bildungsroman, the psychoanalytic case history) built around the container of the individual or the one. Both Eliot and Bion posit a kind of faith in the notion that the strangeness of interpersonal interaction, the thing that it touches on that belongs fully to no one person, can be evoked, if not fully pictured, in writing. Once again, Philip is the one to voice this in *The Mill on the Floss*:

> I don't think any of the strongest effects our natures are susceptible of can ever be explained. We can neither detect the process by which they are arrived at nor the mode in which they act on us. The greatest of painters only once painted a mysteriously divine child—he couldn't have told how he did it—and we can't tell why we feel it to be divine. I think there are stores laid up in our human nature that our understandings can make no complete inventory of. Certain strains of music affect me so strangely—I can never hear them without their changing my whole attitude of mind for a time. (*MF* 317)

Maggie replies: "Ah! I know what you mean about music—*I feel so.*" In this passage, Philip could well be describing Bion's O (ultimate reality, thing-in-itself, truth, the "unknown and the unknowable"): its power and its ineffability, its reality and inaccessibility, its resistance to residing within any single subject or psyche, and its animation, instead, of the space between them. The "strongest effects our natures are susceptible of" can never be explained; "there are stores laid up in our human nature that our understandings can make no . . . inventory of." Philip describes what Bion claims for O: that it cannot be known but that it can be intuited; that it cannot be grasped not by the ordinary "links" of "being known, loved, or hated—K, L or H" (*Tr* 147) but only by a state of mind of receptivity and faith, F, "that there is an ultimate reality and truth—the unknown, unknowable, 'formless infinite'" (*A&I* 31). Bion writes that O "stands for the absolute truth in and of any object; it is assumed that this cannot be known by any human being; it can be known *about*, its presence can be recognized and felt, but it cannot be known. It is [only] possible to be at one with it" (*A&I* 30, emphasis added). Philip's statement can be read as describing this combination of felt truth and unknowability, both in its emphasis on what cannot be "explained," "detected," or "inventoried" by "understanding," and in its somewhat convoluted grammar, which makes "effects" and "process" the main subject of these sentences rather than any more precise descriptor. Philip's recourse to aesthetic experience—painting or seeing a painting, making or hearing music—to evoke the strangeness of something neither fully inside nor fully outside, something that evokes strong personal feeling but could never be fully contained within one person, points to one of Eliot's favored tropes for describing the strangeness of interpersonal relations. In *The Mill on the Floss*, Eliot uses music and romance as Bion uses the psychoanalytic situation: to get at another order of experience that is as uncanny as it is real, as unrepresentable as it is deeply felt.

In the final volume of *The Mill on the Floss*, Maggie Tulliver, now nineteen years old, a "dark lady" (*MF* 386) with "large round" arms and "brown skin" (*MF* 399), is home for a brief visit when her eyes, characteristically, "fill with tears." She is thinking about how dissatisfied she is with her life and position, now that her father has died and she has been forced to seek work outside of the home and outside of her hometown in a "third rate schoolroom" (*MF* 400):

> Memory and imagination urged upon her a sense of privation too keen to let her taste what was offered in the transient present: her future, she thought, was likely to be worse than her past, for after her years of contented renunciation, she had slipped back into desire and longing: she found joyless days of distasteful occupation harder and harder—she found the image of intense

and varied life she yearned for and despaired of, becoming more and more importunate. (*MF* 389)

Again, the characteristic multiple-colon sentence structure signals the force of Maggie's self-overflowing longing. But if memory and imagination agitate Maggie, the arrival in her life of Stephen Guest, her cousin Lucy's suitor, and music do just the opposite, helping to soothe "all her inward consciousness of a painful past and her presentiment of a troublesome future" (*MF* 416). Maggie experiences for a few brief weeks Lucy's more privileged life and

> the new sense of leisure and unchecked enjoyment amidst the soft-breathing airs and garden scenes of advancing Spring, amidst the new abundance of music, and lingering strolls in the sunshine and delicious dreaminess of gliding on the river, could hardly be without some intoxicating effect on her after her years of privation; and even in the first week Maggie began to be less haunted by her sad memories and anticipations. (*MF* 417)

She gets to feel that "she was one of the beautiful things of this spring time" and that "there were admiring eyes always awaiting her now" (*MF* 417). Maggie, briefly lifted above her life of "emphasis," is arguably free to enter into the experiences of music, romance, and sexual attraction.

Music has a powerful effect on Maggie. It throws her into "a wild state of joy" (*MF* 390); she tells Lucy, "Life seems to go on without effort, when I am filled with music" (*MF* 401). Alone at Lucy's piano, she finds "that the old fitness between her fingers and the keys remained and revived, like a sympathetic kinship not to be worn out by separation" (*MF* 417). She plays the tunes to song she has heard over and over again, "until she had found a way of producing them so as to make them a more pregnant, passionate language." And indeed, "the mere concord of octaves was a delight to Maggie, and she would often take up a book of Studies rather than any melody, that she might taste more keenly by abstraction the more primitive sensation of intervals" (*MF* 418). The piano becomes an animated object, friend or family tied to Maggie not only by "kinship" but also by a special bond of "sympathy." Her fingers meet keys that feel familiar and receptive, in a kind of ideal attachment that can never be "worn out by separation." With piano strings vibrating and the sound of octaves (O) and other "primitive" intervals reverberating around her, Maggie's love of music is used to emblematize a greater kind of receptivity: "her sensibility to the supreme excitement of music was only one form of that passionate sensibility which belonged to her whole nature and made her faults and virtues all merge in each other" (*MF* 418). Maggie's "passionate sensibility" not only makes "faults and virtues" merge into each other, but also inside and outside, production and reception (as in Philip's earlier explanation of aesthetic experience), her voice and the voices of others' as they sing together, sound waves and sexual attraction: music concretizes the sensation of something real, pressing, and yet immaterial in the air, something shared between people and yet owned by none of them, a relational "matrix of thought" and feeling. Indeed, music is that which definitionally overflows its container, as a voice emitted from a body, sound emitted from an instrument, in turn filling up and overflowing the listener, the air vibrating in the spaces between them.

Music and romance come together in the novel's productively mixed metaphor of vibrations.[84] Stephen is a singer, and his "fine bass voice" (*MF* 400) seems "to make all the air in the room alive with a new influence" (*MF* 435). Maggie is "taken hold of and shaken" by his voice as if "by an invisible influence," and "borne along by a wave too strong for her" (*MF* 435). Stephen's gaze, too, has a synesthetic influence on Maggie, as she catches him sneaking looks at her "with a glance that seemed somehow to have caught the vibratory influence of the voice" (*MF* 400). Maggie answers vibration with vibration: "In poor Maggie's highly strung, hungry nature . . . these apparently trivial causes had the effect of rousing and exalting her imagination in a way that was mysterious to herself" (*MF* 400). Maggie senses in these notes and glances something else vibrating just outside the sphere of her own experience: the "half-remote presence of a world of love and beauty and delight" (*MF* 400), dreamy and ineffable and real, sensible by way of the "faith and sympathy that were the best organs of her soul" (*MF* 478), and which both music and romance play upon.

This is not the only time the "highly strung" Maggie is figured as a musical instrument. Later, the narrator intimates that Maggie "had little more power of concealing the impressions made upon her than if she had been constructed of musical strings" (*MF* 427). Like an aeolian harp, Maggie is played upon by air and vibration, captive to her "passionate sensibility" to music, to admiration, and to love. Listening to a duet sung by Stephen and Philip, Maggie "thrills" to the song's shift into a minor key:

> Poor Maggie! She looked very beautiful when her soul was being played on in this way by the inexorable power of sound. You might have seen the slightest perceptible quivering through her whole frame, as she leaned a little forward, clasping her hands as if to steady herself, while her eyes dilated and brightened into that wide-open, childish expression of wondering delight which always came back in her happiest moments. (*MF* 434)

"Poor Maggie!": to be so moved by music or to look so beautiful in the process? And yet, the narrator suggests, we should be so lucky as to see her "frame" "quivering" to the music as the sound plays on her, body and "soul." The erotics of vibration are not diminished but enhanced by her "childlike" beauty, "wide-open" and unselfconscious. And, indeed, "clasped" hands and fingers are so often associated with Maggie's childhood relationship to her brother Tom that he too is spectrally on the scene here, bringing with him the novel's reverberating erotics of brother-and-sisterhood.

Romantic rapture too is a form of O. Maggie and Stephen's illicit romance makes life seem, to Maggie, like a "keen vibrating consciousness poised above the pleasure or pain" (*MF* 459). Their interest in each other has not yet been spoken, but is all the more powerful for this fact. They feel each other's gaze from across the room; they imagine touching hands even before they are actually joined in a dance (*MF* 459); when they are left alone together, they do not speak, and yet "each [is] oppressively conscious of the other's presence, even to the finger-ends" (*MF* 420). They communicate without speaking, as in the moment of their "mute confession" of their love for each other (before Stephen concretizes this attraction by kissing Maggie's arm) on an evening walk in a conservatory:

> Something strangely powerful there was in the light of Stephen's long gaze, for it made Maggie's face turn towards it and look upward at it—slowly, like a flower at the ascending brightness. And they walked unsteadily on, without feeling that they were walking—without feeling anything but that long grave mutual gaze which has the solemnity belonging to all deep human passion. The hovering thought that they must and would renounce each other made this moment of mute confession more intense in its rapture. (*MF* 460)

Bion might call Stephen and Maggie's coming together their "valency": the "capacity for spontaneous instinctive co-operation" and the ability to bind with or "enter into combination" with others. Valency indicates, Bion writes, "a readiness to combine on levels that can hardly be called mental at all but are characterized by behaviour in the human being that is more analogous to tropism in plants than to purposive behavior" (*Groups* 116–17). Maggie turns her face to Stephen's "slowly, like a flower at the ascending brightness," as though his face is the sun. Maggie and Stephen trust to their "spontaneous" readiness to turn to each other, to make together not only a mutual gaze but a mutual truth: a heliotropism to the O of their shared experience.

This mutual gaze and mutual consciousness grows more and more encompassing, and culminates when the pair, inadvertently left alone by Lucy and Philip, float down the river together on their way to an accidental elopement, locked into "the sweet solitude of a twofold consciousness that was mingled into one by that grave untiring gaze which need not be averted" (*MF* 484). Alone together, Maggie and Stephen are joined in the kind of consuming contact that Maggie has longed for—although both Maggie and the novel will argue, uncertainly, that this kind of merger, one that places "the past and the future" outside "the enchanted haze in which [Maggie and Stephen] were enveloped" (*MF* 484), is wrong. And multiply so: it becomes at once too "passive," an "automatic" "yielding" (*MF* 487) to pleasure and a withdrawal of "consent" (*MF* 497), and at the same time too driven, too much a product of "wayward choice" (*MF* 491). Arguably, though, such formulations belong to knowing about the experience rather than being in it—to K (knowledge) rather than to O, to what the novel will go on to name as the reduction to maxim of the complexity, and richness, of living.

One of Bion's favorite methods for describing O is a line of poetry: a verse from *Paradise Lost* that reads, "The rising world of waters dark and deep / Won from the void and formless infinite."[85] Bion writes, after citing these lines:

> I am not interpreting what Milton says but using it to represent O. The process of binding is a part of the procedure by which something is "won from the void and formless infinite"; it is K and must be distinguished from the process by which O is "become". The sense of inside and outside, internal and external objects, introjection and projection, container and contained, are all associated with K. (*Tr* 151)

Maggie's hyperbolic formulations of her predicament in relation to Stephen are arguably such reductions of O to K, simple ways of understanding something complex, a "world won" from the "formless infinite"—or, rather, a world of conventional morality and sociality won from the infinity of possible social forms.

Maggie's hyperboles pose strict choices and dire consequences. In an argument with Maggie about the fate of their relationship, Stephen claims that he is not bound to Lucy, nor Maggie to Philip, because they are not officially engaged. But Maggie protests: "The real tie lies in the feelings and expectations we have raised in other minds. Else all pledges might be broken, when there was no outward penalty. There would be no such thing as faithfulness" (*MF* 468). A single pledge carries the weight of all performative language and of all fidelity too. And later, when Stephen claims that their love for each other is a "natural law" that "surmounts any other," Maggie again responds just as dramatically: "If we judged in that way, there would be a warrant for all treachery and cruelty—we should justify breaking the most sacred ties that can ever be formed on earth. If the past is not to bind us, where can duty lie? We should have no law but the inclination of the moment" (*MF* 495–96). If they act cruelly this once, there would be "a warrant for *all* treachery and cruelty," for the breaking of all "sacred ties." In these statements of hyperbolic responsibility, Maggie transfigures a single personal choice (elopement with Stephen) into something powerful enough to destroy the binding forces of time, law, language, and family. Although the exaggeration of such statements is clear when they are spoken by Maggie (and points up the hyperbole implicit in Stephen's way of thinking as well), such statements are reiterated and naturalized later by the novel's moral authorities: first by the narrator, then by Dr. Kenn. In a moment of weakness or "vanity," Maggie feels she wants nothing more than "Stephen Guest at her feet." But, luckily, the narrator intones, "there were things in her stronger than vanity— ... affection, and long deep memories of early discipline and effort, of early claims on her love and pity" (*MF* 455). Later, Dr. Kenn, stepping in as wise commentator on contemporary morality, laments: "at present, everything seems tending towards the relaxation of ties—towards the substitution of wayward choice for the adherence to obligation which has its roots in the past" (*MF* 515). In these instances, Maggie's hyperboles are taken for moral truths, and the divide between her categorical choices (past ties vs. wayward choice, memory vs. momentary inclination, duty vs. passion) are etched deeper in stone.

And yet in another tone of voice the narrator critiques just this kind of rigid moralism:

> The great problem of the shifting relation between passion and duty is clear to no man who is capable of apprehending it: the question ... is one for which we have no master key that will fit all cases. ... The truth [is] that moral judgments must remain hollow and false, unless they are checked and enlightened by a perpetual reference to the special circumstances that mark the individual lot. (*MF* 517)

A magisterial statement of "perpetual" uncertainty, the passage insists on the dialectic between universal law and "individual lot" that is a staple concept of Eliot's essayistic writing. But rather than insisting that one choose "duty" over "passion," the passage intimates that the very capacity to "apprehend" the complexity of the problem is what unfits a person to make a clear choice. (As Bion might put it, by way of his repeated citation of Blanchot, "la réponse est le malheur de la question.") Moral judgments, "hollow and false," are containers inadequate to the experience of ethical life, and "maxims" too mark a kind of cognitive-spiritual incapacity. The passage continues:

> All people of broad, strong sense have an instinctive repugnance to the men of maxims; because such people early discern that the mysterious complexity of our life is not to be embraced by maxims, and that to lace ourselves up in formulas of that sort is to repress all the divine promptings and inspirations that spring from growing insight and sympathy. And the man of maxims is the popular representative of the minds that are guided in their moral judgment solely by general rules, thinking that these will lead them to justice by a ready-made patent method, without the trouble of exerting patience, discrimination, impartiality, without any care to assure themselves whether they have that insight that comes from a hardly-earned estimate of

temptation, or from a life vivid and intense enough to have created a wide fellow-feeling with all that is human. (*MF* 518)

The "mysterious complexity of life" is not to be "embraced" by maxims, by formulas that "lace [us] up" rather than open us out. And maxims, as Nancy K. Miller argues, are doubly inadequate because they are so unmistakably gendered—an insight Eliot doubles down on (and produces) in her phrase "men of maxims." As Miller puts it, critiquing too misogynist estimations of women's literature, "the maxims that pass for the absolute truth of human experience, and the encoding of that experience in literature, are [in fact] organizations, when they are not fantasies, of the dominant culture."[86] Maxims disguise male (more specifically, white middle-class male) experience as "neutral universal" experience, excluding not only "divine promptings and inspirations that spring from growing insight and sympathy," but, more pointedly, women's experience and ways of knowing. Indeed, maxims are often fantasies that such ways of knowing do not exist, and that the "mysterious complexity of life," which maxims cannot "embrace," does not exist either. To put it in Bion's terms: sometimes maxims are not statements of knowledge at all, but rather attacks on linking. Eliotic sympathy is what is named in the final formulation of the passage as precisely that which overflows maxims and "personal lots"—as that which renders experience palpable, if not fully knowable, and renders problems apprehensible, which is to say fully "puzzling" (R.I.P., Mr. Tulliver), if not definitively answerable.

Philip's letter of forgiveness to Maggie following her failed elopement with Stephen, which arrives at the novel's close just before the flood, solidifies the equation of sympathy and "enlarged" overflowing life. He writes:

> The new life I have found in caring for your joy and sorrow more than for what is my own, has transformed the spirit of rebellious murmuring into that willing endurance which is the birth of strong sympathy. I think nothing but such complete and intense love could have initiated me into that enlarged life which grows and grows by appropriating the life of others; for before, I was always dragged back from it by ever-present painful self-consciousness. I even think sometimes that this gift of transferred life which has come to me in loving you, may be a new power to me. (*MF* 523)

What Eliot recommends is not moral relativism, but rather moral openness and self-exertion (even as a kind of self-forgetting). What it recommends is not quietism, but "intensity." As in Adam Phillips's gloss of Bion, this passage asks that we do not assume "omniscience as a substitute for learning from experience," but instead that we think and feel through and with others.[87] Living our lives as enlarged and widened by others is, after all, in a sense all that we can do: as

Bion says of O, a sense of how deeply related we are is on one level impossible to fully understand and, on another level, all that we will ever experience. Thinking through Maggie's hyperbolic pronouncements might mean "redescribing them" such that the "incompatible wants" they put forward can be rendered "compatible," "resdescribing them such that they are no longer mutually exclusive." Phillips writes: "In reality we can have, say, justice and mercy, be children and have adult relationships"—we can have memory and passion alike; we can honor both duty and impulse.[88]

Bion writes that the distinction between knowing and being holds true not only for psychoanalytic experience—the very real difference between knowing about psychoanalysis and being analyzed, of knowing an analyst's interpretation and allowing it to change you—but for reading too. Bion instructs his own readers as follows:

> The reader must disregard what I say until the O of the experience of reading has evolved to a point where the actual events of reading issue in his interpretation of the experiences. Too great a regard for what I have written obstructs the process I represent by the terms "he becomes the O that is common to himself and myself." (A&I 28)

How might we distinguish the O of reading *The Mill on the Floss* from the K of having read it? How might we distinguish our experience of the novel as it, miraculously, enlarges our lives, from a critical interpretation that keeps it self-contained? This is one of the key questions the novel wants and gets us to ask, even if actually answering it could never match scale with the complexity of the question. The reading experience, even more widely relational than Bion intimates (in the merely dyadic "O that is common" to writer and reader—as if these figures were single, as if they were not populated and accompanied by others, or tied to them by multiple links of knowledge, love, hate, and faith), can't be captured as knowledge, but it can be felt and experienced. And it can, I think, be pointed to the future, nascently offering forms and experiences of relationality that cannot yet be thought. Eliot's aim then, perhaps most visibly in *The Mill on the Floss* but valuably considered across her fiction, is not necessarily to strengthen social sympathies in unduly concrete ways, but rather to animate fields of relationality so that new and unpredicted futures can be produced.

Wishful Futures

In case such a claim seems too vague, too indefinite, too implausible, too wishful (code words, perhaps, for "too feminine"—a charge leveled against nineteenth-century novelists as well as twenty-first-century academics), I want to offer in closing a few concrete examples of what the futures embedded in the novel have looked like, and what a few as-yet-unforeseen ones may come to look like. As Bion writes in the quotation I have used as an epigraph for this chapter, "there may be ideas which cannot be more powerfully expressed because they are buried in the future which has not happened." *The Mill on the Floss* "contains" such vaguely expressed ideas—ideas that, as Bion puts it, are not yet available to George Eliot as "thought," ideas that exceed what the novel can clearly formulate. And yet they may come into thought and "powerful" expression when the novel is placed in new circumstances and new social and textual relations: when it arrives in the futures that have been unburied and brought into light.

One of the futures of Eliot's novel, as I began this chapter by indicating, lies in feminist literary criticism in the wide sweep of time from the novel's publication in 1860 to the 1980s. This criticism emphasizes the novel's legacy of wishfulness in the utopian impulse necessary to feminist theory and political activism alike. Feminist critics have used the novel as a privileged object: a text written by a woman who developed a uniquely useful vocabulary (wishing and longing) and series of formal techniques (most notably here, its use of and play on the more conventional male Bildungsroman) for thinking about patriarchy and women's place within it. This sentiment still has an active life in the 2010s, as the writer and social justice activist adrienne maree brown makes clear. Brown argues that the creation of "longing" is the first step to creating political change: it brings the wish for justice and equality into the mind and the body. As an act of both ideation and pleasure-seeking—as an erotic, in Audre Lorde's sense of the term[89]—longing allows us to imagine and to *desire* new forms of love, care, kinship, and sociopolitical relations.[90]

I wonder if it is possible, using brown's work as a starting point, to move from the "future" of the mainstream second-wave feminism of the 1970s to 1990s, including that inflected by French feminist psychoanalysis (emblematized in this chapter by Mary Jacobus's dual reading of *The Mill on the Floss* with Irigaray's *Ce sexe qui n'en est pas un*) to the "futures" of two adjacent critical approaches: women of color feminist writing from the same period and its extensions in more recent queer of color theory. Space does not allow me to fully develop this new genealogy of wishfulness (or, to be more precise, and to borrow from Irigaray's title, this "genealogy which is not one"),[91] but I want to at least sketch out some of its contours. And I want to suggest that our ability to sketch these contours begins and ends with Maggie Tulliver's brown skin.

An important caveat first. In spelling out some of these unpredicted and unpredictable futures of the novel, I do want to be clear that emphasizing what is generative in the novel does not mean ignoring what is precluded or even violently foreclosed in it.[92] Indeed, to act as though these two possibilities—futurity and foreclosure—are fully distinct would be to reinscribe Kleinian splitting, forgetting Bion's insistence on the constant interchange between paranoid-schizoid defenses and their depressive alternatives, which he highlights in his use of a two-way arrow: PS ↔ D. And it would mean forgetting, too, the overlap Sedgwick has so skillfully described between the critical strategies of paranoid and reparative reading. Bion's theories inscribe dual potentials: for linking and for attacks on linking, for learning from experience and for its hateful evasion, for psychological growth and for psychological self-destruction. Projective identification, Bion's contemporary Herbert Rosenfeld explains, can be used to communicate or it can be used, conversely, for "evacuating and emptying out" meaning, effecting a "denial of psychic reality."[93] But even this categorization may be too split. Thomas Ogden's more holistic (and modern) account emphasizes the simultaneity of multiple purposes and effects of projective identification, reminding us that it is a psychological process that is at once "a type of defence, a mode of communication, a primitive form of object relationship, and a pathway for psychological change."[94] Projective identification does not alternate, in other words, between a mode of evacuation and a mode of communication, but always serves both "defensive and communicative functions" at once. The novel's projection of futures is, likewise, not disconnected from its foreclosures; its wishfulness is not separate from its violences; its accomplishments not separate from its acts of destruction, the "repression on which meaning depends."[95]

The Mill on the Floss itself makes this clear. An oracular statement in the novel's short conclusion argues: "Nature repairs its ravages—repairs them with her sunshine and with human labour." Five years after the flood, the world has for the most part returned to normal. But then the narrator's voice intones, as if starting the conclusion all over again: "Nature repairs her ravages—but not all." Not everything can be repaired: "uptorn trees are not rooted again," "hills are left scarred," and "to the eyes that have dwelt on the past, there is no thorough repair" (*MF* 543). Never was a novel more insistent on rejecting in advance a thoroughly reparative reading. And yet the novel insists too on a more-than-minimal efficacy of repair, and it underlines our desire for it too. The final line of the novel is both the epitaph on Maggie and Tom's joint tombstone and, as epigraph, the novel's first line: "In their death they were not divided" (*MF* 544). Destruction is carried forward, even if in fantasy alone, by a reparative impulse that makes the end of the novel circle back to its beginning.

Back to brown skin: Why does the novel insist on figuring Maggie's appearance by recourse to ethnic and racial designations? When, as a child, Maggie runs away to join the "gypsies," she arguably arrives to them as a colonizer, ready to teach them about Geography and Columbus, introduce them to English teatime, and become their queen (*MF* 117). But might the flash of recognition that sparks between Maggie and a young gypsy woman resonate beyond white fantasy, giving itself over to a different experience and use for modern readers of color?[96] Could it be a source of what José Muñoz calls "disidentification"—a way of bending something not created for you, something that is even made specifically to exclude you, into a resource that can be repurposed and made into something sustaining?[97] Constructing this new critical plot for the novel means unearthing ideas "in" the novel that are "buried in the future," uncontained in the novel alone but discoverable in the "matrix of thought" we find by placing the novel in a new relational configuration. In this way of reading plot, the flood is not the end of the novel after all.

Maggie's Skin

In her essay "Dinah's Blush, Maggie's Arm" (1993), Margaret Homans argues that Eliot's novels predicts (and perhaps helps to shape) a major fault in second-wave feminism: its tendency to ignore class and racial difference in its construction of a monolithic (white, middle-class) womanhood. The trademark move of occluding difference in order to consolidate a "universal" (declassed, deracialized) norm of femininity—here, domestic and middle-class—is part and parcel of the ideological labor of the Victorian novel, which works "to consolidate middle-class hegemony in the nineteenth century."[98] Eliot's early novels, Homans argues, make middle-class feminine, domestic morality stand in for morality—they make, in other words, characters like Dinah and Maggie into men of maxims, universalizing their experience by denuding it of markers of gender, sexuality, and class, so that they are "made to represent values that cross all class boundaries."[99] Homans's intervention is important and useful; and yet she too neglects race and ethnicity in her analysis of the construction of Victorian norms of femininity. For all of her focus on the surface of the skin (Dinah's blush) and to Maggie's body (the large, round arms to which our attention is drawn again and again in the novel, and which Homans argues stand in for Maggie's breasts), Homans fails to pay attention to the color of Maggie's skin—which is described as "brown" or "dark" at least seventeen times over the course of the novel (and that's not even including all of the references to her dark eyes, also arguably a kind of racial coding).

The Mill on the Floss is at once emphatic about the fact of Maggie's physical difference and relentless in its attempts to render it metaphorical. Maggie is called a "mullatter" (*MF* 15), a "gypsy" (e.g., *MF* 73, 312), and a "dark woman" like Rebecca, a Jewish woman, in Scott's *Ivanhoe* (*MF* 345). But the possibility of real ethnic or racial difference is subsumed, in a move that critics identify as characteristic of the Victorian novel, into a "mark" of merely individual "difference."[100] Maggie's dark hair, dark eyes, and dark skin are nominally explained as a genetic indication of her closer tie to her father's side of the family, the

Tullivers, with their ramshackle ways and surplus offspring, than to her mother's side, the self-important and more cleanly middle-class Dodsons (and clearly, in this split, the novel ties whiteness to class status, as exemplified in the blonde, blue-eyed, pink-cheeked, and wealthy Dodson cousin Lucy Deane). Maggie's dark skin is also made into a signifier of her wildness, her tendency to play outside more than a girl should, her boyishness, her time in the sun, her preference for the outdoors over domestic space: those aspects of her that reject or are cast out of conventional femininity.

But in the practice of the novel, Maggie's "dark" physical characteristics function more actively as markers not of her lineage, but of her extreme individuality. This individuality ramifies in two opposing directions: a positive and a negative exceptionality. The side of positive exceptionality is what Maggie's cousin Lucy lovingly calls her "general uncanniness" to her world (*MF* 403). Maggie's unusually wide-ranging sympathy, her lack of fit with her backward provincial world, her desire for more: all of these make her uncanny not just to her world but to the novel itself. They also name, in Nathan Hensley's view, Maggie's exceptional modernity, in a reading that identifies Maggie with Hegel's world-historical individual, "asynchronous with her now" and "wishing to break out" of "contemporary existence" into something new.[101] Maggie's positive exceptionality is also tied to her extrafictionality: to her autobiographical relation to Mary Ann Evans, and, reading this connection out from the plot, into Maggie's counterfactual survival into the industrial 1860s through that middle-aged writer.

Her extreme individuality also ramifies in the direction, though, of negative exceptionality: Maggie's brownness renders her an object of debasement, an outcast and a scapegoat, insufficiently English, an outsider within the nation, unable to fit herself into the norms of the community. She is ultimately expelled not just from St. Oggs, but from the social realist novel itself. But, as the critics Alicia Carroll and Deborah Nord point out, even in this violent expulsion, the difference on the surface of Maggie's skin is subsumed by a different kind of bodily distinction: the pronounced secondary sex characteristics—full figure, large round arms, flashing eyes—that declare that she is singled out as a sexualized woman and an object of male attention rather than as a racialized figure.

Carroll and Nord are perhaps the scholars most attentive to questions of race and ethnicity in *The Mill on the Floss*, and both focus on the figuration (and imaginary racialization) of Maggie as a gypsy and on her actual encounter with gypsy characters early in the novel. In chapter 11 of book 1, Maggie attempts to run away in order to join a band of gypsies camping on the outskirts of the town. Because she has "so often [been] told she was like a gypsy and 'half wild'" (*MF* 112), Maggie fantasizes that she will be rejoining her own "unknown kindred" (*MF* 114), a family truer than the false Dodsons with their light complexions and unforgiving hearts.[102] But she does so only to discover that the people she meets do not match up to her romantic image of them. Eliot's depiction of the gypsies is off-putting for modern readers: even while it debunks her characters' blatantly racist views, it instantiates troubling racialized myths of its own. Maggie corrects Tom's perceptions of the gypsies—he thinks they are "thieves and hardly got anything to eat and had nothing to drive but a donkey" (*MF* 112)—only to replace them with her own: she imagines that "the gypsies would gladly receive her and pay her much respect on account of her superior knowledge" (*MF* 112). She plans to teach them "a great many things" (*MF* 116), including stories about Columbus from her "Catechism of Geography," passing on lessons of empire and becoming "the queen of the gypsies" (*MF* 117). The novel mocks Maggie's self-aggrandizing fantasies, ostensibly correcting her racist views just as Maggie corrected Tom's—and yet we see the gypsies from Maggie's angle of vision throughout. We are made to narratively inhabit Maggie's disdain for their dirtiness, her feeling about the incomprehensibility of their "unknown tongue" (*MF* 118), and her disorientation by the strangeness of their social configurations, which do not echo the nuclear family dynamics—brother-and-sister pairs, man-and-wife aunts and uncles—with which Maggie is familiar. The gypsy children are twice referred to as "small sphinxes": the narrator ostensibly refers to their postures—"two small shock-headed children were lying prone and resting on their elbows something like small sphinxes" (*MF* 116–17)—but the descriptor also encodes them as queer creatures, indeterminately sexed/gendered and unlinked from expected paternal/fraternal patterns. They, apparently, have not made the "long forced march" that makes animal babies into sexed human children, crossing over the divide between nature and culture. Rather than real people with a real language, a real culture, and a real sense of geography, space, kinship, and community, the novel makes the gypsies into figures of otherness, difference, unknowability, and unassimilability.

Indeed, both Carroll and Nord argue that the figure of the gypsy as Eliot deploys it, both in *The Mill on the Floss* and in its connected texts—Eliot's dramatic long poem "The Spanish Gypsy" (1868) as well as the "Brother and Sister" sonnet sequence (1869)—is just that: a figure, a cipher for displaced aspects of mainstream middle-class British identity in the process of being made, an Orientalized Other.[103] Both critics argue that racial and ethnic otherness is reduced to a merely figural status in *The Mill on the Floss*: the novel allows us no access to nineteenth-century gypsy life and culture as a historical reality separate from fantasies of British identity. And it allows us, therefore, no access to a world outside of white middle-class England. These claims are, in a sense, indisputable, and certainly Maggie's brown skin remains, in the world of the novel, nothing but a darker shade of white. But I do wonder what might happen if we were to read outside of the novel's plot—if we were to write ourselves into a critical future adjacent to the one already sketched by the existing criticism—by taking Maggie's recognition of herself in the gypsies more seriously, as something that exceeds the novel's own ability to conceptualize it.

Approaching the gypsy camp, Maggie attracts the attention of one of the gypsies, "a young woman with a baby on her arm," who walks over to meet her: "Maggie looked up in the new face rather tremblingly as it approached, and was reassured by the thought that her aunt Pullet and the rest were right when they called her a gypsy, for this face with the bright dark eyes and the long hair was really something like what she was used to see in the glass" (MF 115). Maggie's "trembling" identification with this gypsy mother, her sense of the rightness at being called a gypsy when she looks into her face, the recognition of her own eyes and hair (and skin color?) embodied by someone who may not feel that these are shameful and disqualifying physical characteristics, who may even feel ownership and pride in them: the encounter has an affirmative potential that cannot be ignored. The experience it affirms is not Maggie's per se, nor is it Mary Ann Evans's—but it just may be the experience of another reader, maybe one who is looking for something like Maggie was looking for in her own reading: a guide when there is none other at hand, and who will find it in the book in front of her, no matter how flawed and imperfect it is.

Muñoz's account of "disidentificatory reception" might help to explain what such an encounter might achieve.[104] Explaining this idea, Muñoz creates an imagined scenario of reading. The text he has in mind is Frantz Fanon's *Black Skin, White Masks*, the "great twentieth-century treatise on the colonized mind." Despite the greatness and importance of Fanon's text, it of course contains its own faults and oversights. In a pivotal "chapter on colonial identity," Muñoz writes, Fanon "dismisses the possibility of a homosexual component" in such an identity. And this is where the thought experiment really begins:

> Think, for a moment, of the queer revolutionary from the Antilles, perhaps a young woman who has already been burned in Fanon's text by his writing on the colonized woman. What process can keep an identification with Fanon, his politics, his work possible for this woman? In such a case, a disidentification with Fanon might be one of the only ways in which she is capable of reformatting the powerful theorist for her own project, one that might be as queer and feminist as it is anticolonial. Disidentification offers a Fanon, for that queer and lesbian reader, who would not be sanitized; instead, his homophobia and misogyny would be interrogated while his anticolonial discourse was engaged as a *still* valuable yet mediated identification. This maneuver resists an unproductive turn toward good dog/bad dog criticism and instead leads to an identification that is both mediated and immediate, a disidentification that enables politics.[105]

This kind of enabling disidentification is what I want for my own imaginary reader, the young woman of color who picks up *The Mill on the Floss* and sees herself at once reflected in and reviled by Maggie Tulliver. It is a project of reception and identity formation that I, lacking other books, wish that I had been able to enact as a young reader—just as Mary Ann Evans imagines herself, in Maggie Tulliver, reading what she needed in Thomas à Kempis guided by a reader who left brown marks on the page for her to find. A disidentificatory reading of *The Mill on the Floss* would be able to interrogate the bigotry and racism in Eliot's novel while engaging her feminist and queer-affirmative discourse "as a *still* valuable yet mediated identification." As Maggie can "tremblingly" identify with the gypsy woman—whose interiority, whose daily life, whose very name we are never given access to—my reader can "tremblingly" disidentify with the white brown-skinned Maggie.

We can, of course, understand Maggie's recognition of her own face in that of the gypsy woman as a kind of possessive individualism, an appropriative mirroring, an encounter with difference that is used only to strengthen Maggie's whiteness, even while pronouncing her sexuality and womanhood aberrant. Indeed, this is in some sense all that the word "gypsy" means in the novel—as Nord and Carrol argue, *The Mill on the Floss* makes it impossible to approach gypsy culture as a historical reality separate from British fantasies of identity. And yet Muñoz's disidentification gives us a way in: it allows us to maintain this insight *and* to see how we might use the novel to enable other political projects. George Eliot is not insisting that we think of difference intersectionally: that idea exceeded her. And yet that insight might be found in the new, trembling, vibratory relation that arises between certain readers and the book, where what the O of reading reveals is that femininity cannot in fact be understood outside of class and racial difference, and perhaps even more specifically, outside of the context of its production in the context of empire, nation building, and its many migrations and diasporas.

Discussing the way Michael Eigen draws out Bion's notion of an "area of faith" in psychoanalytic thought and practice, Adam Phillips writes: "If, for Freud, desire was always in excess of the object's capacity to satisfy it, for Eigen our profoundest emotional life is in excess of our capacity to make sense of it." We produce imaginings that are beyond our scope to adequately process; as Eigen puts it, "our mental creations are often ahead of our ability to assimilate them in meaningful and useful ways."[106] Our imaginings are ahead of both our ability to process them and our ability to actualize them. This is perhaps the very definition of "wishing and longing."

Muñoz asks: "What process can keep an identification with Fanon, his politics, his work possible for this woman?" What process can keep an identification with Eliot, her politics, and her work possible for me, for my students of color?

Wishing. Such wishing need not strive toward a universalizing feminism; it need not erase racial or other forms of difference. As bell hooks, "struck by the depths of longing in many of us," puts it: "The shared space and feeling of 'yearning' opens up the possibility" of speaking "across race, class, gender, and sexual practice," a space where "all these differences might meet and engage one another."[107] Wishing can acknowledge failure and hope for something more—it can, and does, as brown argues, ignite the political movements that demand more. I wish that Eliot had imagined the gypsies with the same kind of curiosity and generosity that she imagines most of her other characters with—from Mrs. Glegg to Mr. Pullet to "good Luke" the servant. She didn't or she couldn't, but part of the power of the novel is that it allows for us to wish for things that are not there: to wish, as Maggie does, for things that we should be able to have. Readers should indeed recognize, and even feel pain at, the fact that Eliot, despite all of her imaginative powers as a writer, and all of the force and intensity with which she irradiates the lives of so many of her characters, did not irradiate nonwhite lives. But readers, and especially readers of color, can also use their wishfulness to expand the novel, to let it exceed and overflow itself, to let it make contact with them, in ways that are both "mediated and immediate," such that it answers some—not all—of their needs and concerns. This is not sanitizing or revisionary reading—it is "a disidentification that enables politics."

3

Restlessness

THE RETURN OF THE NATIVE, BALINT, "COLONIAL OBJECT RELATIONS"

Dismissing late distaste for life,
I craved its bleak unrest.
—HARDY, "HER IMMORTALITY"

If often he was wrong and, at times, absurd,
to us he is no more a person
now but a whole climate of opinion
under whom we conduct our different lives
—W. H. AUDEN, "IN MEMORY OF SIGMUND FREUD"

The real origin of change [to rural England] was the developing system of agrarian capitalism, which, as has been characteristic of capitalism throughout its history, succeeded in transforming its environment in a dramatically productive way, by making both men and nature instrumental to a dominating purpose. Capitalism has in this sense always been an ambiguous process: increasing real wealth but distributing it unevenly; enabling larger populations to grow and survive, but within them seeing men only as producers and consumers, with no substantial claim on society except in these abstract capacities.... In this place and that, different ways, different times, could be actually remembered. But under the pressure of the general contradictions of the system this realistic local observation grew to a general historical outline, and then to a myth.... We have heard this sad song for many centuries now: a seductive song, turning protest into retrospect, until we die of time.
—RAYMOND WILLIAMS, THE COUNTRY AND THE CITY

There are many maps of one place, and many histories of one time.
—JULIE FREDERIKSE, NONE BUT OURSELVES

"PERSONS WITH ANY weight of character carry, like planets, their atmospheres along with them in their orbits," Hardy writes in *The Return of the Native* (1878; RN 36). People charge the air around them, carrying around with them moods, views of the world, and ways of being that are palpably felt by others. The phenomenon Hardy is describing, located indeterminately between the physical and metaphysical, would later be of great interest to twentieth-century psychoanalysts as well. The Hungarian-British analyst Michael Balint (1896–1970), an important figure in the Independent group's reimagination of therapeutic technique, points out that transference is not a neutral-universal phenomenon occurring in an "airtight compartment."[1] Instead, "different analytical atmospheres, so to say, [are] created and maintained by the individual analyst's technique and personality."[2] In Hardy's novels and Balint's theories, personality is atmospheric: more vaporous than solid, more surround than essence, personality transforms the space around a person and exerts a gravitational pull on others. I think these ideas pertain to literary experience as well. Novels, too, carry atmospheres along with them, drawing readers into states of feeling and being that, palpably felt while reading, might be difficult describe or reexperience once we have strayed too far beyond a particular novel's orbit.

As readers of Hardy well know, his novels make for particularly weighty planets, drawing readers into their atmospheres—their "characteristic tone or pervading mood[s]"—with an unusual force.[3] As in the fluctuations in *Tess* between violent coercion and quietly sustaining unintegration, between paranoid and reparative orientations to the outside world, the atmospheres of Hardy's novels are as discontinuous as they are powerful—like so many microclimates spread across the surface of their vast globes. The atmosphere of *The Return of the Native* is discontinuous: like the heath itself, the novel is at once "exhilarating" and "soothing" (RN 185), and like the heath, too, it is at once hyperlocal and multiply worlded.[4]

This chapter focuses on Michael Balint, a Budapest-trained analyst who emigrated to England during the political upheavals of the late 1930s, and who is well known not only for his psychoanalytic work on early object relations, but also his wider-reaching contributions to medical practice through his focus on the doctor-patient relationship.[5] What I find most fascinating in his work for the purposes of this chapter is the way that Balint addresses not simply the *objects* of object relations theory, but the *space* around and between these objects. Balint is interested in how people imagine and manipulate both the imagined space between themselves and their objects—are people clingy or distant? Do they enjoy closeness or cultivate detachment?—and real space: that is to say, how people move in the world and how they manipulate the material elements that surround them, particularly the air. One of Balint's central questions becomes: Do people feel the environment around them to be an "open, friendly expanse" or a "horrid, empty space"?[6] Here and throughout his body of work, Balint comes closer than any other thinker to making the spatial metaphors of British psychoanalysis concrete, and to making its geographies explicit. And it is for this reason that I want to read his work in relation to *The Return of the Native*.

This chapter brings Hardy, Balint, and postcolonial theory into conversation in order to illuminate the "colonial object relations" of *The Return of the Native*.[7] The novel's narrator remarks of Tamsin Yeobright that "all similes and allegories concerning her began and ended with birds" (*RN* 209). I want to argue that Hardy's wide-ranging figurations of space in this novel—"all similes and allegories concerning" the heath—begin and end with empire. While *The Return of the Native* is notable for its quasi-dramatic unity of space, circumscribing all of its action within the delimited boundaries of the "vast tract of unenclosed wild" named Egdon Heath (*RN* 9), my reading points to the way the novel refuses to stay put, but rather kaleidoscopes restlessly through settings and geographic locations. Hardy's frequent figurations and re-figurations of the landscape, accomplished through rapid-fire historical and literary allusion, move us all over the globe while keeping us firmly grounded on the heath. Hardy embeds within the novel's hyperdomestic world multiple layers of imperial history: Roman, British, and Ottoman; ancient and modern; European, African, South Asian, and Middle Eastern. I argue that understanding this is crucial to interrupting readings of Victorian fiction, and of British psychoanalysis alike, that ignore their colonial foundations.

My reading also gives us a new way of understanding an issue that has continually confounded the novel's readers and critics: the strange pseudo-racialization of many of the novel's characters. This list includes not only the most dramatically "colored" and racially figured characters—the dyed-red Diggory Venn, whose skin is thoroughly stained from the materials of his trade, the mining and selling of the reddle used to mark sheep, and the "dark" Eustacia Vye, whose racialization is most implicit in her performance as the Turkish Knight (e.g., *RN* 52)—but also a host of other characters we may not have understood as racially marked, but whose skin color too receives an inordinate amount of attention: the "transparent tissue[d]" Tamsin (*RN* 112); the brown laboring body of her cousin Clym, the "native" himself; and even the heath itself, variously labelled "swarthy" (*RN* 11), "Ishmaelitish" (12), "negro" (127), and "ebony" (259).[8] In attending to both the wide geographic reach of the novel and the insistent pseudo-racialization of its white British characters, this chapter reads *The Return of the Native* as a story of black holes and white mythologies: of imperial spaces rendered visible and invisible at the same time, and of the coming into being of "whiteness" as a racial and ethno-nationalist designation that functions precisely by refusing to see the bodies and labor of people of color.[9] I turn to Balint's notion of "the basic fault"—a fracture in early object relations that forms and deforms the self—to help read the novel's anodyne and yet strangely unsettling concluding chapters, in which red and brown skin blanches back to white and Hardy's geographic references settle into a whitewashed world of Maypole dancers, white picket fences, and Merry Old England. I want to argue that the novel's ending can help us see a "basic fault" in the Victorian domestic novel and Victorian studies alike: the tendency to "forget" the colonial object relations constitutive of the period and the field. Criticism has mainly focused on Hardy's local and regional interests in the novel. This chapter will show just how full of the world the heath is from the start.

Atmospheres

The Return of the Native is backdated to the 1840s and set on the heathland of Hardy's "partly-real, partly dream-country of Wessex"—a fictional county that, based on his native Dorset, was just coming into being at this early stage in Hardy's career.[10] At the start of the novel, originally published in twelve monthly parts with accompanying illustrations in the magazine *Belgravia*, Clym Yeobright, who has left his native Egdon Heath to become a jeweler in Paris, comes home with a distaste for Continental life and a plan to educate the heath's rural laborers. Can the native return? Some of the novel's best critics, Gillian Beer and Raymond Williams, have raised this question.[11] Not only has the native changed, but his presence in turn changes the place: How much of the world does he bring back home with him? Clym carries along with him, especially in the world-seeking heart and eyes of Eustacia Vye, the atmosphere of Paris. Clym brings home French songs (*RN* 248); the specter of revolution; the sparkle of glittering gems and Channel crossings; his memories of the gilded, sun-dazzled rooms of the Louvre (*RN* 196); and the internalized rhythms of "all the beating and pulsing that is going on in the great arteries of the world" (*RN* 276). Eustacia, who despises the heath and longs for the seascapes of the nearby tourist town of Budmouth, is attracted to this explicit worldliness. She willfully sets out to fall in love with Clym and to have him fall in love with her. And she, of course, succeeds, ending her earlier love affair with the caddish Damon Wildeve, fiancé to Clym's cousin Thomasin (familiarly, Tamsin), and eventually marrying Clym.

Atmospheres of love are also atmospheres of Paris floating above the heath. In their happiest moments, Clym and Eustacia feel themselves "enclosed in a sort of luminous mist," which "blot[s] out from their eyes" the heath and its July weather, whose bright sun has "fired its crimson heather to scarlet" (*RN* 235). The mist, in fact, "hid from them surroundings of any inharmonious color, and gave to all things the character of light." Together out in the atmosphere, "they were like those double stars which revolve round and round each other, and from a distance appear to be one" (*RN* 235).[12] And yet Clym has a difficult time sustaining this love, or rather his faith in Eustacia's love, outside of her presence. He knows that while he "pore[s] over her lips, her eyes, and the lines of her face," she has "mused and mused on the subject" of Paris, "even while in the act of returning his gaze" (*RN* 236). In Clym's face, Eustacia sees Paris, while in Eustacia's, Clym sees the possibility of "the evanescence of love" (*RN* 235) and the failure of his ambitious plans for scholarship, educational reform, and social justice.

A central innovation of British psychoanalysis is to attend to object relations as just the kind of "atmosphere" Hardy describes. Rather than emphasizing strict boundaries between people, thinkers in the British school want to describe their overlapping orbits. Precisely because their central intervention in classical psychoanalytic theory is to underscore a firm conviction in dependence and merger as the central facts and phenomenology of early life, these analysts look for ways to conceptualize what Balint calls "the harmonious interpenetrating mix-up" (*BF* 67) of subjects and objects that occurs not only in infancy, but well beyond it. They are interested in what it feels like to be in someone else's presence, and even more than this, how the interaction of two people charges the atmosphere in a particular way—like the "luminous mist" that surrounds Clym and Eustacia when they are most in love.

What is felt within the atmosphere of planet Clym-Eustacia can't quite survive outside of its gravitational pull. During their courtship, before their marriage and cohabitation (in a small cottage on the heath, literally, or in the sky as "double stars," figuratively), Eustacia and Clym meet out on the heath to watch a lunar eclipse and revel in each other's company. But as Clym leaves this passionate tryst, he feels himself sobering: "as he walked further and further from the charmed atmosphere of his Olympian girl his face grew sad with a new kind of sadness" (*RN* 198). The farther he walks from Eustacia the less he can feel her force, and the sadder—"with a new kind of sadness"—his face grows, with the realization that Eustacia sees him "rather as a visitant from a gay world to which she rightly belonged than as a man with a purpose" to stay on the heath and to work for its social improvement (*RN* 198). And the closer Clym gets to his mother's home at Blooms-End, the more he remembers too "the widening breach" (*RN* 199) between the two of them: Mrs. Yeobright disapproves of his plans to give up his career in Paris. Hardy writes that as Clym's "sight grew accustomed to the first blinding halo kindled about him by love and beauty" (*RN* 199), he can see that he is in a difficult situation. With Eustacia, he does not feel it; but away from her, the "perception of the dilemma in which his love had placed him came back with full force" (*RN* 198). The same might be said for the feeling of reading: we tend to lose our lived sense of a novel's pull and multiplicity when we step away from it. And yet Balint's work can help us to understand and theorize this phenomenon—and also the fact that some of a novel's most powerful effects are tied less to its plot and characters than to its overall atmospheric conditions.

The Return of the Native flattens out in memory, the richness of the reading experience fading as we float further from its orbit. Given the force of its tragic itinerary, we might remember it as being pervasively dark and gloomy, rather than shot through with moments of pleasure and joy. We might forget that the novel ends not with Eustacia Vye's tragic death by drowning, but with the muted Maypole romance of Thomasin Yeobright and Diggory Venn. I think that it is possible to stay closer to the novel by describing it as a collection of images rather than a single story. Here are some of the images that stand out to me: Eustacia appearing on the barrow of the heath with her iconic telescope, then slipping down the side "with the glide of a water-drop down a bud" (*RN* 18). The first appearance of the "vermillion figure" (*RN* 77) of the reddleman. Hardy's famous description of Clym's face etched with the perception of "the coil of things" (*RN* 138), and of the slow change as Eustacia's face loses its sleepy, "carmine flush" and blanches to a deathly pale (*RN* 318). Clym's blind pleasure in the manual labor of furze-cutting, and the butterflies that sport around his spade (*RN* 247). Mrs. Yeobright lying down to rest on a fragrant patch of wild shepherd's thyme as she stumbles across the heath to her death by sunstroke and snakebite (*RN* 282), and, at the end of the novel, Thomasin taking her baby Eustacia to the same "soft mats" of "green turf and shepherd's thyme" to practice walking (*RN* 381). Susan Nunsuch "warming and kneading, cutting and twisting, dismembering and re-joining" a wax figure to stand for Eustacia in effigy (*RN* 347). The image of Wildeve and Christian Cantle tossing dice on the dark heath on a stump illuminated by bioluminescent glow of a circle of squiggling glowworms (*RN* 239). Charley's arrangement of arrow-heads, mosses, stones, and crystals in Eustacia's home during her sorrow and convalescence (*RN* 330). Diggory Venn combing the grass searching for Tamsin's lost glove (*RN* 379). Tamsin protecting her baby from the stormy weather in her trek across the heath: bundled in clothes, the baby is kept as warm and dry "as the kernel to the husks" (*RN* 351). The splash of a stone in water to signal the arrival of Eustacia's lover (*RN* 63), and the weir that pulls her in, her long dark hair and saturated clothes weighing her down, to her death by drowning (*RN* 363). The novel collects disparate images and feeling-states as much for the intrinsic pleasure in each as for the sake of developing the plot.

British psychoanalysis can help us to keep some of these atmospheres alive. In descriptions of the wordless, ambient feel of object relations and the force exerted on us by others, mid-twentieth-century psychoanalysts also give us a way to theorize and describe the atmospheres of literary texts and our relations to them. Balint's writing on what it feels like to be with another person might be particularly useful in helping us build into our criticism descriptions of what it feels like to be with the novel. In an early essay cowritten with his first wife Alice Balint (née Alice Székely-Kovács, also Hungarian, 1898–1939), "On Transference and Counter-Transference" (1939), the Balints argue that each analyst carries his or her own unique atmosphere.[13] Transference is not uniform, but is instead shaped by the particular qualities of the analyst. Just as a small detail about the analytic setting, like the choice of the pillow on the couch, might change the entire feel of the room, "differences in the analytical atmosphere" are "brought about by the analyst himself." Biographical details—the fact that "the analyst has a name, is male or female, is of a particular age, has a home, etc."—shape this atmosphere, but so do elements that are harder to put a finger on. "Certainly," the Balints write, "it is not a bold inference to conclude that many more such 'personal' elements influence our intangible analytical attitude as well."[14] Already at this early stage of Balint's career, verbal interpretation is beginning to be called into question as the central curative mechanism of psychoanalysis. *How* something is said is just as important as *what* is said, and the analyst's style of speech contributes to their atmospheric particularity:

> The very fine shades present in the formulation of an interpretation or even of a seemingly indifferent communication, . . . the accentuation or nonaccentuation of certain words, even their cadence or intonation, naturally differ from analyst to analyst. The best argument for the existence of a personal element in all of this is the fact that in control analyses [perhaps better known as supervisions] words are very often used by the controlling analyst [supervisor] to the following effect: "What you said to your patient was quite correct; only I should have said it in rather different words, and certainly with a different stress."[15]

In comments like these, the literariness of object relations theory becomes particularly clear: Balint invites us to read not the content of what is said, but the precise phrasing, the "stress" on certain words, the "cadence" and intonation" in the analyst's voice. As his career progresses, Balint will focus more and more on wordlessness: on the necessity of reading not only the sonic, extrasemantic dimensions of speech, but also personality and mood, not just emanating from spoken words but floating in the air itself. I think this is a unique strength of psychoanalytic theory: to be bold enough to make claims about those "intangible," nonsolid things that, by definition, exceed the graspable and precisely locatable.

Balint's final psychoanalytic work, *The Basic Fault* (1967), is by all accounts his magnum opus. Focusing on the formative effects of early disturbances in object relationships and the therapeutic power of regression, Balint forcefully argues for the limited impact of interpretations spoken by the analyst and offered to the patient. He argues instead for the power of the analytic relationship itself. The problem with a dialogue-based method of psychoanalysis is that it "presupposes that interpretations are experienced by both patient and analyst as interpretations and not as something else" (*BF* 9). Interpretations-as-interpretations—that is, as "sentence[s] consisting of words with an agreed meaning"—presuppose, Balint writes, a patient who is able to "take in" ideas and work them through (*BF* 14). And yet many patients—unstable, regressed, or in a vulnerable state—are not able to do this. As Balint describes it, they are not operating on the level of "agreed, conventional, or adult language," but on a level in which interpretations will be experienced as *actions* rather than as statements: as "unwarranted demand, attack, criticism, seduction, or stimulation." For Balint, the patient is not in need of interpretations: "the patient is in need of an environment" (*BF* 180).

The curative mechanism of psychoanalysis for Balint, and for many other British Independent thinkers, is not interpretation, but the object relation itself. This relationship restages early, preverbal states of merger and nondifferentiation. And for this reason, it in fact feels less like a relationship and more like what Balint variously calls an environment, a climate, an atmosphere, "primary love," an *arglos* (unsuspecting, guileless) state, or "harmonious interpenetrating mix-up." Balint is explicit about this proliferating vocabulary, arguing that it is difficult to find precise words for what is by definition wordless:

> It is difficult to find words to describe what it is that is created. We talk about behaviour, climate, atmosphere, etc., all of which are vague and hazy words, referring to something with no firm boundaries and thus reminiscent of those describing primary substances [such as air and water]. In spite of the fact that the various forms of object relationship cannot be described by concise and unequivocal words, that is, the translation of the various object relationships into words must always be subjective, arbitrary, and inexact, the "atmosphere," the "climate," is there, is felt to be there, and more often than not there is even no need to express it in words—although words may be an important contributory factor both to its creation and maintenance. (*BF* 160–61)

Words may never measure up when it comes to describing a unique object relationship: the palpable feel of the consulting room, the shift in atmosphere when words suddenly stop working in conventional ways, the emotion that charges the air with haziness, the way the space itself seems to hold and carry particles of both people, who are no longer separate, fully delineated objects, but rather amorphous clouds, floating around and mixing together.[16] I love the place in the passage above where Balint's writing grows most passionate: with or without words to name it, the climate or atmosphere created by two people together "*is* there, is *felt* to be there."

In a recent essay in *Qui Parle*, the literary scholar Dora Zhang makes a very similar plea. She argues for the power of atmospheres, and for our need to make ourselves sensitive enough to read the ones that surround us—not just as social beings, but as *political* beings as well. Although she does not directly engage Balint, Zhang takes a page from his book when she writes: "For all their seeming haziness, atmospheres have real effects. They alter the kinds of things that can be said in a space, the kinds of actions that are thinkable, and the modes of sociality that are possible."[17] Her analysis extends Balint's claims by moving out of the consulting room and into the political sphere—into spaces as diverse as the classroom, the retail store, the picket line, and the occupied public plaza. Zhang draws from Amador Fernández-Savater, an activist in and theorist of the 15-M, or *indignados*, struggle in Spain, who has called for the need to "organize" not so much a political "movement" as a new political "climate": a collective, far-reaching shift in priorities, demands for justice, and moods of empowerment that can enable "new 'political horizons' across time and distance."[18]

Like Balint and Zhang, I want to advocate for a project of sensitization and trust in realms beyond words. Affective, aesthetic, and political climates alike may be vague, hazy, hard to pin down, but they *are* there, are *felt* to be there. What tools do we have in literary studies to describe how words on the page act on us, rather than what they say? What happens when we see a literary text less as discrete object and more as an environment, a climate, a harmonious interpenetrating mix-up? Analyzing the discontinuous atmospheres of *The Return of the Native*, my aim is to better understand the novelistic production of both particular kinds of object relations and particular kinds of political climates. To do so, I will attend in particular to the apparent discontinuity between the novel's local setting and its wide-ranging descriptive and figurative practices, which take us all over the globe. I want to ask: Can *The Return of the Native* help to make us more sensitive to and aware of colonial object relations, in all of their explicit and implicit violence, even though it seems to obscure and forget them?

Harmonious Interpenetrating Mix-Up

For Hardy, atmosphere is first and foremost a material fact—albeit one that is importantly shaped by literary attention. At the start of the novel, Mrs. Yeobright and her niece Thomasin eagerly prepare for Clym's homecoming for the Christmas holidays. In one remarkable scene, they collect his favorite apples from their winter storage place, the loft in Mrs. Yeobright's fuel-house. As Thomasin climbs into the loft, Hardy directs our attention to atmospheric effects—that is, to the effects of light and to the visible quality or texture of air itself:

The loft was lighted by a semicircular hole, through which the pigeons crept to their lodgings in the same high quarters of the premises; and from this hole the sun shone in a bright yellow patch on the figure of the maiden as she knelt and plunged her naked arms into the soft brown fern, which, from its abundance, was used on Egdon in packing away stores of all kinds. The pigeons were flying about her head with the greatest unconcern, and the face of her aunt was just visible above the floor of the loft, lit by a few stray motes of light, as she stood halfway up the ladder, looking at a spot into which she was not climber enough to venture. (*RN* 112)

The "stray motes of light" that make it possible for Thomasin to see her aunt's face are, in a way, Hardy's misnomer for other, more material motes in the air: the floating specks of dust and hay, downy pigeon feathers, crumpled particles of dried and decaying ferns, and dead skin cells illuminated by the shaft of light coming from the hole in the loft's roof just above Thomasin's head. Atmospherics of air produce atmospherics of mood: the women quietly muse about Clym's impending arrival, with Thomasin expressing her curiosity about how Clym's face may have changed (predicting Hardy's own long description of this some pages later). Pushing aside ferns so that "mellow fruit greeted her sense with its ripe smell," Thomasin wonders aloud: "'Dear Clym, I wonder how your face looks now?' she said, gazing abstractedly at the pigeon-hole, which admitted the sunlight so directly upon her brown hair and transparent tissues that it almost seemed to shine through her" (*RN* 112). Tamsin herself is an airy medium for the light to shine through, her skin so light toned and thin that you seem to be able to see the life flowing within it. Or put differently, Tamsin's remaining materiality is a mote in the air, floating on thoughts of her cousin's face. She directs her words to someone who is not there and, at the same time, abstracts her aunt's material presence into thin air by talking through her.

In *Tess of the D'Urbervilles*, Hardy names the substances floating in the air at a barn dance a "vegeto-human pollen," formed, in the case of the famous Chaseborough scene, by the "floating fusty *debris* of peat and hay, mixed with the perspirations of warmth of the dancers" (*T* 500).[19] This is atmosphere made concrete. It is a way to identify, in the cloud that intermingles wet human substance with dried vegetable debris, something we wouldn't otherwise see, or be able to pin down, but is nevertheless there: a distinct feel, tone, or mood of the environment that is not emanating from any one source in particular, but is rather a product of profound intermixture. This concretization also brings to the foreground something that usually recedes, or that functions as merely a supporting medium. In Hardy's fiction, air takes on a weight and feel all its own.

Racially marked skin, and a politicized atmosphere: Hardy has already underscored Tamsin's skin and complexion, so fair that it is transparent. On our first introduction to her, as she wakens into consciousness and a series of thoughts visibly passes over her face, the narrator remarks: "An ingenuous, transparent life was disclosed; it was as if the flow of her existence could be seen passing within" (*RN* 41). Thomasin's dual-coded sexual and racial purity are designated as a whiteness so white as to be transparent in a vision of normative female sexuality against which Eustacia's own—dark, unruly, restless, exotic—will be contrasted throughout the novel. And while Eustacia will drown, dragged down by the weight of her saturated clothes and living dark tresses, Thomasin's innocence and ingenuousness make her immaterial enough to float on air.

The Basic Fault contains a long excursus on the qualities of air. Balint notes, "in our relationship to the air, there are no sharp boundaries. It is an idle question to enquire whether the air in our lungs, or in our bowels, is us or not us, or where the exact boundary between us and the air is; we still live with the air in an almost harmonious interpenetrating mix-up" (*BF* 67). I will return to spell out some of the significance of this fact for Balint's larger theories, but first I want to point out that Balint's description chimes remarkably well with a famous description of air in *The Return of the Native*. In one of the novel's several lengthy interludes describing the landscape itself, Hardy's narrator describes the wind on Egdon Heath. Blowing over the hilly heath's "pits and prominences," and through its low-growing vegetation of heather and gorse, the wind produces a sound "audible [nowhere] else on earth": a multiple-toned voice made up of the sound of the wind moving through different kinds of vegetable matter. Of all the heath's tones, the narrator remarks, its most distinctive is the voice produced when the winter wind blows through the dried flowers of hibernating heather. Hardy's personification of the sound makes it at once human and vegetable and elemental, material and spiritual:

> It was a worn whisper, dry and papery, and it brushed so distinctly across the ear that, by the accustomed, the material minutiae in which it originated could be realised as by touch. It was the united products of infinitesimal vegetable causes, and these were neither stems nor twigs, neither leaves nor fruit, neither blades nor prickles, neither lichen nor moss. They were the mummified heath-bells of the past summer, originally tender and purple, now washed colourless by Michaelmas rains, and dried to dead skins by October suns. (*RN* 56)

Although the sound from one desiccated heath-bell alone is too quiet to hear, together the bells create a "plaintive" November "recitative" that seems to alter perception itself—both in its scale and its synesthetic possibilities: "One inwardly saw the infinity of those combined multitudes: one perceived that each of the tiny trumpets was seized on, entered, scoured and emerged from by the wind as thoroughly if it were as vast as a crater" (*RN* 56). There are no "sharp boundaries" here—not even between the "multitudes" of heath-bells. Rather than imagining that each bell speaks for itself, Hardy, making them "combined," insists that it is "the single person of something else speaking through each in turn." A "spirit"—of place, of "windy tune," of "song"—moves them and speaks through them (*RN* 57). Hardy's own harmonious mix-up draws in characters too, with the wind scouring the cavities of human ears as well as trumpet-shaped flowers, sounding vocal cords as well as leaves, twigs, and stems. Eustacia Vye, listening on the heath, becomes one more wind instrument among others when she lets out a long sigh and lets it twine in with the winds around her: "The bluffs had broken silence, the bushes had broken silence, the heather-bells had broken silence; at last, so did the woman" (*RN* 57). Sighs and air currents, lungs and climate, combine to create the sounding that describes the very atmosphere of the place.

Several recent critics have written beautifully on Hardy's unique view of the natural world, and the tendency in his fiction to picture the environment as that which melds human and nonhuman worlds. As scholars like William A. Cohen have shown, landscapes in Hardy's hands are as sensate as characters, and people are as permeable as their surroundings. *The Return of the Native*, Cohen notes, "famously exaggerates even Hardy's usual devotion to landscape description," and in the novel, "the natural surroundings of the heath intrude on, and become inseparable from, the bodies of its inhabitants."[20] Balint's "harmonious interpenetrating mix-up" is one way of registering this "intense relatedness" to the "environment," and in particular to what Balint calls the "primary substances"— water, air, earth, and fire—that sustain our existence (*BF* 67).

For Balint, our reliance on the primary substances that surround and support us is both a material fact and a wonderfully illustrative metaphor: this trusting, *arglos* relation to the environment also represents, ideally, our earliest relations to other people. Balint describes a phase of "primary love" in which our first objects, the people who care for us and sustain us in our infancy, feel more like substances or environments than clearly differentiated objects. They support us much like the earth and air do: without our taking notice, without need for conscious thought. "Primary love," a concept that dates back to a paper Balint published in 1937, is in fact a bold intervention in psychoanalytic theory: it replaces the notion of "primary narcissism" (the accepted Freudian conviction that the earliest object is the self) with a "theory of primary relationship to the environment" (*BF* 65). Balint writes:

> The cathexis of the environment by the foetus must be very intense—more intense than a child's or adult's. This environment, however, is probably undifferentiated; on the one hand, there are as yet no objects in it; on the other hand, it has hardly any structure, in particular no sharp boundaries

towards the individual; environment and individual penetrate into each other, they exist together in a "harmonious mix-up." (*BF* 66)

Like a fish in water or a fetus in amniotic fluid, the question of what is inside and what is outside simply does not hold. Substances are there to be used and to be absorbed, and to be absorbed into. Environments are soft and amorphous rather than rigidly demarcated or sharply boundaried. Air is Balint's central example when he argues that first caregivers function more like environments than objects with outlines:

> We use the air, in fact we cannot live without it. We inhale it in order to take parts out of it and use them as we want; then, after putting substances into it that we want to get rid of, we exhale it—without paying the slightest attention to it. In fact, the air must be there for us, and as long as it is there in sufficient supply and quality, we do not take any notice of it. This kind of environment must simply be there, and as long as it is there—for instance, if we get enough air—we take its existence for granted, we do not consider it as an object, that is, separate from us; we just use it. (*BF* 66–67)

Balint's is a theory of dependence and merger, and one in which an object extends out into an aura or atmosphere rather than staying within its own lines.

Part of Balint's interest in this early mix-up is also that it reflects one of the possibilities for later object relations. Unsurprisingly for a thinker so interested in analytic technique, Balint is particularly interested in regression to primary love in analysis itself. Balint encourages the strategic use of such regression, arguing that it is what makes for the therapeutic mechanism itself. In certain phases of the treatment, "the analyst assumes, in fact must assume, the qualities of a primary object" (*BF* 69), and in these phases, "the analyst must do everything in his power not to become, or to behave as, a separate, sharply-contoured object" (*BF* 167). What the patient needs for change to occur is not just another object in his life, but instead:

> an environment that accepts and consents to sustain and carry the patient like the earth or the water sustains and carries a man who entrusts his weight to them. In contrast to ordinary objects, especially to ordinary human objects, no action is expected from these primary objects or substances; yet they must be there and must—tacitly or explicitly—consent to be used, otherwise the patient cannot achieve any change: without water it is impossible to swim, without earth impossible to move on. The substance, the analyst, must not resist, must consent, must not give rise to too much friction, must accept and carry the patient for a while, must prove more or less indestructible, must not insist on maintaining harsh boundaries, but must allow the development of a kind of mix-up between the patient and himself. (*BF* 145)

Analysis creates an objectless space in which the patient "should be able to find himself, to accept himself, and to get on with himself" (*BF* 178) without interference. Rather than an object with stark outlines—an object that might be experienced as demanding, obtrusive, or oppressive—the analyst should function as a "yielding" environment with permeable boundaries, providing not so much words, interpretations, and knowledge as "time and milieu" (*BF* 179), even a silent one. For Balint, the analyst's role is not so much to act or to know as to "create an environment, a climate" (*BF* 177) in which the patient can "discover *his* way to the world of objects—and not be shown the 'right' way by some profound or correct interpretation" (*BF* 180, emphasis added). In these formulations, Balint works to challenge and revise the power dynamics of classical analysis, transforming its asymmetry into a collaboration between "two people who [are] not fundamentally different in importance, weight, and power" (*BF* 171).

Balint's belief in regression is fundamental. The patient must return to primary love in order to enact what Balint calls a "new beginning": that is to say, a "changed relationship to the patient's objects of love and hate." A "regression for the sake of progression," the new beginning stages a return to "a point before the faulty development started," inaugurating new possibilities for object relations and "character changes" as well (*BF* 132). Again, the contribution is significant: Balint argues for the very possibility of novelty in object relations rather than an endless cycle of repetition and reenactment. The transference not only replays earlier relationships, but, by returning to primary love, opens the possibility for entirely new kinds and styles of object relating to develop.[21]

Can novels function as primary substances, as primary objects, as primary love? Hardy believes that they can. He makes his novels highlight their own capacity to do so, underlining their ability to function as sustaining environments and to draw readers into their "harmonious interpenetrating mix-ups." As I have argued in my earlier chapter on *Tess*, a key way in which Hardy's novels operate in this manner is in the long descriptive passages that dissolve the boundaries between subjects and their environments, and that offer, in their lyrical suspensions of anxiety and time, respite from Hardy's shocking plots.[22] In *The Return of the Native*, such a provision is most abundantly clear in Mrs. Yeobright's walk across the heath, on a stiflingly hot summer day, to reconcile with her son Clym and his wife Eustacia after they have married against her wishes. It is the last day in August, in the crush of a heatwave that leaves nothing unwilted: "In Mrs. Yeobright's garden large-leaved plants of a tender kind flagged by ten o'clock in the morning; rhubarb bent downward at eleven; and even stiff cabbages were limp by noon" (*RN* 269). Mrs. Yeobright, despite her more advanced age and imperfect health, pursues her peacemaking visit regardless of the heat, but stops frequently to rest. Hardy describes the pleasures of observation in these moments of rest in such a way that Mrs. Yeobright's sensations spill into our own:

> Occasionally she came to a spot where independent worlds of ephemerons were passing their time in mad carousal, some in the air, some on the hot ground and vegetation, some in the tepid and stringy water of a nearly-dried pool. All the shallower ponds had decreased to a vaporous mud, amid which maggoty shapes of innumerable obscene creatures could be indistinctly seen, heaving and wallowing with enjoyment. Being a woman not disinclined to philosophise, she sometimes sat down under her umbrella to rest and watch their happiness, for a certain hopefulness as to the result of her visit gave ease to her mind, and, between her important thoughts, left it free to dwell on any infinitesimal matter which caught her eyes. (*RN* 270)

Hordes of tiny gnats and insects swarm and swim and crawl, forming busy miniature clouds or crowding tiny pools of hot, algae-filled water, "heaving and wallowing with enjoyment." Their enjoyment spreads to Mrs. Yeobright and to the novel's readers, who take pleasure in their own observation of these "independent worlds of ephemerons," and, as Beer points out, in the way these pauses in the walk also represent pauses in the plot. Happiness arises, she argues, from close observation of the natural world and from the interruption of tragic plot: "Hardy's writing is characterised by creative vacillation, by a shiftiness which survives the determination of plot. Life is devious and resourceful, constantly reassembling about new possibilities which lie just off the path of the obliterative energies of event. Happiness and hap form the two poles of his work." For Hardy, Beer continues, happiness is "almost always at odds with narrative, because it is at odds with succession." Happiness is instead "constellatory, 'a series of impressions' at most."[23] Mrs. Yeobright's happiness here is not only in her projection of happiness on to the "heaving and wallowing" insect life, but in the "ease" given "to her mind" by the lifting of the pressures of plot, of space found "between important thoughts." Enjoyment diffuses from insect to woman to narrator to reader and back again in an atmosphere of pleasure and heat—of primary love. But this pleasure is indeed only temporary: the visit will not go well, and hap will take over where happiness ceases. Shut out from Clym's house by a string of trying coincidences and Eustacia's misapprehension of the situation, Mrs. Yeobright will leave heartbroken, and will die, from sun, stroke, despair, and an adder bite added in for good tragic measure, without seeing her son again. The vegetable clock—the wilting leaves and bending stems of large-leaved plants, rhubarb, and cabbage—has predicted her own doom. Mrs. Yeobright collapses on the heath, which is so hot that it feels as though "every valley" is filled "with air like that in a kiln" (*RN* 269). The atmosphere has shifted, taking on a different palpability and pressure: Mrs. Yeobright feels "the air around her pulsating silently, oppressing the earth with lassitude" (*RN* 269). Entering her lungs, pressing down on her limbs, the heavy atmosphere makes her breath ragged and her gait uneven as she stumbles across the heath, never to make it home.

The Return of the Native is a novel that changes atmosphere, climate, and mood with a dizzying rapidity. Its shifts are dictated not only by the pressures of plot, not only by the pleasures of Hardy's language—which "ricochets across registers" and between "experience-near and experience-far" descriptions[24]— but also by the restlessness of its figurative activity. This restlessness is bent on taking places both as themselves and as other places on the map, other locations in time. Take the long description of the heath that opens the novel: "A Saturday afternoon in November was approaching the time of twilight, and the vast tract of unenclosed wild known as Egdon Heath embrowned itself moment by moment. Overhead the hollow stretch of whitish cloud shutting out the sky was a tent which had the whole heath for its floor" (*RN* 9). The narrative attunes us to both "vast" expanses and enclosed spaces (as the white clouds tent in the brown floor and shut out the blue sky). It shows us the heath as both "unenclosed wild[s]" and gestures forward to its future, dictated by enclosure laws and private ownership. The novel's management of space is multiple and complex, and it contains not just one but a multitude of geopolitical and historical atmospheres (the 1840s of its setting and the late 1870s of its publication, Dorset and Wessex, rural tradition and developing agrarian capitalism). And even more than this, the heath that grows browner and browner as twilight settles beneath a stretch of white clouds is never simply itself: not only because the land literally holds layers of imperial history, in the concrete form of the Roman barrows that dot the landscape and get so much narrative attention, but also because Hardy's description, with all of its figurative movements, continually draws us *away* from the heath in efforts to paint the scene. Arguing that "Haggard Egdon" requires a modern aesthetic sense to appreciate it, one that is helped along because "orthodox beauty" in landscape is slowly losing its appeal, Hardy writes:

> The new Vale of Tempe [in Greece] may be a gaunt waste in Thule [a mythical name for Scandinavia]: human souls may find themselves in closer and closer harmony with external things wearing a sombreness distasteful to our race when it was young. The time seems near, if it has not actually arrived, when the mournful sublimity of a moor, a sea, or a mountain will be all of nature that is absolutely in keeping with the moods of the more thinking among mankind. And ultimately, to the commonest tourist, spots like Iceland may become what the vineyards and myrtle-gardens of South Europe are to him now; and Heidelberg and Baden be passed unheeded as he hastens from the Alps to the sand-dunes of Scheveningen [a seaside resort in

the Netherlands, and the site of a major naval battle between English and Dutch forces in 1653]. (*RN* 10–11)

Oh, the places we go while staying firmly grounded on the heath: from Greece to Scandinavia; from the moor to the sea; from the vineyards of the dusty, hot South of France to the tundra of the icy Arctic Circle; from the peaks of the Alps to the beaches of the Hague. While never actually changing scene, the novel's narration draw us across the globe and back again, far from the heath and right up close, in an energetic to-and-fro, near and far, travel and return.

Black Holes

Textual inscriptions of other places and landscapes can be quick, as when Eustacia, standing in the chimney corner of her grandfather's house and straining to hear a conversation taking place on the roof, peers upward into multiple worlds at once. Eustacia, "listening, looked up the old irregular shaft, with its cavernous hollows, where the smoke blundered about on its way to the square bit of sky at the top, from which the daylight struck down with a pallid glare upon the tatters of soot draping the flue as sea-weed drapes a rocky fissure" (*RN* 108). Overlapping visions of soot and seaweed point to the coexistence of two different worlds within this one chimney, or in this one textual subjectivity. It is as if Eustacia, who detests the heath's rolling hills of heather and gorse and longs to return to Budmouth's seaside bustle, manages to carry with her both atmospheres at once, inhabiting not just the heath but also the seaside, if only imaginatively. The textual subjectivity is not just Eustacia's, but ours too, as Hardy, by way of Eustacia's point of view, makes sense of soot tatters stretched across the flue by seeing them as seaweed draped across rocks. Images like these are one reason we love Hardy: the quality of his eye, the acuity of his description, the strangeness of his mind in creating these links. But the juxtaposition of these images also points to something less familiar: the under-remarked geopolitical imagination of this novel.

The most compelling manipulations of space in *The Return of the Native* are those that write onto the heath histories of empire that are elsewhere disavowed. And so, a final word on air: Hardy being Hardy, what is for Balint a harmonious interpenetrating mix-up will sometimes become menacing. As in Proust's asthmatic fits,[25] Hardy imagines for us the horrors of a limited supply of air. In book 5, Thomasin comes to visit Clym, who has been "out of [his] senses" with grief over the loss of his mother, and is only slowly recovering:

> "Ah, Thomasin! Thank you for coming to-night," said Clym when she entered the room. "Here am I, you see. Such a wretched spectacle am I, that I shrink from being seen by a single friend, and almost from you."

"You must not shrink from me, dear Clym," said Thomasin earnestly, in that sweet voice of hers which came to a sufferer like fresh air into a Black Hole.
"Nothing in you can ever shock me or drive me away." (*RN* 304)

Hardy's quick reference to "a Black Hole" points not to astronomy, but to the history of British Empire. The "Black Hole of Calcutta" is the site where European prisoners of war were held for one fateful night in June 1756, after Bengali forces led by Nawab Siraj ud-Daulah wrested control of Fort William from the British East India Company. The prison—small, hot, airless, and tightly packed—allegedly claimed the lives of 123 prisoners, who died of suffocation after being locked in the prison overnight. The incident was immediately and forcefully commemorated by one of the survivors, John Zephania Holwell (1711–90), in the form of both a written narrative and a white marble obelisk erected near the site after the British reconquest of Fort William in 1757 as a monument to the lives lost.[26] Howell's account emphasizes the "horrid" violence of the Bengali troops and the tyranny of their ruler.[27] Through these accounts, the "tragedy of the Black Hole of Calcutta" became "deeply entrenched in British folk-memory of their rule in India" for centuries to come.[28] *The Return of the Native* stands as evidence of that claim, and is perhaps exemplary of how British imperial "folk-memory" operates: it registers the horror of European losses while relegating memory of South Asian death and expropriation to the void—into a black hole of a different kind.

The historian and postcolonial theorist Partha Chatterjee remarks that the tragedy was so widely known in some parts of the world, thanks to Holwell's narrative and the British desire for tales of Indian "savagery," that the phrase "Black Hole" came to stand in for any "dark and suffocating place."[29] And yet the location of *the* Black Hole (vs. Hardy's *a* Black Hole) is an important one. As Chatterjee explains, Fort William would grow in importance in the centuries after its construction in the early eighteenth century by the East India Company: "In the nineteenth century, Fort William and city of Calcutta that surrounds it became the capital of the British Empire in India. In the twentieth century, Calcutta also became a major place where nationalist modernity was fashioned and mass politics was organized."[30] As the title of Chatterjee's book, *The Black Hole of Empire*, indicates, the incident at Calcutta and its outsized mythology condenses into itself whole stretches of imperial space-time. Reconstructing the local history of the Black Hole of Calcutta and the various phases of its physical memorialization (in 1760, 1902, and 1940, when the monument became a focal point of the Indian independence movement, and when nationalist activists successfully demanded the removal of the monument from Dalhousie Square) allows Chatterjee to narrate not only a larger "history of the

British Empire in India and the national resistance to it," but also "a history of the global practices of empire" writ large.[31]

In *The Return of the Native*, Hardy evokes the Black Hole of Calcutta in order to describe the suffering of two white bodies: the suffering of the central characters Clym, to whom Thomasin arrives as a breath of "fresh air," and, less directly, Mrs. Yeobright, whose death by the stifling heat of a breezeless summer day transforms the sweltering heath into a kind of suffocating chamber, a heat-filled "kiln" (*RN* 269) much like the Fort William prison.[32] This apportioning of suffering to white bodies alone follows the lead of both folk-memory and official British commemoration. On the original Black Hole memorial, erected in 1760, after the reconquest of Calcutta (which Siraj had renamed Alingar) by the British in the Battle of Plassey (Palashi) in 1757, there are two plaques, one on each side, with inscriptions written by Holwell. The first plaque lists forty-eight names of those who died in the Fort's prison,

> with who sundry other Inhabitants,
> Military and Militia to the Number of 123 Persons,
> were by the Tyrannic Violence of Surajud Dowla,
> Suba of Bengal, Suffocated in the Black Hole Prison of Fort William in the Night of the 20th Day of
> June, 1756, and promiscuously thrown the succeeding Morning into the Ditch of the
> Ravelin of this Place,
> This
> Monument is Erected
> by
> Their Surviving Fellow Sufferer,
> J. Z. HOLWELL

The second plaque renders British retaliatory violence both heroic and deserved. It reads:

> This Horrid Act of Violence was as Amply
> as deservedly revenged
> On Surajud Dowla,
> by his Majesty's Arms,
> under the Conduct of Vice Admiral Watson and Coll. Clive
> Anno, 1757

The Bengali soldiers and civilians killed in the reconquest of Fort William are, of course, left uncounted, unnamed, and unmentioned on the monument. This suffering—let alone the suffering of all of those who had been murdered, dispossessed, and politically discounted by British rule since the establishment of Fort William in 1700—never makes it onto the monument or into folk-memory.

Nor onto Hardy's page. *The Return of the Native* never recurs directly to the Black Hole, but it does briefly mention one of its history's players: the "Coll. Clive" named above—Robert Clive (1725-74), that is, who led the British reconquest of Fort William and who went on to become Baron Clive and one of the foremost leaders in British India, famous for firmly establishing the dominance of East India Company rule in southern India and Bengal, amassing an enormous personal fortune from his exploits, and for being at least partially responsible for establishing the economic preconditions for the devastating Bengal famine of 1769-70.[33] Clive enters Hardy's novel in a reference to the unexpected developments in Clym's early career. Hardy writes: "The waggery of fate which started Clive as a writing clerk, Gay as a linendraper, Keats as a surgeon, and a thousand others in a thousand other odd ways, banished the wild and perceptive heath lad to be a shopman to a jeweler" (*RN* 169). Clive and Clym: these are men catapulted from modest beginnings to glamorous circumstances—if, that is, development from a poor clerk for the British East India Company to rich tyrant, destroying the lives of "a thousand others in a thousand other odd ways," counts as a glamourous outcome. What Hardy describes as the "waggery of fate" we might describe as systematic exploitation founded on racist ideology.

The book inscribes a final silent connection to the Black Hole of Calcutta: Lord Curzon, viceroy of India from 1899 to 1905, responsible for rebuilding the Black Hole memorial monument in 1902, was a friend of Hardy's in the 1890s.[34] British Empire is part of the air that Hardy and the novel breathe, and the air the reader breathes in its atmosphere. And the violent history that underwrites Clym's "breath of fresh air," and the ease with which it is mentioned, should, I think, stifle us at least a little. In his epic poem *The Dynasts* (1910), Hardy would write that "war makes rattling good history."[35] But the sounds of this particular history of war—like the "rattling" of the Indian Mutiny of 1857-58 that surely informed Hardy's understanding of British Empire, and provided a historical background for this particular literary reference that was closer to the time of the novel's writing—are not quite spoken aloud, but seem instead to get trapped in the novel's throat.[36]

X Marks the Spot

In his war poem "Embarcation," written twenty years after *The Return of the Native*, Hardy describes the experience of standing on the Southampton Docks in October 1899, watching British troops depart to fight in the Second Boer War. As the soldiers "tramp" "deckward" down the gangplank, "yellow as autumn leaves" in their khaki uniforms but "alive as spring" (9), Hardy's speaker imagines the various histories of war that have converged on this "selfsame" harbor.[37] "Here" marks the spot where the ongoing march of history meets the bloody "stasis" of the accumulation of layers of imperial violence—Roman (Vespasian), Anglo-Saxon (Cerdic), medieval British (Henry), and now South African. Here is the poem in full:

> Here, where Vespasian's legions struck the sands,
> And Cerdic with his Saxons entered in,
> And Henry's army leapt afloat to win
> Convincing triumphs over neighbor lands,
>
> Vaster battalions press for further strands,
> To argue in the selfsame bloody mode
> Which this late age of thought, and pact, and code,
> Still fails to mend.—Now deckward tramp the bands,
>
> Yellow as autumn leaves, alive as spring;
> And as each host draws out upon the sea
> Beyond which lies the tragical To-be,
> None dubious of the cause, none murmuring,
>
> Wives, sisters, parents, wave white hands and smile,
> As if they know not that they weep the while.

Vaster battalions, further shores: and yet, for Hardy, what looks like global expansion is in fact stuck in place. Despite the "late age" of turn-of-the-century modernity, global relations occur "in the selfsame bloody mode" as in 43, 519, and 1422—they are argued not in the language of evolving "thought, and pact, and code," but rather in static mode ("and," "and") of warfare, violence, and settler colonial genocide.[38] And yet despite this knowledge, and despite the countless repetitions of death and bloodletting, Hardy writes that each host of soldiers "draws out upon the sea / Beyond which lies the tragical To-be" without doubt, without murmur, without protest (lines 10–12).

"Embarcation" captures a layered vision of place that subtends many of Hardy's novels, even one understood to be as resolutely local and pastoral as *The Return of the Native*. Hardy's picture of Egdon Heath busily pictures on one local spot the various ingresses and egresses of imperial conquest that shape its history, embedding the British, Roman, and Ottoman empires within the novel's hyperlocal domestic world. Through the dense network of literary and historical allusion Hardy uses to describe and create the novel's landscapes and atmospheres, *The Return of the Native* shows just how worlded one small corner of England necessarily is—and just how worlded novels are too. Hardy's famous heathlands contain, like the dice Christian Cantle marvels at, "a great deal in a small compass" (*RN* 222).

At several points in the novel, Hardy invites us to think of the heath as the globe itself. When Eustacia flees her home on a dark, stormy evening at the novel's climax, her formerly seafaring uncle can't imagine how he could find her:

> To follow her was almost impossible. Had the dwelling stood on an ordinary road, two persons setting out, one in each direction, might have made sure of overtaking her; but it was a hopeless task to seek for anybody on a heath in the dark, the practicable directions for flight across it from any point being as numerous as the meridians radiating from the pole. (*RN* 344)

In Hardy's image, the lonely house on the desolate heath becomes a geographic pole, the plane that surrounds it drawn over with lines of latitude and longitude. The image is a map of the world superimposed onto the heath and folded over into a spherical globe. In *Tess*, Hardy describes the circumscribed existence of rural people as follows: "to persons of limited spheres, miles are as geographical degrees, parishes as counties, counties as provinces and kingdoms" (*T* 99–100). But the geography he draws in *The Return of the Native* has a different effect: it doesn't stretch the "county" out to replace the "kingdom," but rather fixes the entire globe on one spot.

As Eustacia stumbles across the heath in the driving rain and pitch black, tripping over "twisted furze-roots, tufts of rushes, or oozing lumps of fleshy fungi, which at this season lay scattered about the heath like the rotting liver and lungs of some colossal animal," the narrator intensifies her sense of nighttime terror by drawing onto the heath a host of other settings. Hardy writes: "It was a night which led the traveller's thoughts instinctively to dwell on nocturnal scenes of disaster in the chronicles of the world, on all that is terrible and dark in history and legend—the last plague of Egypt, the destruction of Sennacherib's host, the agony in Gethsemane" (*RN* 345). Part Eustacia, part generalized "traveller," *someone's* thoughts are made to dwell, by a combination of "instinct" and education, pathetic fallacy and recalled reading, on "nocturnal scenes of disaster in the chronicles of the world." Through the list of allusions, biblical and Byronic, to all that is "terrible and dark in history and legend," Hardy places the fleeing Eustacia on the heath, but also imaginatively in Egypt, Judah, and Jerusalem by turns.[39] And in general, this is one of the novel's greatest feats: the way Hardy moves us in and out of far-flung geographic and historical spaces even while keeping us firmly grounded on the heath.

The novel's famous bonfire-night scene, through which the action of the novel commences, moves acrobatically through time and tradition even while staying rooted on one spot. Hardy writes of the local "bonfire-makers":

> It was as if these men and boys had suddenly dived into past ages and fetched therefrom an hour and deed which had before been familiar with this spot. The ashes of the original British pyre which blazed from that summit lay fresh and undisturbed in the barrow beneath their tread. The flames from funeral piles long ago kindled there had shone down upon the lowlands as these were shining now. Festival fires to Thor and Woden had followed on the same ground and duly had their day. Indeed, it is pretty well known that such blazes as this the heathmen were now enjoying are rather the lineal descendants from jumbled Druidical rites and Saxon ceremonies than the invention of popular feeling about Gunpowder Plot. (*RN* 20)

X marks the spot of the current fire, of the place to dig to uncover the "ashes of the original British pyre" intermingled with bones and urns of Roman inhabitants, and of ancient "festival fires to Thor and Woden." Trish Ferguson argues that this paragraph (and the novel more generally) "dehistoricizes" Bonfire Night, emptying it of both the "original conservative associations that it had held from [1605], when the plot to blow up Parliament was discovered and the chief conspirator, Guy Fawkes, was hung, drawn, and quartered" and of its more contemporary political associations. "By the 1840s," when the novel is set, "November Fifth had become an annual occasion of radical violence when, throughout England, laborers protested on account of low wages, the effects of Enclosure, the Corn Laws, the suppression of trade unionism, and the introduction of agricultural machinery."[40] For Ferguson, this mytho-historical fantasia, in which men and boys dive into the past and bring back its very flames, releases Hardy from writing about the very real labor unrest that shaped English rural life in the 1840s. As Raymond Williams writes of the pastoral, Hardy's imaginative flight "turns protest into retrospect."[41] But I think that Hardy's description, which mingles the "flames from funeral piles long ago kindled" with the flames shining out now, arguably adds to this history rather than erasing it, stretching the spectator's gaze both back in time and across space. Pagan ritual, dominant religion, and conservative and radical political commitments alike shine out from Hardy's fires.

For Hardy moves his readers variously toward and away from the X on the map that marks the location of the bonfire on the top of a barrow, on top of a hill, in Egdon Heath, Wessex, England. Hardy tells us that the single fire around which are gathered Grandfer Cantle, Christian, Timothy Fairway, and the rest of the Egdon characters marks the "selfsame" spot on which a yearly seasonal fire, marking the start of winter, has always been burned, albeit by different historical players: Celtic, Saxon, and Norse. And yet when Hardy zooms out to describe the network of fires that dot the surrounding landscape, he draws a different kind of map:

While the [Egdon] men and lads were building the pile a change took place in the mass of shade which denoted the distant landscape. Red suns and tufts of fire one by one began to arise, flecking the whole country round. They were the bonfires of other parishes and hamlets that were engaged in the same sort of commemoration. Some were distant, and stood in a dense atmosphere, so that bundles of pale straw-like beams radiated above them in the shape of a fan. Some were large and near, glowing scarlet-red from the shade, like wounds in a black hide.... Perhaps as many as thirty bonfires could be counted within the whole bounds of the district; and as the hour may be told on a clockface when the figures themselves are invisible, so did the men recognize the locality of each fire by its angle and direction, though nothing of the scenery could be viewed. (*RN* 19)

As the earlier "meridians" image made a lonely heath dwelling the fixed pole of a spinning globe, this image makes the local bonfire the center of an illuminated "clockface." The numbers on the clockface are "invisible," the surrounding "scenery" cannot be seen; but the time can be read, and one's location ascertained, by charting the "angle" and "direction" of the surrounding fires. The clockface, then, is also a map, and one that imagines a known and knowable center against an unevenly charted periphery: it is a map of empire. The image of the single bonfire expands into galaxies of "red suns and tufts of fire" that fleck "the whole country round." The fifth of November bonfire custom traveled abroad with British settler colonialists; as historians have noted, Guy Fawkes Day celebrations spread to the United States, Australia, New Zealand, Canada, and the Caribbean in the eighteenth and nineteenth centuries.[42] So when Hardy pictures the constellation of bonfires as pinpricks of light dotting a dark sky, what he is constructing is not simply a *stellar* map—one in which Eustacia's bright fire, "the nearest of any," glows like "the moon of the whole shining throng" (*RN* 32)—but even more importantly, if less explicitly, an *imperial* one. As the bonfire on the barrow sinks low, "most of the other fires within the wide horizon were also dwindling weak." Nevertheless, "attentive observation of their brightness, colour, and length of existence could have revealed the quality of the material burnt; and through that, to some extent, the natural produce of the district in which each bonfire was situate" (*RN* 31). Hardy's bonfire map of materials includes the heath furze of the Egdon district; the light fuel of "straw, beanstalks" and other plant waste from "arable land"; and, finally, fires of wood—"hazel branches, thorn-faggots, and stout billets"—burning brightly, the "steady unfaltering eyes" of "planets" in the stellar metaphor, that are "rising out of rich coppice and plantation-districts to the north" (*RN* 32). Hardy sketches the region, but his insistence on the differences in soil, produce, and raw materials of surrounding lands asks us to imaginatively extend the map, marking off spaces of British colonial extraction of natural resources across the globe.

"Embarcation" ends with Hardy's leaf-like soldiers "draw[n] out upon the sea" (line 10) as their "wives, sisters, [and] parents, wave white hands and smile, / As if they knew not that they weep the while" (lines 13–14). Hardy instructs us to be "dubious of the cause" (line 12) rather than stand with the soldiers and families who deny the reality of "the tragical To-be" (line 11)—an equation of colonial space and death that is reflexive and unexamined, even as it rightly reflects the enormous violence of ongoing colonial war: in the Second Boer War that was waged 1899–1902, it is estimated that there were approximately twenty-two thousand military casualties on the British side, seven thousand military casualties on the Boer side, and over forty-six thousand civilian deaths of Boer and black Africans. But, as in the case of the Black Hole memorial, the poem renders only particular losses legible.

We might use the "white hands" that wave the soldiers goodbye to point us to the hands in *The Return of the Native* that have been overlaid with color: the red hands of Diggory Venn the reddleman, "not temporarily overlaid with the colour" of the dye of his trade but rather fully "permeate[d] with it" (*RN* 13); the gloved hands of Eustacia Vye in her cross-dressing, cross-cultural, and cross-racial role as the Turkish Knight in the ritual mummers' play staging the victory of the crusading Saint George, the patron saint of England, over his Saracen (Muslim Arab) enemy; and the "russet hue[d]" (*RN* 270) hands of Clym Yeobright, once white but now browned and calloused by laboring all day in the sun as a furze-cutter. As these hands wave—and as they clasp, point, work, hold, gesture, and love—what do their colors signal? And what kind of color—real or racial, abstract hues or skin tones—is Hardy trying to show us?

Racial Hands

Diggory Venn's red hands are dyed deep through the skin and even under his fingernails from the material of his trade, an ochre pigment mined from clay pits and used to mark sheep and other livestock. His hands incarnadined, he's not made merely a supernatural figure, ghostly or demonic, but a racialized one, the otherness of blood playing on the surface of his skin. The reddleman is singled out for his itinerant lifestyle, and is twice called an "Arab" (*RN* 79, 122) and once a "gipsy" (*RN* 79). As Aviva Briefel has shown, the "racial hand"—the popular trope of the severed or disembodied hand, acting of its own accord, and its frequent racialization—occupies a special place in the Victorian imagination. As a "compensation" for the fact, troubling to Victorian practitioners of physiognomy, chirognomy, and palmistry, that race "was *not* actually inscribed on the body," Briefel argues, "late-Victorian narratives generated models for how nonwhite hands might offer crucial means of identifying and theorizing racial identity."[43] And so although I'll be talking about sets of hands that are all technically white ones—in color and by race, hands that are only "temporarily overlaid with color"—what I am interested in is their racialized coding: how the hands of Venn, Clym, and Eustacia become the "nonwhite hands" that Briefel argues hold a privileged place in the Victorian imagination (and how, on the other hand, the markedly white hands of Thomasin are treated not as raced, although of course they are, but as neutral, positing whiteness not as hue but as lack of color). In the late Victorian narrative that is *The Return of the Native*, these colored hands mark the places in the novel where whiteness *as* racial identity is at once stabilized and destabilized.

The most direct deployment of the trope occurs early in the novel, and the "racial hand" in question belongs, at least at first, to the little boy Johnny Nunsuch, who is in charge of feeding and stoking Eustacia's Vye's bonfire—which is less a Fifth of November fire than a beacon for Wildeve. Illuminating Eustacia and Johnny only in fits and starts, Hardy writes of the scene:

> Nobody was visible; but ever and anon a whitish something moved above the bank from behind, and vanished again. Close watching would have shown it to be a small human hand, in the act of lifting pieces of fuel into the fire; but for all that could be seen the hand, like that which troubled Belshazzar, was there alone. Occasionally an ember rolled off the bank, and dropped with a hiss into the pool. (*RN* 59)

The hand that "troubled Belshazzar" in the Old Testament Book of Daniel is a severed one, whose writing on the wall prophesies the death of the Babylonian crown prince and the downfall of the empire. In his rendition of the Old Testament scene, Rembrandt paints the hand a startling white, and it pales even more in comparison to Belshazzar's darker hand placed just below it in Rembrandt's painterly composition, Belshazzar's arms spread wide in fear and wonder. But why should we assume that a severed hand writing Hebrew script on neo-Babylonian wall would be stark white and not brown? While Hardy's severed hand is initially a "whitish thing" that visually appears to be disembodied from the boy standing behind the bank, it gets colored in and racialized in a series of revolving comparisons kicked into motion by this initial Biblical allusion. After Johnny pauses in his task to have a conversation with Eustacia, "the little slave went on feeding the fire as before. He seemed a mere automaton, galvanised into moving and speaking by the wayward Eustacia's will. He might have been the brass statue which Albertus Magnus is said to have animated just so far as to make it chatter, and move, and be his servant" (*RN* 61). The passage condenses allusions to the "black" hands of African slaves in the Caribbean and the United States, brass-colored hands of a metal servant, and, with the word "automaton," later used to describe the reddleman during in his late-night gambles on the heath with Wildeve to win back Eustacia's stolen coins, red ones too. Hardy writes of the reddleman in that scene: "He might have been an Arab, an automaton; he would have been like a red-sandstone statue but for the motion of his arm with the dice-box" (RN 226). Johnny and Venn become a paired set of animated statues, bronze and sandstone. And the rapid movement of these passages reveals that hands and bodies in this novel are as wildly figured, transfigured, and transformed as the landscape itself. From white to black to bronze to red, Johnny's "small human hand" points to the racializing movements of Hardy's allusions and transfigurations. And it points too to other hands in the novel that are just as visually salient and just as charged with excess significance as his own fire-feeding ones.

Take Clym's sun-browned hands and their sun-leathered skin. Eustacia laments to her former lover Wildeve over what her husband's work as a furze-cutter has done to his hands:

> Ah! you don't know how differently he appeared when I first met him, though it was but a little while ago. His hands were as white and soft as mine; and look at them now, how rough and brown they are. His complexion is by nature fair, and that rusty look he has now, all of a colour with his leather clothes, is caused by the burning of the sun. (RN 274)

In Eustacia's description, Clym becomes a "rusty" version of a reddleman. His "complexion" has become "all of a colour with his leather clothes": he matches the materials of his trade and his work has "permeated" him, turning him too into someone "singular in colour" (RN 13)—monochrome and unusual. His hands become most rough and brown when Eustacia's hands, soft and white, are laid against them.

The sense of shame and class betrayal Eustacia expresses is echoed by Clym's mother. When Mrs. Yeobright first sees Clym working on the heath, in his "leather-legged and gauntleted" (RN 271) worker-drag, she does not recognize him as her son, but sees him instead as a resolutely nondescript figure, a worker like any other. Once again, his color is of central concern. In the distance, "he appeared of a russet hue, not more distinguishable from the scene around him than the green caterpillar from the leaf it feeds on" (RN 270). Wrapped in protective brown leggings or chaps, his sun-leathered hands covered by thick brown-leather gloves, Clym's skin matches his clothes and both match the heath, like a bright green caterpillar all of a color with a newly unfurled spring leaf. Hardy's narrative, focalized in part through Mrs. Yeobright, runs with this metaphor, turning Clym into an insect several times over and using the image to reflect, stiltedly, on working-class consciousness. As Mrs. Yeobright follows Clym on his path, the narrator observes:

The silent being who thus occupied himself seemed to be of no more account in life than an insect. He appeared as a mere parasite of the heath, fretting its surface in his daily labour as a moth frets a garment, entirely engrossed with its products, having no knowledge of anything in the world but fern, furze, heath, lichens and moss. (*RN* 270–71)

A caterpillar on a leaf, a "parasite of the heath," a moth on a garment, a man utterly familiar with a world of "fern, furze, heath, lichens and moss": the observer for whom Clym "seem[s] to be of no more account in life than an insect" is uncomfortable with insignificance, symbiosis, and singularity of concern. Any indefiniteness as to whom we might attribute these thoughts is clarified along with Mrs. Yeobright's outrage when, a few paragraphs later, she finally recognizes Clym:

> She was scarcely able to familiarise herself with this strange reality. She had been told that Clym was in the habit of cutting furze, but she had supposed that he occupied himself with the labour only at odd times, by way of a useful pastime; yet she now beheld him as a furze-cutter and nothing more—wearing the regulation dress of the craft, and apparently thinking the regulation thoughts, to judge by his motions. (*RN* 271)

The flip of the image by which Clym becomes not her son, a middle-class man with books to study and thoughts of his own, but a "furze-cutter and nothing more," with his "regulation dress" and "regulation thoughts," makes her heart throb, and it should make ours throb too—not at Clym's plight, but at the reduction of subjective experience assumed for working-class people.

Clym's manual labor has indeed altered his body and his mind, but in fuller ways than Eustacia and Mrs. Yeobright, who see it only as downward mobility or degradation, can imagine.[44] As readers, we are in a privileged place to see this, and to critique Mrs. Yeobright's classist impulse, because we have just gotten a glimpse of Clym's experience while at work, and his are hardly "regulation thoughts." That is to say, they are not diminished thoughts; if they are regulated by the rigors and rhythms of his blade swing, this is not to say that they are flat, reduced, or prosaic as a consequence. The moth engrossed with its garment surely knows a close-up richness that might fascinate us too if we could access it. And Clym's physical labor, taken up after he loses his eyesight after long hours of study, affords him a kind of relief in and through its apparent monotony: "Though frequently depressed in spirit when not at work, owing to thoughts of Eustacia's position and his mother's estrangement, when in the full swing of labour he was cheerfully disposed and calm. . . . The monotony of his occupation soothed him, and was in itself a pleasure" (*RN* 247). In the ellipsis that I have inserted above, bookmarked by statements of pleasure achieved despite the bodily demands of difficult manual labor, there is a long paragraph of lyrical description. Thought does not stop, but it does shift focus. Absorption in one's work is not a mindless insect state but one of rich phenomenological attention to one's environment. The narrator remarks of the myopic, hook-swinging Clym:

> His daily life was of a curious microscopic sort, his whole world being limited to a circuit of a few feet from his person. His familiars were creeping and winged things, and they seemed to enroll him in their band. Bees hummed around his ears with an intimate air, and tugged at the heath and furze-flowers at his side in such numbers as to weigh them down to the sod. The strange amber-coloured butterflies which Egdon produced, and which were never seen elsewhere, quivered in the breath of his lips, alighted upon his bowed back, and sported with the glittering point of his hook as he flourished it up and down. Tribes of emerald-green grasshoppers leaped over his feet, falling awkwardly on their backs, heads, or hips, like unskillful acrobats, as chance might rule; or engaged themselves in noisy flirtations under the fern-fronds with silent ones of homely hue.... In and out of the fern-brakes snakes glided in their most brilliant blue and yellow guise, it being the season immediately following the shedding of their old skins, when their colours are brightest. Litters of young rabbits came out from their forms to sun themselves upon hillocks, the hot beams blazing through the delicate tissue of each thin-fleshed ear, and firing it to blood-red transparency in which the veins could be seen. (*RN* 247)

The atmosphere for Clym could not be more different from the atmosphere of labor as Mrs. Yeobright imagines it. To appreciate the biodiversity of "creeping and winged things," and even to be enrolled in their band, is not to be a "mere" insect oneself, and this atmospheric shift is palpable to readers too. It moves us out of fateful forward momentum and into lyrical pause, staging the shift Gillian Beer describes from hap to happiness, and it pulls us out of and away from sharp edges between objects into Balint's "harmonious interpenetrating mix-up," where butterflies quiver on your breath. While the bulk of the novel's embodied movement consists in walking across the heath, linear locomotion gives way here to a different quality of movement: the back-and-forth swing of Clym's hook, the falling of the cut furze, the circling of the bees, the fluttering of insect wings, the acrobatic leaps and tumbles of the grasshoppers.[45]

The class-centered implications of Clym's brown skin in Mrs. Yeobright's and Eustacia's responses are clear: brown is the color of outdoor work, of sun-darkened skin and manual-labor-roughened hands. But Hardy insists on the *racialized* register of brown skin too, and uses the novel's "wild rhetoric" (*RN* 57) of allusion to underscore it. A "brown spot," and "nothing more" (*RN* 247), becomes more and more (handpost, gait, man, dead husband, living son) in Mrs. Yeobright's eyes as she realizes the worker walking the heath just ahead of her is in fact Clym:

> The furze-cutter was so absorbed in the business of his journey that he never turned his head; and his leather-legged and gauntleted form at length became to her nothing more than a moving handpost to show her the way. Suddenly she was attracted to his individuality by observing particularities in his walk. It was a gait she had seen somewhere before; and the gait revealed the man to her, as the gait of Ahimaaz in the distant plain made him known to the watchman of the king. "His walk is exactly as my husband's used to be," she said; and then the thought burst upon her that the furze-cutter was her son. (*RN* 271)

The passage introduces another Old Testament figure: Ahimaaz, a swift runner who brings news to King David of his rebellious son Absalom's defeat in Jerusalem. In Hardy's telling, it is Ahimaaz's gait that distinguishes him, making him "known" even on the "distant plain" to the "watchman of the king." Making Clym non-English, the passage clinches his racialization, making his brown skin read not simply as that of an English worker, but, figuratively, as that of a Middle Easterner. And indeed, Eustacia immediately links the classed demotion of furze-cutting to slavery and forced labor—distributed, of course, along racial lines. While Clym argues that, if he takes up furze-cutting to supplement their income, they will be "fairly well off," Eustacia replies: "In comparison with slaves, and the Israelites in Egypt, and such people!" (*RN* 246).

Moreover, Hardy's evocation of another geographic space in the passage above is succinct but powerful: from the rolling hills of gorse and furze, he quickly transports us to the plains of Israel, evoking, I think, not just another landscape superimposed on the heath, but another political history. At the time of Hardy's writing, British interest in Jerusalem, then held by an Ottoman Empire whose regime was disintegrating throughout the nineteenth century, was growing, leading eventually to British victory in Palestine in World War I and the era of the British Mandate. The British took Jerusalem from the Ottomans in 1917, a date squarely within Hardy's lifetime, as were the Arab uprisings against British rule in the 1920s. It can only enrich our reading to see the heath as holding all of these spaces and histories, and to see *The Return of the Native* holding all of these pasts and futures: how else can we ever really read except atmospherically?[46]

The Return of the Native is not in any sense fully delimited by the time and place of its writing: it is a product of what Eng calls the "racial century" of 1850–1950, the longer span of years encompassing its conceptualization, writing, reception, and insertion into the literary canon. To read the heath as at once

Egdon, Upper Bockhampton, and Jerusalem is also to give weight to other important references in the novel: the quick gloss of the heath as an "untameable," timeless, "Ishmaelitish thing" (*RN* 11–12)—which is to suggest, perhaps, not only a roaming wilderness, but a figure that condenses Jewish, Christian, and Muslim beliefs—and the novel's more extended reflection on the Ottoman Empire embedded in Eustacia's performance of the Turkish Knight.[47]

Ottoman Eustacia

Eustacia is a racialized figure from the start. Hardy introduces her, in the early chapter "Queen of the Night," as a Sphinx, a Pagan, the "raw material of a divinity" (*RN* 68). The light of her "wild dark eyes" (*RN* 53), "full of nocturnal mysteries," "as it came and went, and came again, was partially hampered by their oppressive lids and lashes; and of these the under lid was much fuller than it usually is with English women" (*RN* 68). Non-English, non-Christian, superhuman, Eustacia's presence exudes not the here and now but the remembered exoticism of far-off places: "Her presence brought memories of Bourbon roses, rubies, tropical midnights, and eclipses of the sun; her moods recalled lotus-eaters, the march in 'Athalie;' her motions, the ebb and flow of the sea; her voice, the viola" (*RN* 69). It is a stunning evocation, at once sonic (playing "her voice, the viola," and the music from Mendelssohn's 1843 orchestration of Racine's "Athalie") and squarely in the realm of the moving image (the sea that "ebbs and flows," the sun that gets eclipsed by another moving orb, the light that comes and goes from behind her eyes). As descriptions like this one show, Eustacia is perhaps more wildly figured and coded than any other character in the book— with the possible exception of the heath itself. Ruby and rose, Eustacia is Bourbon and she is tropical; she is Athalie in the Kingdom of Judah, and she is a lotus-eater in coastal Libya. Transposing this last allusion away from Homer and Herodotus into Hardy's present-day, she is an English opium-eater, doubling and redoubling Orientalist images: as De Quincey wrote in 1821, "I question whether any Turk, of all that ever entered the paradise of opium-eaters, can have had half the pleasure I had."[48] Eustacia's soul is "flame-like" in color; her "mouth seemed formed less to speak than to quiver, less to quiver than to kiss" (*RN* 68–69). Colored Eustacia is made to be looked at, from her curving mouth to deep into her eyes, while white Thomasin is not.

Or so Hardy tells us. I am referring to the passage, two chapters before, in which Thomasin's physical appearance is first described—and yet we are told to look away. Diggory Venn stares at her face for a much-extended moment, his own gaze backed by the implicitly male gaze of the narrator and the reader. He stares at her faintly parted lips and lightly closed eyes, which he imagines open: "one could easily imagine the light necessarily shining through them as the culmination of the luminous workmanship around." He stares long before coming to himself and realizing he should not: "One thing was obvious: she was not made to be looked at thus," and the reddleman "cast his eyes aside with a delicacy which well became him" (*RN* 41). And where Eustacia is racialized as resolutely other, Thomasin, once again all "transparent tissues," is racialized as white femininity itself. As the sleeping beauty opens her eyes, her very face emits "an ingenuous, transparent light" (*RN* 41). Eustacia is darkness, "obscurity" (*RN* 92), impenetrability to vision and interpretation, and thus demands wild figuration.[49] Thomasin is luminousness, ingenuousness, and "transparent light," whiteness itself. Nothing needs to be coded or decoded because all can be seen: so white is her skin, so pure is her being, so clear, that the "flow of her existence" can be seen "passing within." Eustacia is exoticism and the elaborate detailing of sexual history; Thomasin is Englishness and virginity, her body just waiting, like the "beautiful feminine tissue" of Tess, "blank as snow," to be "traced with a pattern" (*T* 74).

I take this detour to emphasize the two interlinked points I am trying to build in this section. Not only is Eustacia is more resolutely racially coded than any other character in the book, this racial coding unfailingly subtends the representation of her sexuality as excessive, aberrant, un-English—and desirable. In her critique of the Eurocentric bias of Foucault's *The History of Sexuality*, Ann Laura Stoler argues that "the discursive and practical field in which nineteenth-century bourgeois sexuality emerged was situated on an imperial landscape where the cultural accoutrements of bourgeois distinction were partially shaped through contrasts forged in the politics and language of race."[50] I can think of no better gloss than this for the comparisons I am describing between the depictions of Thomasin's and Eustacia's bodies and sexualities. A turf-cutter who has never seen her asks, is Eustacia "dark or fair?" "Darker than Tamsin," Mrs. Yeobright mutters in response (*RN* 177).[51] Eustacia describes and inscribes the "imperial landscape" against which Tamsin's normative, English, bourgeois sexuality is literally defined; it is the dark ground against which the contrast of Thomasin's whiteness, innocence, and eligibility for life, marriage, and reproduction—rather than Eustacia's solitude, singleness, flight, and suicide—becomes legible and producible as an identity, like a "pearl" on "a table of ebony" (*RN* 259).[52] Stoler argues that none of the figures central to Foucault's portrait of nineteenth-century sexual discourse—the masturbating child, the hysterical woman, the Malthusian couple, the perverse adult—could "exist as objects of knowledge and discourse in the nineteenth century without a racially erotic counterpoint, without reference to the libidinal energies of the savage, the primitive, the colonized—reference points of difference, critique, and desire."[53] I am arguing that Eustacia Vye provides that reference point in the novel, helping to clarify the definition of feminine "whiteness" from within English national borders. Eustacia imports, through Hardy's kaleidoscopic and never-ending figurations of her, "imperial landscapes" into domestic spaces. And this otherness is concretized in Hardy's transformation of Eustacia into a "Terrible Turk."

Given the prominence, early in the novel, of Eustacia's performance as the Turkish Knight in the yearly Christmas mummers' play—a usurpation of the boy Charley's role and therefore a double masculine masquerade: Eustacia does it so she can come to the holiday party and see Clym Yeobright, the promising young man his fellow natives are so eager to see return—it is remarkable how little critical attention the novel's portrayal of the Ottoman Empire has received. A notable exception is Patrick Brantlinger's "Terrible Turks: Victorian Xenophobia and the Ottoman Empire," which explores Victorian perceptions of the Ottoman Empire in light of British "imperial envy" and Islamophobia.[54] The essay briefly glances at Eustacia's performance in *The Return of the Native*, contextualizing it in light of changing British foreign policy toward the Ottoman Empire around the central nineteenth-century events of the Greek war for independence (1821–32), the Crimean War (1853–56) and the "Bulgarian Crisis" of 1876, shortly before the novel was originally published. Brantlinger describes how each of these points of competing interest between the Ottoman and British empires reinvoked the "ancient stereotype" of the Terrible Turk, "with its roots"—as in the mummers' play that stages his death at the hands of Saint George, patron saint of England—"in the anti-Islamism that inspired the Crusades." For the Victorians, Brantlinger writes, the Turk was "terrible" in the "twin senses of awful and of powerful and awe-inspiring." Turkish rulers were stereotyped as "cruel" and "despotic," "even though Ottoman rule was for many of its subjects peaceful, prosperous, and tolerant of various races, cultures, and religions."[55] And in literature and performance, Turkish fighters were stereotyped as both fierce and powerful and lascivious: according to Andrew Wheatcroft, British writers deployed tropes of both the Terrible and the "Lustful" Turk.[56] Cast in this role, cross-dressed, her hands embrowned and masculinized by the gloves that make part of her costume, and pursuing Clym, Eustacia's aberrant sexuality is rerouted into registers of religious, racial, and cultural difference.

Stoler makes an argument for a "hidden fault line" of racial difference within sexual discourse:

> Imperial discourses that divided colonizer from colonized, metropolitan observers from colonial agents, and bourgeois colonizers from their subaltern compatriots designated certain cultural competencies, sexual proclivities, psychological dispositions, and cultivated habits. These in turn defined the hidden fault lines—both fixed and fluid—along which gendered assessments

of class and racial membership were drawn. Within the lexicon of bourgeois civility, self-control, self-discipline, and self-determination were defining features of bourgeois selves in the colonies.... These discourses of self-mastery were productive of racial distinctions, of clarified notions of "whiteness" and what it meant to be truly European.[57]

Expelled from the novel, whitened by death, and purified only in her exquisite corpse beauty, the fate of Eustacia Vye clarifies not only "whiteness," but the concomitant category of explicitly *sexual* definitions of "civility, self-control, and self-discipline." Eustacia asks: "But do I desire unreasonably much in wanting what is called life—music, poetry, passion, war, and all the beating and pulsing that is going on in the great arteries of the world?" (*RN* 276). Does she desire unreasonably much in wanting what is called a sex life? In one key, the novel answers: yes, she does. As a sexual and sexualized being, she is cast not as an English woman, but as a Turkish Knight: masculinized, racialized, exoticized, and part of a larger discourse of Victorian xenophobia and "imperial envy."[58] As such, this racialization of Eustacia, which concretizes the wild figurative movements through which she is drawn from the start, also illustrates Stoler's redrawing of the imperial map. The "racial configurations" of the "imperial world" become not "peripheral" but, rather, internal.[59] As Anne McClintock puts it in *Imperial Leather*:

> Imperialism is not something that happened elsewhere—a disagreeable fact of history external to Western identity. Rather, imperialism and the invention of race were fundamental aspects of Western, industrial modernity. The invention of race in the urban metropoles ... became central not only to the self-definition of the middle class but also to the policing of the "dangerous classes": the working class, the Irish, Jews, prostitutes, feminists, gays and lesbians, criminals, the militant crowd and so on.[60]

Imperialism happens at home: in the metropole and in domestic spaces, in the systems that produce and police difference within them. Just as the "vast, fissured architecture of imperialism" is gendered and split,[61] a "basic fault" renders non-normative feminine sexuality as non-English and non-Christian, transforming Eustacia into a "Terrible Turk."

To reiterate and expand on my earlier claim, in describing *The Return of the Native* as a novel of black holes and white mythologies, I am describing how domestic space is also always imperial space,[62] how questions of gender and sexuality are also always questions of racialization, and how Victorian novels and mid-twentieth-century psychoanalysis alike inscribe colonial object relations even while ostensibly occluding them. In Hardy's rendering, Eustacia does not belong to the same world order as other characters in the novel. Indeed, she does not belong to the same *characterological* order. Eustacia says that she does not have the "gift of content" (*RN* 275). She means that she is not someone who is able to be happy, but I prefer to read the line as the gift of "*content*" rather than "con*tent*": Eustacia cannot contain herself, and she cannot be contained in the novel except as wild racial and imperial figuration. Eustacia asks, "Do I desire unreasonably much?" and in another key from the one I have previously described, the novel answers: of course not. It is not too much for a woman to desire a life, a sex life, a life of activity and agency and satisfaction. But the novel she is in cannot provide it for her. To close this chapter, I want to turn from the red, brown, and bronze hands whose appearance punctuates *The Return of the Native* to the white hands that are all that remain at the novel's close. In an underscoring of the novel's white mythology, colored hands and hands of color are expelled or bleached, and the question of an active and alive sexuality gets muted out, too, in favor of traditional, fenced-in family units.

White Mythologies

The hands that close the novel are the lovely white hands of Thomasin Yeobright, hands that are joined in marriage to the newly whitened ones of Diggory Venn. Their coupling begins with a missing glove: a glove borrowed from Thomasin, without her permission, by her waiting-girl Rachel for the occasion of the May Day dance, and then misplaced during the outdoor celebration. Diggory, who has "manage[d] to become white" (*RN* 374), "turn[ing] so by degrees" after giving up his trade in reddle (*RN* 375), assiduously searches for the lost glove. Thomasin watches from a second-story window, not yet knowing that the glove he is searching for belongs to her, and that his search is a sign of love for her. "Gently lift[ing] the corner of the white curtain" to look out, she saw that

> Venn was still there. She watched the growth of the faint radiance appearing in the sky by the eastern hill, till presently the edge of the moon burst upwards and flooded the valley with light. Diggory's form was now distinct on the green; he was moving about in a bowed attitude, evidently scanning the grass for the precious missing article, walking in zigzags right and left till he should have passed over every foot of the ground. (*RN* 379)

Eventually he finds it, stands up, and presses it to his lips. Later, he will present it to Thomasin, and propose to her. I am interested in this marriage, and interested in their happiness; but I am just as interested in the stunning whitening process that precedes and enables it. The white curtain, the white moonlight, and Diggory's now-white skin point to a process of lightening—in mood, in color, and in racial purification—that seems to subtend the novel's ability to end. Clym is the first to fully see Diggory in his new aspect, just a few pages before:

> To his astonishment there stood within the room Diggory Venn, no longer a reddleman, but exhibiting the strangely altered hues of an ordinary Christian countenance, white shirt-front, light-flowered waistcoat, blue-spotted neckerchief, and bottle-green coat. Nothing in his appearance was at all singular but the fact of its great difference from what he had formerly been. Red, and all approach to red, was carefully excluded from every article of clothes upon him; for what is there that persons out of harness dread so much as reminders of the trade which has enriched them? (*RN* 374)

The earlier Diggory Venn, the "lurid red" (*RN* 13) man of the "Arab existence" (79), of the "mark of Cain" (79), and the life of a "gipsy" (79)—in other words, the wildly and irregularly racialized "blood-coloured" figure (70), who is not only red like blood but colored by nonwhite blood—is gone, and in his place stands a man of the ordinary hues of "an ordinary Christian countenance." Cleared away along with his red color are all of the codings of racial, ethnic, cultural, and religious difference.

And it's not just Diggory who has changed. The very heath has too. What was initially "an untameable, Ishmaelitish thing" (*RN* 11–12)—Semitic, heathen, uncivilized—is now cultivated, Christianized, Anglicized; no longer brown and barren, but all green and white. The springtime celebration that ends the novel erects not just a Maypole, but an entire white mythology of Merry Old Unmixed England. Hardy writes of the preparations: "It was a lovely May sunset, and the birch trees which grew on the margin of the Egdon wilderness had put on their new leaves, delicate as butterflies' wings and diaphanous as amber." These are leaves "alive as spring": the brightest, most transparent of spring greens unfurling against the stark white of the birch branches. The passage continues,

> Beside Fairway's dwelling was an open space recessed from the road, and here were now collected all the young people from within a radius of a couple of miles. The pole lay within one end supported by a trestle, and women were engaged in wreathing it from the top downwards with wild flowers. The instincts of merry England lingered on here with exceptional vitality, and the symbolic customs which tradition has attached to each season of the year were yet a reality on Egdon. (*RN* 375–76)

Old England is alive and well on Egdon Heath, unchanged by modernity or miscegenation. Clym, feeling aged and withdrawn after the loss of his mother and of Eustacia—"every pulse of loverlike feeling that had not been stilled during Eustacia's lifetime had gone into the grave with her" (*RN* 377)—hangs back from the festivities. But in Thomasin both the "instincts of merry England" and the "pulse of loverlike feeling" have a mild spring awakening:

> The next morning, when Thomasin withdrew the curtains of her bedroom window, there stood the Maypole in the middle of the green, its top cutting into the sky. It had sprung up in the night, or rather early morning, like Jack's bean-stalk. She opened the casement to get a better view of the garlands and posies that adorned it. The sweet perfume of the flowers had already spread into the surrounding air, which, being free from every taint, conducted to her lips a full measure of the fragrance received from the spire of blossom in its midst. At the top of the pole were crossed hoops decked with small flowers; beneath these came a milk-white zone of Maybloom; then a zone of bluebells, then of cowslips, then of lilacs, then of ragged-robins, daffodils, and so on, till the lowest stage was reached. Thomasin noticed all these, and was delighted that the May-revel was to be so near. (*RN* 376)

It is through this old tradition—and the purity it spreads into the "surrounding air," creating around it a "milk-white zone" that is "free from every taint"—that Thomasin and Diggory will come together and form a conventional nuclear family within the "white palings" (*RN* 375) that separate the house at Blooms-End from the wild heath.

And "white paling" does indeed seem to be the action that best describes the end of the novel: Diggory is washed white; Clym, who no longer works outdoors, loses his tan; and the lovers Wildeve and Eustacia are dead, their corpses blanched. In her death, the dark beauty Eustacia is cleansed of color and of dangerous sexuality: "as she lay there still in death, [Eustacia] eclipsed all her living phases. Pallor did not include all the quality of her complexion, which seemed more than whiteness; it was almost light" (*RN* 367). White skin, white atmospheres—like the one in which Hardy's rustics, making a down bed as a wedding gift for the new couple, find themselves immersed in: "As bag after bag was emptied airy tufts of down and feathers floated about the room in increasing quantity till, through a mishap of Christian's, who shook the contents of one bag outside the tick, the atmosphere of the room became dense with gigantic flakes, which descended upon the workers like a windless snowstorm" (*RN* 388). Like the one in which English men and women dance around a Maypole in a white nationalist celebration that takes no heed of imperial conquest or contact. And like the one at the end of the novel, from which all foreign coloring and xenophobic panic has been cleansed. Part of my point about all of this emphasis on white skin, white paling, and white picket fences is that these designations too are racializations: this may go unnoticed because it is the very essence of white mythology, as "the history writing of the West," to render whiteness as neutrality, as universality, as the absence of racial designation. White mythology turns whiteness from a color into an ideology of clarity, innocence, truth, and beauty.[63] Over there, black holes, suffocation, savagery; at home, white skin, fresh air, and friendly expanses.

The Basic Fault

And yet there is a brittleness to the novel's ending that undermines its resolution, like a crack in the depths of one of Charley's faceted crystals. We feel the flattening out of existence that comes with Eustacia's death and the loss of her desire as driving force; we are left with Clym's sorrow for his mother and his lingering glances at her empty chair (*RN* 395), the "muffled" sound of Thomasin's daughter Eustacia's footfalls on the heath (*RN* 381), and the "neutral tone[s]" (*RN* 385) of Clym—he who had once had such ambitions plans— mildly preaching to a small crowd of listeners who idly "pull heather, strip ferns, or toss pebbles down the slope" of the heath (*RN* 395). Something that Ian Duncan writes about the ending of Wilkie Collins's *The Moonstone* (1868) strikes me as serving equally well as a description of *The Return of the Native*: "When a conventional English domestic order is finally restored it appears reduced, artificial, bright but fragile; while the horizons of the world around it, opened by the deeds of empire, are sublime and alarming."[64] This is exactly how I feel about this novel's ending—and I suspect that it is exactly what Hardy hoped we might feel. Gone is Eustacia's outsized desire,[65] gone are bright colors, gone are now-outmoded ways of life, replaced by a "conventional English domestic order" that appears "reduced, artificial, bright [white] but fragile." It is an order marked by loss, by exclusion, by violence, and by a "blanching process" (*RN* 318) that renders life safe but artificial.

Balint describes something fundamentally akin to this brittle resolution in his guiding concept of "the basic fault." He uses the term to discuss disturbances that arise in the earliest phases of development and object relation— disturbances that forever after shape the personality. In keeping with other object relations theorists, Balint sets out to describe life before Oedipal stages, and life before even two-body relationships are firmly established: a time of "definitely simpler, more primitive" relations, when one is just learning differentiation from and relation to first objects at all. His wording is precise: "I propose to call [this] the level of *the basic fault*, and I wish to stress that it is described as a fault, not as a situation, position, conflict, or complex" (*BF* 16). Balint offers a description of "the level of the basic fault" as a list of its "chief characteristics":

> (a) All the events that happen in it belong to an exclusively two-person relationship—there is no third person present; (b) this two-person relationship

is of a particular nature, entirely different from well-known human relationships of the Oedipal level [the nature of these early relations are what Balint calls "primary love" or "harmonious interpenetrating mix-up," as I have already described them]; (c) the nature of the dynamic force operating at this level is not that of a conflict, and (d) adult language is often useless or misleading in describing events at this level, because words have not always an agreed conventional meaning. (*BF* 16–17)

In the benign regression, patients return to the level of the basic fault so that they might heal, and enact what Balint calls "a new beginning": a way to "establish—or, probably, re-establish—an all-embracing harmony with one's environment, to be able to love in peace" (*BF* 65). The idea is that what Balint is calling healing cannot be encompassed by the idea of resolving a conflict or removing a hang-up. Something deeper is at stake. Returning to his word choice, Balint stresses that "basic" refers to the pre-Oedipal and the preconflictual. "But why fault? First, because this is exactly the word used by many patients to describe it. The patient says that he feels there is a fault within him, a fault that must be put right. And it is felt to be a fault, not a complex, not a conflict, not a situation" (*BF* 21). Something is missing; something is off; something is, internally, misaligned. The patient might feel that "the cause of this fault is that someone has either failed the patient or defaulted on him," but even this "someone" and the failure or default are nebulous and undefined. Balint continues:

> The term fault has been in use in some exact sciences to denote conditions that are reminiscent of that which we are discussing. Thus, for instance, in geology and in crystallography the word fault is used to describe a sudden irregularity in the overall structure, an irregularity which in normal circumstances might lie hidden but, if strains and stresses occur, may lead to a break, profoundly disrupting the overall structure. (*BF* 21)

A fault in a diamond, a crack in the golden bowl, the mid-trunk burl up from which a tree keeps on growing: what Balint is talking about are the faults that shape us, subtly deforming the personality but forming it too—livable compromises that lie deep in the structure and remain hidden, unless the strains and stresses of living become too much. And yet, as Balint emphasizes, patients *feel* these faults, and feel them not as exacerbated conflict but as the persistent sense that something is not quite right, that something is off—a dull ache rather than a sharp pain. Balint's revision of classical psychoanalytic theory by way of the term "fault" pertains to both Oedipus and instinct:

> We are accustomed to think of every dynamic force operating in the mind as having the form either of a biological drive or of a conflict. Although highly dynamic, the force originating from the basic fault has the form neither of

an instinct nor of a conflict. It is a fault, something wrong in the mind, a kind of deficiency which must be put right. It is not something dammed up for which a better outlet must be found, but something missing either now, or perhaps for almost the whole of the patient's life. An instinctual need can be satisfied, a conflict can be solved, a basic fault can perhaps be merely healed provided the deficient ingredients can be found; and even then it may amount only to a healing with a defect, like a simple, painless scar. (*BF* 21–22)

We are left, I think, with this kind of simple scar at the end of *The Return of the Native*, a pale line stretched across its skin. We have the May Day celebration, yes, but only as the kind of "confetti triumph" that conceals much deeper wounds—something like what Anne McClintock described when she asked, almost thirty years ago, of the quincentenary celebration of the "discovery" of the Americas: "By what fiat of historical amnesia can the United States of America, in particular, qualify as postcolonial—a term that that can only be a monumental affront to the Native American peoples currently opposing the confetti triumph of 1992?"[66] Hardy's own "confetti triumph" only thinly papers over faults that the novel itself has uncovered: Mrs. Yeobright's and Eustacia's deaths, and the impossibilities of filial and romantic love in constraining social conditions that those deaths represent; Clym's failures—not his failures to meet his potential, but to create a measure more of social justice in his world; Hardy's failure to fully render rural life and agricultural labor protest as anything more than "pastoral" reduction and Shakespearean antics; and his failure, too, to render a world much wider than the heath's enclosure would indicate.

And yet what I am trying to reflect here is that this paper-thin veneer does more than simply cover over Eustacia's racialized sexual restlessness, rural workers' political unrest, and the horrors of colonial violence. The novel makes us *feel* the basic fault underlying its fragile, brittle ending. We can read Hardy's novel not simply as a white mythology, but as an *allegory* (in the sense of possible critique) of this white mythology, making us sensible to all that is lost in the reduction of global histories of empire to the stories of "conventional English domestic order," white Western victory, and pastoral simplicity.

Balint, of course, is interested in individual psychic development and the hazards and benefits of the basic fact of early dependence and merger: "the origin of the basic fault may be traced back to a considerable discrepancy in the early formative phases of the individual between his bio-psychological needs and the material and psychological care, attention, and affection available during the relevant times. This creates a state of deficiency whose consequences and after-effects appear to be only partly reversible" (*BF* 22). But here I am interested, as I am throughout *Novel Relations*, in thinking about these developmental concepts in a different register. I am interested in thinking about the basic fault in the novel's constitution, and in the literary study of Victorian domestic fiction more largely. The originary scar in the structure of both runs along the same fault line: the tendency to ignore the transimperial relations that shape British identity, British domestic ideology, and the ideology of the British domestic novel. Colonial object relations subtend all nineteenth-century British cultural production. But the frequent failure to acknowledge this fact, both in the nineteenth century and into the twenty-first, in our literary critical practices and products, constitutes the "basic fault" in the Victorian novel as it has been institutionalized in Victorian studies.

But the basic fault of the Victorian novel need not be ours. Wide-ranging colonial object relations are implicitly embedded in Victorian domestic novels, and are therefore at least partially recoverable. *The Return of the Native* makes this particularly clear. Hardy's allegory of white mythology—a critique that exposes the papering-over of colonial atrocity in the making of Western identity and that exposes the racially loaded metaphorics of the color white itself— exposes faults below the surface of his pastoral, domestic novel. Like the "cracks" that appear "in clayey gardens" on 31 August, the hottest day of the summer, "and were called 'earthquakes' by apprehensive children" (*RN* 269), these fault lines are small but significant, and they are there to be read. They are legible like scars, and like scars they encode both histories of violence and possibilities for healing, albeit incomplete.

I want to point as well to the inscription of a similar constitutive fault in British object relations psychoanalysis. Thinkers like Winnicott, Bion, Balint, and others rarely, if ever, speak to issues of empire, race, ethnicity, and the making of national identity in their theories, or even in their wider writings. However, I argue that these issues necessarily subtend their theories of subject formation and object relations, and are legible if we are willing to read their theories carefully and critically enough—and, I'll add, to read them at moments, strategically, as I am doing here, nonpsychologically. Empire subtends the very lives of these analysts. Bion was born to English parents in colonial India, was a tank officer in World War I, treated soldiers and veterans of World War II, and at the end of his life spent a significant amount of time in Brazil: as I have described in more detail elsewhere, he is a true son of British Empire and witness to its long decline, and a participant in colonial and decolonial efforts alike.[67] Masud Khan was born in pre-Partition Punjab, and struggled his whole life, I think, to be accepted as a true equal to his analytic community peers as a Pakistani man in England.[68] Balint was an assimilated Hungarian Jew who was forced to leave his native Budapest in 1938 when the Nazi German government was gaining political control over the country. Although he made it safely to England, his parents committed suicide in Budapest in 1944 to avoid being arrested by the Nazis.[69]

It is remarkable how frequently we separate psychoanalytic ideas from their atmospheres—from their geopolitical scenes of production. Think, for instance, of the scene of the "Controversial Discussions." These debates took place in Tavistock Square buildings shaken by the falling bombs of the London Blitz of 1940–41.[70] A famous anecdote features Winnicott interrupting a heated debate between the Kleinians and Anna Freudians to suggest everyone take shelter.[71] And these debates were caused, in part, by the in-pouring of analysts from other centers of psychoanalytic thought—Budapest, Berlin, and Vienna—due to political upheaval and Nazi persecution of Jewish people. Analysts with different training and different points of view all converged in London. And they shouted at each other about child analysis, about technique, about women's sexuality, about certification, and bracketed the war. The psychoanalytic historians Pearl King and Riccardo Steiner have explored what Anna Freud, in a 1934 letter to Ernest Jones, called "a new kind of diaspora," adding: "you surely know what the word means: the spreading of the Jews over the world after the destruction of the temple of Jerusalem."[72] In describing this "new kind of diaspora," she was also gesturing to the efforts of the psychoanalytic community to shape it, relocating analysts at risk not only to London, but also to the United States and Latin America.

This gesture to a larger global framework is vital. In an essay that has served as powerful inspiration for my work here, "Colonial Object Relations," David Eng looks beyond Europe to situate psychoanalytic ideas within more extensive colonial histories. Freud's theorization of the death drive, for instance, is hardly a tie tethered solely to individual psychology nor even a product of the lives Freud saw taken by World War I in Europe.[73] Rather, Eng argues, "the genealogy of Freud's death drive [is] embedded in a haunting, though unacknowledged colonial history," one that stretches from "the string of colonial genocides in Africa, Asia, and the Americas" to "the Holocaust and its accelerated violence" to form the "racial century" of the years 1850–1950.[74] In Eng's analysis, acknowledging these disavowed colonial histories makes it possible to understand not only the genesis of psychoanalytic ideas but also their uneven, Eurocentric applications. In the example at the center of the essay, Eng critiques the bad conscience of the reparative impulse as it has descended from Klein to Sedgwick, arguing that "reparation," read in its fuller colonial and postcolonial contexts, "appears as the differential production of the human through the affective distribution of precarious life, as it constitutes and separates good objects [read: white European] deserving of care and redress from bad objects [read: nonwhite colonial subjects] meriting no consideration."[75]

Eng's careful reading of the work of Melanie Klein (drawing as it implicitly does on the insights of Wynter, Rancière, and Butler) gives weight to a much quicker gloss of British object relations thought offered by Adam Phillips: "In its twilight, the British Empire produced a theory of good-enough mothering as the antithesis, the guilty critique, of what was always a bad-enough imperialism."[76]

These are important critiques of object relations thought, and I have little doubt in their veracity. What I want to push on here is my conviction that there are indeed insights and gestures of thought within object relations theory that can be used to recover these colonial histories, even as the interpersonal theories fail to explicitly acknowledge them or give them their full due. Without ignoring the colonial complicities of many psychoanalytic thinkers, we need to remember the multiplicity of political possibilities embedded in their texts. Failure to do so flattens out not only their work, but also the possibilities of our own.

In her recent essay "Therapeutic Criticism," Amanda Anderson critiques the psychological and affective orientation of much recent literary scholarship.[77] Surveying the influx in novel studies in the last twenty years of demands for new methodologies that move away from ideology critique, Anderson argues that calls for reparative, surface, and other forms of nonsymptomatic reading reflect "the rise of therapeutic culture and its influence on literary and cultural studies."[78] Anderson sees this therapeutic impulse as most forcefully emblematized, and indeed as most influential in these fields, in two places: in "Foucault's turn from the analysis of disciplinary power to practices of the self" in his later career, and in Sedgwick's 1997 essay "Paranoid and Reparative Reading," which, as I have spent some time discussing in earlier chapters of this book, uses Klein's theory of fundamental positions in relation to one's objects, and to the world more largely, as archetypes for different modes of critical practice. Anderson is troubled by the way these approaches narrow the methodological field of novel studies, first by overprivileging the encounter between critic and text (highlighting in particular the critic's own intellectual and affective disposition) and second by either failing to address the larger political systems in which these relations take place, or by treating those systems as irremediable. Discussing both Sedgwick's essay and the current popularity of Winnicott in literary studies, Anderson argues that while object relations thought carries the potential for a thoroughgoing investigation of how "our most basic relations and practices—including our early development—might condition and enable our engagement with social and political life," as yet critics have failed to make good on that possibility. "Sedgwick's account," Anderson argues, "does not clearly advance our understanding of political psychology. Insofar as it is reparative . . . it retains a therapeutic quality, which is to say it addresses the immediate needs of the subject and its practices rather than the system itself."[79] I find Anderson's intervention to be timely and important, especially as it raises the question of the relationship between "therapeutic" approaches and politically responsive and responsible work. And yet I find her readings of Winnicott and Sedgwick alike to be too monolithic. Anderson argues at one point that "the difference between Klein and Winnicott lights up the difference between the two leftist positions, the radical and the liberal."[80] If the aim for Anderson is to flesh out the connections between personal and political psychology, and between our orientation to texts and our orientation to the systems that define our world, it is difficult to see how such reductionist formulations will further that project. To assume that a rich corpus of thinking can be put to only one political use seems to miss the complexity of textuality and of critical practice alike.

And this is precisely what Balint's theories offer: ways of thinking about positioning our objects, managing our distance and closeness from them, and using them to create productive atmospheres. What follows the benign regression for Balint is the "new beginning": "*an attempt to create something better, kinder, more understandable, more beautiful, and above all, more consistent and more harmonious than the real [original] objects proved to be*" (*BF* 68). It is not always possible to do so. But it is the very "*attempt*" that inaugurates the political: the urge to create something "better, kinder, more understandable," and more just. As Jordy Rosenberg understands it, the political impulse begins with social relations—that is to say, with object relations in a different key. "Political life," writes Rosenberg, is "the extension of ourselves into the world" and "the forming and care for the collectivities that we will need to survive this world, and that, perhaps more importantly, we want to survive us into a different future."[81] And atmosphere, as the kind of nonbordered subjectivity that both Hardy and Balint describe, is what subtends those new relations, collectivities, attachments, and solidarities.

Victorian novels and British object relations psychoanalysis can certainly appear to be limited in their emphases and ideologies. In some sense, they certainly are. And yet our engagement with these textual objects and ideas need not be limited or singular. We can use them to open up wider relational networks than they may immediately avow, but that, as in Hardy's practice of imperial figuration, turn out to open the text at every turn. To put it in Balint's language, there are so many ways we can position ourselves in relation to these textual objects, so many degrees of distance to take and negotiate and, Hardyesquely, constantly adjust,[82] that I think object relations psychoanalysis, when it is read carefully and its methods are used to their fullest extensions and advantages, can help us to unpack the very colonial contexts in which it was produced—including the Victorian literary tradition out of which many of its tactics and techniques are drawn. Just as Hardy's references to empire and transimperial politics in *The Return of the Native* demand a more extended reading than they have received in the past, so too do the realities of empire and transimperial politics in the lives and writings of object relations theorists. Such work wouldn't promise, as in the parlance of Hardy's poem "Embarcation," to fully "mend" ongoing atrocities of "thought, and pact, and code" in the world. Nor would it promise to thoroughly "repair," as in Klein and Sedgwick's work, the damaging ideological effects of Victorian and mid-century psychoanalytic texts as products of empire that, often, work to disavow their own histories and complicities. But such work could, I think, move Victorian studies in the direction of a new beginning.

4

Aliveness

MIDDLEMARCH, JOSEPH, HEIMANN, OGDEN

"Es ist dafür gesorgt dass die Bäume nicht in den Himmel wachsen [Care is taken that the trees do not grow into the sky]," says the German proverb; in other words, everything on this Earth has its limits which may not be overpassed. Even Imagination which used to be in high repute for its immensity, is seen nowadays to be no more than a worker in mosaics, owing every one of its glinting fragments & every type of its impossible vastness to the small realm of experience. . . . To every thing human there are limits.

—GEORGE ELIOT, UNPUBLISHED ESSAY[1]

I write (I pronounce) this sentence: "The forces of life suffice only to a certain point." As I pronounce it I think of something very simple: the experience of weariness that constantly make us feel a limited life; you take a few steps on the street, eight or nine, then you fall. The limit set by weariness limits life. The meaning of life is in turn limited by this limit: a limited meaning of a limited life. But a reversal occurs. . . . Language modifies the situation.

—MAURICE BLANCHOT, "NARRATIVE VOICE"

I have always felt that an important function of the interpretation is the establishment of the *limits* of the analyst's understanding.

—D. W. WINNICOTT, "COMMUNICATING AND NOT COMMUNICATING"

GEORGE ELIOT'S *MIDDLEMARCH* (1871–72) begins by celebrating ardor. The prelude's ode to Saint Theresa is an ode to ardor, celebrating Theresa's "passionate, ideal nature": "her flame . . . soared after some illimitable satisfaction, some object which would never justify weariness, which would reconcile self-despair with the rapturous consciousness of life beyond self" (*M* 3). But little passes through Eliot's hands unironized, and Saint Theresa's ardor quickly becomes as outmoded an expressive style for the novel's narrator as it is unsustainable for Dorothea Brooke, "foundress of nothing" (*M* 4). *Middlemarch* attempts to document the subtlety of failure, telling the story not of ardor but of its limits, not of enthusiasm but enervation, and of foreclosure precisely where possibility once seemed limitless.

The Reverend Edward Casaubon, the novel's failure among failures, steps in to set the dominant affective tone of the novel. Sequestered in his library, lost in a labyrinth of research, the aging scholar labors in vain and shrinks from contact with others, even his young new wife Dorothea. Instead of ardor, Casaubon embodies a kind of "weary experience" (*M* 85) that seems unique in the initial chapters of the novel, but later becomes quite universal. Gravity or something that resembles it becomes a figure for the weariness that overtakes us all:

> Suppose we turn from outside estimates of a man, to wonder, with keener interest, what is the report of his own consciousness about his doings or capacity: with what hindrances he is carrying on his daily labours; what fading of hopes, or what deeper fixity of self-delusion the years are marking off within him; and with what spirit he wrestles against universal pressure, which will one day be too heavy for him, and bring his heart to its final pause. (*M* 84)

The "universal pressure" that the human heart pushes against at each and every beat creates an inevitable fatigue, prelude to a "final pause." The body wears out and the mind tires, and even the simple effort of wondering about the inner lives of others runs up against the obstacle, quotidian but unavoidable, of exhaustion. The novel cannot sustain the energy of its opening, and not only because the "dim lights and tangled circumstances" (*M* 3) of modern life produce ordinary failures rather than epic achievements. More than this, the celebration of ardor in *Middlemarch* flags because the narrative is just as powerfully drawn to another center of gravity: to exhaustion itself.

In this chapter, I want to explore both "weary experience" and the role that Eliot gives to her own narrative voice and technique as a source of enlivening energy. To do so, I am going to turn to a psychoanalytic vocabulary that I argue is closely related to the novel's focus on the opposing feelings and forces of ardor and weariness: these are the terms "aliveness" and "deadness," brought to the fore by Melanie Klein and picked up and deployed in creative ways by the next generation of British analysts, including Winnicott, Bion, Joan Riviere, Paula Heimann, and Betty Joseph, and foregrounded too in recent relational thought, especially by Thomas Ogden in a series of papers published in the 1990s. Aliveness and deadness are terms used to describe aspects of the experience of one's internal object world—are one's internal objects alive and thriving?—and, even more pointedly, the workings of transference and countertransference in psychoanalytic practice—does the analysis feel alive to both participants? Ogden's definitions of aliveness and deadness make them central to the psychoanalytic project: "every form of psychopathology," he writes, "represents a specific type of limitation of the individual's capacity to be fully alive."[2] For Ogden, this means that the goal of the analysis becomes "larger than that of the resolution of unconscious intrapsychic conflict, the diminution of symptomatology, the enhancement of reflective subjectivity and self-understanding, [or] the increase of sense of personal agency." Instead, the goal is to extend "the experience of aliveness"—a "quality" that is difficult to define and yet "superordinate" to all of the other capacities in his list.[3] This chapter argues that *Middlemarch* can help us to define and to feel what Ogden and other psychoanalytic thinkers call the sense of aliveness—and the sense of deadness that threatens it as well.

Weariness, writes Blanchot, limits life. We can stay awake for a certain number of hours and no more. To put it in language closer to the novel's, our heart will beat only so many times before it stops. And in *Middlemarch*, even beyond depleting the vital "forces of life," weariness threatens to deplete it of its interest— that is to say, both life's meaning and its potential to be meaningful. When another character deridingly calls Dorothea's designs for architectural improvements to the workers' housing on her uncle's estate her "favourite fad for drawing plans," Dorothea moodily asks herself: "What was life worth—what great faith was possible when the whole effect of one's actions could be withered up into such parched rubbish as that?" (*M* 37). There is a bit of gentle mockery in the narrator's restatement of Dorothea's thoughts, poking fun at both Dorothea's inflation of her reforming projects and her hyperbolic reaction to criticism. And yet Dorothea's response expresses a concern that the novel does in fact take extremely seriously in its unfolding. What *is* life worth when earnest attempts to create change, when ardent impulses to promote social justice, are made laughable?

"Scepticism, as we know, can never be thoroughly applied, else life would come to a standstill; something we must believe in and do" (*M* 240), Eliot's narrator later reflects, pointing to the way Fred Vincy, college dropout and merchant middle-class family "scapegrace" (*M* 127), maintains a kind of boundless faith in his own limited abilities. And yet such skeptical, "standstill" states of mind threaten even the novel's most ardent and believing characters, and indeed, threaten the narrative itself. *Middlemarch* is a novel that reflects on the fact that the world can be brought to a "standstill"—that blueprints can be "withered up" into "parched rubbish," that life can so easily be made to feel flat, stale, and unprofitable—on the basis of an interpretation, or rather an interpretive mood, alone. And indeed, the novel shows that this feeling isn't a mere depressive projection, or an empty cynicism, but is rather an accurate understanding, among others, of the possibilities for effective ethical and political action within the confines of developing nineteenth-century capitalist imperialism, especially for women. (Dorothea may not be able to do anything to make her uncle's estate, or her world, a better place.) The novel wants to show both what brings life to a standstill and what puts it back in motion. In fact, it wants to put life back in motion itself.

Against the threats of life- and interest-draining weariness, *Middlemarch* posits the enlivening effects of highly mobile figurations and reconfigurations of meaning. Specifically, these processes play out as metaphor-making (on the level of narrative voice) and idealization (on the level of the relation of literary figures, character to character and reader to narrator). Both of these processes depend upon mobility: the mobility of mind, of psychic investments, and of figurative possibilities that the narrative voice models in its own ongoing movement. The narrator turns gemstones seen through Dorothea's eyes into "little fountains of pure colour" (*M* 14), turns Mr. Brooke's thought about the flightiness of young women into "the broken wing of an insect" laying lightly in his mind among other "fragments" and picked up by a breeze to alight on Dorothea (*M* 20), turns an unloving marriage into the act of handing your spouse a glass of water without looking at him (*M* 201–2), and turns Mary Garth into a "brown patch" in the mirror next to her bright blond cousin Rosamond (*M* 113). These images are striking. Each gives us, to repurpose one of the novel's most famous descriptions of sympathy as a definition of metaphor, an "idea wrought back to the directness of sense, like the solidity of objects" (*M* 211). But my interest here is less in the power of individual metaphors than in the activity of the narrative voice that generates them. By continuously "changing the metaphor" (*MF* 147) the narrative voice makes it possible to read and feel a situation differently, over and over again. This makes *Middlemarch* a novel that not only generates metaphors, but generates metaphorical possibilities, in and through the activity of a narrative voice that, for instance, reads one metaphor through another, or allows the metaphors elaborated by a character and by the narrator to refine and complicate one another.[4]

This kind of mobility of mind and meaning-making are values that are celebrated by the psychoanalytic theorists I focus on in this chapter. The mid-century analysts Paula Heimann (1899–1982) and Betty Joseph (1917–2013), practicing in England and building on the work of Melanie Klein and Joan Riviere, pivotally reconfigured psychoanalytic understandings of transference and countertransference dynamics. They urged a more sensitive attunement to the subtle shifts in feeling, energy, and voice that take place in any analytic session. They modelled the use of "here and now" interpretations, which showed how tracing moment-to-moment shifts in tone and feeling in the session could yield rich insights into a patient's psychic life.[5] And, crucially, they reconceived the emotional responses of the analyst, arguing that they were not impediments to treatment, as traditional thinking of countertransference held, but rather an extremely useful tool. This chapter argues that the style of interpretation practiced and described by Heimann and Joseph, and by present-day analysts like Ogden and Bollas who build on their work, can make us more attuned readers of George Eliot, allowing us to track the movements of metaphor-making that shape Eliot's narrative voice and to better sense their enlivening force. The practice-based theories of these analysts help us to see that *Middlemarch* may ultimately be less about what the novel says—the big lessons of sympathy and moral perfectionism it is often used to demonstrate—and more about what happens to you when you read the book.

In her groundbreaking paper "On Counter-Transference" (1950), Paula Heimann argues that what has not been "sufficiently stressed" about the analytic situation is that "it is a *relationship* between two persons"—meaning that it involves the feelings not only of the patient, but of the analyst too. Rather than shutting down their emotional responses for fear of destroying analytic neutrality or detachment, Heimann argues that analysts need to tune in to them more deeply. Just as important as cultivating the "evenly hovering attention" of classic Freudian theory, Heimann argues that analysts need to cultivate not only "freely working attention" but also, crucially, "a freely roused emotional sensibility so as to follow the patient's movements and unconscious phantasies."[6] Reading *Middlemarch* following this directive, this chapter offers not simply a new account of George Eliot's narrator, celebrated as magisterial and removed, but, more precisely, a new account of the *relationship*, to borrow Heimann's italics and insight, it is possible to have with this narrator.

The George-Eliot-Narrator

There is a long critical history of making George Eliot's narrative voice monolithic, and of doing so by identifying it with the voice of the author. The publication of the first of *Middlemarch*'s eight parts, on 1 December 1871, was timed to coincide with the publication of Alexander Main's *Wise, Witty, and Tender Sayings in Prose and Verse, Selected from the Works of George Eliot*, an anthology of memorable quotations pulled from their original context and presented as universal truths emanating from a sage-like author. In his preface, Main writes that Eliot elevates "the Novel" as a genre "by making it the *vehicle* of the grandest and most uncompromising moral truth."[7] As Leah Price notes, Main published three more editions of *Sayings* over the years, "updated like clockwork each time a new book by Eliot herself appeared," as well as the *George Eliot Birthday Book*, a quotation-a-day diary "decorated with a 'thought' from George

Eliot for every day of the year."[8] Price argues that Main and others made a market for Eliot's fiction by, in part, changing its genre. The notion of Eliot's lyric- or aphorism-like "quotability" came to shape, Price shows, not only critical responses to Eliot's work but even her fiction itself.[9]

The construction of the persona of George Eliot the author coincides with the stabilization of her narrative voice. And the problem with that is that it can lead not only to missing or mishearing the fluctuations in the narrative voice on the page, in all of its variousness and variety of tones, but also to overlooking the strangeness, in terms of ontology and fictionality alike, of narrators "themselves" (a strangeness that is reflected in our language, which does not allow us to assign a narrator a stable pronoun—it, he, she, they—without a great deal of awkwardness). Catherine Gallagher argues (in the same essay I invoked in connection with *Tess*) that we are not drawn to literary characters because they are like us, but rather because they are ontologically distinct from us.[10] Their appeal arises not from identification, but from what we might call, following José Esteban Muñoz's powerful definition of the term, disidentification: a force that shapes subjectivity around what it cannot be, around what it has to repurpose and reshape in order to make use of. How might Gallagher's argument—developed in both her "Fictionality" essay and a reading of our relation to Dorothea Brooke in the companion essay entitled "George Eliot: Immanent Victorian"—be extended to help us think through our relations to those even stranger literary beings we call narrators?

Arguably, we read Eliot's fiction as much for the narrator as for character or plot. We want to know not only what Dorothea thinks and feels, but what Eliot's narrator thinks and feels about what Dorothea thinks and feels. The narrator describes, for instance, both Casaubon's "uneasy lot" and his/her/their/its personified response to this predicament: "For my part I am very sorry for him" (*M* 280). And yet this seemingly personal disclosure does not make the narrator a character among others, but rather a different kind of "novelistic nonentity," one that has the privilege of moving in and out of subject positions and degrees of personification while maintaining a distinctive voice and angle of vision.[11] Repurposing Gallagher's inquiries into the pleasures of ontological difference or disidentification from characters allows us to ask: Why are we so powerfully drawn to Eliot's narrators and the patterns of language that define them?

I want to argue that it is less the George-Eliot-narrator's quotability—the culling of "wise, witty, and tender sayings" that turns the unfolding of the novel into time-stopped series of disconnected aphorisms—than its *mobility* that draws us in. The narrative voice of *Middlemarch* pulses, like the heartbeat that forms the implicit soundtrack of the novel (emanating from a squirrel, from Saint Theresa's transverberated heart, from Casaubon's slowly stopping one), in and out of personification, beating out rhythms of intimacy and distance, privacy and publicity, ardor and weariness, and knowledge and nescience that shape the reading experience precisely as movement.[12] As movement and as *relationship*: the narrative voice that keeps turning over new thoughts, new interpretive possibilities, and new metaphors also continually repositions the reader, framing shifting possibilities for intellectual and emotional responsiveness in relation not simply to the action described, but also to the narrator him-/her-/them-/itself, as literary figure or as voice.[13]

"Freely Roused Emotional Sensibility"

Heimann's "On Counter-Transference," originally delivered as a paper in 1949 and first published in 1950, was foundational for the reshaping of modern psychoanalytic practice. In it, Heimann argues that while previous theories of the countertransference, including Freud's own, regarded the analyst's feelings as an obstacle to psychoanalytic work, in her own estimation, these feelings are in fact what makes it possible. Heimann worries about how new psychoanalysts, urged on by conventional recommendations to strive for neutrality, have felt the need to dull their sensibilities: "Many candidates [in psychoanalytic training] are afraid and feel guilty when they become aware of feelings toward their patients and consequently aim at avoiding any emotional response and at becoming completely unfeeling and 'detached.'"[14] For Heimann, though, any and "all of feelings which the analyst experiences toward his patient" constitute the countertransference as a tool, as an instrument, as a sensitization device where the goal is to become more rather than less feeling. She writes: "The analyst's emotional response to his patient within the psychoanalytic situation represents one of the most important tools to his work. The analyst's counter-transference is an instrument of research into the patient's unconscious."[15] Advocating for a "freely roused emotional sensibility" that will follow the patient's own "emotional movements and unconscious" life, Heimann argues, clearly and matter-of-factly, but nevertheless movingly, for the power, reality, and reliability of unconscious communication: "Our basic assumption is that the analyst's unconscious understands that of his patient. This rapport on the deep level comes to the surface in the form of feelings which the analyst notices in response to his patient, in his 'counter-transference.' This is the most dynamic way which his patient's voice reaches him."[16] These are striking claims, and must have been even more so at the time of their original statement and publication, when they cut against the grain of so much received psychoanalytic wisdom.[17] Another mind, another voice, another's experience reaches you through your own feeling. The "basic assumption" is belief in deep, ongoing unconscious rapport.

Heimann's conception of countertransference as an "instrument of research into the patient's unconscious" resounds most readily, perhaps, with Freud's own recommendations for analytic technique. The psychoanalyst, writes Freud, "must turn his own unconscious like a receptive organ towards the transmitting unconscious of the patient. He must adjust himself to the patient as a telephone receiver is adjusted to the transmitting microphone. Just as the receiver converts back into sound waves the electric oscillations in the telephone line which were set up by sound waves," so the doctor's unconscious can reconstruct the unconscious of the patient.[18] But I hear reverberating just as strongly George Eliot's own formulations of the role of the artist as instrument, a technological device that amplifies the barely perceptible and extends the range of the reader's sensitivities: a microscope, a microphone, a radio receiver. In an early, and well-known, essay for the *Westminster Review*, Eliot argues that artists give us their "higher sensibility as a medium, a delicate acoustic or optical instrument, bringing home to our coarser senses what would otherwise be unperceived by us"[19]—the sound of the grass growing, the squirrel's heart beating, the "transmitting unconscious of the patient," and the patient's "voice," sounded and unsounded.

For Eliot as for Heimann, feeling enriches rather than impairs one's interpretive abilities. "If an analyst tries to work without consulting his feelings," Heimann writes, "his interpretations are poor."[20] In *Middlemarch*, Eliot urges a similar lesson in a scene close to the end of the book in which Dorothea argues she cannot explain the story of her romance with Will Ladislaw to her sister Celia in any detached way: "you would have to feel it with me," Dorothea says, "else you would never know" (*M* 822). Nothing in the novel can be "known" except in its unfolding, moment to moment, on the page, in the movement not just of plot, but in the life of narration. And this means not simply feeling it with Dorothea, or with any other one of the novel's characters; it means getting a specific feel of and for the voice on the page, a voice that at once belongs and does not belong to George Eliot, or to Mary Ann Evans, and a feel for its movement and multivocality. Heimann writes: "the analyst's emotional sensitivity needs to be extensive rather than intensive, differentiating and mobile."[21] This insight can also serve as an instrument for reading *Middlemarch*: how do we cultivate a mobile and extensive emotional sensitivity that allows us to pick up on all of the subtleties of the novel's narrative voice?

In the preface to *The Shadow of the Object* (1987), Christopher Bollas describes, in what strikes me as one of the most succinct and powerful descriptions of object relations psychoanalysis out there, as well one of the most potentially fruitful for literary analysis, just how British psychoanalysts reworked and rethought analytic practice. The piece is in large part a tribute to Heimann—an analyst of Russian Jewish descent who was born in Poland, trained in Germany, and who moved to London, with her daughter, as a refugee in 1933, and spent the rest of her life there. Bollas writes:

In the early 1950s Paula Heimann, a member of the British Psycho-Analytical Society, posed a question that became crucial to the practice of psychoanalysis in what has come to be called the "British School" of psychoanalysis. When listening to the patient's free associations (or broken speech), and tracing the private logic of sequential associations as all psychoanalysts had done up until then, she asked: "Who is speaking?" We can say that up until this moment it had always been assumed that the speaker was the patient who had formed a therapeutic alliance with the analyst, and therefore that he was a neutral or working speaker who was reporting inner states of mind. This assumption comprised the classical view of analytic narrative. But Heimann knew that at any one moment in a session the patient could be speaking with the voice of the mother, or the mood of the father, or some fragmented voice of a child self either lived or withheld from life.[22]

In the psychoanalytic situation, as in life, a speaker never speaks neutrally, never simply "report[s] inner states of mind" or desires; indeed, never speaks simply as him- or herself. Because the self for thinkers in the British School is precisely a record of its object relations—the history of its internalizations—the patient speaks (and, indeed, thinks and feels) from a series of different subject positions, giving voice to the various objects within a densely populated inner world. Who is speaking? The answer shifts from moment to moment. And just as the voice, voicings, moods, and assumed identities, at once historical and fantasized, of the patient shift, so too does the role assigned to the analyst as addressee. Bollas continues his history by describing the way Heimann adds a crucial second question of address to her first:

> "To whom is this person speaking?" Heimann then asked. The unconscious admits no special recognition of the neutrality of the psychoanalyst and, given the unending subtleties of the transference, Heimann realized that at one moment the analysand was speaking to the mother, anticipating the father, or reproaching, exciting, or consoling a child—the child self of infancy, in the midst of separation at age two, in the oedipal phase, or in adolescence. Heimann and other analysts in the British School, all of whom had been deeply influenced by the work of Melanie Klein, analyzed the object relations implied in the patient's discourse. The patient's narrative was not simply listened to in order to hear the dissonant sounds of unconscious punctuation [as in classical Freudian analysis] or the affective registrations that suggested the ego's position and availability for interpretation [as in Anna Freudian ego psychology]. The British analyst would also analyze the shifting subjects and others that were implied in the life of the transference.[23]

The patient speaks as a series of objects *to* a series of objects, bringing alive in the room, through nothing but modulations of voice and body language, the "shifting subjects and others" newly understood to be "implied in the life of the transference." To tune into what Bollas calls "the unending subtleties of the transference," the analyst must be responsive to range—must have a sensibility that is, in Heimann's words, extensive, differentiating, mobile.[24] Voice itself is incredibly rich and resonant in Bollas's account. Object relations are present in the patient's very discourse. And the presence of these "shifting subjects and others" is revealed not only by the way a patient speaks the desires of others, but even echoes and emulates their very intonations, recreating their objects' rhythms of speech and conversational habits as fully as their patterns of thought.

I want to take these insights and imperatives as "instruments of research" for reading the novel as well.[25] In my relational reading of *Middlemarch*, I take this to mean listening for moment-to-moment shifts in the narrator's voice and its readerly address. Who is speaking? To whom is this person/literary figure/novelistic nonentity speaking? I take it to mean allowing for the way the voice on the page shifts register from chapter to chapter and from sentence to sentence. I take it to mean listening for the numerous tones of voice in which Eliot's narrator "reproaches," "consoles," or "excites" us—these are Bollas's terms, but I find them remarkably fitting descriptions of the most common rhetorical moves of Eliot's narrator. And, finally, I take reading this way to mean taking seriously the unevenness of Eliot's narrative voice rather than attempting to smooth it out by recourse to knowingness (the Eliot we think we know) or normativity (a set of ideas about what we think the Victorian novel or a serious work of realism should be and do).

Before returning to *Middlemarch* and trying to read it in just this way, a final word on *The Shadow of the Object*: when I read the remarkable passage that I've quoted at length, I can't help but hear another voice in the background. Alongside Bollas, who himself ventriloquizes Heimann, I cannot help but hear Roland Barthes and the uncannily similar set of questions he asks to open "The Death of the Author," his own meditation on narrative voice:

> In his story *Sarrasine* Balzac, describing a castrato disguised as a woman, writes the following sentence: "This was Woman herself, with her sudden fears, her irrational whims, her instinctive worries, her impetuous boldness, her unprovoked bravado, her fussings, and her delicious sensibilities." Who is speaking thus? Is it the hero of the story, bent on remaining ignorant of the castrato hidden beneath the woman? Is it Balzac the individual, furnished by his personal experience with a philosophy of Woman? Is it Balzac the author professing "literary" ideas on femininity? Is it universal wisdom? Romantic psychology?[26]

Who is speaking? Barthes asks the same question as Bollas, concerned not with the voice in the session but rather the voice on the page. How can we identify, Barthes asks, just who it might be that "speaks" a single sentence in a work of fiction? Barthes lists several possibilities for the given work at hand—the hero of the story *Sarrasine*, Balzac the man or Balzac the author, "universal wisdom" or "romantic psychology"—but settles on a different kind of response. Who is speaking? The answer, he writes, is that "we shall never know, for the good reason that writing is the destruction of every voice, of every point of origin. Writing is that neutral, that composite, oblique space where our subject slips away, the negative where all identity is lost, starting with the very identity of the body writing."[27] Rather than stay with his list of possible speakers, rather than arguing that in literature several voices speak together at once (even if, curiously, Richard Howard's freer translation of Barthes's French would render it so: "It will always be impossible to know" who is speaking, his sentence runs, "for the good reason that all writing is itself this special voice, consisting of several indiscernible voices, and that literature is precisely the invention of this voice"),[28] Barthes argues that, in writing, voice is destroyed, identity is lost, origin annihilated. In the place of voice, Barthes describes "neutrality": the text as a tissue of quotations without origin, but with an assured destination in the reader who gathers those quotations together. The death of the author, he famously argues, guarantees the birth of the reader.

It is so important to be able to read according to Barthes's instruction here. But the psychoanalytic version of this insight, and rejoinder to Barthes, is not to rush to neutrality, but instead to stay with the multiplicity of voices, intonations, and possible speakers that comprise narrative voice. And that is what this chapter, contra-Barthes and following Bollas and Heimann, aims to do: to follow Eliot's narrative voice in and out of its various voicings and personifications, rhetorical gestures and tones of voice, personalities and impersonalities, the "wisdom[s]" and "psycholog[ies]" of its various literary figures, and the feeling-states it variously describes and imposes. Doing so "changes the lights" for us, giving us not a monolithic, "wise and witty" author-narrator, but the "shifting subjects and others implied in the life" not of the transference but of novelistic form: it gives us an object relations of reading.

Alongside and beyond Words

In *Middlemarch*, "ardent outsets" end in "declension" (*M* 832). The failure (spectacular or, even worse, ordinary) of the novel's characters to achieve their grand ambitions is echoed in the narrative's inability to escape routinized plots and established literary conventions.[29] By demoting Dorothea's search for useful social action into a mere personal romance, the novel begs the question whether the marriage plot signifies narrative success or rather the succumbing, in exhaustion and fatigue, to convention and tradition.[30] Understood to be a more "mature" novel than *The Mill on the Floss* in several senses—written later in Eliot's career, a description of adulthood rather than childhood and adolescence, and a novel that Virginia Woolf famously argued is "one of the few English novels written for grown-up people"—*Middlemarch* is still deeply concerned with longing, but urgently wants to explore what happens in its ebb. That is to say, in the threatened ebb of longings as diverse as religious feeling, romantic desire, sexual attraction, professional ambition, and political activism. The novel wants to show us how life and literature can be drained of their potential to be meaningful, and how that capacity can be restored.

These are experiences that the novel works to enact as much as to describe. Take this description of Casaubon—one of the novel's most wrenching set pieces—which begins with the narrator's announcement, "For my part I am very sorry for him":

> It is an uneasy lot at best, to be what we call highly taught and yet not to enjoy: to be present at this great spectacle of life and never to be liberated from a small hungry shivering self—never to be fully possessed by the glory we behold, never to have our consciousness rapturously transformed into the vividness of a thought, the ardour of a passion, the energy of an action, but always to be scholarly and uninspired, ambitious and timid, scrupulous and dim-sighted. (*M* 280)

In the narrator's description, Casaubon becomes the very ground against which rapture, energy, ardor, and action gain their value. And yet the syntax of the sentence makes the reader subject to the same obstacles as Casaubon in reaching possession by glory: slow, deliberate thought and laborious effort. The sentence's long series of modifying clauses slows our reading down and brings us to continual halts before its many commas, colons, and dashes. It creates a motion of narrative that Rosemarie Bodenheimer identifies as typical of Eliot's prose: each clause "rereads and responds" to the "implications" of the one before.[31] In this passage, Eliot's narrator simultaneously exalts ardor and exhausts the reader, urging us into epiphany and yet holding us at the level of language's opacity. The passage makes us feel Casaubon's weariness with him.

Middlemarch is a notoriously exhausting read. Its sheer length, its "diffuseness" (in Henry James's famous characterization),[32] the multiplicity of its characters and plots, the difficulty of its prose, the frequency of its attempts to draw readers into moral self-reflection: the novel demands a level of intellectual and emotional exertion that has been noted since the time of its original serial publication. Victorian critics frequently discussed Eliot's fiction, according to Nicholas Dames, in the "language of physiological exhaustion" and the "rhetoric of nervous fatigue."[33] Reading *Middlemarch* wears the reader out. But it does so, perhaps, as a kind of promise, delimiting the kinds of comfort and consolation, the modified forms of energy and ardor, that Eliot's novels and her unique narrative voice can offer.

Betty Joseph (1917–2013), a British analyst and important figure in the "contemporary Kleinian" circle, can help us to conceptualize the force of language as enactment rather than simple statement. In her stunning and important paper, "Transference: The Total Situation" (1985), Joseph defines the transference in a way that picks up on and develops her teacher Paula Heimann's insights on the countertransference. Opening the paper, Joseph writes: "My stress will be on the idea of transference as a framework, in which something is always going on, where there is always movement and activity."[34] Even the syntax stresses ongoing movement. For Joseph, like Heimann before her, the analyst's mobility of mind and of emotional sensibility is paramount. And this is because the transference—the charged relationship between analyst and analysand that makes these figures always more than simply themselves, not singular but rather the location of "shifting subjects and others" that make up their entire long histories of object relating—is itself constantly changing and shifting. Things happen in the consulting room: different voices speak, different objects appear, different gravities and atmospheres descend, and different purposes are put to words beyond simply expressing ideas. It is Joseph's notion that *that* is what gives itself to be interpreted in the session: not simply what is said, but "everything that the patient brings into the relationship," which "can best be gauged by our focusing our attention on what is going on within the relationship, how [the patient] is using the analyst, alongside and beyond what he is saying."[35] What is going on "alongside and beyond" what is being said, "alongside and beyond" words, in the "total situation"? The question is as apt for literary criticism as for psychoanalysis.

Betty Joseph was born and raised, like George Eliot one hundred years before her, in the English Midlands. Her engagement with psychoanalysis began in Manchester, where, in 1940, as a social worker treating children and helping with the evacuation effort, she began psychoanalytic treatment with Michael Balint (the Hungarian analyst who would eventually become a leader of the Independent group of the British Psychoanalytical Society, and whose work I discuss at length in chapter 3). Joseph then moved to London to pursue her own psychoanalytic training. There, she became part of a distinctly Kleinian lineage: she was analyzed by Paula Heimann (then Klein's student), held regular consultations with Klein, and became close friends with a group of analysts, Hanna Segal, Wilfred Bion, and Herbert Rosenfeld, who would become known as the "contemporary Kleinians." Joseph's biographers report that she considered herself a "late developer," and it was not until the 1970s that she began to trust her own ability to make distinctive contributions to psychoanalytic thought with her published work.[36] Writing about analytic technique and the mechanisms of psychic change, her contributions from that period until her death in 2013 were substantial indeed.[37]

What Joseph describes in her paper is above all a technique for reading. Her instruction to attend to what happens both "alongside and beyond" what is said is such a powerful phrase because it acknowledges that enactments occur not only in extralinguistic dimensions ("beyond"), but also in paralinguistic ones, "alongside" what is spoken—that is to say, in aspects of language that function not simply semantically but also, for Joseph, as action, as tonality, as sound, and as enlivening or deadening force. In naming transference a "total situation," Joseph indicates a way of keeping all of these dimensions of language in play with one another. Joseph borrows this phrase from a remark by Melanie Klein: "It is my experience that in unravelling details of the transference it is essential to think in terms of *total situations* transferred from the past into the present, as well as emotions, defences and object relations."[38] But in characteristic fashion, Joseph extends this statement in several surprising directions. Most basically, the "total situation" reflects the fact that transference is not restricted to direct remarks about the analyst, but is diffused into the entirety of what happens in the session: everything from the patient's "reports about everyday life" to the shifts in his tone of voice to the "atmosphere" he "build[s] up" in the room give "clue[s] to the unconscious anxieties stirred up in the transference situation."[39]

The "total situation" reflects, more fundamentally still, the very fact that things like atmospheric shifts and the "pressures brought to bear on the analyst" themselves convey meaning: they are elements of projective identification that are played out in the session, making the "here and now" of the transference the analyst's best chance to reconstruct earlier histories of object relating.[40] Joseph writes:

> Much of our understanding of the transference comes through our understanding of how our patients act on us to feel things for many varied reasons; how they try to draw us into their defensive systems; how they unconsciously act out with us in the transference, trying to get us to act out with them; how they convey aspects of their inner world built up from infancy—elaborated in childhood and adulthood, experiences often beyond the use of words, which we can often only capture through the feelings aroused in us, through our countertransference, used in the broad sense of the word.[41]

The broad sense of that word is, of course, a definition borrowed from Heimann. Countertransference encapsulates the totality of an analyst's feelings toward the patient. And for Joseph, too, these feelings are a kind of tool and sensory technology, capturing "experiences" that are "beyond the use of words." Projective identification is a form of communication, unconscious speaking to unconscious, that plays out in the extra- and paralinguistic dimension of feeling. And all of this valuable communication of a patient's history and "inner world" is lost, Joseph shows, if we do not look to transference as a "total situation" that occurs "alongside and beyond" words. And lost then too is the possibility for real and significant "psychic change"—the center of some of Joseph's most powerful theoretical interventions.[42] She continues:

> I am assuming that this type of projective identification is deeply unconscious and not verbalized. If we work only with the part that is verbalized, we do not really take into account the object relationships being acted out in the transference; here, for example, [in a case history she has just briefly described] the relationship between the uncomprehending mother and the infant who feels unable to be understood, and it is this that forms the bedrock of her [the patient's] personality. If we do not get through to this, we shall, I suspect, achieve areas of psychic understanding, even apparent shifts in the material, but real psychic change, which can last beyond the treatment, will, I think, not be possible.[43]

What interpretation needs to account for is not just what is said in the session, but what is lived through. I believe the same is true for reading novels—especially, perhaps, a novel like *Middlemarch*, which is explicitly designed, in its length, its difficulty, its wide scope, and in its epic ambition and the weight of its disappointments, to be experienced and felt rather than just understood. As Joseph puts it, "analysis to be useful must be an experience, in contrast, for example, to the giving of understanding or explaining."[44] As Dorothea puts it, "you would have to feel it with me. Else you would never know" (*M* 822).

C. Is for . . .

Joseph writes that "if one sees transference" as "basically living, experiencing, and shifting—as movement—then our interpretations have to express this."[45] Interpretation has to move: it has to be nimble, mobile, and sensitive to moment-to-moment shifts in tone and atmosphere. I am arguing that our interpretations of *Middlemarch* have to move as well. We can learn a great deal about this literary practice from Joseph, whose analytic technique, as it appears in her papers in the form of both detailed description of her sessions and reported dialogue, is so minutely focused we might call it microanalysis. Reading the case material she includes in her papers is indeed one of the great pleasures of reading her work: there, you can see her idiosyncratic and amazingly focused interpretive style in action, and begin to pick up some of its idiom yourself.

In the transference paper, for example, Joseph describes a patient whom she calls "C." In their sessions together, C. describes in "great and obsessional detail" his worries about getting from London to Manchester for work—"his worries about catching the train, getting through the traffic, and so on, and how he had safeguarded these problems. He also discussed," Joseph continues, "an anxiety about losing his membership in a club because of nonattendance, and spoke about a friend being slightly unfriendly on the phone." In a first attempt at interpretation in the session, Joseph offers "detailed interpretations," based on these reports, about "feeling unwanted" and "feeling shut out"—but these interpretations "do not seem to make real contact or to help him." But as Joseph stresses "his need to be *inside* and safe," C. begins talking in a very different way.[46] I am going to quote the passage that follows at some length, both to get across the shifts in tone in which Joseph is interested and the skillful way she describes them. In the first paragraph below, she uses free indirect discourse to convey particularities of C.'s tone and her experience of it. Previously talking in an obsessional, disconnected way,

> in relation to my showing [C.] his need to be inside and safe he started to talk, now in a very different and smooth way, about how similar this problem was to his difficulty in changing jobs, moving his office, getting new clothes, how he stuck to the old ones, although by now he was short of clothes. Then there was the same problem about changing cars. . . .
>
> At this point I think that an interesting thing had occurred. While all he was saying seemed accurate and important in itself, the thoughts were no longer being thought, they had become words, concrete analytic objects into which he could sink, get drawn in, as if they were the mental concomitant of a physical body into which he was withdrawing in the session. The question of separating off, mentally as physically, could be evaded since our ideas could now be experienced as completely in tune and he had withdrawn into them.[47]

The ellipsis and paragraph break mark the space of Joseph's realization of the shift, of emerging from the trance of C.'s smooth speech, into which she too has been entering. From obsessional talk to self-interpretations intended to help him merge with the analyst, C.'s words have taken on a fantastic, and defensive, function. The notion of words as "concrete analytic objects" used to avoid thinking evokes Bion and his "attacks on linking." But Joseph gives this notion her own unique inflection by emphasizing how she has accessed this insight: tapping into her own experience as a method for understanding what is happening in the patient's own psyche.

Joseph writes: "Having heard certain of my interpretations and their meaning correctly, he used the words and thoughts not to think with, but unconsciously to act with, to get into and try to involve me in this activity, spinning words but not really communicating with them."⁴⁸ Joseph's interpretations are originally experienced as such—"i.e., a sentence consisting of words with agreed meaning," as Balint puts it (*BF* 13)—but then turned to a different purpose. Words are used to "act with," as things to spin and sink into rather than use for communication. C.'s words attempt to draw the analyst into the enactment, so that she too is "spinning words but not really communicating them." And yet Joseph argues that this is not simply a problem, but more importantly a vital source of information from which to draw. Joseph writes:

> My stress throughout this contribution has been on the transference as a relationship in which something is all the time going on, but we know that this something is essentially based on the patient's past and the relationship with his internal objects or his belief about them and what they were like.... [W]hat we can do, by tracing the movement and conflict within the transference, is bring alive again feelings within a relationship that have been deeply defended against or only fleetingly experienced, and we enable them to get firmer roots in the transference. We are not completely new objects, but, I think, greatly strengthened objects, because stronger and deeper emotions have been worked through in the transference.⁴⁹

Transference as dynamic, moving, total situation enables the analyst not simply to reconstruct the past, but to bring dead and deadened feelings back "alive again."

C. is for Betty Joseph's patient, but we could read it this way too: C. is for Casaubon, and C. is for Casaubon's own Concrete words. In a passage describing Casaubon's devastating inability to take pleasure in his new marriage to Dorothea, *Middlemarch* shows that metaphor too can be used as a concrete thing and a way *not* to think. Eventually, this chapter is going to argue for the novel's implicit promotion of the enlivening effects of metaphor. But *Middlemarch* gets us there through movement: by pointing first to the "fatal" effects of having one's thoughts "entangled in metaphors" (*M* 85) when they stop ideas and ideation rather than moving them forward. Casaubon, unsurprisingly, sparks the narrator's insight of the deadening effects of end-stopped metaphor. Once again reporting his/her/their/its own feeling before turning to a longer reflection, the narrator reports:

> I feel more tenderly towards [Mr Casaubon's] experience of success than towards the disappointment of the amiable Sir James [Dorothea's rejected suitor]. For in truth, as the day fixed for his marriage came nearer, Mr Casaubon did not find his spirits rising; nor did the contemplation of that matrimonial garden-scene, where, as all experience showed, the path was to be

bordered with flowers, prove persistently more enchanting to him than the accustomed vaults where he walked taper in hand. He did not confess to himself, still less could he have breathed to another, his surprise that though he had won a lovely and noble-hearted girl he had not won delight,—which he had also regarded as an object to be found by search. (*M* 85)

It is less Casaubon's lack of "delight" than his internal figuration of it as "an object to be found by search" that pulls focus and, purportedly, garners the narrator's sympathy. Casaubon's concrete metaphorical thinking works as a pitifully stultifying force:

> Poor Mr Casaubon had imagined that his long studious bachelorhood had stored up for him a compound interest of enjoyment, and that large drafts on his affections could not fail to be honoured; for we all of us, grave or light, get our thoughts entangled in metaphors, and act fatally on the strength of them. And now he was in danger of being saddened by the very conviction that his circumstances were unusually happy: there was nothing external by which he could account for a certain blankness of sensibility which came over him just when his expectant gladness should have been most lively, just when he exchanged the accustomed dulness of his Lowick library for his visits to the Grange. (*M* 85)

Casaubon's metaphor is economic: he has been thinking that because he has forgone "enjoyment" in his youth, it must be stored up in a savings account waiting to be withdrawn in older age, and not only to the amount in which it was originally deposited, but a number increased by the steady accrual of interest. The crushing disappointment of Casaubon's realization is twofold. First, because now there is no excuse for his blank sensibility: his unhappiness can no longer be attributed to external circumstances, but only to his own incapacity to enjoy. And second, Casaubon discovers too that his defining metaphor was poor, an inaccurate description of life and a "fatal" misunderstanding of the nature of joy and the consequences of its deferment. There was nothing to save up, not "enjoyment" nor "affections" nor sexual pleasure, and now there is nothing to withdraw. There is, however, a real cost to having become so attached to this flawed figure of speech: continued dullness and, in his desire to hide his experience from Dorothea, isolation. The narrator notices in Casaubon's self-narration what Betty Joseph noticed in C.'s: that words are no longer being used to think with, but are being used instead as concrete objects to hide in and manipulate. In Casaubon's case, the "thoughts that were no longer being thought with" have become metaphor—to be more precise, *concrete* metaphor, in two senses of the word: concrete in the sense that metaphor translates an abstraction into a distinct, material image (life as a bank account, enjoyment as a thing to save, delight as an object to be found by search), and concrete in the sense that the metaphor is "congealed, coagulated, solidified, solid"—it has lost its fluidity, its ability to flow and shift and change form.[50]

Stuck in his metaphor, Casaubon stagnates in lonely despair. But, you will notice, the narrative description of him does not. The passage continues:

> Here was a weary experience in which he was as utterly condemned to loneliness as in the despair which sometimes threatened him while toiling in the morass of authorship without seeming nearer to the goal. And his was that worst loneliness which would shrink from sympathy. He could not but wish that Dorothea should think him not less happy than the world would expect her successful suitor to be; and in relationship to his authorship he leaned on her young trust and veneration, he liked to draw forth her fresh interest in listening, as a means of encouragement to himself: in talking to her he presented all his performance and intention with the reflected confidence of the pedagogue, and rid himself for the time of that chilling ideal audience which crowded his laborious uncreative hours with the vaporous pressure of Tartarean shades. (*M* 85–86)

Authorship as "morass," ideal audience as "chilling," "Tartarean shades," expected reactions as "vaporous pressure": the narrative voice rapidly cycles through metaphors and images, showing that what is "fatal" is not metaphor itself, nor even its tendency to get mixed up with thought, but only the kind of "entanglement" in metaphor that brings thinking to a standstill. Where Casaubon's metaphor is concrete, George Eliot's narrator models the movement of metaphorical thinking.

In his 1997 essay "Reverie and Metaphor: Some Thoughts on How I Work as a Psychoanalyst," Thomas Ogden argues that just as metaphorical thinking is essential to psychoanalytic theory, metaphorical language is essential to psychoanalytic practice. For Ogden, it is the nature of the unconscious itself, in its irreducible otherness, that demands the use of metaphor. He writes:

> The unconscious is not simply a type of thinking and of organising feeling regulated by a different way of creating linkages (i.e. primary process modes of linking); rather, it is a form of experiencing that by its nature cannot be directly brought into conscious awareness. When we say that an experience that had once been unconscious has "become" conscious, we are not talking about moving something into view that had formerly been hidden behind the screen of the repression "barrier." Instead, we are talking about the creation of a qualitatively new experience, one that is not simply brought into

the "view" of the conscious awareness. Since we can never consciously "know" or "see" unconscious experience, the transformations creating derivatives of unconscious experience (for example, the operation of the dream work or the "reverie work") do not create new forms of unconscious experience, but create expressions of what unconscious experience *is like*.[51]

Inaccessible by definition, unconscious experience comes to us only in mediated forms. In keeping with his claim, Ogden turns to an example from his clinical practice to explain what a presentation of the unconscious "is like":

> For example, a patient told me that he had had a dream in which he saw a tidal wave approaching, but was unable to move or cry for help. This rendering of his dream did not represent a glimpse into the patient's unconscious internal object world; it was a psychological expression of what the patient's experience was *like*. It is a metaphor. Dreams are metaphors, reveries are metaphors, symbols are metaphors for the individual's unconscious experience. Consequently, to the degree that we as analysts are interested in unconscious experience, we are students of metaphor. It is therefore incumbent upon us to develop an intimate familiarity with the workings of metaphor so that we may come to know its expressive power as well as its limits.[52]

The patient's dream is a rendering of his unconscious world, and his telling of it a rendering of his dream, as Ogden's presentation of case material is again a rendering of the analytic situation. What is important for Ogden, as for Heimann and Joseph before him, is motion: the continual creation of such "expressions of what unconscious experience *is like*."

Metaphor has both enormous "expressive power" and clear "limits"—Ogden borrows from Robert Frost to explain that "all metaphor breaks down somewhere."[53] This insight plays out in *Middlemarch* too: it is Casaubon's failure to *let* his metaphor break down that creates the problem. He makes it an overly concrete vision of the world rather than a malleable expression of what the world *may* be like. Metaphors break down, but usefully so: this is why they need to continually evolve and change, as does our picture of the unconscious, and even our picture of our own early experience.[54] For Ogden, analysis facilitates this evolution by functioning precisely in and through an interchange of representations: "a very large part of the way in which patients speak to their analysts, and analysts speak to their patients, takes the shape of introducing and elaborating upon the other's metaphors."[55] What animates analysis for Ogden, what makes it feel "most alive and most real," is the *movement* from metaphor to metaphor—a movement that *Middlemarch* also enlists to ward off Casaubon's weariness and to keep life, and narrative, from coming to a standstill.

Exhaustion and Recuperation

Ogden specifies that he is not necessarily talking about "a particularly rich or imaginative set of metaphors," or poetic language per se, but rather ordinary language and ordinary efforts to describe "what despair or loneliness or joyfulness feel *like*." He writes: "each time a patient speaks to us or we speak to a patient about feeling 'under pressure,' 'tongue-tied,' 'feeling worn-out,' 'being deaf,' 'torn,' 'divided,' 'wracked with pain,' 'emotionally drained,' 'not giving a shit' etc., the patient and analyst are introducing metaphors that might be elaborated, modified, 'turned on their ear,' and so on."[56] Feeling "worn-out" is, indeed, one of *Middlemarch*'s most used metaphors of ordinary speech. Characters in the novel feel worn, worn out, over-worn, winter-worn, weather-worn, grief-worn, and weary (*M* 396, 196, 708, 360, 74, 825, and 129, respectively). And these metaphors are the antithesis to alive and enlivened experience. On their honeymoon in Rome, Dorothea realizes that Casaubon will not be an ideal tour guide in this foreign city, nor indeed through life: "What was fresh to her mind was worn out to his; and such a capacity of thought and feeling as had ever been stimulated in him by the general life of mankind had long shrunk to a sort of dried preparation, a lifeless embalmment of knowledge" (*M* 196).

In Eliot's best-known formulations, the artist is an amplifying acoustic or optical instrument, whose sensitivity picks up and amplifies textures of everyday existence others cannot detect.[57] And yet at other times Eliot worries about the technical flaws in this instrument, and her own fallibilities as an artist. In an 1857 letter to her editor John Blackwood, Eliot wrote: "I undertake to exhibit nothing as it should be; I only try to exhibit some things as they have been or are, seen through such a medium as my own nature gives me."[58] The problem, however, is that the "medium" of one's "own nature" is colored by feeling, and may refract representation. She continues: "The moral effect of [my] stories of course depends on my power of seeing truly and feeling justly; and as I am not conscious of looking at things through the medium of cynicism or irreverence, I can't help hoping that there is no tendency in what I write to produce those miserable mental states."[59] "Cynicism" and "irreverence" are, to Eliot, not only "miserable mental states" but also "standstill" ones: they lock the world into one particular angle of vision. They are a medium of feeling, a filter or tinted lens, off limits to the author who wants to "see truly" and "feel justly." And yet part of the power of *Middlemarch* is precisely its ability to perceive and channel such "miserable mental states"—if only to be able to fend off the views of art and life they produce.

By giving weariness such a prominent place in her novel, Eliot considers, and makes us feel, the very real possibility of an existence that feels empty and meaningless: one in which all of our enormous capacities of thought and feeling are "shrunk to a sort of dried preparation, a lifeless embalmment of knowledge"—withered into so much "parched rubbish." And it makes us feel as though this view would not even be the effect of the discoloring medium of "cynicism" or "irreverence," but rather an accurate view of life. Realism may not have redemptive power. And novels—deploying the same old words, the same old marriage plot—might exhaust rather than create meaning. Against her typical formulations of the good, sympathy-building work of which novels are capable, in *Middlemarch*, Eliot uses figurations of weariness and deadness to frame the possibility that novel reading may not be revelatory or redemptive, but simply resigned. Rather than a form of ethical education or a means of moral self-improvement, novel reading may function as escape, as ideology pure and simple—telling us to stay home, to get married, to reconcile ourselves to the fact that we cannot change the political orders of our world—or, even worse, as tedium pure and simple.[60] "Oh the world is a thing whose lover disappoints / who is tired of the news that is no news / who toils for silly people doing silly things," writes the poet Clarissa Pinkola Estés.[61] And this is precisely the condition of feeling the novel simultaneously fears and wants to evoke—the one that it needs to evoke in order to more fully dispel. Lovers disappoint, toil is wasted, and marriage is a bore. When asked why she killed her husband, the French actress Laure deadpans, "because he wearied me" (*M* 153). What if *Middlemarch* wearies us too?

The tiredness of language is one of Eliot's great themes. Whatever great variety of thought, whatever richness of feeling we many find in ourselves or in others, we are forced to represent it to ourselves in what are, quite simply, the same old words. Language therefore threatens to reduce not only the complexity of thought and feeling, but also the vast difference between any two people. As Balint puts it: "words [at times] cease to be vehicles for free association; they have become lifeless, repetitive, and stereotyped; they strike one as an old worn-out gramophone record, with the needle running endlessly in the same groove" (*BF* 176). Words wear out. And yet the very fact that Eliot *thematizes* this problem in *Middlemarch* turns it to productive use. She describes this recuperative movement in *Leaves from a Note-Book*, where she initially points to words as an overfamiliar "medium of understanding and sympathy," but then recuperates their potential by praising, as in the passage's title, the "Value in Originality":

> Great and precious origination must always be comparatively rare, and can exist only on condition of a wide, massive uniformity. When a multitude of men have learned to use the same language in speech and writing, then and then only can the greatest masters of language arise. For in what does their mastery consist? They use words which are already a familiar medium of

understanding and sympathy in such a way as greatly to enlarge the understanding and sympathy. Originality of this order changes the wild grasses into world-feeding grain. (290)

In the hands of the best writers, Eliot argues, the weariness of language is overcome, making old words new again and using them to cultivate deeper "understanding and sympathy." She demonstrates this herself by reanimating the tired medium of language with her own "original" metaphor: she "changes the wild grasses into world-feeling grain." I have spoken about the pulsations that animate this novel, and this, I think, is one of them: *Middlemarch* moves us between the absolute losses of language and their redemption, between a perception of the weariness of the novel form and its recuperation, and between, too, standstill states of mind and the renewed urgency of metaphorical and idealizing movement.

In his essay "The Narrative Voice," the opening of which I use as one of the epigraphs to this chapter, Blanchot asks what happens when the sentence "the forces of life suffice only up to a certain point" is spoken or written. The answer is that it becomes impossible. Borrowing meaning from language, the sense of the sentence changes. Life is now only *said* to be limited. Blanchot writes:

> The sentence I pronounce tends to draw into the very inside of life the limit that was only supposed to mark it from the outside. Life is said to be limited. The limit does not disappear, but it takes from language the perhaps unlimited meaning that it claims to limit: the meaning of the limit, by affirming it, contradicts the limitation of meaning, or at least displaces it. But because of this, the knowledge of the limit understood as a limitation of meaning risks being lost. So how are we to speak of this limit (say its meaning), without allowing meaning to un-limit it? (379)

Blanchot's question is one that *Middlemarch*, I am arguing, also raises: How are we to portray the weariness of life within a language that always, recuperatively, turns weariness into interest?[62] And in particular, how do we portray the weariness of life within a literary form, the realist novel, that attempts to endow ordinary life, down to the smallest, faintest heartbeat, with representational significance?

Blanchot extends the thought experiment by asking what happens when the same sentence, instead of taken alone, is understood to be the final sentence (the "accomplishment") of a written narrative. What are the further recuperations offered by narrative form? *Middlemarch* could well be Blanchot's imaginary written narrative: "the forces of life suffice only to a certain point" makes for a decent plot summary of the novel. The reader hopes that Dorothea will be able to find an "epos" that will give form to her enthusiasm and transform her vague longing into some great social work. But instead, she marries Will Ladislaw, and her life, the novel's finale tells us, is "absorbed into the life of another" (*M* 836), and her effect on the world is "incalculably diffusive" (*M* 842) at best. The novel concludes by making Dorothea just one of the untold "number" of others who, like her, "lived faithfully a hidden life, and rest in unvisited tombs" (*M* 838). The forces of life, and the forces of commemoration, suffice only to a certain point. *Middlemarch*—a novel about weariness, about ordinariness, about unoriginality, about aging, about failure, about not being special, about life's limited meaning—faces up squarely to the dilemma Blanchot articulates: the question of how to gesture to the fact of a "limited meaning of a limited life" in narrative without erasing or sublimating that limit.

The novel calls Dorothea a modern-day Theresa—that is, a Theresa who cannot achieve anything, a "foundress of nothing, whose loving heart-beats and sobs after an unattained goodness tremble off and are dispersed among hindrances, instead of centering in some long-recognizable deed" (*M* 4). Elisha Cohn argues that Eliot's novel "creates an alliance" with "the ephemeral and the abjected," and lines like this certainly make that case.[63] And yet the fact that the rest of the novel wonders about those trembling heartbeats and sobs, and arguably succeeds in registering them, points to the fact that the novel also creates an alliance with the permanent and the integral. Blanchot's writing on narrative voice helps us to see that the literary act of depicting weariness might unwittingly recuperate it, drawing the "ephemeral and the abjected," Eliot's "loving heart-beats and sobs," into the circle of meaning rather than underscoring a limit.

But this is precisely what Eliot's novel sets out to thematize and to intelligently affirm: the possibility of recuperation and redemption, even in a modern, secular world. In order to do so, it has to make us feel both poles of existential and novelistic possibility: meaninglessness and meaning; abjection and hope; incapacity and enormous, almost limitless, capacity; deadness and aliveness. In testing new vocabularies for novelistic, interpersonal, and psychological recuperation, the novel needs a foil for these possibilities. Just as Casaubon's weariness is the ground against which Dorothea's ardor gains meaning, absolute exhaustion of interest in life is the ground the novel needs to set in order for its alternative to really mean something. The novel needs us to feel with it that weariness, that a sense of inner deadness, has been really felt and considered and apprehended as a possibility for life before it can truly matter that other possibilities have been found. In *Middlemarch*, states of deadness need to feel real and possible in order for the sense of aliveness the novel creates (by way of metaphorical movement, idealization, narrative voice and novel reading itself) to mean as much as it does.

In the remainder of this chapter, I want to draw out some of the tensions in the recuperative possibilities that animate *Middlemarch*—and I want to do so, in part, because I am struck with the ways they seem not only to resonate with British psychoanalysis, but to form some of its baseline premises. In what follows, then, I will discuss these tensions in the form of the oscillations of omniscience that form and frame the narrator as literary figure; the shuttle between projection and introjection that is posited as a basic psychic mechanism by Ludwig Feuerbach, Eliot, and British school psychoanalysts alike; and the animating force of idealization that I argue powers both of these movements. These explorations are shaped by the directives I take Heimann and Joseph to be issuing not simply for analytic technique but also for literary reading: that we read and interpret with an "emotional sensitivity" that is extensive, differentiating, and mobile (Heimann), that we take the novel's narration and the reader's relation to it as "basically living, experiencing, and shifting—as movement" (Joseph),[64] and that we listen to the shifts in narrative voice and to what the novel conveys "alongside and beyond" language. This chapter tries to draw out less-noted aspects of the "total situation" of the *Middlemarch* reading experience. As in all of this book's chapters, I am interested in how novelistic form shapes psychoanalytic theory and our conception of psychic experience. The specific aspect of that phenomenon that I want to explore here is how we internalize some of the enlivening capacities of George Eliot's narrative voice: that is to say, how novels and novelistic narrators work to form our multivocal self-narration and to make it more interesting.

Omniscience: Poor Bulstrode, Proud Mary

One long-celebrated source of the psychic and affective pull of Eliot's narrators is their assuring knowingness. Early in the novel, Dorothea reads a letter from Casaubon to discover his proposal of marriage. Despite the letter's "frigid rhetoric," which the narrator describes as being "as sincere as the bark of a dog or the cawing of an amorous rook" (*M* 50), Dorothea is overcome with emotion. Eliot writes:

> Dorothea trembled while she read this letter; then she fell on her knees, buried her face, and sobbed. She could not pray under the rush of solemn emotion in which thoughts became vague and images floated uncertainly, she could but cast herself, with a childlike sense of reclining in the lap of a divine consciousness which sustained her own. She remained in that attitude until it was time to dress for dinner. (*M* 44)

The curious incompleteness you hear in the passage's key sentence is Eliot's own. Dorothea does not cast herself down, does not cast herself onto the floor or onto a piece of furniture. For this moment, she is not really located in physical space at all, but only in the imaginary space outside the scene described in the final clause of the sentence: Dorothea has "a childlike sense of reclining in the lap of a divine consciousness which sustained her own." The image describes a felt sensation at once material and immaterial: it pictures a child casting herself onto the lap of a mother or father only to dissolve embodiment into "a divine consciousness" which sustains Dorothea's own *consciousness* rather than her body. Dorothea imagines, in other words, two registers of experience at once: being physically held and being held in mind, resting on another's body and resting on another's awareness of her. The novel suggests that even if we can't believe, alongside Dorothea, in a divine consciousness, we can believe in a narrative consciousness, there to sustain Dorothea's consciousness and perhaps to sustain the reader's too, observing, if not with infinite capacity, with seemingly infinite effort and care.[65] We cast ourselves on secular omniscience. We come to feel, as readers of *Middlemarch*, that we are, like characters, observable and potentially narratable, and just knowing this can ease our minds: not only because someone out there might know us, but because we might borrow that structure of omniscience as a way of knowing ourselves.

And yet, as several critics have pointed out, *Middlemarch* is as interested in staging lapses of omniscience as in omniscient narration itself.[66] And not just lapses into total stupidity or unfeelingness—although those possibilities are pictured too—but also, crucially, by staging transitions from omniscience into other modes of perception and feeling. I think of a crucial moment in *Daniel Deronda* (1876) that dramatizes one such deliberate sidestepping of omniscience. Describing the title character's generous interest in others, the narrator suddenly stops short to declare, in an uncharacteristic one-word sentence, that in some circumstances language is not enough: "Enough. In many of our neighbors' lives there is much not only of error and lapse, but of a certain exquisite goodness which can never be written or even spoken—only divined by each of us, according to the inward instruction of his own privacy" (*DD* 175). Eliot posits here something that can be sensed but not described, experienced but not turned into knowledge-text.[67] While *Middlemarch* so often urges us to hear "the report" of the other's "consciousness," it also clears spaces for not reporting, not transcribing, not explicitly knowing or putting into words: "Enough." Continuing to build on Heimann's insights on shifting registers of voice and personality, we might argue that we are so powerfully drawn to Eliot's narrators not because they perform an unfailing omniscience, but precisely because they move in and out of knowing—between, for instance, the impulse to think of characters and ourselves as fully and exhaustibly knowable and the contrasting impulse to regard other minds as essentially unknowable. The narrative voice not only describes but performs this movement, moving between, too, ardor and weariness, deadness and aliveness, and between stagnation in thought and relief at the possibilities of one's own psyche to animate and enrich the world.

And indeed, in Audrey Jaffe's astute analysis, oscillation is precisely what defines novelistic omniscience. This is particularly notable, for Jaffe, in the narrative swing between impersonality and personality. While omniscient narrators are typically contrasted with characters, whose knowledge is necessarily limited, these two types of literary figures are not, Jaffe argues, strictly opposed, but rather mutually constitutive. Omniscience is a "narratorial configuration" that simultaneously "*refuses* character"—constructing itself as "a voice that implies presence and a lack of character to attach it to"—and *requires* characters to define it. Jaffe writes:

> Knowledge appears to us only in opposition to its absence; an effect of unboundedness is created in contrast to one of limitation. Thus when omniscient narration demonstrates the ability to transcend the boundaries that confine characters, it must construct the very boundaries it displays itself transcending. Rather than being a static condition, then, the evidence of an unquestioned authority, omniscience is the inscription of a series of oppositions which mark a difference between describer and objects of description: oppositions between sympathy and irony, involvement and distance, privacy and publicity, character and narrator, self and other—and, most generally, the assertion of narratorial knowledge and its absence in characters.[68]

There are two central points I want to draw from Jaffe's argument. I'll list them here before expanding on each in the paragraphs below. The first is Jaffe's observation that omniscient narration marks off its own "unbounded" knowledge only by pointing out its "limitation" in a character. The second is her insight into the mobility of the narrative voice, and her rich description of its pulsating movements between "sympathy and irony, involvement and distance, privacy and publicity, character and narrator, [and] self and other."

Elaine Freedgood builds on the first point in her essay "The Novelist and Her Poor," which highlights the antiegalitarian structure of nineteenth-century fiction: its omniscience relies upon the enforced stupidity of its characters. In Freedgood's analysis, free indirect discourse works to humiliate as much as to elevate.[69] And, surely, the ever-intelligent "George Eliot" is the nineteenth-century narrator-author who most solidifies our sense that "the thoughts any of us might think and not speak are very often thoughts that are less original, acute, smart, ironic, and knowing than those of a narrator who can invent, narrate, ironize, and refine them."[70]

Nowhere are Jaffe's and Freedgood's claims about the enforced ignorance of characters in comparison to the omniscient narrator clearer than in the case of the banker and religious hypocrite Bulstrode. A man of "subdued tone" and "sickly air" (*M* 92), Bulstrode is a particularly apt target for this kind of narrative takedown precisely because he plays at omnipotence and omniscience himself, both in his attempts to manage the affairs of the town and its people and in his aggressive self-narration, which takes the form of prayer. The word omniscience is used only twice in the novel, and in both instances it concerns Bulstrode: "Omniscience," capital O, names the God to whom Bulstrode prays, and more precisely, the God whom Bulstrode secretly hopes does not quite know his innermost motives (*M* 687, 824). Reflecting, at one remove, on Bulstrode's self-exculpatory prayers as he makes the decision, half-hidden even from himself, to let Raffles die for his own benefit, the narrator remarks: "Does any one suppose that private prayer is necessarily candid—necessarily goes to the roots of action? Private prayer is inaudible speech, and speech is representative: who can represent himself just as he is, even in his own reflections? Bulstrode had not yet unraveled in his thought the confused promptings of the last four-and-twenty hours" (*M* 710). Bulstrode has not unraveled his own motives—but the narrator, of course, has. And, unlike Bulstrode, the narrator can speak from a place of universal truth ("private prayer is inaudible speech, and speech is representative") rather than a place of false self-representation—precisely because the place of *self* here is erased altogether, in the remove separating omniscient narrator from limited character that Jaffe has described. This is dramatically rendered in the grammar of the sentences, which take as their subject nonexistent persons: "Does *any one* suppose?" and "*who* can represent himself?" The narrator reveals, in the form of questions that are really accusations, truths that Bulstrode could never see, truths that his entire personality (and/or his existence as a literary character) is constructed around occluding: that our ways of talking about ourselves will never fully represent us.

Prayer, for Ludwig Feuerbach (1804–72), the German philosopher who was so important to Eliot (and to whom I'll return in the next section), is "the absolute relation of the human heart to itself," a form in which "man speaks undisguisedly of that which weighs upon him."[71] Bulstrode's prayers are, to the contrary, pure disguise—of his past, of his murderous intentions and actions toward the dying alcoholic Raffles, and of worldly motives wrapped up in the language of the next life. Prayer here is nothing but an alibi. Bulstrode's "inaudible speech," then, is not only lapsed prayer, but also bad self-narration and poor self-analysis.[72] Poor Bulstrode indeed.

And yet what the novel gives us to imitate and introject is not only an omniscience that enriches itself by impoverishing character, and not only the aphoristic voice of the passage's universal truths, but also movement itself. If there is any one character who gets to embody this aliveness of mind in the novel, it is Mary Garth, plain and droll, the love interest of Fred, caretaker of her awful dying uncle Featherstone, and daughter of honest, hard-working parents Caleb and Susan Garth—two characters the novel also clearly celebrates and adores. Mary's active mind and sense of humor sparkle through her difficulties: Mary "was fond of her own thoughts, and could amuse herself well" by simply sitting with them in the twilight, "revolving" the scenes of the day (*M* 314). Her thoughts are not prayer, are not petition, are not self-representation—indeed, it is less their content than their movement, their revolutions, that make Mary fond of them. In spite of the ugly scenes she sees playing out between Featherstone and his hopeful heirs, Mary "liked her thoughts: a vigorous young mind not overbalanced by passion, finds a good interest in making acquaintance with life, and watches its own powers with interest" (*M* 315). Watching the powers of the mind with interest: this is perhaps one way we can account for the pleasures of reading the novel and what it can do to us.

Mary notices the greed that motivates the obsequious visitors to Stone Court, but can laugh at their ridiculousness too: at the way they walk about "thinking their own lies opaque while everybody else's were transparent, making themselves exceptions to everything, as if when all the world looked yellow under a lamp they alone were rosy" (*M* 314). Mary's own lamp seems to be uncolored by "yellow" (Eliot's feared cynicism or irreverence) or "rose" (what the passage describes as unmerited "solemnity or pathos"): instead, "Mary had plenty of merriment within" (*M* 314). Mary's enjoyment is most directly a function of her youth, her intelligence, and the fact of her solid education despite her modest upbringing. (Her equally admirable father, Caleb, worships "the indispensable might of that myriad-headed, myriad-handed labour" [*M* 250] as Lydgate worships science—and the narrator in turn worships this healthy reverence of work in both of them.) But it is a function of something else besides: the powers of observation, humor, and metaphor-making that make Mary a stand-in for both the writer Mary Ann Evans/George Eliot and the narrator too.

Earlier, the novel praises Mary Garth's ability to move from a serious admonition of her would-be fiancé Fred to a joke in the space of a short conversation. She begins with a heartfelt reproach to Fred for his failure to find a vocation: "How can you bear to be so contemptible, when others are working and striving, and there are so many things to be done—how can you bear to be fit for nothing in the world that is useful?" (*M* 255). Her remarks are forceful because she loves Fred, and because they express one of the novel's own heartfelt moral imperatives: work—do good work—although it will be a given that what constitutes good work will be hard to define. In Fred's case, and arguably in Dorothea's and Will Ladislaw's too, *Middlemarch* mockingly describes the perils of class (and racial) privilege.[73] But when Mary's lecture continues by picturing Fred "learning a tune on a flute" rather than doing anything worthwhile, she can't help but smile: "Mary's lips had begun to curl with a smile as soon as she had asked that question about Fred's future (young souls are mobile), and before she ended, her face had its full illumination of fun" (*M* 255). If Mary gets to speak one of the narrator's lessons about being useful in the world, the quick parenthetical praise points to a quality of Mary's that the narrative voice aspires to embody as well: to have a "mobile" voice and view (and face). Mobility is what enlivens thought and feeling, preventing the world from coming to a dead "stand-still." And it, in the form of mobile projections of value and appreciation and worth, is what makes faith and loving possible too, as I'll address in the next sections on idealization in religion (Feuerbach), in romance (Eliot), and in the transferential structures of psychoanalysis and novelistic narration.

Secularism and Psychoanalysis

Both the prelude and finale of *Middlemarch* emphasize the novel's place in a modern context in which "the medium" that shaped the "ardent deeds" of Saint Theresa and Antigone is "for ever gone" (*M* 838)—that is to say, in a secular context in which the familiar religious orders will not provide life with its shape and meaning. It will not furnish life with what Jacques Derrida calls an "alibi": an excuse or defense that would defer life's meaning to another time, another place, another register, and that would make it possible to say: life may be limited here, but it is unlimited elsewhere; life's meaning may not be immanent, but it can be located in transcendence.[74] Understood as a religious emotion, earthbound weariness is redeemed in heavenly rest; but, understood as a secular emotion, what weariness renders is the fact that life simply wears itself out, and wears us out along the way—as in the prelude's description of the weary lapse from the epic to the everyday, and from religious ecstasy to ordinary sexual and reproductive desire.

And yet the tension the novel enacts between secularism and faith is far more dynamic than settled. The novel concludes by thanking "the number who lived *faithfully* a hidden life" (*M* 838, emphasis added)—pointing to the difficulty, assuredly quite marked for the former Evangelical Mary Ann Evans and for many in her generation and intellectual milieu, of thinking and living without religious guarantees to fall back upon. Indeed, Nancy Henry argues that Eliot was particularly preoccupied with the question of a secular afterlife in the years during which she wrote *Middlemarch*. Her 1867 poem "O May I Join the Choir Invisible" articulates one possibility in the same "diffusion" of good deeds that shapes the conclusion of *Middlemarch*. "May I," asks the poetic speaker:

> Be the sweet presence of a good diffused,
> And in diffusion ever more intense,
> So shall I join the choir invisible
> Whose music is the gladness of the world
>
> (LINES 40–44)

The poem, like *Middlemarch*, offers the possibility of "living on in others through the influence we have on their lives,"[75] contributing to the overall "gladness of the world" or, in *Middlemarch*, to the more modest fact "that things are not so ill with you and me as they might have been" (*M* 838). The poem and the novel alike set the possibility for a secular afterlife in religious terms (living "faithfully," joining a heavenly choir), but hope to significantly alter their valences. In *Middlemarch*, there is gravity and there is grace. But that grace is of a very human kind: it is the heart pushing back against universal pressure.

In *The Essence of Christianity* (1841), Ludwig Feuerbach argues that religion is nothing other than human feeling projected onto a divine object: "The divine nature which is discerned by feeling is in truth nothing else than feeling enraptured, in ecstasy with itself—feeling intoxicated with joy, blissful in its own plenitude."[76] George Eliot became the first English translator of Feuerbach's text in 1853, and it impressed her deeply.[77] For Feuerbach, divinity is essentially human, a projection of human nature and its basic capacities onto an external object that is only then exalted. "God is [nothing more than] the manifested inward nature" of man, and religion nothing more than "the revelation of [man's] intimate thoughts, the open confession of his love-secrets."[78] Focusing throughout this work on feeling as the most salient example of the-human-as-the-divine, Feuerbach describes the strange play of immanence and transcendence that makes up our lived experience of the capacity to feel: "Feeling is thy own inward power, but at the same time a power distinct from thee, and independent of thee; it is in thee, above thee; it is itself that which constitutes the objective in thee—thy own being which impresses thee as another being; in short, thy God."[79] Our capacity to feel is so powerful that we cannot believe it is ours alone. This is what makes feeling, for Feuerbach, one definition of the essence of religion. Feeling stands in for all that we are capable of: "It is the same with every other power, faculty, potentiality, reality, activity—the name is indifferent."[80] Religion gives us a chance to experience and make salient the capacities within us that are so striking that they do not quite feel like our own.

Feuerbach's insistence that "the antithesis of divine and human is altogether illusory" highlights an interplay between projection and internalization that also animates much of object relations thought. In his 1995 essay "What Is This Thing Called Self?" Christopher Bollas identifies a similar dynamic driving psychoanalytic inquiry. Concerned with questions surrounding sense of self, or what he calls "being a character," Bollas argues that self is best described as "an aesthetic intelligence," the unfolding of a personal "idiom of being" that is an inborn style of engaging with oneself, with others, and with the world.[81] Bollas's "idiom" feels as strangely located as Feuerbach's description of feeling— "in thee" and "above thee" at the same time. Bollas writes: "The feel of an inner logic, the movement of desire, the dissemination of interests, do yield a feeling that one is invested by an intelligence that guides one through existence."[82] Our idiom feels in us and above us at the same time. Interestingly, Bollas turns precisely to the history of religion and of religious feeling, and the projective/introjective dynamic that Feuerbach argues comprises it, as an explanatory analogy:

> We may see how intelligent an act of projective nomination it was to believe from inner experience that some kind of deity was looking over us. The notion of a God living within each of us is, strangely, an unconscious return of the projection: God as that organizing intelligence that informs our existence and leaves us with a sense of there being something that transcends and yet looks after us. Sometimes the self feels like a kind of transcendental presence, an authorizing agency, greater than the sum of those self experiences which we can know in life but unknowable as a thing-in-itself.[83]

For Bollas, the thing we are used to calling God is exactly the thing called self; the organizing intelligence we are accustomed to calling divine is the very definition of what makes us humans and that makes us who we are. The sense of something "that transcends us and yet looks after us"—what Bollas calls idiom— might even be something like the "report of [one's] own consciousness" Eliot describes in *Middlemarch*. It arguably feels similarly: inside and outside, emanating from within but spoken in the voice of another—a voice, perhaps, learned by reading Eliot's novels and internalizing her own narrative voice.

Bollas goes on to collapse the distinction, like Feuerbach before him, between "God" and the "self" by arguing that they are both merely placeholders, words whose function it is to mark off sites of mystery and interrogation:

> These days in psychoanalysis we perplex ourselves with the question of the self, but in a certain sense this word suits our secular profession and its patients because it is a personal way of objectifying the unknown. When we ask: What is the self? we interrogate the meaningful unknown.... In previous centuries, the signifier occupying the place of the self was very likely the word "God," serving our need to objectify the place of the meaningful unknown; the Protestant concept of the God who lives inside us all served

as a bridge to the concept of the self, something that lives in us and yet seemingly transcends us.[84]

I think that George Eliot's novels are also important bridges in the historical shift Bollas identifies between God and the self as signifiers of the "meaningful unknown," between religion and the "secular profession" of psychoanalysis.[85] *Middlemarch* in particular, the home of so many of Eliot's most famous sympathetic appeals, is an important part of that intellectual history, contributing to a notion of self at once urgently demanding examination and just out of reach—something to "wonder" about, to feel, but to never fully know, an "object which [will] never justify weariness" (*M* 3).

Like the pulse of omniscient narration as Jaffe describes it, the sense of self for Bollas is something that comes into focus and fades, obtrudes and recedes; is something that can be sensed but never fully represented: quoting Jaffe again, something located "not in presence or absence, but in the tension between the two."[86] This insight helps to flesh out what recent critics, using a variety of different names, have pointed to as an important underside of Eliot's fiction: "vagueness" in Daniel Wright's phrase, "nescience" in Elisha Cohn's, "disquiet" in David Kurnick's, the "unnarratable" in D. A. Miller's.[87] Eliot's voice is less knowing than we have believed, but perhaps all the more appealing in the ways it gets us to "wonder" rather than to know, affording us both objects to put in the place of a meaningful unknown and an idiom in which to question them. Wearying from all-knowingness, the novel works to create sites of productive unknowing without lapsing into unregulated, or unbelievable, mysticism. And it tests the possibilities of unknowing in sites that constantly want to suppose knowledge, recuperate loss, find redemption, create meaning, erase limits, provide alibis, and install omniscience: novels yes, narrative yes, prayer yes, and psyches too. *Middlemarch* helps to construct, in and through novelistic form, the kind of subjectivity object relations psychoanalysis will later explore precisely as "idiom."

Idealization

Middlemarch is a romance. Part of what this means is that the novel wants to press on the way that we use others both as sites of the "meaningful unknown" and to instill a sense of self within us. One of the novel's weariest episodes is experienced by its most ardent character: midway through the novel, Dorothea, worn out by the "perpetual effort demanded by her marriage" to Casaubon (*M* 475), and slowly realizing there may not be a way to keep Will Ladislaw in her life without seriously displeasing her husband, who jealously senses flirtation and affection between them, is scared to find the whole world feeling dull and meaningless. She looks for consolation in her favorite books, but opens "one after another" only to find that she "could read none of them":

> Everything seemed dreary: . . . devout epigrams—the sacred chime of favourite hymns—all alike were as flat as tunes beaten on wood: even the spring flowers and the grass had a dull shiver in them under the afternoon clouds that had the sun fitfully: even the sustaining thoughts which had become habits seemed to have in them the weariness of long future days in which she would still live with them for her sole companions. (*M* 475)

Dorothea longs for "a fuller sort of companionship," and yet "the thing that she liked, that she spontaneously cared for, seemed to be always excluded from her life" (*M* 475). The "thing" that she "liked," this thing that is animating her, is Will Ladislaw, both in her as-yet not fully realized love for him, and the cause that he provides: Dorothea wishes to right the past injustice that disinherited Will and his parents, keeping them from the family property and wealth that Casaubon now holds. The passage makes it clear that, for Dorothea, the animation of being with Will—the liveliness of their conversations, their pleasure in each other's company, their physical attraction to each other—is linked to a larger animation of life, both of which feel temporarily drained on this gray day:

> This afternoon [Dorothea's] helplessness was more wretchedly benumbing than ever: she longed for objects who could be dear to her, and to whom she could be dear. She longed for work which would be directly beneficent like the sunshine and the rain, and now it appeared that she was to live more in a virtual tomb, where there was the apparatus of ghastly labour producing what would never see the light. To-day she had stood at the door of the tomb and seen Will Ladislaw receding into the distant world of warm activity and fellowship—turning his face towards her as he went. (*M* 475)

Following this bleak vision, in which Will's Orpheus leaves Dorothea's Eurydice behind in the underworld, forever missing warmth and "activity," the passage incorporates two of the novel's shortest sentences. Their rhythms and repetition bang out, as if on a wooden drum, the flatness Dorothea feels: "Books were of no use. Thinking was of no use. . . . There was no refuge from spiritual emptiness and discontent, and Dorothea had to bear her bad mood, as she would have borne a headache" (*M* 475). These are surely horrors for George Eliot: that thinking is of no use to make the world feel alive, that *books* are of no use to make the world feel alive—and headaches.[88] The novel links three things together in Dorothea's stand-still state of mind: the lack of a love object; an inability to do good, world-changing work; and "spiritual emptiness and discontent." On the one hand, this may be the Victorian novel's chief mystification: making romance the category of experience through which all other intentions and ambitions will rise or fall. On the other hand, perhaps this isn't a mystification at all, but rather an acknowledgment of just how much we need someone to admire, and someone who admires us in turn, in order to maintain our faith in the world and its objects and endeavors. In the romance between Dorothea and Will, *Middlemarch* wants us to understand how much belief in another person "changes the lights for us" (*M* 762).[89] This is the force of idealization as it is played out in the secular, sexual, and distinctly marital context of *Middlemarch*.

We come to find out that Dorothea's darkest moment is not when she learns the truth about Casaubon, nor is it this "dreary" afternoon when she thinks she is losing Will because Casaubon has forbidden her to see him. It is instead the moment later in the novel when she loses faith in Will, and therefore loses faith in much else besides. (And in the novel, to be abandoned by or lose faith in someone while that person remains in close proximity is a worse nightmare than any other kind of loss: it is the horror of a bad marriage.) After seeing Will and Rosamond together, and imagining they are having an affair, Dorothea's entire picture of Will changes. Indeed, "there were two images" of him at once. The first is in the form of the man she loved and idealized: "Here, with the nearness of an answering smile, here within the vibrating bond of mutual speech, was the bright creature whom she had trusted—who had come to her like the spirit of morning visiting the dim vault where she sat the bride of a worn-out life" (*M* 786). The second is in the form of someone who has deluded her: "And there, aloof, yet persistently with her, moving wherever she moved, was the Will Ladislaw who was a changed belief exhausted of hope, a detected illusion," a man who has "brought his cheap regard" and "lip-born words to her who had nothing paltry to give in exchange" (*M* 786–87). More than someone who has deluded or disappointed her, he is someone who is exhausted belief incarnate, "detected illusion" itself. Everything that Dorothea has been sending to him, her belief and her hope, her thoughts and her feelings, her narrations and self-narrations, have been sent to someone who didn't exist, at least not in the form she had believed in. She imagined Will as someone who could understand and love her, but she was sending all of these things—her very subjectivity directed toward him—it turns out, to no one.

This is perhaps the ultimate form of weariness—novelistic, theological, psychic—in *Middlemarch*: the intimation that for all we want to send an account of our experience out into the world, we know that there is no one there to receive it. Whomever we might imagine in the place of a recipient—an omniscient God, a novelistic narrator, an analyst, a husband, a wife, a lover—is placed there by way of fantasy, projection, idealization: by way of wish or alibi. Subjectivity, in the conceptualization of *Middlemarch* and psychoanalysis, becomes a form of address—something to send out, something directed toward the understanding, if not mercy or intervention, of another: subjectivity is a letter or a prayer. And yet both discourses also suggest, through their interrogations of idealization and related transferential operations, that this understanding of subjectivity is, in fact, a fantasy. There may be no one to collect our experience for us, to hold it and to gather it together, except for ourselves, and even then, only imperfectly.

Feuerbach's *The Essence of Christianity* makes an argument akin to this one: prayer never arrives at its destination because there is no destination at which to arrive. Since God is in a sense an idealization, a projection of human nature and what is best in it, our prayers have nowhere to go: they are simply "feeling speaking to feeling." And so, taken in reverse perspective, we could also say that, for Feuerbach, prayer *always* arrives at its destination: it keeps us in the medium of feeling. Feuerbach writes: "Only a trusting, open, hearty, fervent prayer is said to help; but this help lies in the prayer itself. As everywhere in religion the subjective, the secondary, the conditionating, is the *prima causa*, the objective fact; so here, these subjective qualities are the objective nature of the prayer itself."[90] What is remarkable and moving about Feuerbach's thinking is that he makes the idea of forgone transcendence a cause for celebration rather than for misery, a site of richness rather than poverty. The prayer is its own help, the "human soul, giving ear to itself."[91] What man praises in God is the extraordinariness of his own capacities—and, especially, the extraordinary capacity of his own feeling. Feuerbach's writing, in Eliot's translation, is as expansive as the feelings he describes, marveling at man's emotional range and flexibility. And this includes too the capacity for projection. What we feel is so immense that we can't help but think it must in some sense be transcendent: but it is in us. What we experience is so intense that surely there must be someone else to help us register and contain it: but that person is only there because we imagine them to be. While for Derrida, this slide of attribution is a cause for lament (we cannot seem to think without installing transcendental authority somewhere), for Feuerbach, it is a cause for celebration.

And it may be a cause for celebration in *Middlemarch* as well. Dorothea's decision to marry Casaubon is clearly based on a mistaken idealization. Dorothea's early outsized comparisons make this abundantly clear: "here was living Bossuet, whose work would reconcile complete knowledge with devoted piety; here was a modern Augustine who united the glories of the doctor and saint" (*M* 25). The comparison is laughable: Causabon is not Augustine or Bossuet but Concrete words and Cawing rooks. And yet what makes her subsequent reflections so striking is that that they so precisely confuse her own capacities for his: " 'He thinks with me,' said Dorothea to herself, 'or rather, he thinks a whole world of which my thought but a poor two-penny mirror. And his feelings too, his whole experience—what a lake compared to my little pool!' " (*M* 25).

Dorothea is, of course, sorely mistaken—hers is the whole wide world of thought and feeling and experience, his the painfully narrow one. The form of the revelation makes this clear: "said Dorothea to herself." Without knowing it, it is her own capacity to think and feel that she is admiring. She is the one with the imaginative capacity to make the world large, to conjure up the vastness of thought and feeling she then attributes to Casaubon. The narrator's ensuing speculation on interpretation and its expansive possibilities ensure that understanding. In extrapolating so much from the little she knows about Casaubon,

> Miss Brooke argued from words to dispositions not less unhesitatingly than other young ladies of her age. Signs are small measurable things, but interpretations are illimitable, and in girls of sweet, ardent nature, every sign is apt to conjure up wonder, hope, belief, vast as a sky, and coloured by a diffused thimbleful of matter in the shape of knowledge. (*M* 25)

Surely, one aspect of the affective labor of this passage is to despair: Casaubon is not who Dorothea thinks he is; she is going to be disappointed; she is misreading her way into a loveless, sexless, childless, and confining marriage. "Signs are small measurable things," and perhaps people are too. But the other function of the passage is to lead us to marvel: at the capacities of "wonder, hope, and belief" to make signs and lovers "illimitable" and to color an entire sky with a few drops of dye. Dorothea has a hard lesson to learn about idealization in and through her marriage to Casaubon. But I am trying to make clear that the novel hardly speaks against idealization in and of itself. The novel does something far more complicated: it points to the necessity of idealization as a force that animates meaning-making and that animates life. Without idealization, no romance, and no love. Without idealization, no good work. Without idealization (in a lesson Eliot draws from Feuerbach), no faith, no religious feeling. And finally, without idealization, no "psychic change" (to recall Betty Joseph's phrase): novel reading and analysis alike effect psychic change through transferential relations, which invest narrator and analyst, respectively, with an imaginary power—to make meaning, yes, but also to keep meaning moving.[92]

There may be no one to send your subjectivity toward. And yet we imagine that there is, and continue sending out our subjectivity—praying, self-narrating, idealizing, dreaming up "objects that never justify weariness," going to therapy, making metaphors—even when we know this to be the case. This phenomenon is what fascinates Feuerbach, and what fascinates the writer of *Middlemarch* as well: our insistence on constructing more-knowing objects and directing narrations of our own lives and experiences toward them. It is what makes us feel alive, and what makes novel reading feel alive as well. *Middlemarch* cannot make this happen without the equipment of romance, nor without the equipment of omniscient narration. But it moves us in and out of each, getting us to feel both their driving pull and the calamity of their loss, which enervates, deadens, and drains of wonder. If the novel shows us how belief in a love object can "change the lights for us," it also shows how monumentally darkening it can be to lose someone in whom we have believed, even if we lose that person in thought alone. And it gives us a new kind of narrator, just as British psychoanalysis gives us, in its reconceptualization of transference/countertransference dynamics and the mechanisms of psychic change, a new kind of therapist. *Middlemarch* gives us a narrator that is more movement than concrete sayings, more object relation than subject.

Dorothea ultimately learns that she can let herself hold on to the first image of Will: his feelings for her are real, he is an object in which she can invest her hopes and beliefs. In the love scene in which they come together, Dorothea talks about how shaken she was when she doubted him: almost nothing could have challenged her feelings for him, "but thinking you were different—not so good as I believed you to be" (*M* 808). Will responds by acknowledging and accepting her idealization—and his own dependence on it:

> "You are sure to believe me better than I am in everything but one," said Will, giving way to his feeling in the evidence of hers. "I mean, in my truth to you. When I thought you doubted of that, I didn't care about anything that was left. I thought it was all over with me, and there was nothing to try for—only things to endure." (*M* 809)

Life without Dorothea's belief in him to animate it was, for Will, pure weariness: a world in which there is nothing left to try for, "only things to endure." The narrator had questioned whether there was any "good work or fine feeling" in Casaubon—those things do reside in Will, in part through Dorothea's own projection, her own emotional labor, and the fantasy/reality the two together co-create. What Will and Dorothea offer each other—what marriage (less than as institution than as a relation) can sometimes do—is to hold up an image of the other person in mind that does in fact help to keep that person feeling alive. What does the novel, according to *Middlemarch*, offer to do? To hold experience, primarily, but even more pressingly, to animate it. I want to repeat that *Middlemarch* pictures gravity and man-made grace: the heart pushing against pressure, the mobility of young (and middle-aged, and narrative) souls, of exchanging metaphors, and narrating together in order to feel alive.

I want to close with a final small point: the suggestion that using the psychoanalytic terminology of aliveness and deadness may also be useful to literary interpretation in another way. This vocabulary and way of thinking may help us to see what can and can't be animated in Victorian novels and in critical responses to them, marking off areas over which idealization and metaphor can range and those that are rendered off-limits. It can help us register what we have cared to bring alive in the book, and what remains to be animated. I'll end the chapter with a preliminary list. Alive in *Middlemarch*: subjectivity, interpersonal relations, romance, the finding of vocation, the gradual cooling of ardor, reform, class privilege and its discontents, longing, coded sexuality, the very real yearning for maternity, "brown patches" when they are white girls, the "bloom" and fade of youth (*M* 93), aging, "extravagance" and "lapse." Dead in *Middlemarch* (and here I list things mentioned in the novel but not fully energized there—nor, I think, in the novel's criticism): agitation, machine-breaking, rick-burning, looms, Dissent, revolution, communal living, "Negro Emancipation" (*M* 459), colonial spaces, the "migrations of races," and the "clearing of forests" (*M* 214).[93] Also alive in *Middlemarch*, and alive precisely because the narrative voice expends an enormous amount of energy making them so: broken insect wings, "candlelight tinsel and daylight rubbish" (*M* 539), and weariness.

Coda

IN "THE ABSENT OBJECT" (1964), Edna O'Shaughnessy makes a stunning claim: that "absence is a natural and essential condition of a relationship."[1] What a relationship *means*, what distinguishes it from "a simple association" or a fantastic state of merger, is that it "spans presence and absence."[2] A relationship is sustained even when the object is not physically present. I cried when I first read this essay, not long before finishing manuscript revisions on this book. I have read a great deal of psychoanalytic theory over the last fifteen years, but it took these sentences to make me understand just how fundamentally object relations psychoanalysis resignifies presence and absence. It makes presence more complex and multiple, a dappled light, and it makes absence a condition of possibility rather than one of loss or absolute limitation, a "piercing shaft of darkness."[3]

O'Shaughnessy's essay explicates, simply and movingly, foundational object relations thought on absence: Klein's identification of the powerful impulse in us to turn the absent object into a bad object—a neglecting one, a destructive one, a nonsustaining one—and Bion's revisionary response that makes absence inaugurate the very processes of thought. But I am most interested in O'Shaughnessy's own spin, which focuses on "how the absent object can cease to be a bad object." She argues that this is "a most intricate and slow process"—a painstaking cognitive and emotional labor that involves a desire for separation ("a child always, in part, wants even to be weaned," she writes); a lessening need for "a bad absent object" so that "the object can be allowed to keep its good qualities when away" and "can be trusted to return when needed"; growing "concern for the object in its own right," so that it can be given "freedom for a life of its own" or simply "allowed to rest"; and finally a recognition that periods of absence are needed to have true closeness.[4] The essay made me understand, on the level of feeling, something I had imagined I understood all along. We can believe in relationality precisely because we can trust in absence: we can trust that we continue to be in relationship to our objects even when they are not there, even when they are gone, even when they are "only" internal objects.

What this means for lived experience is that we can think of relationships as having far longer lives than we may have previously supposed: relationships last beyond separation, beyond prolonged absence, and beyond even death—so that we can say our relationships with lost loved ones go on sounding and shaping us and evolving, like ever-vibrating piano strings, even when those people are long gone from the physical world.[5] What this means for novel reading is that we can believe in the power of our relationships to literary figures of various kinds (characters, narrators, authors, and readers), allowing their and our own fictionality to be productive and enriching rather than somehow disqualifying. What this means for psychoanalytic theory is a new conception of absence: one that is not predicated on absolute loss, and that, consequently, suggests the possibility of developing a model of psychic formation that does not rely so exclusively on mourning and melancholia. What this means for literary studies is an interruption of traditional notions of historicity and a more porous sense of geographic and disciplinary boundaries, such that we can start to build wider relational networks between our fields and our objects of study, and learn to think and write using a wider range of knowledges and methodological approaches.[6]

Object relations thought is studded with alternative pictures of loss, mourning, and absence. Describing how the child gradually stops using her transitional object, Winnicott writes that "its fate is to be gradually allowed to be decathected." The object is not internalized, and the child's feelings about it do not get repressed; "it is not forgotten and it is not mourned." It is simply allowed to fade, relegated to an affectionate "limbo" from which it and its original meaning can certainly return, if the child needs it to—although most often we simply don't.[7] Balint describes "a kind of regret or mourning" that comes along with the basic fault, the "unalterable fact of a defect or default in oneself" that has "cast its shadow over one's whole life." The basic fault may heal off, but it will leave a scar, evidence that the "unfortunate effects" of early failures of the first object and the environment can "never fully be made good," that "the basic fault cannot be removed, resolved, or undone." And yet this regret also brings it with it a recognition that has significant actuality and beauty to it: healing the fault into a "simple, painless scar" means "giving up for good the hope of attaining a faultless ideal of oneself" (*BF* 183). What Balint calls regret we might describe, in another key, as a profound and useful inauguration into reality.

These small moments pull focus because they catch the light, like faceted crystals, of the revisionary understanding of presence and absence that defines object relations thought. They give psychoanalysis a language for loss beyond mourning and melancholia. A great deal of important work in cultural and literary theory has centered, building from Freud, on grief and grieving as constitutive of the subject. Foundational texts like Judith Butler's *Gender Trouble* and Anne Cheng's *Melancholy of Race* use psychoanalytic mourning to theorize aspects of identity structured on socially constructed exclusions and oppressions.[8] In a similar vein, Paul Gilroy's *Postcolonial Melancholia* addresses the "social pathology of neoimperialist politics" as one of failed mourning. Postcolonial melancholia makes it difficult for the British social body to acknowledge "the pains and gains" of its past "imperial adventures" and their continuation in "lingering but usually unspoken colonial relationships and imperialist fantasies." Its nationalist and anti-immigrant manifestations refuse to recognize migration as a logical consequence of colonial history: that "the immigrant is here because Britain, Europe, was once out there."[9] All three of these writers have given us invaluable and productive theories of psychic and social life. And yet I wonder what happens when we shift lenses from mourning and melancholia. I wonder if considering the ongoing, rather than ghostly, lives of foreclosed aspects of identity changes the lights for us, allowing us to think in terms more multiple and less binaristic (Butler's m/f or normative/transgressive, Cheng's white American/racialized other, Gilroy's citizen/immigrant). I wonder, too, if it might enable new critical practices, closer in spirit to what José Esteban Muñoz is able to yield in his disidentificatory reading: innovations of thought and method that also produce renovations of feeling, toward both our literary objects and the writing we produce around them.[10]

In "A Theory of Resonance," Wai Chee Dimock has called for her own method of relational reading that re-evokes *The Mill on the Floss* in its emphasis on vibration and reverberation. Dimock argues that the term "resonance," "modeled on the traveling frequencies of sound," usefully describes the diachronic dimensions of literary history, or the "traveling frequencies of literary texts." These frequencies, she writes, are "received and amplified across time, . . . causing unexpected vibrations in unexpected places."[11] The text changes in its new context: how it sounds shifts in relation to new ears and new listening. The "literary," then, "is not an attribute resident in a text, but a relation, a form of engagement, between a changing object and a changing recipient, between a tonal presence and the way it is differently heard over time."[12] Here, as in O'Shaughnessy's definition of relationship, absence is definitive. As Dimock explains, time is both "a medium of unrecoverable meaning" and "a medium of possibly new meaning."[13] Relationality is what reframes temporality. It is not simply that the loss of meaning precedes its recovery, or is redeemed in it. More radically, both "unrecoverable" and "possibly new" meaning permanently coexist, in the layers of loss and novelty, of presence and absence, that make up both psyches and texts.

This permanent coexistence of presence and absence (not a fort/da, and not an act of mourning) is the true meaning of psychoanalytic redescription: the need not simply to return to an experience over and over again, but to create it anew, again and again, in your own voice and in the voice of your analyst. And it is the meaning of literary criticism, which is itself a kind of redescription that makes and remakes novels, sounding and resounding them in new contexts and with new interlocutors. It may also help us picture aspects of twenty-first-century identity that seem to require this more complex thinking of relationship: Modern conditions of having multiple racial, ethnic, or cultural identities, and sometimes feeling an imperfect affinity with any single one of them. Of exile, estrangement, and dislocation, such as when one has never seen or been to one's homeland, or when that homeland has been so decimated by war or climate-change-induced natural disaster or poverty that it is no longer recognizable. Of "colonial cacophony," when competing settler colonial oppressions and claims to social justice create feedback and static in addition to song.[14] Of transnationality, mass migration, and globalization rather than cartographies of national borders and center/periphery organizations and hierarchies.[15] And the condition, too, of having to grapple with ancestries that span colonizer and colonized, Indigeneity and indenture and invasion, and resistance and complicity alike.[16]

In one of the most beautiful essays on internal objects I have read, Adela Pinch argues that Victorian readers' adoration for the deceased poet Percy Bysshe Shelley predicted a "modern version of love": one in which "love or attachment" is enacted "as a highly mobile, manipulable and manipulated relation to a vague, shifting object that is understood, in essence, to be an internal object." Pinch describes how the poet appeared to Victorian and modern Shelley lovers in his afterlife, in séances or simply in their thoughts, as a "diaphanous, porous, abstracted" shape—a "shape all light," in one of his own phrases. This "vague" and "shifting" shape prefigures, for Pinch, internal objects as they were theorized in the twentieth century.[17] But those abstract concepts become stand-ins too: for authors, who are themselves, at least to the readers who love them and develop imaginary relationships with them, insubstantial, internalized, and adored. Pinch writes: "Authors are not-really-persons who move within us, objects of love that stand for, and make sense of, obscure parts of our inner lives. Author love lets us live."[18] It is a stunning insight, and one that we, as literary critics, would do well to let ourselves believe. I would add that if author love lets us live, it lets authors do so too, living on in us, inhabiting our minds in ways that are not simply imaginary and do not make them infinitely manipulable, but are rather predicated on a real and durable relationship, and on real words.

I like Shelley-Pinch's uneven light as a representation of the multilayeredness and unevenness of presence: not a presence that steadily shines, nor one that flickers, but one that modulates, that shifts, that layers different depths of shadow, like sunlight falling on a forest floor or reflected at the bottom of a watery well.[19] And I like Freud-Bion's "piercing shaft of darkness" as a picture of the possibilities of absence. In a letter to Lou Andreas-Salomé, Freud wrote, "I know that in writing I have to blind myself artificially in order to focus all the light on one dark spot, renouncing cohesion, harmony, [and] rhetoric."[20] Bion's interpretation of this remark is typically strange and fascinating: he imagines a "piercing shaft of darkness" that "can be directed on the dark features of the analytic situation" (*A&I* 57). For Freud, eyes that block out peripheral sights can better focus, and eyes adjusted to darkness begin to distinguish gray shapes in the dark. But for Bion, darkness itself forms a beam, a place where the *absence* of knowledge and, in its place, blind faith (F) can illuminate matters that are, after all, beyond the realm of the sensible—such as the feeling of two minds meeting, when the space between them becomes thick and charged, like walking in the dark when you think there might be an object in front of you.

The object relations intuition of a more complex layering of presence and absence (and of more complex visions of presence and absence themselves) is, as I hope I have been able to show, what Victorian novels are able to produce as experience. Reading *Tess of the D'Urbervilles*, we feel gender to be mobile and "internally varied"—sometimes salient and pressing, and sometimes porous and insubstantial, and we feel ourselves able to move in and out of fictionality as well, sometimes present to ourselves, sometimes as self-absent as Tess. Reading *The Mill on the Floss*, we understand that it is not just author love, but also character love, that lets us live, even despite the false stops of plot and authorial blind spots. This is a novel that truly lives in its relation to new readers, who reshape the novel so that it has something to give them even as they give of themselves back to it for the sake of future readers. Reading *The Return of the Native*, we understand that it is not only the earliest object relations that remain embedded in the psyche, but also colonial relations that remain embedded in the novel. Even after attempts to relegate them to the black hole of oblivion, there they still are, insisting on real geographies that resist imperial forgetting, and that exceed psychic manipulations. Reading *Middlemarch*, we move in and out of states of belief, in and out of states of being in love (with objects of love that, as in Pinch's description, figure and stand in for both the most radiant and the most obscure parts of ourselves), and in and out of metaphorical language that makes us see things as always and essentially there and not there, themselves and more than themselves (like Dorothea's gems that are both glittering stones and liquid pools of light).[21] Relational reading as I have framed it depends on both the reality and fictionality of internal objects, and on the countless shades of presence and absence that structure our psychic and our literary experiences.

In this book, I have tried to show how much Victorian fiction and British psychoanalysis together have to teach us about relationality. But in keeping with the spirit of the book, and in keeping methodological faith with its ideas, I want to keep inviting new connections and new links and new futures. Finishing this book, I have realized that there is one story that presses particularly strongly to be told alongside this one: the story of the almost parallel development in the mid-twentieth century of another strand of relational thought in the colonies, where anticolonial thinkers like Frantz Fanon, Édouard Glissant, and C. L. R. James were writing theories of skin as well as psyche, of the politics and poetics of relation alike.[22] I hope that someone will write that expanded history—thinking about shared as well as competing insights, thinking about nineteenth-century British literature and its various legacies in colonial and postcolonial education in England and across the globe, thinking across archival ruptures, thinking about which aspects of history are allowed to come alive in mainstream Victorian studies and which are not, and pushing toward a more fully postcolonial psychoanalysis—whether that person is me or someone else. And I hope, more broadly, that we can encourage faith (F) in relationality in the field of Victorian studies. A faith that opens the field up to new methods and ideas, and that extends, in fact, into a new and newly expansive "we."

NOTES

Introduction

1. *A&I* 117.

2. There are of course many exceptions to this universalizing claim—and I should add that, in using this sweeping writing style, I am borrowing from both the Victorian novelists I study (as in George Eliot's famous pronouncement from *Middlemarch*, "we all of us, grave or light, get our thoughts entangled in metaphors, and act fatally on the strength of them" [8]) and the British object relations psychoanalysts I engage, whose very project is to make universalizing claims about the psyche (as in D. W. Winnicott's statement, which I love, that he does need to give many case examples of children at play with transitional objects, because "for anyone in touch with parents and children, there is an infinite quantity and variety of illustrative clinical material," and "illustrations are merely given to remind readers of similar material in their own experience" ["Transitional Objects," 8]). In using Eliot's "we" myself, I am trying to point to both its utility and its limitations. The universalizing truth claims of Victorian literature and British psychoanalysis do at times have something to offer, and, as readers, we can be well served not to reject them out of hand. On the other hand, this project aims to point out the forceful and violent exclusions of the "we" in both of these discourses, which construct in particular a white, British, middle-class reader as supposedly neutral universal subject only by excluding colonial subjects and people of color. And so, in revisiting the powerful and exclusionary "we" of both mid-nineteenth-century British novels and mid-twentieth-century British psychoanalysis, my aim is to both describe and expand it: *Novel Relations* constructs a different "we"—the more inclusive and future-oriented readership this book turns to and calls into being.

3. I am thinking, for instance, of works as diverse as D. A. Miller's *The Novel and the Police*, Eve Kosofsky Sedgwick's *Between Men*, Edward Said's *Culture and Imperialism*, and more recently Caroline Levine's *Forms: Whole, Rhythm, Hierarchy, Network*.

4. Invoking a current unspoken critical consensus in Victorian studies, I want to both speak its biases out loud and push against them where I can. I am inspired by recent calls to action in Victorian studies that comment on the exclusions and shortcomings of the field and advocate for revisionary practices, including for instance Manu Samriti Chander's "'Oh My God, I Think America's Racist,'" and Ronjaunee Chatterjee and Amy Wong's "Politics, Inclusion, and Social Practice." I hope that *Novel Relations* can amplify these calls, and start to answer to them too in its own methodologies and practices.

5. To name just a handful of very recent works that are helping to expand the relational networks of Victorian novels, geographically and temporally, see Robert D. Aguirre, *Informal Empire: Mexico and Central America in Victorian Culture*; Joselyn M. Almeida, *Reimagining the*

Transatlantic, 1780–1890; Zarena Aslami, *The Dream Life of Citizens: Late Victorian Novels and the Fantasy of the State*; Elaine Freedgood, *The Ideas in Things: Fugitive Meaning in the Victorian Novel*; Daniel Hack, *Reaping Something New: African American Transformations of Victorian Literature*; Nathan K. Hensley, *Forms of Empire: The Poetics of Victorian Sovereignty*; and Tim Watson, *Caribbean Culture and British Fiction in the Atlantic World, 1780–1870*.

6. I think, for instance, of Hardy's haunting and sweeping claim from *Tess of the D'Urbervilles* (which also helps to illustrate Hardy's own fascinating use of "we"): "In the ill-judged execution of the well-judged plan of things, the call seldom produces the comer, the man to love rarely coincides with the hour for loving. Nature does not often say 'See!' to her poor creature at a time when seeing can lead to happy doing; or reply 'Here!' to a body's cry of 'Where?' till the hide-and-seek has become an irksome outworn game. We may wonder whether at the acme and summit of the human progress these anachronisms will become corrected by a finer intuition, a closer interaction of the social machinery than that which now jolts us round and along; but such completeness is not to be prophesied, or even conceived as possible" (43).

7. On the critical codification of nineteenth-century British realism, aspects of fiction that this codification has overlooked and occluded, and sketches of alternate histories and twentieth- and twenty-first-century genealogies, see Elaine Freedgood, *Worlds Enough*, and Lorri G. Nandrea, *Misfit Forms*.

8. For an illuminating (and very readable and teachable) overview of psychoanalytic history and thought, see Stephen A. Mitchell and Margaret J. Black, *Freud and Beyond: A History of Modern Psychoanalytic Thought*. Two chapters of particular interest for readers looking to learn more about the British analysts I study here include chapter 4, "Melanie Klein and Contemporary Kleinian Theory" (85–111), and chapter 5, "The British Object Relations School: W. R. D. Fairbairn and D. W. Winnicott" (112–38). That chapter title makes this a good time to explain why Fairbairn is not a large part of my own book: I have chosen to focus on thinkers who lived and worked primarily in London, and while Fairbairn's work and thought were important to the development of object relations theory, the fact that Fairbairn lived and worked in Edinburgh, in relative isolation from the community in London, led me to bracket his work (which is indeed quite fascinating) from this particular project.

9. The following two works provide very useful overviews of British psychoanalytic thought: Eric Rayner, *The Independent Mind in British Psychoanalysis*, and Gregorio Kohon, ed., *The British School of Psychoanalysis*. In addition to collecting many important psychoanalytic essays, Kohon's introduction to that volume provides a very useful overview of the history of the psychoanalytic movement in Great Britain (19–82). For more on that history, especially its first two decades, see Philip Kuhn, *Psychoanalysis in Britain, 1893–1913*. *Essential Papers on Object Relations*, ed. Peter Buckley, is another volume of note. Also useful are works that help to explain how innovations in British object relations thought have helped to build modern "relational" psychoanalytic approaches. See Jay Greenberg and Stephen Mitchell's *Object Relations in Psychoanalytic Theory*, which synthesizes work not only from the "British" school of object relations, but also from "Freud, the American 'ego psychologists,' and [the influential American psychiatrist and originator of 'interpersonal psychoanalysis' Henry Stack] Sullivan" (vii), and Mitchell's *Relational Concepts in Psychoanalysis*.

10. Riviere, "Those Wrecked by Success," 145.

11. Winnicott in particular has become a popular figure in US and British culture in recent years—he has been made into a character in Alison Bechdel's graphic novel *Are You My Mother?*, and into a central thinker of maternity in Maggie Nelson's *The Argonauts* (Nelson jokes, alluding to his recent popularity, that her book could be subtitled "Why Winnicott Now?"), and has been picked up by academics ranging from Barbara Johnson to Martha Nussbaum. And yet a reading that fully situates him in his intellectual milieu without blurring his ideas together with other theorists' is still needed.

12. By Mary Jacobus, see in particular *The Poetics of Psychoanalysis: In the Wake of Klein*, *Psychoanalysis and the Scene of Reading*, and *Romantic Things*. By Eve Kosofsky Sedgwick, see in particular *Touching Feeling*, *The Weather in Proust*, *Tendencies*, and "Melanie Klein and the Difference Affect Makes."

13. Literary criticism that builds on the work of psychoanalysts in the British object relations tradition is relatively rare compared with criticism that builds on post-Freudian thinkers like Lacan and Klein, but there is excellent work in this field by (in addition to Mary Jacobus and Eve Kosofsky Sedgwick, whom I've mentioned) Gabriele Schwab, Peter Rudnytsky, Barbara Ann Schapiro, Nancy Yousef, and, in Victorian studies more particularly, Carolyn Betensky, John Kucich, Adela Pinch, John Jordan, David Russell, Amanda Anderson, and Ben Parker. Closest to the ambitions of this book is perhaps Mary Jacobus's stellar *The Poetics of Psychoanalysis*, which explores the "literary aspects of the twentieth-century psychoanalytic tradition in England" and draws out its connections with Romantic literature. *The Poetics of Psychoanalysis* is the most thorough examination of the British psychoanalytic thinkers in literary and cultural studies that I know. In *Novel Relations*, I want to build on and complement Jacobus's study by addressing not the influence of Romantic tropes in object relations theory, but, instead, the two-way conversation between Victorian fiction and object relations psychoanalysis. I want to draw out in particular the ways object relations thought is shaped by novelistic form.

14. I am extremely grateful to the late Muriel Dimen for suggesting the phrase "relational reading" to describe my methodology at the American Psychoanalytic Association (APsaA) annual meeting in January 2013, when she served as a respondent on a conference panel where I presented an early version of my work on Winnicott and Hardy's *Tess of the D'Urbervilles*. I was a fellow of APsaA that year, and it proved to be an invaluable opportunity: it connected me with Muriel Dimen and also the wonderful Robin Renders, PhD, a practicing psychoanalyst and teacher at Berkshire Psychoanalytic Institute at Austen Riggs in Stockbridge, MA. Taking Robin's courses for therapeutic practitioners and psychoanalysts in training over the last several years has been essential to my education in psychoanalytic thought, and to my understanding of it as live practice.

15. These papers were recently collected in Thomas H. Ogden, *Creative Readings*.

16. For more on this subject see, Didier Anzieu, "Beckett and Bion"; Steven Connor, "Beckett and Bion"; Hunter Dukes, "Beckett's Vessels and the Animation of Containers"; and Ralph Schoolcraft, "Beckett et le psychanalyste."

17. Quoted in Phillips, *Winnicott*, 5.

18. As Rita Felski voices a related sentiment on the impossibility of art's autonomy (building not from object relations psychoanalysis, but from Bruno Latour's actor network theory), "There never was an isolated self-contained aesthetic object to begin with, because any such object would have long since sunk into the black hole of oblivion rather than coming to our attention. Artworks

can only survive by making friends, creating allies, attracting disciples, inciting attachments, attaching on to receptive hosts." Artworks live by "soliciting and sustaining attachments" (Felski, "Context Stinks!" 584).

19. "No decision on this point is expected," Winnicott writes, and in fact, "the question is not to be formulated" ("Transitional Objects," 17).

20. Winnicott, 20, 3.

21. Winnicott, 7, 19.

22. Hardy, "Profitable Reading of Fiction," 58.

23. Felman, "Turning the Screw."

24. For a fascinating (and certainly not overly concrete) study of nineteenth-century interest in child development and how it shaped pictures of subjectivity, see Carolyn Steedman's *Strange Dislocations: Childhood and the Idea of Human Interiority*.

25. Winnicott, "Fear of Breakdown" (1974), 104, and "Ego Integration" (1962), 57–58.

26. Shapira, *War Inside*, 3. See also Riccardo Steiner, "'It Is a New Kind of Diaspora....,'" which discusses the correspondence between Anna Freud and Ernest Jones in their efforts to help relocate persecuted or displaced analysts to England during what Anna Freud terms "a new kind of diaspora," and which Steiner glosses as "the forced emigration of German and Austrian psychoanalysts during the Nazi regime and its persecution of the Jews" (35).

27. On Ernest Jones (1879–1978), who is often considered responsible for bringing psychoanalysis to Britain, see Kohon, *British School of Psychoanalysis*; Rayner, *Independent Mind*; and King, "Contributions of Ernest Jones." To clarify: the society Ernest Jones founded in 1913 was named the London Psycho-Analytic Society, which was dissolved and reformed, in 1919, as the British Psycho-Analytical Society. However, it makes sense for our purposes to conceive of the society as founded in 1913—the change in name and some fluctuations in its membership were minor changes mainly undertaken to ensure Jones's ongoing control. John Rickman (1891–1951), who would later train Winnicott, Bion, and others, was also instrumental to the community's formation and institutionalization: he helped to found the *International Journal of Psycho-Analysis* in 1920, and the Institute of Psycho-Analysis (to handle the society's legal and business matters) and the International Library of Psycho-Analysis in 1924 (see Rayner, *Independent Mind*, 11–12).

28. For a full record of these conversations, see Pearl King and Riccardo Steiner, eds., *The Freud-Klein Controversies, 1941–45*.

29. For works that cover wider intellectual histories of psychological thought in Britain and that interrogate the contributions of psychology and psychoanalysis to constructions of British character and culture, see Nikolas Rose, *The Psychological Complex: Psychology, Politics, and Society in England, 1869–1939*, and *Inventing Our Selves: Psychology, Power, and Personhood*; G. C. Bunn, A. D. Lovie, and G. D. Richards, eds., *Psychology in Britain*; and Mathew Thomson, *Psychological Subjects: Identity, Culture, and Health in Twentieth-Century Britain*.

30. See, for instance, Lyndsey Stonebridge, *The Destructive Element: British Psychoanalysis and Modernism*; Perry Meisel, *The Literary Freud*; Esther Sánchez-Pardo, *Cultures of the Death Drive: Melanie Klein and Modernist Melancholia*; and Jennifer Spitzer, "On Not Reading Freud," as well as her forthcoming book, *Secret Sharers: Modernism and the Debate with Psychoanalysis*.

31. Eng, "Colonial Object Relations," 2.

32. McClintock, *Imperial Leather*, 8. For a contemporary iteration of the call to think psychology and politics together, see Maria Christoff, "First 100 Days: The Ethics of Big Data."

33. I want to clarify here that it is not my intention to collapse distinctions between distinct colonial situations, nor the differences between the dislocations of empire and the dislocations of the refugee experience. I am merely trying to sketch some of the various ways in which the wars and forced migrations of the twentieth century shaped the lives of many of the British School analysts I examine in this book. For an important theorization of twentieth-century conditions of dislocation and the difference between the exile, expatriate, and refugee experience and political condition, see Edward W. Said, "Reflections on Exile."

34. Fatimah Asghar's stunning poetry collection *If They Come for Us* begins with the following definition of Partition: "At least 14 million people were forced into migration as they fled the ethnic cleansings and retributive genocides that consumed South Asia during the India/Pakistan Partition, which led to India's and East and West Pakistan's independence from colonial Britain. An estimated 1 to 2 million people died during the months encompassing Partition. An estimated 75,000 to 100,000 women were abducted and raped. Partition remains one of the largest forced migrations in human history; its effects and divisions echo to this day" (front matter).

35. Heimann, "On Counter-Transference," 57. Heimann's refugee status surfaces not only by way of a patient's dream but also a parenthetical aside: "the dream showed that the patient wished me to be damaged (he insisted on my being the refugee to whom applies the expression 'rough passage' which he had [earlier] used for [a] new friend)" (57).

36. I explore this approach and some of its potentials in my essay "Linking with W. R. Bion."

37. Important studies linking nineteenth-century psychological and physiological discourse to nineteenth-century literature include: Sally Shuttleworth, *The Mind of the Child: Child Development in Literature, Science, and Medicine, 1840–1900*, as well as her earlier monograph, *George Eliot and Nineteenth-Century Science*; Rick Rylance, *Victorian Psychology and British Culture, 1850–1880*; Nicholas Dames, *The Physiology of the Novel: Reading, Neural Science, and the Form of Victorian Fiction*; Michael Davis, *George Eliot and Nineteenth-Century Psychology*; Jill L. Matus, *Shock, Memory and the Unconscious in Victorian Fiction*; Benjamin Morgan, *The Outward Mind: Materialist Aesthetics in Victorian Science and Literature*; and Jenny Bourne Taylor and Sally Shuttleworth, eds., *Embodied Selves: An Anthology of Psychological Texts, 1830–1890*.

38. See a longer discussion of Bion's idea in chapter 2, and in Ogden, "On Holding and Containing," 1355.

39. In his biography of Winnicott, Adam Phillips mentions "the great nineteenth-century novels that Winnicott read so keenly," and makes a reference to *Middlemarch* in particular (Phillips, *Winnicott*, 34–35). Rodman's biography records that during his military service in 1917, Winnicott read the novels of Henry James and George Meredith (Rodman, *Winnicott*, 34–35).

In her biography of Masud Khan, *False Self*, Linda Hopkins documents that Khan, who received his BA and MA in English literature, was an expert on "Shakespeare, Joyce, Virginia Woolf, and Doestoevsky," but that he "was also a scholar of the works of Oscar Wilde, T. S. Eliot, Thomas Hardy," and others (455n6). During these studies and preparing for further education at Oxford (which Khan ended up forgoing when he moved to London in 1946, choosing to pursue psychoanalytic training instead), Khan worked with an Oxford-trained tutor, under whose guidance he "abandoned an interest in Persian and Urdu poetry, in order to immerse himself in Shakespeare and Western literature." Hopkins quotes a letter Khan wrote in 1970 that reads: "If anyone wants to know the matrix of my sensibility, he shall have to look to . . . the climate of these books that created that tension in me in the years 1940–1946 which actualised itself in my becoming an analyst

204   NOTES TO CHAPTER 1

and living the life I do in London" (13). For more on Khan's life, see also Judy Cooper, "Khan, (Mohammed) Masud Raza (1924–1989)."

40. For important work on the formation of English literary studies in colonial settings, and in South Asia in particular, see Gauri Viswanathan, *Masks of Conquest: Literary Study and British Rule in India*. For histories of English literary education in Britain, and the institutionalization of the nineteenth-century English novel in particular, see Carol Atherton, *Defining Literary Criticism: Scholarship, Authority and the Possession of Literary Knowledge, 1880–2002*; Catherine Belsey, "Re-reading the Great Tradition"; and Meredith Martin, *The Rise and Fall of Meter: Poetry and English National Culture, 1860–1930*.

41. To name just one concrete connection: in her article on Ernest Jones, Pearl King records that "one of the first achievements of the newly formed Institute of Psycho-Analysis [in 1924] was to co-operate with Leonard Woolf and the Hogarth Press to form the International Psycho-Analytical Library for the publication of psychoanalytic literature" ("Contributions of Ernest Jones," 281). They published, for instance, some of the first English-language translations of Freud, by Joan Riviere and others. For more on these connections, see James Strachey and Alix Strachey, *Bloomsbury/Freud: The Letters of James and Alix Strachey*.

42. The extended timeline I trace in bringing Victorian fiction and British psychoanalysis together shares contours with the intellectual history of twentieth-century modernism: Victorian novels are part of the intellectual tradition that shaped the Bloomsbury writers and thinkers, who then too had numerous crossings with figures in British psychoanalytic circles. For this reason, too, Victorian fiction and later British psychoanalysis have a special fit.

43. One literary historical reason for this is that Victorian writers, Eliot and Hardy foremost among them, have been foundational in the realist novel tradition that in many ways remains dominant in the Anglophone literary world.

44. Ablow, *Feeling of Reading*.

45. For a resonant but distinct approach, see the work of film and media studies scholar Eugenie Brinkema, who writes: "The turning to affect in humanities does not obliterate the problem of form and representation. Affect is not where reading is no longer needed.... I am claiming that we require a return to form precisely because of the turn to affect, to keep its wonderments in revolution, to keep going" (*Form of the Affects*, xiv, xvi).

46. I think here, of course, of Lacanian approaches to language. See, for instance, Jacques Lacan's "The Function and Field of Language in Psychoanalysis" (also known as "The Rome Discourse," originally published 1953), and the very useful summaries of Lacan's work by Bruce Fink in *The Lacanian Subject*, my favorite text to use when teaching Lacan to undergraduates.

47. Bollas, "Psychic Genera," 58–59.

Chapter 1

1. I am thinking of how often Tess is alone throughout the novel: walking through the woods during her pregnancy to avoid being looked at by people she imagines are judging her, her stunning summertime walks at Talbothays Dairy in which she can almost hear the "rush of juices" and "hiss of fertilization" (*T* 149), her solitary search for work after being abandoned by Angel, how she sleeps alone under a tree one night and finds herself mercy killing a flock of injured pheasants (*T* 279–80), how she defaces herself by cutting her eyebrows to avoid "aggressive

admiration" (*T* 280), on her flight from Alec. Other readers, though, may recall how much Tess is in groups, especially in groups of other women. Part of what I am interested in is how readily she is singled out from these groups, and made to be alone. So, for example: In our initial introduction to Tess as one of the many in a band of girls dressed in white, she is singled out by the red ribbon in her hair and by narrative attention (*T* 14). In the memorable scene in which Angel carries four dairymaids across a stream, "flies and butterflies" brushed up from the grass caught up and fluttering in their "gauzy skirts," he saves Tess for last and gives her a special attention that makes the other girls jealous (*T* 143). And even in scenes of communal work, Tess is differentiated, as when she is given a special position on top of the corn-threshing machine, where she is "shaken bodily by its spinning, and this incessant quivering, in which every fibre of her body participated," and which "throw[s] her into a stupefied reverie" (*T* 333). A Kleinian reading, building on her essay, "On the Sense of Loneliness" (1963), might take up these moments in more detail. Klein's interest is on an inner sense of loneliness: on how one can feel alone even when in the company of others. She writes: "By the sense of loneliness I am referring not to the objective situation of being deprived of external companionship. I am referring to the inner sense of loneliness—the sense of being alone regardless of external circumstances, of feeling lonely even when among friends or receiving love. This state of internal loneliness, I will suggest, is the result of a ubiquitous yearning for an unattainable perfect internal state." Klein theorizes loneliness as a kind of pathology, be it "one which is experienced to some extent by everyone" (300). Klein's formulation, compelling as it is, is precisely what Winnicott pushes against in his own essay "The Capacity to Be Alone." While for Klein loneliness is a sensation of felt deficit, for Winnicott it can be a feeling of satisfaction. Winnicott takes being alone as an acquired ability and a sign of emotional health. In keeping with this emphasis, my readings focus not on Tess being singled out or feeling alone while with others, but, instead, on moments when she is actually alone but imaginatively feels herself to be in the company of others—including at times the company of literary figures who occupy different ontological and metaleptic frames, such as the narrator, author, and reader.

2. Winnicott, "Capacity to Be Alone," 30.

3. See the biographies of Winnicott by Brett Kahr, *D. W. Winnicott*; F. Robert Rodman, *Winnicott*; and Adam Phillips, *Winnicott*.

4. Thanks to Samuel Baker for this phrase, and for his extremely helpful comments on an early version of this chapter at the Dickens Universe Winter Conference at Rice University in 2011. His insights about what that short paper could eventually be, and the larger literary critical conversations to which it could contribute, were central to my writing of this chapter.

5. Munger, *On the Threshold*, 182.

6. Phillips, *On Kissing*, 41.

7. Freud, "Civilization and Its Discontents," 64.

8. Hardy, "Tess's Lament."

9. Ruskin, "Pathetic Fallacy," 1284.

10. Ruskin, 1286.

11. For further work on the relationship between Tess and her environment, see Elaine Scarry, "Participial Acts: Working: Work and the Body in Hardy and Other Nineteenth-Century Novelists"; William Cohen, "Faciality and Sensation in Hardy's *The Return of the Native*"; and Elisha Cohn, "'No Insignificant Creature': Thomas Hardy's Ethical Turn."

12. As Elaine Freedgood points out, "Hardy's appeal is precisely that he invents all kinds of terrible feelings and then makes them so lyrically appealing" (e-mail to the author, 14 May 2011).

13. Silverman, "Female Subjectivity," 28.

14. Silverman, 23.

15. When I speak of Hardy as author this way throughout the book, I am attributing to him agency but not necessarily intentionality. As Marjorie Levinson writes of Hardy's oeuvre, "One might say that it has Hardy's name all over it yet lacks the intentionality we associate with signature" ("Object-Loss and Object-Bondage," 550).

16. Winnicott's fellow object relations psychoanalyst W. R. D. Fairbairn phrases this imagination of the psyche vividly as an " 'inner reality' peopled by the ego and its internal objects." Quoted in King and Steiner, *Freud-Klein Controversies*, 359.

17. Sixty years later, it would seem as if the problem still has not been solved. Modern psychoanalytic thinkers comment that loneliness remains underemphasized and undertheorized in psychoanalytic work, even though it is a central concept that underlies so many others. See the collection *Loneliness and Longing*, edited by Brent Willock, Lori C. Bohm, and Rebecca C. Curtis.

18. Winnicott, "Capacity to Be Alone," 29.

19. Winnicott, 30.

20. Winnicott, 30.

21. Winnicott, 31.

22. Winnicott, 36.

23. Winnicott, 36.

24. "Holding" and its function in both maternal care and later in the analytic situation (itself a "holding environment") are most fully laid out in Winnicott's essay "The Theory of the Parent-Infant Relationship" (1960). Winnicott writes that in the earliest stages of life, "The alternative to being is reacting, and reacting interrupts being and annihilates [it].... The holding environment therefore has as its main function the reduction to a minimum of impingements to which the infant must react with resultant annihilation of personal being" (47). For further explanation of the role of the mother and her state of being while caring for the infant, see Winnicott's "Primary Maternal Preoccupation" (1956).

25. Winnicott, "Capacity to Be Alone," 34.

26. Winnicott, 34.

27. There is an immense body of work on the subject of sympathy in nineteenth-century fiction. See, in particular, Rachel Ablow, *The Marriage of Minds: Reading Sympathy in the Victorian Marriage Plot*, and Rae Greiner, *Sympathetic Realism in Nineteenth-Century British Fiction*. My approach builds on this work not only by pointing out the ways in which Hardy complicates the discourse of sympathy but also by emphasizing, beyond the Victorian novel's resonance with contemporary psychological theories, its anticipation of twentieth-century psychoanalysis. A recent strand of criticism on nineteenth-century sympathy dwells in particular on the Victorians' obsession with imagining other minds, the difficulty inherent to this practice, and the convergence of Victorian psychological discourse and the novel. See Adela Pinch's *Thinking about Other People in Nineteenth-Century British Fiction*, which, significantly, includes a brief reference to Bion. Debra Gettelman's review essay "The Psychology of Reading and the Victorian Novel"

provides a very useful overview of the growing body of critical literature converging around the history of reading, affect theory, psychology, and the Victorian novel.

28. We might think of these sounds as a kind of song, and, as Bryan Doniger points out, in *Tess* music frequently points the way "into unfamiliar, disorienting, or extravagant places" ("Time for Song," 2). Indeed, what follows this scene is a literal disorientation that causes the horse Prince's death, the pool of his blood reflecting "a million prismatic hues," and Tess's anguished insight that she is living on a "blighted star" (*T* 33).

29. For further work on the subject of the dominance of states between waking and sleeping in the novel, see Philip Weinstein, *The Semantics of Desire: Changing Models of Identity from Dickens to Joyce*, 112.

30. Clementina Black, "Review," *Illustrated London News*, 9 January 1892, repr. in Cox, *Critical Heritage*, 187.

31. Beer, *Darwin's Plots*, 231, 222.

32. W. P. Trent writes in the *Sewanee Review*: "Never has Mr. Hardy's knowledge of nature stood him in better stead than in the descriptive passages which here and there break the tense thread of the action" ("The Novels of Thomas Hardy," *Sewanee Review* 1, no. 1 (1892): 22, repr. in Cox, *Critical Heritage*, 245).

33. Beer, *Darwin's Plots*, 239.

34. Black, "Review," 187.

35. Beer, *Darwin's Plots*, 231.

36. Gallagher, "Rise of Fictionality," 357.

37. Gallagher, 356–57.

38. Bayley, *Essay on Hardy*, 168–69, 173.

39. See also Marcelle Clements, who points to Hardy's complex emotional relationship to his heroine, "alternating respect, voyeurism, and an almost voluptuous compassion" (introduction to *Tess of the D'Urbervilles*, by Thomas Hardy, xiii).

40. Gallagher, "Rise of Fictionality," 356.

41. I am also implicitly arguing, in this chapter and in the chapter on *The Return of the Native* as well, for a different account of Hardy's form and style, in which those elements of his artistic practice that have long been construed as flaws or failures in fact amount to self-conscious experimentation with literary form. Terry Eagleton argues that Hardy is "blithely unconcerned with that great fetish of literary art, unity" ("Buried in the Life," 92). Hardy scholars have recently taken up this claim: rather than trying to smooth over the "stylistic unevenness" and "fractures of representation" that characterize his fiction, they celebrate what Linda Shires calls its "radical aesthetic." By staging multiplicity and incongruity "at every narrative level," Shires argues, Hardy "questions the very foundations of traditional representation and belief" and trains the reader to "become conditioned into thinking simultaneously in terms that are multiple and even contradictory" ("Radical Aesthetic," 147). Critics like Peter Widdowson, Simon Gatrell, Penny Boumelha, and Zena Meadowsong make similar claims. The "ruptures of formal coherence" and "narrative dissonances" that characterize Hardy's fiction are not mistakes, nor lapses in narrative realism (Meadowsong, "Hardy and the Machine," 227), but rather intentional demonstrations of the work's "resistance to reduction to a single and uniform ideological position" (Boumelha, *Thomas Hardy and Women*, 7). Hardy's novels do not say one thing; they intone many. A

particularly stunning iteration of this argument appears in Marjorie Levinson's essay, "Object-Loss and Object-Bondage," on Hardy's poetry, which argues that the "non-coherence" of Hardy's work as a "critico-aesthetic project" is the source of both our pleasure in reading and its resistance to easy critical conclusions or recapitulations (550). I quote Levinson at greater length later in this chapter. See also Terry Eagleton, "Buried in the Life: Thomas Hardy and the Limits of Biographies"; Linda M. Shires, "The Radical Aesthetic of *Tess of the d'Urbervilles*"; Simon Gatrell, introduction to *Tess of the D'Urbervilles*, by Thomas Hardy; Zena Meadowsong, "Thomas Hardy and the Machine: The Mechanical Deformation of Narrative Realism in *Tess of the d'Urbervilles*"; Peter Widdowson, "Hardy and Critical Theory," and *On Thomas Hardy*; Penny Boumelha, *Thomas Hardy and Women: Sexual Ideology and Narrative Form*; and Marjorie Levinson, "Object-Loss and Object-Bondage: Economies of Representation in Hardy's Poetry."

42. Freedgood, "Fictional Settlements," 398.

43. Freedgood, 402.

44. Woloch writes that the purpose of his study is to "redefine literary characterization in terms of this distributional matrix." He sets out to show "how the discrete representation of any specific individual is intertwined with the narrative's continual apportioning of attention to different characters who jostle for limited space within the same fictive universe" (*One vs. the Many*, 13). In my approach to character I am also drawing on the important work of Deidre Lynch, whose book *The Economy of Character: Novels, Market Culture, and the Business of Inner Meaning* draws attention both to historical shifts in literary character and our practices of reading and understanding it and to the social construction and historicity of subjectivity itself (7–10). Importantly, I distinguish my own work from recent cognitive approaches to literary character, which in my view efface some of the dimensions of fictionality and form—as well as psychodynamic effects between reader and text—that I most want to draw out here. For interesting work in the cognitive vein, see Blakey Vermeule, *Why Do We Care about Literary Characters?*, and Lisa Zunshine, *Why We Read Fiction: Theory of Mind and the Novel*.

45. Winnicott, "Capacity to Be Alone," 417.

46. In the same preface, Hardy divides the novel in much the same way as his critics, distinguishing between its "scenic parts" (moments of action and dialogue, which he calls "representative simply") and its "contemplative" ones, which he writes are "oftener charged with *impressions* than with opinions" (*T* 462; emphasis added). Hardy uses this word again when he writes: "Let me repeat that a novel is an *impression*, not an argument" (*T* 463; emphasis added). In his preface to *Poems of the Past and the Present* (1901), Hardy makes a similar argument for the effect of his literature when he writes, "unadjusted impressions have their value" (84).

47. Work in the history of reading charts the shift from vocalized to silent reading and from public to private reading in the nineteenth century. See, for instance, Patrick Brantlinger, *The Reading Lesson: The Threat of Mass Literacy in Nineteenth Century British Fiction*; Kate Flint, *The Woman Reader, 1837–1914*; Jon P. Klanchner, *The Making of English Reading Audiences, 1790–1832*; and the edited collections John O. Jordan and Robert L. Patten, eds., *Literature in the Marketplace: Nineteenth-Century British Publishing and Reading Practices*; and James Raven, Helen Small, and Naomi Tadmor, eds., *The Practice and Representation of Reading in England*. Leah Price's "Reading: The State of the Discipline" offers a useful overview of the field as well as the nineteenth-century shift in reading practices I am describing here. In *Physiology of the Novel*, Dames argues that Victorian reviewing practices, which focus on emotional and physiological reactions to

reading, also help to set the norm for discussing the *solitary* rather than *collective* consumption of a work of art (12). This practice is certainly visible in the small set of reviews of *Tess* that I cite here.

48. Phillips, *On Kissing*, 29.

49. Sedgwick, "Paranoid and Reparative Reading." Sedgwick writes that "reparative reading" is a critical practice that "undertakes a [wholly] different range of affects, ambitions, and risks" from paranoid reading (150). While paranoid reading seeks to demystify and to expose, the "desire of a reparative impulse" (149) is to seek joy, pleasure, love, surprise, hope, and amelioration (137, 144).

50. Sedgwick, 124.

51. For a different critique of Sedgwick's essay—one that concentrates on the mutual inscription of the two polarities of paranoid and reparative reading and the need to reexamine the place of aggression in love—see Heather Love, "Truth and Consequences: On Paranoid Reading and Reparative Reading."

52. Sedgwick, "Paranoid and Reparative Reading," 149.

53. In the debates between Anna Freud and Melanie Klein that shook the psychoanalytic world in the early 1940s, and especially the British Psychoanalytic Society in London, where the debates took place, Winnicott was one of the psychoanalytic thinkers who did not take sides but rather carved out a "Middle" or "Independent" group between the two figureheads and their approaches.

54. For Winnicott's declaration of these principles, see, for instance, "Transitional Objects and Transitional Phenomena" (1951/1971), in which he includes a statement about looking at the phenomenology of pleasurable sensation that is not strictly centered on sexual satisfaction, and "The Theory of the Parent-Infant Relationship" (1960), in which he expresses his disbelief in the notion of an original death drive. Sedgwick makes a similar point about moving from drive to affect in her essay "Melanie Klein and the Difference Affect Makes." In my view, however, the description of Kleinian theory in this essay sounds more like Winnicott and other followers in the Independent tradition than like Klein herself. And indeed, Sedgwick comments that she prefers to read *about* Klein than to read Klein's own work. I wonder to what extent Sedgwick's image of Klein in this essay is colored by others' later interpretations of Klein's work—including those put into play by Winnicott himself.

55. See Winnicott's essays "Communicating and Not Communicating Leading to a Study of Certain Opposites" (1963) and "Primitive Emotional Development" (1945).

56. Winnicott, "Ego Integration" (1962), 58.

57. Winnicott writes: "It is sometimes assumed that in health the individual is always integrated, as well as living in his own body, and able to feel that the world is real. There is, however, much sanity that has a symptomatic quality, being charged with fear or denial of madness, fear or denial of the innate capacity of every human being to become unintegrated, depersonalized, and to feel that the world is unreal" ("Primitive Emotional Development," 140). In a striking footnote, he adds: "we are poor indeed if we are only sane" (140n3).

58. Levinson, "Object-Loss and Object-Bondage," 572, 575. Hardy's poems, Levinson writes, reverse the standard Kantian definition of aesthetic experience: while "full of purposes," they lack "any overall or integral or, as it were, formative purposiveness" (556). I want readers to hear too echoes of Winnicott's formulations of rest, which is for him the basis of aesthetic experience as

a "non-purposive state, as one may say a sort of ticking over of the unintegrated personality" ("Playing," 74).

59. Levinson argues that Hardy's poetry resists "reading"—it blocks our ability to "mobilize textual material into value-form and a form of intention, however dispersed and conflictual" ("Object-Loss and Object-Bondage," 550–51).

60. See, for instance, the seminal Foucauldian-inflected account of the ideological work of the novel, in D. A. Miller's *The Novel and the Police*.

61. See Laura Green's account of feminist identificatory reading practices in "'I Recognized Myself in Her': Identifying with the Reader in George Eliot's *The Mill on the Floss* and Simone de Beauvoir's *Memoirs of a Dutiful Daughter*." Articulating traditional views of readerly identification and its ideological work, Green writes: "literary identification cements an ontological alliance between protagonist and reader," thereby aggrandizing "the individual consciousness." Thus, "the realist novel's representation of identification" is "central to the charge of ideological conservatism and bourgeois hegemony leveled at classical realism more generally in the Brechtian tradition of Marxist aesthetics" (57). Green identifies the Althusserian process of interpellation as a basis for her critique, as well as Etienne Balibar and Pierre Macherey, who, "drawing out the implications of Althusser's argument specifically for literature," write: "Any process of identification is dependent on the constitution and recognition of the 'subject.' . . . In literature, the process of constituting subjects and setting up their relationship of mutual recognition necessarily takes a detour via the fiction world and its values" (Balibar and Macherey, "On Literature," 90, quoted in Green, "I Recognized Myself," 58). Green pushes against these views of identification in her essay, as do I in this chapter—I resist in particular the notion of a solidified subject and ontological sameness, and do so by drawing on the alternate models of object relations psychoanalysis. See Louis Althusser, "Ideology and Ideological State Apparatuses (Notes toward an Investigation)," and Etienne Balibar and Pierre Macherey, "On Literature as an Ideological Form." For other important and beautiful work spelling out and complicating Freudian notions of identification, see Diana Fuss, *Identification Papers: Readings on Psychoanalysis, Sexuality, and Culture*.

62. Lisa Brocklebank, in her very interesting article on what the theories of nineteenth-century psychic researcher Frederic Myers might contribute to theories of novel reading, argues that "Victorian fiction," in addition to being a "tool for social control" via "the production and regulation of subjectivity," also "served as a means of expanding the field of sensations, the possibilities for sympathetic identification, and therefore the kinds and qualities of feelings one could experience" ("Psychic Reading," 238).

63. I have drawn inspiration for this reading from Stanley Cavell's moving essay on the death of a son in Shakespeare's *The Winter's Tale*, "Recounting Gains, Showing Losses: Reading The Winter's Tale."

64. Indeed, just after this scene, Hardy uses the same synecdochic conceit to describe Tess herself and her limited "radius of movement and repute": "To persons of limited spheres, miles are as geographical degrees, parishes as counties, counties as provinces and kingdoms" (99–100). For an interesting take on this quotation, see Daniel Williams, "Rumor, Reputation, and Sensation in *Tess of the d'Urbervilles*."

65. Curiously, pregnancy and motherhood do not arise even in Kaja Silverman's excellent exploration of female subjectivity in the novel. We could read this (generously) as a motivated elision that sheds light on Hardy's blind spot: Silverman focuses on the "dominant scopic regime

of the novel" ("Female Subjectivity," 20), which does not, she argues, allow us access to Tess apart from the way she is structured by the male gaze. Indeed, no part of her, neither body nor interiority, escapes the "figural coercion" of male vision and male desire, a coercion that "extends 'inward' in the guise of an unhappy consciousness of being watched" (27). Importantly, this is Silverman's own answer to the question of why Tess cannot feel alone: because she is always being watched, and not because she is a literary character, but, instead, because she is a woman. As the art critic John Berger puts the same argument, because "how she appears to men is of crucial importance for what is normally thought of as the success of her life," "a woman must continually watch herself" (Berger, "*Ways of Seeing*," 37). A woman is always watched, and a woman is always made to internalize that male gaze and to watch herself, to treat herself as an object for visual consumption. What Winnicott's writing introduces is a different take on watching, theorizing not the *male* but the *maternal* gaze—defined as a presence as much as a look, a "holding environment" as much as a figure.

66. The classic articulation of this view is by James Strachey, "The Nature of the Therapeutic Action of Psycho-Analysis."

67. Winnicott, "Dependence," 251–52.

68. Winnicott, 251.

69. Fetterley, *Resisting Reader*, xii.

70. Boumelha, *Thomas Hardy and Women*, 120.

71. Are we feeling the sticky sap on Tess's skin with our own fingertips? Or do we feel the surface of Tess's skin as if it were our own? The multiplicity of our positions in any fantasy scenario, as conceived in the Freudian and post-Freudian imagination, is powerfully described by Lise Shapiro Sanders in *Consuming Fantasies: Labor, Leisure, and the London Shopgirl, 1880–1920*.

72. For more on the subject of narrative lulls in Hardy, see Beer, *Darwin's Plots*; Cohn, *Still Life*; and David James, "Hearing Hardy: Soundscapes and the Profitable Reader." See also the psychoanalyst Masud Khan's wonderful essay "On Lying Fallow."

73. Bollas, "Transformational Object," 97, 104.

74. Bollas, 98–99.

75. Bollas, "Aesthetic Moment," 386.

76. In a series of fascinating essays, Gabriele Schwab also works to extend Bollas's work on aesthetic theory into an exploration of literature and literary theory: see "Cultural Texts and Endopsychic Scripts," "Genesis of the Subject, Imaginary Functions, and Poetic Language," and "Words and Moods: The Transference of Literary Knowledge."

77. Bollas, "Psychic Genera," 61.

78. Dimen, "Deconstructing Difference," 349; Harris, "Gender as Contradiction," 212. Both of these writers are cited in Jessica Benjamin's "In Defense of Gender Ambiguity," which argues for the importance of understanding gender as coming in and out of focus in order to develop "a broader view of gender identifications" beyond our standard definitions of femininity and masculinity, a view "which transcends the simple, oedipal logic of opposites and recognizes the multiplicity of sexual life" (27). Dimen, describing the complicated relationship between gender and sense of self, writes, "Gender, as an internally varied experience, is sometimes central and definitive, sometimes marginal and contingent. Consequently, it is fundamentally and inalterably paradoxical" ("Deconstructing Difference," 349). While Dimen describes how feeling out of gender can lead to anxiety, *Tess* poses something like the opposite scenario: when Tess and

the reader alike are out of gender, in the novel's quiet, reparative, or "maternal" moments, they are released from the anxiety of the novel's driving forces.

Chapter 2

1. Bion's citation of Isaac Luria is drawn from Gershom Scholem, *Major Trends in Jewish Mysticism* (London: Thames and Hudson, 1955), 254.

2. Beer, "Beyond Determinism," 88.

3. Bion was born in colonial India to English parents, and educated in England, where he spent almost his entire adult life before moving to Los Angeles in his final years.

4. Originally formulated in essays written in the late 1950s and early 1960s—"On Arrogance" (1957), "Attacks on Linking" (1959), and "A Theory of Thinking" (1962) chief among them—Bion continued to develop the container/contained concept throughout his career, continually expanding and reformulating it in his major works, the books *Learning from Experience*, *Elements of Psychoanalysis*, *Transformations*, and *Attention and Interpretation*, published in the 1960s and early 1970s. The notion of a person or a setting being "containing" has become ubiquitous in analytic and pop-psychological terminology. Indeed, some writers believe that the container/contained concept has become so popular that it risks being misused. Lynne Zeavin writes, in her review of a 2011 book on Bion's legacy called *Bion Today*: "In the last years, Bion has become so popular in the United States that often it seems that psychoanalytic rigor is under threat, if not altogether lost. Bion's radical formulations have become catch phrases in some circles, their meaning diluted and their specificity lost. This volume [*Bion Today*] goes a long way toward restoring the particularity and originality of Bion's ideas and reminding us of the value of rigorous thought, particularly in relation to concepts that now verge on the cliché: container/contained, reverie, projective identification, countertransference, and thinking" (Zeavin, review of *Bion Today*, by Chris Mawson). In this chapter, I hope to both take up Zeavin's charge by helping to restore the rigor of these concepts and, in keeping with the book's larger project, to situate them in a longer literary and psychological history that includes Victorian fiction.

5. A notable exception is the literary scholar Mary Jacobus, who has written extensively and compellingly on both connections between British psychoanalysis and literature (particularly Romantic literature) and the "poetics" of psychoanalytic writing itself. See in particular *Scene of Reading* and *Poetics of Psychoanalysis*, the latter of which includes two chapters on Bion's life, his work, and its connections with Romantic literature. Other notable exceptions include Adela Pinch and Hunter Dukes. Adela Pinch engages Bion's theories of thinking with nineteenth-century literature and philosophy, including George Eliot's *Daniel Deronda*, in her fascinating book *Thinking about Other People in Nineteenth-Century British Fiction*. In "Beckett's Vessels and the Animation of Containers," Dukes explores figures of containers throughout the writing of Samuel Beckett, who was in therapy with Bion for a brief period beginning in December 1933. Dukes argues that Bion may have drawn inspiration for his psychoanalytic concept from Beckett's *Murphy*, written concurrently with his analysis with Bion (82, 87n).

6. Ogden, "On Holding and Containing," 1357.

7. As the analyst Edna O'Shaughnessy movingly puts it, Bion's work has "in a quiet way in the consulting room caused a revolution in how an analyst may try to know his patient" (review of *Wilfred Bion*, 859).

8. Beer, "Beyond Determinism," 88.

9. Byatt, introduction (1979) to *MF*, xxxix.

10. Sir Edward Bulwer-Lytton wrote that the novel's final "tragedy was not adequately prepared" (*George Eliot Letters*, 3: 317). Another of Eliot's contemporaries complained in an 1860 review that "the authoress does not know how to bring her story to a natural ending," and that "there is an exhaustion, a dim and unfinished appearance, about her last chapters, which contrasts more than it ought to do with the vehemence and vividness" of the earlier parts (unsigned review, *Guardian*, 25 April 1860, 377–78, repr. in D. Carroll, *Critical Heritage*, 127). And in *The Great Tradition: George Eliot, Henry James, Joseph Conrad* (1948), F. R. Leavis famously dismisses the novel's inconsistencies as a product of the autobiographical nature of *The Mill on the Floss*, making them signs of Eliot's own desire surfacing through her main character. He writes: "the presence of the author's own personal need" is both a salient and "embarrassing" aspect of Eliot's fiction (32).

11. N. Miller, "Emphasis Added."

12. Woolf, "George Eliot," 358.

13. Beer, "Beyond Determinism," 80.

14. Susan Fraiman usefully synthesizes much of this criticism in her excellent essay "*The Mill on the Floss*, the Critics, and the Bildungsroman."

15. Beer, "Beyond Determinism," 81–82.

16. Jacobus, "Men of Maxims."

17. Jacobus, 211.

18. Jacobus, 222.

19. Beer, "Beyond Determinism," 81.

20. Hack, *Reaping Something New*, 122–23. See his excellent work on Eliot's fiction and its futures in African American literature throughout that book, as well as in his essay "The Last Victorian Novel: II. *The Quest of the Silver Fleece*, by W.E.B. Du Bois."

21. Green, "I Recognized Myself," 62–63. The quotation is drawn from Moi, *Simone de Beauvoir*, 1.

22. Green, "I Recognized Myself," 60.

23. Ahmed, *Willful Subjects*. See also *The Promise of Happiness* and *Living a Feminist Life*, 68–70. Ahmed writes that Maggie Tulliver, as a "willful heroine," inspired her to write *Willful Subjects*. "Maggie Tulliver has been the object of considerable feminist desire and identification over time. We might share affection for Maggie as feminist readers, as we might share affection for many of the willful girls that haunt literature. . . . My hunch . . . in moving from the figure of the feminist killjoy to the willful subject was that willfulness and unhappiness share a historical trajectory. We learn from our traveling companions"—here, from Maggie (*Willful Subjects*, 3).

24. Bion's essay "On Arrogance" (1957) is the starting point of his rewriting of the Oedipus myth, and in it he states these themes quite precisely: "I shall rehearse the Oedipus myth from a point of view which makes the sexual crime a peripheral element of a story in which the central crime is the arrogance of Oedipus in vowing to lay bare the truth at no matter what cost. This shift of emphasis brings the following elements into the centre of the story: the sphinx, who asks a riddle and destroys herself when it is answered, the blind Tiresias, who possesses knowledge and deplores the resolve of the king to search for it, the oracle that provokes the search which the prophet deplores, and again the king who, his search concluded, suffers blindness and exile.

This is the story of which the elements are discernible amongst the ruins of the psyche, to which the scattered references to curiosity, arrogance, and stupidity have pointed the way" (86).

25. Relevant here too is Rachel Bowlby's excellent book *Freudian Mythologies: Greek Tragedy and Modern Identities*, which both explores Freud's use of Greek myth and seeks out new models beyond Oedipus for modern identity, family, and family making.

26. Brooks, *Reading for the Plot*.

27. I am very grateful to Zachary Samalin for his help with this formulation, and to Nasser Mufti as well, who organized a work-in-progress seminar at the University of Illinois at Chicago in April 2017 to workshop an earlier draft of this chapter. Thanks to all the attendees of that seminar for the careful readings and pointed questions that helped me to clarify my claims on Bionic plot.

28. Nebbiosi and Petrini, "Concept of 'Common Sense.'" Nebbiosi and Petrini clarify the split in contemporary psychoanalytic approaches between drive and relational models, but argue that Bion articulates a unique and prescient middle ground: "Bion's theories on drive are significantly different from those of either Freud or Klein, who are his two real and only psychoanalytical referents. Today they take on a role of great interest compared to that which seems to be the most important epistemological argument in contemporary psychoanalytical thought: to opt for a drive or a relational paradigm. We would like to clarify that the two paradigms arose not so much because the drive paradigm did not consider the relationships—or, conversely, because the relational paradigm did not consider psychic biological and drive-derived elements—but rather because a paradigm sees the drives as being superordinate to the relationships, and the other sees the relationships superordinate to the drives. In neither case do we speak of minimizing or eliminating certain phenomenologies or concepts, but of explaining them in terms of different theoretical co-ordinates. The particular meaning of Bion's theory is that of having suggested, rather precociously, a drive-and-relationship-coordinated view" (174–75).

29. Sally Shuttleworth argues that the novel's opening and closing are linked by their ties to "dream narrative" rather than "conscious narration," and goes on to argue that "the primacy placed upon dreams and the unconscious in the novel subverts the traditional theory of man as a unified rational actor which sustains theories of history as linear progression" (*George Eliot*, 66).

30. Weber, *Legend of Freud*, 7.

31. Phillips, *Becoming Freud*, 15.

32. Ogden, "On Holding and Containing," 1355.

33. Bion, *Cogitations*, 43.

34. Bion, 37–38, 43.

35. See in particular Bion's *Learning from Experience*. These ideas are also extremely powerfully paraphrased and fleshed out in the work of the contemporary psychoanalyst Lucy LaFarge. See, for example, "Interpretation and Containment" and "The Imaginer and the Imagined."

36. Ogden, "On Holding and Containing," 1359.

37. Beer, "Myth," 100.

38. In quotes including ellipses in square brackets, those are the only ellipses that have been added to indicate omission; other ellipses are present in the original.

39. Gettelman, "Reading Ahead." In her essay, Gettelman refers to fraught scenes of wishing within Eliot's fiction (primarily *Adam Bede* and *Daniel Deronda*). Perhaps the most emblematic

instance occurs in *Daniel Deronda* (1876): when her husband drowns, the protagonist Gwendolen Harleth remarks, "I saw my wish outside me." The rest of the novel revolves on the question of her innocence or culpability in this death on the basis of her "cruel wishes" (*DD* 691–92). For detailed readings of this scene and its deliberate confusion of murderous wish and deed, see in particular Jacqueline Rose, "George Eliot and the Spectacle of Woman," and Stefanie Markovits, "'That Girl Has Some Drama in Her': George Eliot's Problem with Action." Gettelman, however, is primarily concerned with wish-fulfillment on the level of reader response: she explores nineteenth-century serial publication, Eliot's readers' tendencies to forecast happy endings as they read early parts of her fiction, and George Eliot's harassed resistance to fulfilling those desires as she wrote the ends of her novels with early readers' responses in mind.

40. Byatt, introduction to *MF*, xxxix. "Puzzling" is Mr. Tulliver's word. It describes, repeatedly throughout the novel, his experience of the world and his description of it to himself, as in this passage describing his reluctance to write a letter: Mr. Tulliver "found the relation between spoken and written language, briefly known as spelling, one of the most puzzling things in this puzzling world" (*MF* 138).

41. While Bion's theories of unconscious communication help to illuminate some of the novel's more "puzzling" formal qualities and thematic cruxes, the novel underscores the distinct literariness of his theories—not simply in Bion's style of writing and frequent references to literature, but more importantly in the very forms of relation and subjectivity that nineteenth-century fiction allows him to think.

42. Freud, "Two Principles," 219.

43. Phillips, "On Frustration," 25, 28.

44. In her response to Bulwer-Lytton's critique regarding the tragedy of the ending being inadequately prepared for, Eliot wrote: "This is a defect which I felt even while writing the third volume, and have felt ever since the MS left me. The '*epische Breite*' [epic breadth] into which I was beguiled by love of my subject in the first two volumes, caused a want of proportionate fullness in the treatment of the third, which I shall always regret" (*George Eliot Letters*, 3: 317).

45. Eliot, "Art and Belles Lettres," *Westminster Review* 65, no. 128 (April 1856): 625–50, cited in Byatt, introduction to *MF*, xxxvii.

46. *George Eliot Letters*, 6: 241–42.

47. For Klein, the parts of the psyche that are "expelled and projected into the other person" are either, in her bipolar terminology, good or bad. Bad parts of the self "are meant not only to injure the object, but also to control and take possession of it." Describing the mother-infant relationship as the earliest locus of projective identification, Klein writes: "In so far as the mother comes to contain bad parts of the self, she is not felt to be an individual but is felt to be part of the bad self." When she is made to contain good parts, they are "used to represent the good, i.e. the loving part of the self" ("Schizoid Mechanisms," 102).

48. See Jaffe, *Victorian Novel Dreams*.

49. Edna O'Shaughnessy puts this in a very clear and usefully commonplace way: the mother is there "to receive and care for" the child's "unwanted parts." "This capacity of the mother, in her reverie with her child, as W. R. Bion calls it, to absorb for him what he does not want to go on containing, and return it to him in better shape, is as important on the emotional plane as the giving of love, just as the removal of urine and faeces is as important as the provision of nourishment on the physical plane" ("Revisiting," 213–14).

50. In *Learning from Experience*, Bion asks: "When the mother loves the infant what does she do with it? Leaving aside the physical channels of communication, my impression is that her love is expressed by reverie" (35–36).

51. Though perhaps verging on a commonsense usage that Lynn Zeavin has cautioned against, I find Ruth Stein's explanation of containing (or "containment," as she puts it) helpful, as it makes a certain everyday, interpersonal aspect of its operations clear: "Containment means a deep, encompassing consonant delineation of the person through mirroring, mentalization, or empathy" (Stein, "Otherness of Sexuality," 66).

52. Dames, *Physiology of the Novel*, 64.

53. Ogden, "On Holding and Containing," 1356.

54. Ogden, 1355.

55. Ogden, 1355n1.

56. Gettelman, "Reading Ahead," 43.

57. *George Eliot Letters*, 1: 105–9.

58. Eliot, *Selections*, 217.

59. Albrecht, "Sympathy and Telepathy," 438.

60. J. Miller, "Reading Writing," 76.

61. See Ogden, "On Projective Identification," 357.

62. Bion, *Learning from Experience*, 42.

63. Armstrong, *How Novels Think*, 4.

64. Mary Ann Evans was Eliot's birth name, but not its permanent form. As Laura Green writes of Eliot's pen name and personal names, as she hashes out too the possibilities for readerly identification with character and author in reading *The Mill on the Floss*: "The ontological status of 'George Eliot' is more than usually unclear. The name is a public fiction whose announced gender is at odds with the identity of the biographical person to whom it is attached; and the 'real' name used, for example in signing her letters, by the person behind the pseudonym—Marian Evans Lewes—is equally fictitious. Since Marian Evans could not marry the already-married G. H. Lewes, Marian Evans Lewes had no legal existence" (Green, "I Recognized Myself," 65).

65. See Michael Eigen, *The Electrified Tightrope*, a selection of his most important papers edited by Adam Phillips.

66. For more on Maggie's childhood doll or "Fetish," which she abuses and punishes as much as she loves, see Vanessa Smith's "Toy Stories." Smith engages *The Mill on the Floss* with Kleinian psychoanalysis, arguing that the novel is less a failed Bildungsroman than a "toy story": a story of broken toys, childhood destructiveness, and negative affect that gestures to "an alternative narrative"—radically immature, regressive, and recursive—"working within and against the imperatives of the bildungsroman" (39). Smith argues that we need to reimagine Maggie's "objects not as the fetishized 'things' of Victorian realism but as signs of *Mill*'s proleptic engagement with a dynamics of object relations" (52). My reading and Smith's share several concerns and approaches. Smith, however, focuses on Klein rather than Bion, and her approach tends to be more concrete and concretizing than my own. Smith focuses on wooden toys in Klein's practice of child psychoanalysis and wooden toys in *Mill*, argues that the novel is a proleptic forecasting of the truths of Kleinian theory (Maggie is "the vector of an impending modernity, awaiting another language to make sense of her" [38]), and ends up recruiting Kleinian theory to a familiar take on Eliotic sympathy, arguing that the outcome of the novel features Maggie "arduously and

reflexively" seeking "to substitute empathetic for projective identification" (51). I value the fact that a relational reading of Eliot and Bion both disrupts the determinism of this chronology and gives us a less-routinized picture of Eliotic sympathy.

67. Descartes, *Meditations*, 113.

68. Woolf, "George Eliot," 658. Woolf is quick to point out, though, that Eliot (Mary Ann Evans) does not share a tragic fate with her heroines: "Save for the supreme courage of their endeavour, the struggle ends, for her heroines, in tragedy, or in a compromise that is even more melancholy. But their story is the incomplete version of the story that is George Eliot herself. For her, too, the burden and the complexity of womanhood were not enough; she must reach beyond the sanctuary and pluck for herself the strange bright fruits of art and knowledge. . . . Triumphant was the issue for her, whatever it may have been for her creations, and as we recollect all that she dared and achieved, how with every obstacle against her—sex and health and convention—she sought more knowledge and more freedom till the body, weighted with its double burden, sank worn out, we must lay upon her grave whatever we have it in our power to bestow of laurel and rose" (658).

69. Hertz, *George Eliot's Pulse*, 74.

70. Benedict Anderson, *Imagined Communities*.

71. For a modern take on this style of Kleinian interpretation, updated in large part by its reference to Bion's theories, see Lucy LaFarge's wonderful paper "The Imaginer and the Imagined."

72. Esty, *Unseasonable Youth*, 63.

73. Esty, 56.

74. Esty argues that Eliot's novel betrays just this tension. Taking *The Mill on the Floss* as the first case study in historical changes in the genre wrought by British imperialism, Esty argues that the novel is a "deliberately failed bildungsroman" (52): a coming-of-age story that nevertheless excludes the possibility of Maggie's emergence as "a fully formed woman" (61). Pointing to the "soul-nation allegory" that founds the genre, Esty argues that this dual impulse is apparent on both levels of the story. The novel both meticulously charts Maggie's growth and stops it short. And the novel also carefully charts national progress and calls it into question. Esty writes that the "strain" of opposing impulses "is even more apparent in the historical frame of *The Mill on the Floss*, where Maggie Tulliver's story is embedded in a tale of social and economic reorganization that take us, in a single narrative, from the pre-Reform Bill agrarian world of St. Ogg's" (the 1820s) to the modern industrial England of the novel's narrative frame (the 1860s), a world of "global traffic and commerce" (53). The novel at once celebrates this movement as national progress and mourns it as "absolute loss": the plot pushes us to the industrial 1860s while also speaking to "the quietly devastating logic of a historicism without recuperation" in which a "rural English core" is not assimilated in national consolidation nor the global-capitalist system, but is rather entirely lost (56–57). Like Maggie's childhood, with its special "moods, sensations, relationships, and experiences," an entire way of life, rural English experience, is gone forever. The end of *The Mill on the Floss*, then, betrays how not just this particular novel but an entire genre— Esty's colonial and postcolonial literature of arrested development—is "hopelessly committed" to both maturation and a longing to evade it, to both rehearsing and trying to stop a historical trajectory that has already occurred in the time of writing.

Nathan Hensley builds on the soul-nation allegory when he argues that *The Mill on the Floss* is not simply concerned with "the birth of the modern subject," but is, "more, the story of the birth of liberal modernity itself" in mid-nineteenth-century England and "the entire political regime understood to coincide with the new contractual individualism" (*Forms of Empire*, 55).

75. Esty argues that Maggie's permanent immaturity is in a sense a saving grace. While in Eliot's "mature" fiction, such as *Middlemarch* (Esty plays on F. R. Leavis's designation of *The Mill on the Floss* as an "immature" novel), characters are forced to accommodate themselves to their social environments, *The Mill on the Floss* does not ultimately "subject Maggie to her Victorian norms of class, gender, region and religion." Esty writes: "Other Eliot heroines grow up and make their peace with social exigencies, but *Mill* represents Maggie's childhood in and for itself, not as mere prelude to the demands of full Victorian womanhood. *Mill* refuses the socialization plot in order to forestall the conversion of Maggie into a mature 'angel of the house.'" (Esty, *Unseasonable Youth*, 63). Death is, of course, a high price to pay for this immaturity. But it's true that in one way of reading, learning from experience is so hated in *The Mill on the Floss* that Maggie would sooner die than have to endure it. In the prayer that brings the flood, she says that she will bear suffering until death, but demands to know "how long it will be before death comes!—has life other trials as hard for me still?" (*MF* 536). Maggie *wants* to believe in learning from experience: "Surely there was something being taught her by this experience of great need; and she must be learning a secret of human tenderness and long-suffering, that the less erring could hardly know?" (*MF* 536). But this sentence's devolution from certainty to uncertainty in the question mark that unexpectedly punctuates the sentence—transforming the "surely" of the narrator's knowledge to the "surely?" of the character's doubtful questioning of the order of things through the use of free indirect discourse—points to Maggie's "lack of faith" in "such a kind of learning." Resorting to the deus ex machina of a flood—water starts rushing in at just this moment—means that Maggie will not have to trust to learning. In this reading, the novel's ending trades the fantasy of the "longed-for" alternative of arriving to the world fully formed for the fantasy of permanent immaturity, definitively short-circuiting the novel's "socialization plot." And yet Esty's reading, though usually so sensitive to the loss inherent to development, might miss here not only the socialization that has already occurred in Maggie's childhood, but also its enormous violence. If there is one thing the novel wants to get across, it is that childhood is not easy, innocent, or pain-free. The narrator insists again and again on the intensity of childhood experience and its suffering, so that if "*Mill* represents . . . childhood in and for itself," this is in part precisely to register the rigors of socialization, not to evade them.

76. Althusser, "Freud and Lacan," 140.

77. Althusser, 140–41.

78. "It was a totally new idea to [Maggie's] mind, that Tom could have his love troubles. Poor fellow!—and in love with Lucy too!" (*MF* 406).

79. Bollas, "Why Oedipus?" 109.

80. Bollas, 108–9.

81. Cohen, *Sex Scandal*, 133.

82. Cohen shows that Maggie's (female heterosexual) scandalous love affair is only one of the Victorian sex scandals in which *The Mill on the Floss* was implicated at the time of its publication. These scandals include not only the "passionate" love story of the novel, but also the "real life" of Marian Evans. Readers' reactions to the novel frequently connected Maggie's elopement with Stephen Guest to both the revelation of the author Marian Evans's identity and, consequently, the fact of her extramarital relationship with George Henry Lewes, a man legally married to

another woman. "The scandal of Eliot's adulterous relationship with George Henry Lewes, and the inextricability of it from the secret of her authorship," Cohen writes, "resonate with the themes of illicit sexuality, alienation from community, and the invidiousness of public opinion in *The Mill on the Floss*" (*Sex Scandal*, 153). Gillian Beer also explores these various scandals in her book *George Eliot*, which includes one of the most compelling discussions I know of on "George Eliot's" decision to use a male pen name and its consequences. She writes: "One goal of writing may be the escape from gender, and it would be a mistake to loop all imaginative writing back into the ghetto of gender, what the Marxist-Feminist Collective describes as criticism that subsumes 'the text into the sexually-defined personality of its author, and thereby obliterates its literality.' But though the arc of desire may be escape from gender, the pre-conditions of writing are bound to the writer's experience as social, sexual, historical being and the writing itself is part of its culture. In the case of George Eliot we have a striking example of a writer who sought to slough off the contextuality of her own name and enter a neutral space for her writing." She adds, revising herself: "That is an abstract and an idealized description of a process which cost much" (Beer, *George Eliot*, 25).

83. The most notable review to this effect is worth citing at length: "Passion, and especially the passion of love, is so avowedly the chief subject of the modern novel that we can scarcely quarrel with a novelist because the passion she chooses to describe is of a very intense kind. We all know that love is neither a smooth-going nor a strictly decorous and prudential affair, and there are many emotions in female breasts, even when the sufferer is judged by her acquaintance to be an ordinary sort of person, which would shock friends and critics if put down in black and white. But there is a kind of love-making which seems to possess a strange fascination for the modern female novelist. Currer Bell and George Eliot, and we may add George Sand, all like to dwell on love as a strange overmastering force which, through the senses, captivates and enthralls the soul. They linger on the physical sensations that accompany the meeting of hearts in love. Curiously, too, they all like to describe these sensations as they conceive them to exist in men. We are bound to say that their conceptions are true and adequate. But we are not sure that it is quite consistent with feminine delicacy to lay so much stress on the bodily feelings of the other sex.... [Eliot] lets her fancy run on things which are not wrong, but are better omitted from the scope of female meditation.... In points like these, it may be observed that men are more delicate than women. There are very few men who would not shrink from putting into words what they might imagine to be the physical effects of love in a woman" (unsigned review, *Saturday Review* 4 [14 April 1860]: 470–71, repr. in D. Carroll, *Critical Heritage*, 118–19).

84. I want to note here that vibrations and reverberations are also ways of conceptualizing Bion's container/contained. As the modern psychoanalyst Lucy LaFarge puts it, "containment may be conceptualised as a mutual process, a *reverberating exchange* between patient and analyst in which affects and fantasies are elaborated and modified as they are transmitted back and forth by projective identification" ("Interpretation and Containment," 69, emphasis added.)

85. Milton, *Paradise Lost*, bk. 3, st. 1, lines 11–12.

86. Nancy Miller, "Emphasis Added," 46. Miller argues that when the plots of eighteenth- and nineteenth-century women's fiction (including Eliot's) are condemned for their implausibility, their "extravagance," their added "emphasis," their sensitivity and sensibility, it is not because they are departing from life, but rather breaking with gendered norms of storytelling.

87. Phillips, "On Frustration," 26.

88. Phillips, 3.

89. See Audre Lorde's "Uses of the Erotic," originally delivered as a paper in 1978. Lorde calls "the erotic a source of power and information." She writes: "The erotic is a measure between the beginnings of our sense of self and the chaos of our strongest feelings. It is an internal sense of satisfaction to which, once we have experienced it, we know we can aspire.... The erotic is not only a question of what we do; it is a question of how acutely and fully we can feel in the doing" (54). I would like to pursue a reading of Eliot's fiction and Lorde's essay more fully, because I think the picture of feminine sexuality Lorde offers resonates there in very illuminating ways. I can imagine the following lines from Lorde as being extremely helpful to our reading of *Middlemarch*, especially the way I read it and its secular interests in the last chapter of this book: "Another important way in which the erotic connection functions is the open and fearless underlining of my capacity for joy. In the way my body stretches to music and opens into response, hearkening to its deepest rhythms, so every level upon which I sense also opens to the erotically satisfying experience, whether it is dancing, building a bookcase, writing a poem, examining an idea. That self-connection shared is a measure of the joy which I know myself to be capable of feeling, a reminder of my capacity for feeling. And that deep and irreplaceable knowledge of my capacity for joy comes to demand from all of my life that it be lived within the knowledge that such satisfaction is possible, and does not have to be called *marriage*, nor *god*, nor *an afterlife*" (56–57). I am grateful to my dear friend, the late Manuel Matos (1981–2018), for first introducing me to Lorde's essay through his own profound engagement with black feminist thought. Rest in power, Manuel.

90. For further elaboration of these ideas, see adrienne maree brown's book *Emergent Strategy: Shaping Change, Changing Worlds* and the speculative fiction collection she coedited with Walidah Imarisha, entitled *Octavia's Brood: Science Fiction Stories from Social Justice Movements*. Since May 2017, she also been writing a biweekly column for *Bitch* magazine. Brown's work in "generative somatics" links individual healing from trauma with larger projects in social justice, and in this way builds from Lorde's work. For a useful introduction to that concept, see the Healing Justice podcast episode entitled "Trauma, Healing, & Collective Power with Generative Somatics" (Kate Werning).

91. This both is and is not a "genealogy" of wishfulness, and it is certainly not singular. I am by no means arguing that the origin of all feminist thought, let alone all women of color feminist thought, is in the writing of George Eliot. Her work has certainly enabled many feminists and feminist desires, as I earlier quoted Sara Ahmed as arguing, but it is of course not their only source. I am just as interested in the wishfulness that flows in the other direction: wishing, as I'll go on to clarify, that George Eliot had been able to think more incisively about racial difference, and working to mediate and remediate her work by reading it in conversation with black and woman of color feminism as well as queer and queer of color theory. What I am sketching obeys a different notion of plot, development, and futurity whose priority is reading relationally rather than chronologically or causally—as in the relational reading Bion models in his approach to the Oedipus myth.

92. Christopher Bollas has a language for understanding this too: psychic trauma and psychic genera, which I reference in this book's introduction. See Bollas, "Psychic Genera."

93. Rosenfeld, "Psychopathology of Psychotic States."

94. Ogden, "On Projective Identification," 362.

95. Jacobus, "Men of Maxims," 209.

96. I follow Eliot's usage of "gypsy" throughout my argument in order to stay consistent with the novel and to represent the Victorian reliance on this word and trope (for a fuller history of Victorian engagements, see Deborah Epstein Nord, *Gypsies & the British Imagination, 1807–193*). I do not want, however, to replicate the discursive violence of a misnaming the Roma people or using a racially charged epithet that is now considered, by some although certainly not all, to be offensive (the word "Gypsy" has been reclaimed for self-identification by some). By way of a small countermeasure to the novel's exclusionary violence, I want to cite here a few websites and articles by and on the modern Romani community, offering readers ways of informing themselves about this community (including hearing their own voices). See the International Romani Union website, https://iromaniunion.org/index.php/en/; the Unión Romaní website, https://unionromani.org/en/; and Margareta Matache's three-part blog series, *The White Norm in Gypsy and Romani Studies*: "Word, Image and Thought: Creating the Romani Other," "The Legacy of Gypsy Studies in Modern Romani Scholarship," and "Dear Gadjo (non-Romani) Scholars . . ."

97. Muñoz, *Disidentifications*.

98. Homans, "Dinah's Blush," 156. Homans writes that she is building on the work of Nancy Armstrong, Mary Poovey, and Cora Kaplan: all of these critics sought, in the mid-1980s, to offer a corrective to mainstream academic feminist criticism by "articulat[ing] the relation of gender to class" (156). Maggie's overt sexuality (and, indeed, her sometimes lower-class status) initially seems to pose a challenge to Homans's argument, as her claim operates on the logic that, in Victorian fiction, female sexual desire is coded as lower-class (as in Hetty's seduction, pregnancy, and infanticide in *Adam Bede*), and only made viable, in middle-class women, in attenuated, domestic forms (as in Dinah's blush in the same novel). But in *The Mill on the Floss* Eliot does manage, "by the same ideological program," to turn "the heroine's trembling, vibrating sexuality into the chief source of her identification as simultaneously middle class and class-transcendent" (168). Homans convincingly argues that while Maggie "is not normally read in class or economic terms," but more often taken as a stand-in for "timeless female sexuality"—as in, we should note, Jacobus's reading—Maggie's desire for Stephen is distinctly and consistently "classed." Her desire for him resonates with his connections to luxury, to consumer culture, and to upper-middle-class industry (170).

99. Homans, 162.

100. See, for instance, Elaine Freedgood, who, in *The Ideas in Things: Fugitive Meaning in the Victorian Novel*, describes this move by way of another paradigmatic Victorian novel: "*Jane Eyre* and *Jane Eyre* do a quintessentially Victorian ideological thing: the novel and its narrator-heroine begin to make an actual historical problem into a part of a newly constructed human condition. In rendering a problem transhistorical, and thereby spiritual and psychological and, above all, individual, its solution lies also in the realm of the spiritual and what will become the psychological—the realm of individual interiority" (48–49).

101. Hensley, *Forms of Empire*, 58.

102. As Deborah Nord points out, this notion references the inaccurate but pervasive Victorian (and perhaps ongoing) myth that gypsies steal British babies or swap them out for their own. See her book *Gypsies & the British Imagination, 1807–1930*.

103. In Nord's compelling claim, Eliot uses the gypsy to figure "the kind of individual to whom she returned again and again: the alien or inexplicably aberrant member of a community that

is otherwise homogenous, organic, and traditional" (99). The gypsy—the "internal alien," the "other within"—becomes a mere stand-in for a figure like Maggie, allowing Eliot to mark her difference and allowing Maggie to both feel this difference herself (as when she "tries on" gypsy identity in her half-day escape) and, disposing of it (when she discards this identity and returns back home), to re-enter the community. The gypsy, then, helps to define George Eliot's famously "knowable community" precisely by being rejected or expelled. Nord argues that Maggie's encounter with the gypsies is not primarily an encounter with others, but a way of dramatizing aspects of the self: it is for Maggie an acting out of a "reverse" family romance, a dream not of high birth but of lowly or culturally debased origins that will help to explain her emotional distance from her family of origin. So while in Eliot's later work this "fantasy" of family romance will become a concrete "plot"—as characters like Feldama in *The Spanish Gypsy* and Daniel Deronda discover actual parentage in other ethnic groups, and respond by entering into plots of expatriation and new-nation making (107)—in *The Mill on the Floss*, ethnic and racial difference is a mere metaphor, and the actual historical gypsy "impossible" in its world. As James Buzard puts a similar claim, the novel engages a fantasy of the community and indeed the larger nation at times partially active in Eliot's work, including *Daniel Deronda*, with its focus on Jewish culture and its proto-Zionist plot: a fantasy in which the "category of race" determines "which culture and which nation" properly belong to a person/character, and whose final extension is "the wholesale ethnic cleansing of each nation and the clean partitioning of the civilized world into airtight container-nations for the occupation of single races" (Buzard, *Disorienting Fiction*, 294).

Alicia Carroll takes Nord's de-concretizing reading of race in Eliot's fiction even further, arguing that feminine "desire is figured through images of darkness and ethnic Otherness throughout [her] canon" (*Dark Smiles*, 3)—that Eliot uses racialized figures to stand in for Victorian women's sexual desire as it is disowned and suppressed by middle-class norms of domesticity and respectability. While Carroll's argument looks to both expose the underlying racism in the operation of "portray[ing] the erotic through Otherness" (40) and to show that "Eliot's trope of Otherness" includes "a critique of empire and Englishness" (28), it tends to undercut itself by continually referring race back to figurations of white female desire. Carroll writes of *The Mill on the Floss*: "discourses of race, both whiteness and blackness [and including the 'rebellious female challenge' which the Gypsy woman presented to domestic ideology], clarify Maggie Tulliver's struggle with women's compulsory innocence" (40). As in Nord's more pointed critique of the same problem (and indeed in Said's and Spivak's foundational critiques of Victorian literature in the same vein), the gypsy is used as a mirror to Maggie's sexual desire even while confirming her in her whiteness. See also Said, *Orientalism*, and Gavatri Chakravorty Spivak, "Three Women's Texts and a Critique of Imperialism."

104. Muñoz, *Disidentifications*, 6.

105. Muñoz, 9.

106. Phillips, introduction to *The Electrified Tightrope*, by Michael Eigen, xv. Phillips quotes Eigen's writing in the same volume (234–35).

107. hooks, *Yearning*, 12–13. The longer passage, resonant and consonant with the work of Lorde, brown, and, I argue, George Eliot in refusing the separation between erotic and political desire, begins: "I gathered this group of essays under the heading *Yearning* because as I looked for common passions, sentiments shared by folks across race, class, gender, and sexual practice, I was struck by the depth of longing in many of us. Those without money long to get rid of the

endless sense of deprivation. Those with money wonder why so much feels so meaningless and long to find the site of 'meaning.' . . . All too often our political desire for change is seen as separate from longings and passions that consume lots of time and energy in daily life. Particularly the realm of fantasy is often seen as completely separate from politics. Yet I think of all the time black folks (especially the underclass) spend just fantasizing about what our lives would be like if there was no racism, no white supremacy. Surely our desire for radical social change is intimately linked with the desire to experience pleasure, erotic fulfillment, and a host of other passions. Then, on the flip side, there are many individuals with race, gender, and class privilege who are longing to see the kind of revolutionary change that will end domination and oppression, even though their lives would be completely and utterly transformed." These remarks are followed by the sentence I quote in the body of the chapter, which argues for yearning as a way to create community even across difference.

Chapter 3

1. A. Balint and Balint, "Transference and Counter-Transference," 224.
2. A. Balint and Balint, 227.
3. I draw this definition from Dora Zhang, whose "Notes on Atmosphere" begins with the following preliminary definition of the term "atmosphere": "Deriving from the Greek *atmos*, vapor or steam, combined with *sphaira*, ball or globe, in its basic sense the word refers to the envelope of gas surrounding the earth or any other celestial body. Used figuratively, it has a much wider reach, indicating the characteristic tone or pervading mood of a surrounding environment" (121).
4. The perception of the heath as at once exhilarating and soothing is Clym's. When Eustacia, a native of the English seaside town of Budmouth who longs for more stimulation than Egdon Heath and its small community can offer, tells him she "cannot endure the heath, except in its purple season," Clym responds: "Can you say so? . . . To my mind it is most exhilarating, and strengthening, and soothing. I would rather live on these hills than anywhere else in the world" (*RN* 185). The conversation articulates the organizing conflicts of the novel: the local and the global, mobility and immobility (and their gender- and class-based distribution), stasis and change, rest and restlessness, and the novel's own opposing abilities to exhilarate and to soothe. Penny Boumelha describes *The Return of the Native* as a novel about restlessness, centered on "incoherent aspiration and a restless dissatisfaction with the material conditions of life" on Egdon Heath (*Thomas Hardy and Women*, 51). While Freud discusses the antithetical meanings implied in single words, Winnicott reminds us that a single word has more than one opposite. The novel flips rest into both restlessness and "unrest"—itself one of Hardy's most relied-upon words.

Unrest appears, famously, in *Jude the Obscure*, in the memorable phrase "the modern vice of unrest" (*J* 85): the pull away from accustomed places and vocations that arguably ruins Jude and which, Hardy wants to argue, shapes the modern condition. In Hardy's poetry, the phrase "bleak unrest" describes life itself: its refusal to stop and slow, to offer any respite from motion and agitation except in death. As these signal phrases suggest, Hardy uses "unrest" in a curious way: not to convey a precise social or political condition—as in, for instance, the labor uprisings of the Swing riots of the 1830s, the period immediately preceding the one in which *Return* is set—but rather, drawing on the word's more concrete etymology, a more generalized condition: unrest for Hardy speaks to the disharmony, discord, turmoil, trouble, or coil "of things" (one of

Hardy's favorite generalizing phrases). This Hardyan vision is spelled out, as we have seen, in *Tess of the D'Urbervilles*, as well: what hounds Tess throughout the novel is not simply death or disgrace, but rather "the pulse of hopeful life" that will not let her rest. As Michael Wood remarks, only Hardy could make "celebratory phrases" like this one and its recurring analogues, such as "the appetite for joy that pervades all creation," sound like so many "damning accusations" ("Greatness and Melancholy"). Hardy at once emphasizes modern life as a condition of restlessness and, as I have argued in the introduction to this book, offers his novels as so many counterbalances, staging moments of rest on the level of both story and narrative form, and making rest one of the most powerful, albeit punctual, atmospheres of *The Return of the Native*. While my earlier chapter on *Tess* showed how Hardy's fiction alternates the unrest of plot, with its melodramatic turns of event, its cliffhangers, its narrowly missed encounters, its "satires of circumstance," and their attendant heightened emotional pitch, with the restfulness of lyrical descriptive passage, this chapter explores Hardy's descriptive practice from another angle: it follows the busy movement of the novel's prolific allusions, references, similes, and metaphors to argue for the presence of a wider world inscribed in the novel and its heath, and a clearer picture of actual colonial unrest than we have previously acknowledged.

5. Balint (born Mihály Bergsmann) was a Hungarian analyst who trained in his native Budapest under Sándor Ferenczi (as well as in Berlin under Hans Sachs) before moving to England in 1939. There, he worked with central British school thinkers and published his major works: *Primary Love and Psycho-Analytic Technique* (1952; a collection of earlier papers, some originally published in Hungarian or German and now translated into English, and many written in collaboration with his first wife, the psychoanalyst Alice Balint), *The Doctor, His Patient, and the Illness* (1957, written in English, as all of his later works), *Thrills and Regressions* (1959; published in collaboration with the psychoanalyst Enid Balint, his second wife, whose sole-authored work closes the book), and, most notably, *The Basic Fault: Therapeutic Aspects of Regression* (1967), his magnum opus on the formative effects of early disturbances in object relationships and the therapeutic power of regression. Trained as a doctor before becoming an analyst, Balint is perhaps most famous for developing "Balint groups," in which medical doctors discussed the psychodynamic aspects of medical practice and the patient-doctor relationship. In *Doctor*, a popular and influential work outside the psychoanalytic world that has been translated into fourteen languages, Balint writes: "the most frequently used drug in general practice [is] the doctor himself, i.e. it [is] not only the bottle of medicine or the box of pills that matter[s], but the way the doctor [gives] them to his patient—in fact, the whole atmosphere in which the drug [is] given and taken" (1). For more on Balint's work on medicine, see Jonathan Sklar, *Balint Matters: Psychosomatics and the Art of Assessment*. Arguing for the ongoing importance of Balint's work, Sklar writes that Balint "kept alive Ferenczi's analytic traditions in Budapest and brought them to London, where they became a vital part of the Independent Group's theory and practice." Sklar then goes on to point out that Balint's life and theories help us to see how much psychoanalysis has to contribute to general medical practice, and to family medicine in particular (xv–xvi, and elsewhere).

6. See M. Balint, "Friendly Expanses—Horrid Empty Spaces," later collected in and expanded upon in *Thrills and Regressions*.

7. As I have mentioned in the introduction, I borrow the phrase "colonial object relations" from David Eng, who argues for the importance of situating psychoanalytic concepts (for

instance, Freud's death drive and Melanie Klein's reparation) within the larger histories of war and colonial violence. Eng, "Colonial Object Relations." I return to his essay and discuss it in more detail later in the chapter.

8. For more on depictions of race in Hardy's work, see Patricia O'Hara, "Narrating the Native: Victorian Anthropology and Hardy's *The Return of the Native*"; Angelique Richardson, "Hardy and Biology"; and Brett Neilson, "Hardy, Barbarism, and the Transformations of Modernity."

9. I am drawing my definition of white mythology from Jacques Derrida's essay "White Mythology: Metaphor in the Text of Philosophy" and from Robert J. C. Young's *White Mythologies: Writing History and the West*, and I use it to refer to, first, Western history writing that effaces the fact of colonialism, trying to erase it from the construction of Western space, Western culture, and Western identity, and second, to the construction of racial whiteness as a neutral universal category of being, as subjectivity itself. I am arguing that Victorian novels and British psychoanalysis are complicit in both of these projects of mythologization and forgetting. For a particularly helpful exposition of the enormous and ongoing violence of the Western philosophical project of constructing a neutral universal definition of "Man" (the dominant ethnoclass) at the expense of the human, see Sylvia Wynter, "Unsettling the Coloniality of Being/Power/Truth/Freedom."

10. This description is Hardy's own from 1912, cited in Gatrell, "Wessex," 30. As Simon Gatrell notes, in an earlier formulation, Hardy calls Wessex "a merely realistic dream-country" (30).

11. Beer, "Can the Native Return?" and R. Williams, *The Country and the City*.

12. For more on Hardy's engagement with astronomy, as fact and as figure, see Anna Henchman, *The Starry Sky Within: Astronomy and the Reach of the Mind in Victorian Literature*.

13. I want to note here how frequently Balint's work depends upon collaboration with women—here, his first wife Alice, and later, after she passed away and Balint remarried, his second wife Enid Flora Balint (née Albu, later Balint-Edmonds, 1903–94), who was a psychoanalyst and social worker, and who contributed in particular to *Thrills and Regressions* (1959). Despite the thanks he gives to these women and his acknowledgments of their labor in the prefaces to his books, it is notable that Michael Balint's work is generally signed with his name alone, and that his fame and reputation far surpasses their own. Alice Balint is not listed in the *Oxford Dictionary of National Biography*, and Enid Balint's entry comprises a single paragraph contained within the entry on Michael Balint. I have not figured out how to fully avoid replicating that problem and its erasure of women's intellectual labor and contributions here, which I very much regret. But I do at least want to signal the problem and my awareness of it, on the way to doing fuller justice to these women and their work.

In the next chapter, I focus more fully on women psychoanalysts in the British circle, engaging the work of Paula Heimann (1899–1982) and Betty Joseph (1917–2013) in particular. Literary scholar Adela Pinch has also emphasized the contributions of women to object relations thought: in her paper "Preserving Attachments" for the 2017 NAVSA conference, she highlighted the work of Marjorie Brierly (1893–1984), Susan Isaacs (1885–1948), Marion Milner (1900–1998), Joan Riviere (1883–1962), Ella Freeman Sharpe (1875–1947), and Alix Strachey (1892–1973). Pinch argues: "From its origins in 1913 at the Medico-Psychological clinic in London, psychoanalysis turned out to be a hospitable career for imaginative women, many of whom were incredibly great, and very literary, writers. British women psychoanalytic writers were the Victorian novelists of the twentieth century" (4).

14. A. Balint and Balint, "Transference and Counter-Transference," 224–25.

15. A. Balint and Balint, 226–27.

16. And to be clear, for Balint, the aim of psychoanalysis itself is also wordless: it is not to help the patient to a greater degree of expressivity, or to be able to articulate his conflicts, but rather "to help the patient have feelings, emotions, and experiences that he was incapable of having before" (*BF* 160).

17. Zhang, "Notes on Atmosphere," 121. Importantly, Zhang notes that an analysis of atmosphere calls for different analytic and theoretical tools and methods. She writes that accomplishing her aim of "generat[ing] precise descriptions of those hard-to-pin-down but influential aspects of our environments that exist ubiquitously but often go unnoticed" entails "a mode of theorizing that aims less at defining or stabilizing a concept than at sensitizing us to it." She recognizes that such work might seem imprecise: "The up-in-the-air quality, as it were, of such theorizing will no doubt be frustrating to some, but it is occasioned by the fact that this phenomenon defies our desire for conceptual integrity and resists our usual models of causality." And yet "none of this means that it is not worth taking seriously, even if it eludes our standard modes of analysis" (124).

18. Zhang, 123. While focusing on Fernández-Savater and the 15-M movement in Spain, Zhang attends as well to linked Occupy, anti-capitalist, and anti-austerity struggles and strategies across the world.

19. As editor Tim Dolin explains in the Penguin edition (*T* 489), this dance scene and the subsequent rape of Tess were cut for the bowdlerized version of the novel first published in *Graphic*, and the excised chapters were published instead under the title "Saturday Night in Arcady" in the *National Observer*. While Hardy reinstated most of the material for the first volume edition in 1891, the Chaseborough dance scene remained missing, and is thus printed as an appendix at the end of the novel (*T* 490–502). Hardy reinstated it in the 1912 Wessex edition.

20. Cohen, *Embodied*, 99. See also his essay "Arborealities: The Tactile Ecology of Hardy's Woodlanders," as well as Cohn, "No Insignificant Creature," and the longer version of that article in her book *Still Life: Suspended Development in the Victorian Novel*; Elaine Scarry, *Resisting Representation*; and Rachel Ablow, *Victorian Pain*.

21. Readers interested in psychoanalytic literary criticism may recognize Balint's "harmonious interpenetrating mix-up" from Eve Kosofsky Sedgwick's deployment of it in one of her final essays, "The Weather in Proust." There, Sedgwick uses this phrase, and Balint's notion of a benign regression to that stage of object relating in psychoanalytic treatment, interchangeably with Winnicott's "holding environment": both thinkers are gesturing to the way other people can serve as sustaining forces rather than distinct objects. These ideas, Sedgwick argues, illuminate an underexplored side of desire in *À la recherche du temps perdu*. Proust depicts, she argues, a desire that is not appropriative, envious, or even distinctly sexual, but that is instead existential—alternately terror inducing and taken for granted, just as Balint describes. In her reading, the narrator's intense longing for a goodnight kiss from his mother is likened not to a jealous lover's desire for a woman's body, but rather to an asthmatic's need for air. Accordingly, Sedgwick's larger claim is that Balint and other object relations thinkers help us to dislodge the traditional Oedipal narratives that have become "commonsense" approaches to both "psychic life and

textuality." Sedgwick argues that traditional Freudian and Lacanian approaches, founded in sexual rivalry, dualistic gender difference, and the "closed system[s] of either/or and zero sum" logics, are inadequate to a full exploration of the "meaning and structure" of the "more complex energies in Proust" ("Weather in Proust," 5).

There is much to admire and learn from in Sedgwick's essay. And yet the quick conflation of Balint and Winnicott keeps us from seeing some of the unique capacities of Balint's theories. This is important because Sedgwick's account of object relations theory has been so influential. Her account, compelling but incomplete (and self-avowedly mystical in this particular essay), has led, I think, to a somewhat limited vision of the potential uses of object relations thought in literary analysis, which I am hoping to both build from and extend. Sedgwick's use of Balint does not take full advantage, I think, of his description of the various *uses* of space—just as ecocritical views of the fundamental mix-up of person and landscape in Hardy's fiction frequently fail to take full account of the many layers of culture and history Hardy embeds in his "uncouth" heath through his restless practice of figuration, references, and allusion.

Some of this is opened up for me by turning to aspects of Balint's writing beyond the "harmonious interpenetrating mix-up" that is so easily collapsed into Winnicott's holding environment. The benign regression that Sedgwick uses to stand in for all of Balint's theory is, after all, just one part of the process for Balint. Treating the analyst as an environment is a means to effect change, the "new beginning" Balint argues analysis is capable of inaugurating, and in which entrenched habits of relating to objects can be renovated. In times of benign regression, the "unobtrusive analyst" is in fact doing a great deal of work—not just offering himself up to become an object of primary love, or a facilitating environment, as in Winnicott's formulations, but actively manipulating distances in order to make this happen. Balint writes: "Emphatically, [regression] does not mean that in these periods the analyst's role becomes negligible or is restricted to sympathetic passivity; on the contrary, his presence is important, not only in that he must be felt to be present but must be all the time at the right distance—neither so far that the patient might feel lost or abandoned, nor so close that the patient might feel encumbered and unfree—in fact, at a distance that corresponds to the patient's actual need; in general the analyst must know what are the patient's needs, why they are as they are, and why they fluctuate and change" (BF 179). It is the analyst's responsibility to constantly modulate distances according to the patient's changing needs so that objects can be felt in new ways, neither too far nor too close. Balint's emphasis on finding "the right distance" between analyst and patient has an even more interesting secondary effect: it charges the space between them in a way totally unique to Balint's way of thinking and describing object relations.

22. In making this claim, I am gesturing back to readings I offered in earlier chapters of this book, and briefly revisiting too Winnicott's theories of "transitional space" and the "holding environment." Balint is explicit in linking his own terminology to that of other psychoanalytic thinkers who have also tried to theorize "this sort of . . . environment-patient relationship." His list of such terms, ranging from Anna Freud's "need-satisfying object" to Hartmann's "average expectable environment" to Bion's container/contained to Margaret Little's "basic unit" and more, spans several competing psychoanalytic traditions (including ego-psychology, Kleinian, and Independent approaches), and yet gives Winnicott pride of place as "the most versatile inventor of such terms." Balint nevertheless argues that his own terms are the most useful, as they are the most comprehensive of the ideas suggested by others (BF 168). This chapter will go on to keep

spelling out the particularities of Balint's thinking and its particular offerings to literary theory and theories of the novel—and this will involve looking beyond the "harmonious interpenetrating mix-up" and benign regression to investigate both specific manipulations of space and distance and the "new beginning" inscribed in his theories.

23. Beer, *Darwin's Plots*, 246.

24. Wild movements in voice add to the sense of a discontinuous reading experience. As Beer so skillfully describes it, Hardy vacillates between "experience-near and experience-far language." She writes: "His vocabulary ricochets across registers, between language close as touch and removed as latinate legal documents. As readers, we are shifted unendingly between microscopic and telescopic, between very old dialect words and very up-to-date references" ("Can the Native Return?" 516). Hardy moves us rapidly between a character's angle of vision to an anonymous (and sometimes ostentatiously learned) narrator's erudite references to landscape description vividly rendered from, as Elisha Cohn puts it, "no particular point of view" ("No Insignificant Creature," 502). One moment, we are inside a heath-bell; the next, looking down over vast swaths of land as the light slowly changes from dusk to evening.

25. Sedgwick, "Weather in Proust," 12.

26. For a remarkable history of these events, see Partha Chatterjee, *The Black Hole of Empire: History of a Global Practice of Power*.

27. P. Chatterjee, 4–5.

28. The full explanatory footnote in the Penguin edition of *The Return of the Native* edited by Slade reads: "On the 20 June 1756, at the fall of Calcutta to Indian forces, 146 European men and one woman were herded into a hot and airless room only eighteen feet long and fourteen wide; when released the following morning, only twenty-three were still alive. The tragedy of the Black Hole of Calcutta became long and deeply entrenched into British folk-memory of their rule in India" (421n3).

29. P. Chatterjee, *Black Hole of Empire*, xi.

30. P. Chatterjee, xi.

31. P. Chatterjee, xi.

32. Here is how their suffering is rendered in this passage: Clym's grief is described as more agonizing in silence than in speaking it aloud, "for in silence he endured infinitely more, and would sometimes remain so long in a tense, brooding mood, consuming himself by the gnawing of his thought, that it was imperatively necessary to talk aloud, that his grief might in some degree expend itself in that effort" (*RN* 304). And Clym describes his mother's death in this way: "she died on the heath like an animal kicked out, nobody to help her until it was too late. If you could have seen her, Thomasin, as I saw her—a poor dying woman, lying in the dark upon the bare ground, moaning, nobody near, believing she was utterly deserted by all the world, it would have moved you to anguish, it would have moved a brute" (*RN* 305).

33. Bowen, "Clive, Robert."

34. Hardy, *Personal Notebooks*, 79, 93.

35. Hardy, *Dynasts*, cited in Chakravarty, *Indian Mutiny*, 19. Terry Eagleton describes the Victorian period as "an era badly rattled" by world-changing geologic, evolutionary, and political revolutions—and, we should add, by the ongoing, if disavowed, imperial violence of the era of *Pax Britannica*. The formulation echoes Hardy's description of war and an earlier formulation that describes the condition of life itself. In *Jude the Obscure*, Hardy writes: "All around you there

seemed to be something glaring, garish, rattling, and the noises and glares hit upon the little cell called your life, and shook it, and scorched it" (J 18). Famously, little Hardy lived through a very similar childhood scene, as recorded in Florence Emily Hardy, *The Early Life of Thomas Hardy, 1840–1891*, 19–20. Undoubtedly, Hardy's novels work to both picture and to recreate for readers the "rattling" condition of late-Victorian life, drawing them into its "noises and glares," its painful hyperesthesia, its upheavals of faith and feeling, its sense that traditional ways of life were ending. And yet as I have argued in the introduction and chapter 1 on *Tess of the D'Urbervilles*, Hardy's fiction also works to still the rattling, to attenuate the blows of sense perception through aesthetic representation, and to offer moments of rest amidst the "bleak unrest" that Hardy writes is definitive of life itself.

36. For further writing on the violence that undergirded the era of the *Pax Britannica*, see Hensley, *Forms of Empire*, and Antoinette M. Burton, *The Trouble with Empire: Challenges to Modern British Imperialism*, where she describes repeated challenges to British imperial rule in the era rather than a monolithic or firmly settled power.

37. Hardy, "Embarcation," 86.

38. Violence the poem arguably occludes. Jane Bownas writes: "By comparing imperial Britain's war in South Africa with imperial Rome's invasion of Britain in his poem 'Embarcation,' [Hardy] is demonstrating that there is in fact no progress in history and that the methods used by both powers are the same" (*Thomas Hardy and Empire*, 51). As Bownas points out, Hardy's interest in this particular war may be tied to its nonindigenous combatants. See also "Empire" by Jane Bownas and Rena Jackson.

39. The novel's interest in how mood alters atmosphere and environment alike is perhaps nowhere better marked than in the contrast between Eustacia's nighttime flight across the heath and Thomasin's travels that same night. What is menacing and awful to Eustacia is ordinary bad weather to Thomasin.

40. Ferguson, "Bonfire Night," 88.

41. R. Williams, *The Country and the City*, 83. For an important critique of the way Williams's analyses tend to ignore the larger imperial contexts in and through which the English economy developed, see Gauri Viswanathan's "Raymond Williams and British Colonialism: The Limits of Metropolitan Cultural Theory."

42. See Sharpe, *Remember, Remember*.

43. Briefel, *Racial Hand*, 2.

44. In *Resisting Representation*, Elaine Scarry beautifully articulates the complexities of Hardy's description of bodily work in his novels, and, in particular, the way workers in Hardy are shaped by and to their tools and materials.

45. I am interested too in the pride of place given here to bright colors, rather than the camouflaging greens and browns that Mrs. Yeobright observes. The "brightest" and "most brilliant" colors emerge before Clym's partially dimmed eyes: the "emerald-green" of grasshoppers, the "strange amber" of Egdon butterfly wings, the raw "yellows and blues" of new-skinned snakes, the "blood-red" veins of a rabbit's sun-pierced ears. These are bright spots for the reader's eyes too, dimmed as they are by the black-on-white printed page. In a journal entry from 1897, Hardy wrote: "Today has length, breadth, thickness, colour, smell, voice. As soon as it becomes *yesterday* it is a thin layer among many layers, without substance, colour, or articulate sound" (quoted in Hardy, *Life and Work*, 302). Hardy's writing, as Beer puts it, "seeks the palpable" (*Darwin's Plots*,

244). In Hardy's terms, it looks to recover the substance, sound, and color of the day. Surely, one function of bright color in the passage is to give today-ness to Clym's experience and the natural world. But I wonder too if the bright colors in the passage might also work to prepare us for the revelation of the brownness of Clym's skin in the pages that follow, making it pop.

46. I am re-echoing here, from chapter 2, Bion's insight regarding O: while in one sense we can never fully access O, in another, O is all that we are ever actually experiencing.

47. These links are solidified in other sections of the novel. Eustacia, in the first throes of love, her thoughts refusing to stay within her own personality and venturing instead to Clym, "full of her passionate and indescribable solicitude for one to whom she was not even a name," cannot be contained in her house either, and goes for a walk outside: "she went forth into the amplitude of tanned wild around her, restless as Ahasuerus the Jew" (*RN* 147). Eustacia and the heath, refusing to be tamed by "white paling," are "tanned wild," and Eustacia is figured as the "Wandering Jew" to the figuration of Diggory Venn, on the same page, as "Israel in Zin" (*RN* 147).

48. Quincey, *English Opium-Eater*, 96.

49. A later description reads: "There was a certain obscurity in Eustacia's beauty, and Venn's eye was not trained. In her winter dress, as now, she was like the tiger-beetle, which, when observed in dull situations, seems to be the quietest neutral color, but under a full illumination blazes with dazzling splendour" (*RN* 92). See also Jules David Law's "Sleeping Figures: Hardy, History, and the Gendered Body."

50. Stoler, *Education of Desire*, 5.

51. I am grateful to Truth Murray Cole for pointing this passage out to me, and for the inspiring essay on Eustacia Vye she wrote for my Victorian novel course in spring 2018. Cole writes: "Mrs. Yeobright's tone implies that being associated with darkness implies blemishes to Eustacia's character in a way being fair does not. One blemish we are made to assume is Eustacia's advanced sexual knowledge. We are never explicitly told, but instead made to assume through Eustacia's movements: 'Eustacia sighed: it was no fragile maiden sigh, but a sigh which shook her like a shiver' [*RN* 68]. Because of her assumed sexual knowledge, Eustacia is both able and desires to intensely experience the physical in a manner unbefitting an innocent woman; she gives herself over to the sigh, letting it shake her. The intense physicality of the sigh cannot be contained within a single clause and thus spills through the colons into another clause. Throughout the novel, Eustacia becomes marked by sexually coded words like 'shiver' and 'quiver,' that relay the sense that if she is not in a constant orgasm (of experience) that she has at least experienced one before" (Cole, "Narrative Policing of Eustacia," 1–2). Cole's larger argument in the essay is also apposite to my claims: "Simultaneously attracted and threatened by Eustacia's lack of conventional femininity, the narrator both supports and polices her" (1).

52. The full passage describes a pair of human figures made white and visible by the racialized background of the heath: "The moon had now waxed bright and silvery, but the swarthy heath was proof against such illumination, and there was to be observed the striking scene of a dark, rayless tract of country, under an atmosphere charged from its zenith to its extremities with whitest light. To an eye above them their two faces would have appeared amid the expanse like two pearls on a table of ebony" (*RN* 259).

53. Stoler, *Education of Desire*, 7.

54. Brantlinger, "Terrible Turks," 208–30.

55. Brantlinger, 208–9.

56. Wheatcroft, *Ottomans*, cited in Brantlinger, 209.
57. Stoler, *Education of Desire*, 8.
58. Brantlinger, "Terrible Turks," 208.
59. Stoler, *Education of Desire*, 8.
60. McClintock, *Imperial Leather*, 5.
61. McClintock, 6.
62. While I do not have room here to keep elaborating these claims, an extended discussion of place and space in *Return of the Native* would usefully engage Simon Gikandi's *Maps of Englishness: Writing Identity in the Culture of Colonialism* and Ian Baucom's *Out of Place: Englishness, Empire, and the Locations of Identity*. Gikandi points to the construction of English identity in times of crisis, especially in times of anxiety about its borders and peripheries. Gikandi recognizes Englishness as "a product of the colonial culture that it seemed to have created elsewhere" and recognizes "English cultural identity" as being "driven by disputes about the perimeters of the values that defined Englishness—the nature of civil society, subjectivity, the meaning of the past, and the structure of feelings" (x). Baucom discusses place-based identity and the torturous routes by which Englishness and Britishness were distinguished and defined in colonial contexts.
63. See Stoler, *Education of Desire*, 12.
64. Duncan, "*Moonstone*," 300.
65. Also known as her "luxuriance" (*RN* 70) and "luxurious[ness]" (*RN* 197).
66. McClintock, *Imperial Leather*, 13.
67. I write about this at greater length in my essay "Linking with W. R. Bion."
68. Devastatingly, the end of Khan's life was marked by a psychotic break that included an anti-Semitic rant in one of his final publications. I want to acknowledge how inexcusable this action was, and to take stock too of the incredible racism Khan must have experienced throughout his time in England. See Cooper, "Khan," and Linda Hopkins's biography, *False Self: The Life of Masud Khan*.
69. P. Hopkins, "Balint."
70. As the historian Michal Shapira describes in detail in her book *The War Inside*, many analysts and social workers in this circle took part in wartime efforts to relocate children from heavily bombed cities to safer homes and institutions in the English countryside. Many also worked at institutions that housed children who had been rescued from Nazi Germany and relocated to England. These experiences in orphanages and group homes fundamentally shaped mid-century psychoanalysis and attachment theory.
71. "100 Years of History."
72. Steiner, "New Kind of Diaspora," 44.
73. See, for instance, Freud, "Why War?"
74. Eng, "Colonial Object Relations," 2.
75. Eng, 16.
76. Phillips, *On Kissing*, 61.
77. See Amanda Anderson, "Therapeutic Criticism," as well as her latest book, *Psyche and Ethos*.
78. A. Anderson, "Therapeutic Criticism," 321.
79. A. Anderson, 326.
80. A. Anderson, 325.

81. Rosenberg, "Gender Trouble on Mother's Day."

82. I am quoting here from Hardy's sonnet "The Sleep-Worker" (1901), the last line of which suggests a careful revisionary labor that we might also try when it comes to the exclusion of colonial history from the dominant critical accounts of the novel: not to destroy, but to "patiently adjust, amend, and heal" (14).

Chapter 4

1. In an essay from one of Eliot's notebooks from the mid-1870s, published by K. K. Collins in "Questions of Method: Some Unpublished Late Essays," 387–89.

2. Ogden, "Analysing Forms," 695.

3. Ogden, 696.

4. J. Hillis Miller, tracking the cointrication of the totalizing metaphors that guide the novel, writes: "Th[e] interpretation of one metaphor by another metaphor is characteristic of Eliot's use of figure" ("Optic and Semiotic," 133–34). For other important works on Eliot's use of figure, also in a deconstructive vein, see Jonathan Arac, "Rhetoric and Realism in Nineteenth-Century Fiction," and Cynthia Chase, "The Decomposition of the Elephants: Double-Reading *Daniel Deronda*."

5. See for example Joseph, "Here and Now."

6. Heimann, "On Counter-Transference," 56.

7. Main, preface to *Sayings*, iv.

8. Price, *Anthology*, 106.

9. See the entire chapter of Price's *Anthology* entitled "George Eliot and the Production of Consumers," 105–56. See also Beer, who describes the construction of George Eliot as sage or Sybil (*George Eliot*), and Jesse Cordes Selbin, "'Interpretations are Illimitable' : George Eliot and the Challenge of Common Reading."

10. Gallagher, "Rise of Fictionality."

11. Gallagher, 356.

12. For more on this heartbeat and other "figures of minimal distance or difference" (140) that preoccupy George Eliot throughout her fiction, and that illustrate her "persistent drive toward rudimentary structures" (141), see Neil Hertz, *George Eliot's Pulse*.

13. For an extended study in a different vein from my own of the narrator's manipulation of the reader, see Garrett Stewart's *Dear Reader: The Conscripted Audience in Nineteenth-Century British Fiction*.

14. Heimann, "On Counter-Transference," 55. I am reminded too of a quip from the novel that takes down Dorothea's practical sister Celia: "To have in general but little feeling, seems to be the only security against feeling too much on any particular occasion" (*M* 64).

15. Heimann, "On Counter-Transference," 56.

16. Heimann, 56.

17. And, indeed, Heimann's paper caused a stir, both for its paradigm-shifting view of countertransference and for what it meant to the psychoanalytic community: the paper represented Heimann's break from her one-time teacher Melanie Klein, in preference for aligning herself with the Independent group and her own independent thinking (C. Taylor, "Heimann").

18. Freud, "Recommendations to Physicians," 115–16. For a brilliant reading of this passage from Freud in conjversation with the postcolonial novel, see Ankhi Mukherjee, "Fissured Skin, Inner-Ear Radio, and a Telepathic Nose: The Senses as Media in Salman Rushdie's *Midnight's Children*."

19. Eliot, "*Westward Ho!* and *Constance Herbert*," *Westminster Review* 64 (July 1855): 288–96, repr. in Pinney, *Essays of George Eliot*, 123–36. Eliot expresses similar notions of the novelist's duty in "The Natural History of German Life: Riehl," *Westminster Review* 66 (July 1856): 51–79, repr. in Pinney, *Essays of George Eliot*, 266–99; and in "Leaves from a Note-Book."

20. Heimann, "On Counter-Transference," 56.

21. Heimann, 56.

22. Bollas, *Shadow of the Object*, 1.

23. Bollas, 1–2. The passage goes on to highlight the contributions of psychoanalyst Margaret Little (1901–94), followed by those of Balint, Winnicott, Marion Milner, Khan, and Bion. Little's *Psychotic Anxieties and Containment: A Personal Record of an Analysis with Winnicott* (1977) is a wonderful book and an essential historical document of mid-century British psychoanalysis.

24. Heimann, "On Counter-Transference," 56.

25. Heimann, 56.

26. Barthes, "Death of the Author" (trans. Heath), 142.

27. Barthes, 142.

28. Barthes, "Death of the Author" (trans. Howard).

29. In Catherine Maxwell's reading, the novel depicts "the slow but pressured adaptation of [Dorothea's] visionary desire to the normative demands of nineteenth-century marriage and motherhood" ("Brooking of Desire," 125).

30. In David Kurnick's cleverly phrased take, which plays on the novel's split between epic (Saint Theresa) and novelistic (Dorothea) lives, "Dorothea's achievement of domestic bliss is thus a failure, we might say, of epic proportions" ("Erotics of Detachment," 589).

31. Bodenheimer, *Real Life*, 38.

32. Reviewing the novel in 1873 for the *Galaxy*, Henry James remarked that, although a "very splendid performance," the novel's "diffuseness" makes it "too copious a dose of pure fiction." *Middlemarch*, he wrote, "sets a limit . . . to the development of the old-fashioned English novel" (Henry James, "George Eliot's *Middlemarch*," *Galaxy*, March 1873, repr. in Haight, *George Eliot Criticism*, 80–87).

33. Dames, *Physiology of the Novel*, 123, 125. The length of Eliot's novels, Dames has shown, led to comparisons with other works of "extended duration" across nineteenth-century media. Dames concentrates in particular on comparisons between *Daniel Deronda* and Wagnerian opera, both of which provoked fears of overstrain, boredom, and exhaustion for readers and listeners. These fears are registered in Victorian criticism, where they are only sometimes resolved into a higher valuation of the "aesthetic and even ethical demands" that such "elongated forms" impose upon their audiences (124).

34. Joseph, "Transference," 157.

35. Joseph, 157.

36. In his entry on Joseph for the *Oxford Dictionary of National Biography*, Michael Feldman writes: "Joseph saw herself as a 'late developer,' who had initially struggled to 'find her feet' as

a psychoanalyst, unlike her close friends and colleagues, Hanna Segal, Wilfred Bion, and Herbert Rosenfeld, whom she regarded as 'born analysts' (interview, 5). As her work developed, however, she evolved her own analytic voice, and became more confident about the importance of her own distinctive contribution, and its impact on psychoanalysis." See also Pick and Milton's 2006 interview with Betty Joseph for the Melanie Klein Trust.

37. Feldman, "Joseph." She was also, according to Robin Anderson writing for the Melanie Klein Trust, "internationally known as a brilliant teacher whose capacity to see the patient through the supervisee was legendary" ("Betty Joseph").

38. Klein, "Origins of Transference" (1952), quoted in Joseph, "Transference," 157.

39. Joseph, "Transference," 157–59.

40. Joseph, 159.

41. Joseph, 157.

42. See in particular her papers "The Patient Who Is Difficult to Reach" (1975), "Towards the Experiencing of Psychic Pain" (1981), and "Psychic Change and the Psychoanalytic Process" (1986/89).

43. Joseph, "Transference," 158–59.

44. Joseph, "On Understanding" (1983), 142.

45. Joseph, "Transference," 160.

46. Joseph, 165, emphasis added.

47. Joseph, 165.

48. Joseph, 166.

49. Joseph, 164.

50. *Oxford English Dictionary Online*, s.v. "Concrete, adj.," accessed 31 October 2018, http://www.oed.com/view/Entry/38398.

51. Ogden, "Reverie and Metaphor," 728.

52. Ogden, 728–29.

53. Ogden, 723.

54. In *The Argonauts*, Maggie Nelson writes, "sometimes one has to know something many times over" (18).

55. Ogden, "Reverie and Metaphor," 724.

56. Ogden, 722, 724.

57. See Tom Sperlinger, "'The Sensitive Author': George Eliot."

58. *George Eliot Letters*, 2: 362. These lines predict the famous description of the "mirror" of the novelist's "mind" in *Adam Bede*.

59. *George Eliot Letters*, 2: 362.

60. In other words, despite Eliot's promises to the contrary, the rigors of difficult reading need not issue in reward. By posing this dilemma, however, *Middlemarch* both inscribes and questions the work of moral perfectionism that Andrew H. Miller argues in *The Burdens of Perfection: On Ethics and Reading in Nineteenth-Century British Literature* is so essential to Victorian thought and so thoroughly enacted by the narrative techniques of the Victorian novel.

61. Estés, "Abre la puerta!"

62. For more on the metaphor of "interest" in the novel and in Freudian and Lacanian psychoanalysis, see Anna Kornbluh's *Realizing Capital: Financial and Psychic Economies in Victorian Form*.

63. Cohn, *Still Life*, 108.

64. Joseph, "Transference," 160.

65. In the traditional criticism of *Middlemarch* in particular, we are called upon again and again to admire the narrator's reach and psychological penetration. To Eliot's narrator, no mind is inaccessible, no motivation undetectable, no pattern of thought irreproducible by way of free indirect discourse. There is no personality so complex (or, for that matter, so unsympathetic) that it cannot be captured by Eliot's capacious understanding and held by her magisterial narrative voice. In place of an all-knowing God, or so the story goes, Eliot's novels offer an all-knowing narrator, one who holds out to us a similar comfort: the promise that your experience might be fully known, perhaps not by someone immediately present, but by a powerful observing intelligence off in the distance. As critics have long pointed out, the very use of "omniscience" as a literary critical term is founded on "the presumed analogy between the novelist as creator and the Creator of the cosmos, an omniscient God" (Jaffe, *Vanishing Points*, 4). Jaffe builds her point by citing many other critics and narrative theorists: Robert Scholes, Robert Kellogg, Shlomith Rimmon-Kenan, Gérard Genette, Dorrit Cohn, and Seymour Chatman.

66. Critics have grown increasingly interested in exploring lapses of omniscience in Eliot's novels. Perhaps most famously and foundationally, Gillian Beer links efforts in realist fiction to renounce omniscient narration to a growing culture of Victorian secularism epitomized in the evolutionary writings of Charles Darwin: "Victorian novelists," she writes in *Darwin's Plots*, "increasingly seek a role for themselves within the language of the text as observer or experimenter, rather than designer or god. Omniscience goes, omnipotence is concealed" (40). In Beer's formulations, writers seek a "substitute for the god-like . . . omniscience open to the theistic narrator" in scientific methods of knowledge production and authentication. In *Realism, Ethics, and Secularism: Essays on Victorian Literature and Science*, George Levine describes "the felt inadequacy of strictly omniscient narration" to novelists like George Eliot writing in a newly secular age, and argues that this "felt inadequacy" helped to spur the recourse to free indirect discourse that became so central to development of the nineteenth-century novel. In Levine's formulations, however, nineteenth-century writers articulate an ethical project in which unknowability itself becomes a positive value, a way of respecting "the absolute otherness of other beings without attempting to assimilate [that] otherness into us, without making it an aspect of ourselves" (192). Most recently, Elisha Cohn's *Still Life* picks up on this interest in "unknowingness" and takes it further: Cohn urges scholars to resist turning renunciations of knowingness in George Eliot's fiction to any positive account, pointing to scenes in which Eliot's "narrators drift away from the position of knowing omniscience into a moody voice that resonates sensations" without seeking to understand or conceptualize them (94–95).

67. In "Beyond the Dreaming Experience" (1976)—which is to my mind one of the most imaginative and paradigm-shifting essays on dream interpretation in post-Freudian psychoanalysis—Masud Khan argues that a dream as it is *remembered* (the "dream text") is quite distinct from the dream as it is *experienced* (the "dreaming experience") (45). The dream text "gets hold of some aspect of th[e] dreaming experience" and works it into "a narrative that can be communicated, shared, and interpreted" (47). It can therefore function defensively, as a false omniscience: "the remembered dream, what I am calling here the dream text, can be a negation of dreaming" (45). But the dreaming experience—with its emphasis, through the gerund form, on the activity of dreaming itself—is "beyond interpretation" (47). Dreaming is a paradoxical form of self-experience: it is at once unconscious and definitive—so much so that Khan proposes

revising Pontalis's famous linguistic aphorism, "the speaking subject is the entire subject," to read, "the dreaming subject is the entire subject" (46). Dreaming is both at the core of the subject and utterly private, utterly incommunicable—the dreaming experience can never quite become an object of knowledge or of articulation. And yet Khan stresses its vitality and its potentiality for the unfurling of the self: "a person in his dreaming experience can actualize aspects of the self that perhaps never become overtly available to his introspection or his dreams. And yet it enriches his life and its lack can impoverish his experience of others, himself, and his sleep" (50). Khan's essay points, as Eliot's work does in perhaps more surprising ways, to verbalization as a medium inadequate to the mystery and unknowability of the self. In a question that echoes a question in *Middlemarch* about prayer ("who can represent himself just as he is, even in his own reflections?" (*M* 710)—a passage I'll go on to discuss), Khan asks, "Who can communicate the whole of his self-experience through verbalization, to himself or the other?" The answer, of course, is no one: "An essential part remains inaccessible" (50).

68. Jaffe, *Vanishing Points*, 6.

69. Freedgood's argument is political: she argues, engaging Rancière's *The Philosopher and His Poor*, that nineteenth-century novelists are particularly prone to treating their working-class characters this way, constructing them as "physically, materially, intellectually, and emotionally less than their narrators" ("Novelist and Her Poor," 211).

70. Freedgood, 219.

71. Feuerbach, *Essence of Christianity*, 103.

72. If Jaffe and Freedgood show how omniscient narration can impoverish or limit characters, psychoanalysis can do this too: as Michael Balint puts it, analysis can create "a picture of the world consisting of a rather insignificant subject confronted with mighty, knowledgeable, and omnipresent objects who have the power of expressing everything correctly in words, an impressive example of whom is the analyst" (*BF* 169).

73. Dorothea to Lydgate: "Only think. I am very uncomfortable with my money.... What I should most rejoice at would be to have something good to do with [it].... It makes me very uneasy" (*M* 765). Poor Dorothea! Her money feels like a burden to her. Urging Lydgate to accept her money as a yearly income in addition to her endowment of his fever hospital itself, Dorothea says: "Think how much money I have; it would be like taking a burden from me if you took some of it every year till you got free from this fettering want of income. Why should not people do these things? It is so difficult to make shares at all even. This is one way" (*M* 767). Is it really so difficult? The novel certainly trains us to think so. The emphasis *Middlemarch* places on the difficulty of spending money justly and of "making shares even" helps the novel to remain, as so many critics have pointed out, on the side of political meliorism rather than radicalism, on the side of reform rather than revolution. As Terry Eagleton puts it, the novel ends in "wide-eyed liberal disillusionment which, with the collapse of more ambitious commitments, is compelled to find solace in the humble reformist tasks near to hand" (*Criticism and Ideology*, 119).

74. Derrida, *Without Alibi*.

75. Henry, "*Middlemarch*," 182.

76. Feuerbach, *Essence of Christianity*, 8.

77. For more on George Eliot's engagement with Feuerbach, see Moira Gatens, "The Art and Philosophy of George Eliot"; Moira Gatens and Stacy Douglas, "Revisiting the Continental Shelf: Moira Gatens on Law, Religion, and Human Rights in Eliot, Feuerbach, and Spinoza"; and

Cristina Richieri Griffin, "George Eliot's Feuerbach: Senses, Sympathy, Omniscience, and Secularism."

78. Feuerbach, *Essence of Christianity*, 10–11.
79. Feuerbach, 9.
80. Feuerbach, 9.
81. Bollas, "What Is This Thing?" 166.
82. Bollas, 165.
83. Bollas, 165.
84. Bollas, 175.
85. Adam Phillips critiques the British Independents for instantiating a "negative theology of the Self." He argues, in an essay on Khan, that for Winnicott and his inheritors, the self comes to stand in the place of the unconscious, "displacing an unavoidable division in the subject" with something that, while unknown, is somehow more centered and more definable. An idiom, a style—an alibi. The self functions as a site of mystery, but also as firm ground on which to anchor meaning and knowledge. Phillips reflects: "In the context of psychoanalysis as a hermeneutics it is difficult not to hear this 'permanently non-communicating' element, like the fabled 'silence of God,' as offering us a powerful message; but of what and for whom, of course, it is impossible to say. Winnicott makes the impossibility of knowing quite clear" ("Returning the Dream," 60). Phillips's critique points to an oscillation with which we are already familiar: the tendency to posit sites of meaning even when we have reconciled ourselves to the fact that no such guarantee is possible, ways we have of finding consolation in the face of more absolute loss, replacing religious modes of thinking we have decided are ineffectual, inaccurate, or misguided with secular modes of knowledge or faith that we come to find simply reinstate old theologies in new forms. What Phillips calls a negative theology we could also call a weary knowledge.
86. Jaffe, *Vanishing Points*, 4.
87. See Daniel Wright, *Bad Logic: Reasoning about Desire in the Victorian Novel*; Cohn, *Still Life*; Kurnick, "Erotics of Detachment"; and D. A. Miller, *Narrative and its Discontents: Problems of Closure in the Traditional Novel*.
88. Oliver Sacks writes briefly of these frequent and recurrent headaches: "George Eliot, similarly, spoke of herself as feeling 'dangerously well' before the onset of her migraine attacks" ("Summer of Madness," 58).
89. This expression comes from an instance in which the novel puts this interpersonal aspiration most piously, describing the good that Dorothea's faith in Lydgate does for him: "The presence of a noble nature, generous in its wishes, ardent in its charity, changes the lights for us: we begin to see things again in their larger, quieter masses, and to believe that we too can be judged in the wholeness of our character" (M 762). My interest here, however, is in the concurrent charges of idealization and sexual desire.
90. Feuerbach, *Essence of Christianity*, 103.
91. Feuerbach, 102.
92. I am arguing for a vision of psychoanalytic transference that is related to but distinct from Lacan's "subject supposed to know." As Shoshana Felman parses Lacan's idea, the "patient's transferential fantasy attributes to the analyst a knowledge which is really his own story as *unknown*" ("Turning the Screw," 135). This is a compelling description, and one that accounts for ordinary acts of idealization and love as they are framed in the novel. And yet I think object relations

psychoanalysis posits a different transferential mechanism: one in which patients internalize the meaning-making and enlivening capacities of the analyst. Together, both patient and analyst feel interested and interesting. See also Kohon's account of these processes, which argues that analysis does not truly start until this special interest is produced (*British School of Psychoanalysis*, 71).

93. I am referring to Dorothea's "delightful plans" for her wealth, before she forfeits her inheritance from Casaubon by marrying Will. She describes these plans to Celia: "I should like to take a great deal of land, and drain it, and make a little colony, where everybody should work, and all of the work should be done well. I should know every one of the people and be their friend" (*M* 550). Worker's colony, commune, intentional community, "home colony," "school of industry," socialist utopia, phalanstery, factory, model working-class society, cooperative: whatever form the "little colony" might have taken, we will never know. Dorothea's fleeting utopian vision is not treated with the same representational protocols as other things in the novel. We hear about it exactly three times: in this brief dialogue, when we hear by way of a letter that Dorothea is away scouting locations (we don't follow her on these travels to Yorkshire—which Heather Miner points out is an area linked to radical working-class politics), and finally in her own brief report to Lydgate announcing her plans have fallen through. Dialogue and letter: unlike so much else in the novel, we never get to see Dorothea or the narrator think or think through this communitarian scheme. And to compound the problem of this potentially revolutionary idea's underrepresentation in the novel, in turn, few critics have written about this "little colony" (let alone its colonial valences). Two interesting exceptions, however, include Mark Allison, "Utopian Socialism, Women's Emancipation, and the Origins of *Middlemarch*," and Heather Miner, "Reforming Spaces: The Architectural Imaginary of *Middlemarch*."

Coda

1. O'Shaughnessy, "Revisiting," 216. "The Absent Object" was first published in 1964; I quote throughout from the more widely available republication of the essay in 2016.

2. O'Shaughnessy, "Revisiting," 208.

3. I am using here a phrase that Bion coins, building from on an image from Freud, in *Attention and Interpretation* to explicate his concept of faith (F). I will return to this phrase and explicate it more fully in what follows; for now, let me just set it in the context in which it appears. Given that psychic phenomenon are "mental and not sensible," how, Bion asks, "are we to 'observe' and 'record' the patient's state of mind?" His response is remarkable: "Since I wish to discuss this but do not know the answer, I shall say 'by F.' Freud said that he had to 'blind myself artificially to focus all the light on one dark spot.' This proves a useful formulation for describing the area I wish to cover by F. By rendering oneself 'artificially blind' through the exclusion of memory and desire, one achieves F; the piercing shaft of darkness can be directed on the dark features of the analytic situation. Through F one can 'see', 'hear', and 'feel' the mental phenomena of whose reality no practicing psychoanalyst has any doubt though he cannot with any accuracy represent them in existing formulations" (*A&I* 57–58).

4. O'Shaughnessy writes, "It is not that the child, grudgingly, in the end, tolerates the absent object, but that he has need of its absence" ("Revisiting," 216).

5. And so that my sister, a naturopathic doctor and shamanic healer, can say she is treating our father even nineteen years after his death, and doing healing work on our Mexican ancestors

too, colonizers and colonized alike. Diana Quinn Inlak'ech, ND, "Healing Our Ancestors: The Importance of Ancestral Relationships."

6. I write at greater length about the need to connect Victorian studies to adjacent fields in my essay "Linking with W. R. Bion." As Tim Watson puts it, Victorian studies "remains too focused on Britain." He urges in particular (to take just one instance of the wider relational networks I am advocating for) a deeper engagement with the Caribbean: "Victorianists should be spending more time discussing work in nineteenth-century Caribbean studies." New scholarly works from that field, "with their emphases on creolization, racial formation, imperial identities, and multilingual literary connections, would add significantly to Victorian studies" (Watson, "Caribbean," 602–3).

7. Winnicott, "Transitional Objects," 7.

8. See also Claudia Rankine, "The Condition of Black Life Is One of Mourning," and Sonya Posmentier, "A Language for Grieving."

9. Gilroy, *Postcolonial Melancholia*, 100.

10. In addition to *Disidentifications: Queers of Color and the Performance of Politics*, see Muñoz's essay "Feeling Brown, Feeling Down: Latina Affect, the Performativity of Race, and the Depressive Position."

11. Dimock, "Theory of Resonance," 1061.

12. Dimock, 1064.

13. Dimock, 1062.

14. Byrd, *Transit of Empire*, xvii, xxvii, 65–66, et al.

15. For writing on the new subfield of Neo-Victorian studies and how it might grapple with the modern afterlife of the British empire and related issues of imperial memory and forgetting, see Elizabeth Ho's *Neo-Victorianism and the Memory of Empire* and her essay "The Neo-Victorian-at-Sea: Towards a Global Memory of the Victorians," as well as Susan Zieger's review essay on three books in that subfield for *Victorian Studies*. Zieger notes, "Drawing on Paul Gilroy's idea of the Black Atlantic, and Michel Foucault's concept of heterotopia, Ho calls for an end to center-periphery imaginations of empire in favor of a global memory of the Victorian attuned to transnationality and mass migration" (132).

16. Jodi A. Byrd complicates the binary colonizer/colonized relationship when she focuses instead, in the context of the Americas, on the relations between "Indigenous peoples, settlers and arrivants—a term I borrow from African Caribbean poet Kamau Brathwaite to signify those people forced into the Americas through the violence of European and Anglo-American colonialism and imperialism around the globe" (*Transit of Empire*, xix). I have learned a great deal about the complexity of these relations and positions as well from Nicole M. Guidotti-Hernández and her book *Unspeakable Violence: Remapping U. S. and Mexican National Imaginaries*, and from Yu-ting Huang, including her essay "Writing Settlement: Locating Asian-Indigenous Relations in the Pacific."

17. Pinch, "Shape All Light," para. 115.

18. Pinch, para. 155.

19. These are images that Pinch draws from Shelley's "last, unfinished, gorgeous, apocalyptic, trippy poem," "The Triumph of Life" (para. 112).

20. Sigmund Freud, letter to Lou Andreas-Salomé, 25 May 1916, in Freud and Andreas-Salomé, *Letters*, 45.

21. For a moving explication of "image as method" that is not unlike what I am trying to describe here and the rethinking of presence and absence it inscribes, see Lisa Stevenson, *Life Beside Itself: Imagining Care in the Canadian Arctic*.

22. I am thinking in particular of Fanon's *Black Skin, White Masks*, Glissant's *The Poetics of Relation*, and James's *The Black Jacobins*.

BIBLIOGRAPHY

Ablow, Rachel, ed. *The Feeling of Reading: Affective Experience & Victorian Literature*. Ann Arbor: University of Michigan Press, 2010.
———. *The Marriage of Minds: Reading Sympathy in the Victorian Marriage Plot*. Stanford, CA: Stanford University Press, 2007.
———. *Victorian Pain*. Princeton, NJ: Princeton University Press, 2017.
Aguirre, Robert D. *Informal Empire: Mexico and Central America in Victorian Culture*. Minneapolis: University of Minnesota Press, 2005.
Ahmed, Sara. *Living a Feminist Life*. Durham, NC: Duke University Press, 2017.
———. *The Promise of Happiness*. Durham, NC: Duke University Press, 2010.
———. *Willful Subjects*. Durham, NC: Duke University Press, 2014.
Albrecht, Thomas. "Sympathy and Telepathy: The Problem of Ethics in George Eliot's The Lifted Veil." *ELH* 73, no. 2 (2006): 437–63.
Allison, Mark. "Utopian Socialism, Women's Emancipation, and the Origins of *Middlemarch*." *ELH* 78 (2011): 715–39.
Almeida, Joselyn M. *Reimagining the Transatlantic, 1780–1890*. Burlington, VT: Ashgate, 2011.
Althusser, Louis. "Freud and Lacan." In *Lenin and Philosophy*, 133–50.
———. "Ideology and Ideological State Apparatuses (Notes toward an Investigation)." In *Lenin and Philosophy*, 85–126.
———. *Lenin and Philosophy and Other Essays*. Translated by Ben Brewster. New York: Monthly Review, 2001.
Anderson, Amanda. *Psyche and Ethos: Moral Life after Psychology*. Oxford: Oxford University Press, 2018.
———. "Therapeutic Criticism." *Novel: A Forum on Fiction* 50, no. 3 (2017): 321–28.
Anderson, Benedict. *Imagined Communities: Reflections on the Origin and Spread of Nationalism*. Rev. ed. New York: Verso, 2006.
Anderson, Robin. "Betty Joseph." Melanie Klein Trust. N.d., accessed 2 July 2018. http://www.melanie-klein-trust.org.uk/joseph.
Anzieu, Didier. "Beckett and Bion." *International Journal of Psychoanalysis* 16 (1989): 163–68.
Arac, Jonathan. "Rhetoric and Realism in Nineteenth-Century Fiction: Hyperbole in *The Mill on the Floss*." *ELH* 46, no. 4 (1979): 673–92.
Armstrong, Nancy. *Desire and Domestic Fiction: A Political History of the Novel*. Repr. ed. New York: Oxford University Press, 1990.
———. *How Novels Think: The Limits of British Individualism from 1719–1900*. New York: Columbia University Press, 2005.

Asghar, Fatimah. *If They Come for Us: Poems*. New York: One World, 2018.

Aslami, Zarena. *The Dream Life of Citizens: Late Victorian Novels and the Fantasy of the State*. New York: Fordham University Press, 2012.

Atherton, Carol. *Defining Literary Criticism: Scholarship, Authority and the Possession of Literary Knowledge, 1880–2002*. New York: Palgrave Macmillan, 2005.

Balibar, Etienne, and Pierre Macherey. "On Literature as an Ideological Form." In *Untying the Text: A Post-Structuralist Reader*, edited with an introduction by Robert Young, 79–99. Boston: Routledge and Kegan Paul, 1981.

Balint, Alice, and Michael Balint. "On Transference and Counter-Transference." *International Journal of Psychoanalysis* 20 (1939): 223–30.

Balint, Michael. *The Basic Fault: Therapeutic Aspects of Regression*. New York: Tavistock, 1979. Originally published 1967.

———. *The Doctor, His Patient, and the Illness*. New York: International Universities Press, 1957.

———. "Friendly Expanses—Horrid Empty Spaces." *International Journal of Psychoanalysis* 36 (1955): 225–41.

———. *Primary Love, and Psycho-Analytic Technique*. New York: Liveright, 1952.

———. *Thrills and Regressions*. New York: International Universities Press, 1959.

Barthes, Roland. "The Death of the Author." In *Image, Music, Text*, translated by Stephen Heath, 142–48. New York: Hill and Wang, 1978.

———. "The Death of the Author." Translated by Richard Howard. *Aspen* 5–6 (1967). http://www.ubu.com/aspen/aspen5and6/threeEssays.html#barthes.

Baucom, Ian. *Out of Place: Englishness, Empire, and the Locations of Identity*. Princeton, NJ: Princeton University Press, 1999.

Bayley, John. *An Essay on Hardy*. New York: Cambridge University Press, 1978.

Bechdel, Alison. *Are You My Mother?: A Comic Drama*. New York: Houghton Mifflin Harcourt, 2012.

Beer, Gillian. "Beyond Determinism: George Eliot and Virginia Woolf." In *Women Writing and Writing about Women*, edited by Mary Jacobus, 80–99. New York: Barnes and Noble Books, 1979.

———. "Can the Native Return?" In *Open Fields: Science in Cultural Encounter*, 31–54. Oxford: Oxford University Press, 1996.

———. *Darwin's Plots: Evolutionary Narrative in Darwin, George Eliot, and Nineteenth-Century Fiction*. Boston: Routledge and Kegan Paul, 1983.

———. "Finding a Scale for the Human: Plot and Writing in Hardy's Novels." In *Darwin's Plots*, 236–58.

———. *George Eliot*. Key Women Writers. Bloomington: Indiana University Press, 1986.

———. "Myth and the Single Consciousness: *Middlemarch* and The Lifted Veil." In *This Particular Web: Essays on "Middlemarch,"* edited by Ian Adam, 91–115. Buffalo, NY: University of Toronto Press, 1975.

Belsey, Catherine. "Re-reading the Great Tradition." In *Re-reading English*, edited by Peter Widdowson, 121–35. New York: Methuen, 1981.

Benjamin, Jessica. "In Defense of Gender Ambiguity." *Gender and Psychoanalysis* 1 (1996): 27–43.

Berger, John. "*Ways of Seeing*, Excerpted." In *The Feminism and Visual Culture Reader*, edited by Amelia Jones, 37–40. New York: Routledge, 2003.

Betensky, Carolyn. *Feeling for the Poor: Bourgeois Compassion, Social Action, and the Victorian Novel*. Charlottesville: University of Virginia Press, 2010.

Bion, Wilfred R. "Attacks on Linking." In *Second Thoughts*, 93–109. Originally published 1959.

———. *Attention and Interpretation*. New York: Karnac Books, 1984. Originally published 1970.

———. "Caesura." In *Two Papers: "The Grid" and "Caesura,"* 35–56. London: Routledge, 1989.

———. *Cogitations*. London: Routledge, 1991.

———. *Elements of Psychoanalysis*. New York: Karnac Books, 1984.

———. *Experiences in Groups and Other Papers*. London: Routledge, 1968.

———. *Learning from Experience*. London: Karnac Books, 1984.

———. "Making the Best of a Bad Job [1979]." In *Clinical Seminars and Other Works*, 321–32. London: Routledge, 1994.

———. "On Arrogance." In *Second Thoughts*, 86–92. Originally published 1957.

———. *Second Thoughts: Selected Papers on Psychoanalysis*. London: Routledge, 1984.

———. "A Theory of Thinking." In *Second Thoughts*, 110–19. Originally published 1962.

———. *Transformations*. New York: Karnac Books, 1984.

Blanchot, Maurice. "The Narrative Voice." In *The Infinite Conversation*, translated by Susan Hanson, 82: 379–87. Theory and History of Literature. Minneapolis: University of Minnesota Press, 1993.

Bodenheimer, Rosemarie. *The Real Life of Mary Ann Evans: George Eliot, Her Letters and Fiction*. Ithaca, NY: Cornell University Press, 1994.

Bollas, Christopher. "The Aesthetic Moment and the Search for Transformation." *Annual of Psychoanalysis* 6 (1978): 385–94.

———. *The Christopher Bollas Reader*. New York: Routledge, 2011.

———. "Psychic Genera." In *Christopher Bollas Reader*, 57–78.

———. *The Shadow of the Object: Psychoanalysis of the Unthought Known*. New York: Columbia University Press, 1987.

———. "The Transformational Object." *International Journal of Psychoanalysis* 60, no. 1 (1979): 97–107.

———. "What Is This Thing Called Self?" In *Cracking Up: The Work of Unconscious Experience*, 146–79. London: Routledge, 1995.

———. "Why Oedipus?" In *Christopher Bollas Reader*, 94–111.

Boumelha, Penny. *Thomas Hardy and Women: Sexual Ideology and Narrative Form*. Totowa, NJ: Barnes and Noble, 1982.

Bowen, H. V. "Clive, Robert, First Baron Clive of Plassey (1725–1774)." In *Oxford Dictionary of National Biography*. Oxford University Press, 2008. https://doi.org/10.1093/ref:odnb/5697.

Bowlby, Rachel. *Freudian Mythologies: Greek Tragedy and Modern Identities*. Oxford: Oxford University Press, 2007.

Bownas, Jane. *Thomas Hardy and Empire: The Representation of Imperial Themes in the Work of Thomas Hardy*. New York: Routledge, 2012.

Bownas, Jane, and Rena Jackson. "Empire." In *Thomas Hardy in Context*, edited by Phillip Mallett. New York: Cambridge University Press, 2013.

Brantlinger, Patrick. *The Reading Lesson: The Threat of Mass Literacy in Nineteenth Century British Fiction*. Bloomington: Indiana University Press, 1998.

———. "Terrible Turks: Victorian Xenophobia and the Ottoman Empire." In *Fear, Loathing, and Victorian Xenophobia*, edited by Marlene Tromp, Maria K. Bachman, and Heidi Kaufman, 208–30. Columbus: Ohio State University Press, 2013.

Briefel, Aviva. *The Racial Hand in the Victorian Imagination*. Cambridge: Cambridge University Press, 2015.

Brinkema, Eugenie. *The Forms of the Affects*. Durham, NC: Duke University Press, 2014.

Brocklebank, Lisa. "Psychic Reading." *Victorian Studies* 48, no. 2 (2006): 233–39.

Brooks, Peter. *Reading for the Plot: Design and Intention in Narrative*. New York: A. A. Knopf, 1984.

brown, adrienne maree. *Emergent Strategy: Shaping Change, Changing Worlds*. Oakland, CA: AK Press, 2017.

brown, adrienne maree, and Walidah Imarisha, eds. *Octavia's Brood: Science Fiction Stories from Social Justice Movements*. Oakland, CA: AK Press, 2015.

Buckley, Peter, ed. *Essential Papers on Object Relations*. New York: New York University Press, 1986.

Bunn, G. C., A. D. Lovie, and G. D. Richards, eds. *Psychology in Britain: Historical Essays and Personal Reflections*. Leicester: British Psychological Society Books, 2001.

Burton, Antoinette M. *The Trouble with Empire: Challenges to Modern British Imperialism*. New York: Oxford University Press, 2015.

Butler, Judith. *Gender Trouble: Feminism and the Subversion of Identity*. New York: Routledge, 1990.

Buzard, James. *Disorienting Fiction: The Autoethnographic Work of Nineteenth-Century British Novels*. Princeton, NJ: Princeton University Press, 2005.

Byatt, A. S. Introduction to *The Mill on the Floss*, by George Eliot, xi–xliii. Penguin Classics. New York: Penguin Books, 2003. Originally published in 1979 edition.

Byrd, Jodi A. *The Transit of Empire: Indigenous Critiques of Colonialism*. First Peoples: New Directions Indigenous. Minneapolis: University of Minnesota Press, 2011.

Carroll, Alicia. *Dark Smiles: Race & Desire In George Eliot*. Athens: Ohio University Press, 2003.

Carroll, David. *George Eliot and the Conflict of Interpretations: A Reading of the Novels*. Cambridge: Cambridge University Press, 1992.

———, ed. *George Eliot: The Critical Heritage*. Critical Heritage Series. London: Routledge and Kegan Paul, 1971.

Cavell, Stanley. "Recounting Gains, Showing Losses: Reading The Winter's Tale." In *Disowning Knowledge in Seven Plays of Shakespeare*, updated ed., 193–222. Cambridge: Cambridge University Press, 2003.

Chakravarty, Gautam. *The Indian Mutiny and the British Imagination*. Cambridge: Cambridge University Press, 2005.

Chander, Manu Samriti. "'Oh My God, I Think America's Racist.'" *V21: Victorian Studies for the 21st Century* (blog), 5 June 2018. http://v21collective.org/oh-god-think-americas-racist/.

Chapman, John, ed. "Art and Belles Lettres." *Westminster Review* 65, no. 128 (1856): 625–50.

Chase, Cynthia. "The Decomposition of the Elephants: Double-Reading *Daniel Deronda*." *PMLA* 93, no. 2 (1978): 215–27.

Chatterjee, Partha. *The Black Hole of Empire: History of a Global Practice of Power*. Princeton, NJ: Princeton University Press, 2012.

Chatterjee, Ronjaunee, and Amy R. Wong. "Politics, Inclusion, and Social Practice." *V21: Victorian Studies for the 21st Century* (blog), 9 December 2016. http://v21collective.org/vtn-chatterjee-and-wong/.

Cheng, Anne Anlin. *The Melancholy of Race: Psychoanalysis, Assimilation, and Hidden Grief*. New York: Oxford University Press, 2000.

Christoff, Alicia Jean Mireles. "Linking with W. R. Bion." *Victorian Literature and Culture* 47, no. 1 (2018): 1–20.

Christoff, Maria. "First 100 Days: The Ethics of Big Data." *Psychoanalytic Activist*, 13 April 2017. https://psychoanalyticactivist.com/2017/04/13/first-100-days-the-ethics-of-big-data/.

Clements, Marcelle. Introduction to *Tess of the D'Urbervilles*, by Thomas Hardy, vii–xiv. New York: Signet Classics, 2006.

Cohen, William. "Arborealities: The Tactile Ecology of Hardy's Woodlanders." *19: Interdisciplinary Studies in the Long Nineteenth Century* 19 (2014). https://doi.org/10.16995/ntn.690.

———. *Embodied: Victorian Literature and the Senses*. Minneapolis: University of Minnesota Press, 2008.

———. "Faciality and Sensation in Hardy's *The Return of the Native*." *PMLA* 121, no. 2 (2006): 437–52.

———. *Sex Scandal: The Private Parts of Victorian Fiction*. Durham, NC: Duke University Press, 1996.

Cohn, Elisha. "'No Insignificant Creature': Thomas Hardy's Ethical Turn." *Nineteenth-Century Literature* 64, no. 4 (2010): 494–520.

———. *Still Life: Suspended Development in the Victorian Novel*. New York: Oxford University Press, 2015.

Cole, Truth Murray. "The Narrative Policing of Eustacia." Unpublished manuscript, last modified 23 February 2018. Microsoft Word file.

Collins, K. K. "Questions of Method: Some Unpublished Late Essays." *Nineteenth-Century Fiction* 35, no. 3 (1980): 385–405.

Connor, Steven. "Beckett and Bion." *Journal of Beckett Studies* 17, no. 1–2 (2008): 9–34.

Cooper, Judy. "Khan, (Mohammed) Masud Raza (1924–1989)." In *Oxford Dictionary of National Biography*. Oxford University Press, 2004. https://doi.org/10.1093/ref:odnb/51070.

Cox, R. G. *Thomas Hardy: The Critical Heritage*. Critical Heritage Series. London: Routledge and Kegan Paul, 1970.

Dames, Nicholas. *The Physiology of the Novel: Reading, Neural Science, and the Form of Victorian Fiction*. New York: Oxford University Press, 2007.

Davis, Michael. *George Eliot and Nineteenth-Century Psychology: Exploring the Unmapped Country*. Nineteenth Century Series. Burlington, VT: Ashgate, 2006.

Derrida, Jacques. "White Mythology: Metaphor in the Text of Philosophy." In *Margins of Philosophy*, translated by Alan Bass, 207–72. Chicago: University of Chicago Press, 1982.

———. *Without Alibi*. Edited and translated by Peggy Kamuf. Meridian: Crossing Aesthetics. Stanford, CA: Stanford University Press, 2002.

Descartes, René. *Discourse on Method and The Meditations*. Translated by F. E. Sutcliffe. New York: Penguin Books, 1968.

Dimen, Muriel. "Deconstructing Difference: Gender, Splitting, and Transitional Space." *Psychoanalytic Dialogues* 1, no. 3 (1991): 335–52.

Dimock, Wai Chee. "A Theory of Resonance." *PMLA* 112, no. 5 (1997): 1060–71.
Doniger, Bryan. "A Time for Song." Unpublished manuscript, last modified 21 March 2016. Microsoft Word file.
Dukes, Hunter. "Beckett's Vessels and the Animation of Containers." *Journal of Modern Literature* 40, no. 4 (2017): 75–89.
Duncan, Ian. "*The Moonstone*, the Victorian Novel, and Imperialist Panic." *Modern Language Quarterly* 55, no. 3 (1994): 297–319.
Eagleton, Terry. "Buried in the Life: Thomas Hardy and the Limits of Biographies." *Harper's Magazine* 315, no. 1890 (2007): 89–94.
———. *Criticism and Ideology: A Study in Marxist Literary Theory*. New York: Verso, 2006.
Eigen, Michael. *The Electrified Tightrope*. Edited by Adam Phillips. New York: Jason Aronson, 1993.
Eliot, George. *Daniel Deronda*. Edited with an introduction and notes by Terence Cave. New York: Penguin Books, 1995. Originally published 1876.
———. *Essays and Leaves from a Note-Book*. Edited by Charles Lee Lewes. New York: Harper, 1884.
———. *The George Eliot Letters*. Edited by Gordon Sherman Haight. New Haven, CT: Yale University Press, 1954.
———. "Leaves from a Note-Book." In *Essays and Leaves*, 272–95.
———. *Middlemarch*. Edited with an introduction and notes by Rosemary Ashton. Penguin Classics. London: Penguin Books, 2003.
———. *The Mill on the Floss*. Penguin Classics. New York: Penguin Books, 2003.
———. "O May I Join the Choir Invisible." In *George Eliot: Collected Poems*, edited with an introduction by Lucien Jenkins, 49–50. London: Skoob Books, 1989.
———. *Selections from George Eliot's Letters*. Edited by Gordon Sherman Haight. New Haven, CT: Yale University Press, 1985.
———. "Value in Originality." In *Essays and Leaves*, 290.
Eng, David L. "Colonial Object Relations." *Social Text* 34, no. 1 (126) (2016): 1–19.
Estés, Clarissa Pinkola. "Abre la puerta! Open the Door!" *National Catholic Reporter. El río debajo del río* (blog), 28 April 2008. https://www.ncronline.org/blogs/el-rio-debajo-del-rio/abre-la-puerta-open-door.
Esty, Jed. *Unseasonable Youth: Modernism, Colonialism, and the Fiction of Development*. Modernist Literature and Culture. New York: Oxford University Press, 2012.
Fanon, Frantz. *Black Skin, White Masks*. Translated by Richard Philcox. New York: Grove Press, 2008. First published 1952.
Feldman, Michael. "Joseph, Betty (1917–2013), Psychoanalyst." In *Oxford Dictionary of National Biography*. Oxford University Press, 2017. http://www.oxforddnb.com/view/10.1093/ref:odnb/9780198614128.001.0001/odnb-9780198614128-e-106822.
Felman, Shoshana. "Turning the Screw of Interpretation." *Yale French Studies* 55/56 (1977): 94–207.
Felski, Rita. "Context Stinks!" *New Literary History* 42, no. 4 (2011): 573–91.
Ferguson, Trish. "Bonfire Night in Thomas Hardy's *The Return of the Native*." *Nineteenth-Century Literature* 67, no. 1 (2012): 87–107.
Fetterley, Judith. *The Resisting Reader: A Feminist Approach to American Fiction*. Bloomington: Indiana University Press, 1978.

Feuerbach, Ludwig. *The Essence of Christianity*. Translated by George Eliot. Library of Religion and Culture. New York: Harper, 1957.
Fink, Bruce. *The Lacanian Subject*. Princeton, NJ: Princeton University Press, 1995.
Flint, Kate. *The Woman Reader, 1837–1914*. Oxford: Oxford University Press, 1993.
Fraiman, Susan. "*The Mill on the Floss*, the Critics, and the Bildungsroman." *PMLA* 108, no. 1 (1993): 136–50.
Freedgood, Elaine. "Fictional Settlements: Footnotes, Metalepsis, the Colonial Effect." *New Literary History: A Journal of Theory and Interpretation* 41, no. 2 (2010): 393–411.
———. *The Ideas in Things: Fugitive Meaning in the Victorian Novel*. Chicago: University of Chicago Press, 2006.
———. "The Novelist and Her Poor." *Novel: A Forum on Fiction* 47, no. 2 (2014): 210–23.
———. *Worlds Enough: The Literary Critical Construction of British Realism*. Princeton, NJ: Princeton University Press, forthcoming.
Freud, Sigmund. "Civilizations and Its Discontents." In *Complete Psychological Works*, 21:54–145.
———. "Formulations on the Two Principles of Psychic Functioning." In *Complete Psychological Works*, 12:215–26.
———. "Recommendations to Physicians Practicing Psycho-Analysis." In *Complete Psychological Works*, 12:109–20.
———. *The Standard Edition of the Complete Psychological Works of Sigmund Freud*. 24 vols. Translated by James Strachey. London: Hogarth, 1958.
———. "Why War?" In *Complete Psychological Works*, 22:195–216.
Freud, Sigmund, and Lou Andreas-Salomé. *Letters*. Edited by Ernst Pfeiffer. Translated by William and Elaine Robson-Scott. International Psycho-Analytical Library 89. New York: Norton, 1985.
Fuss, Diana. *Identification Papers: Readings on Psychoanalysis, Sexuality, and Culture*. New York: Routledge, 1995.
Gallagher, Catherine. "George Eliot: Immanent Victorian." *Representations* 90, no. 1 (2005): 61–74.
———. "The Rise of Fictionality." In *The Novel*, vol. 1, *History, Geography, and Culture*, edited by Franco Moretti, 336–63. Princeton, NJ: Princeton University Press, 2006.
Gatens, Moira. "The Art and Philosophy of George Eliot." *Philosophy and Literature* 33, no. 1 (2009): 78.
Gatens, Moira, and Stacy Douglas. "Revisiting the Continental Shelf: Moira Gatens on Law, Religion, and Human Rights in Eliot, Feuerbach, and Spinoza." *Feminist Legal Studies* 19, no. 1 (2011): 75–82.
Gatrell, Simon. Introduction to *Tess of the D'Urbervilles*, by Thomas Hardy, xiii–xxvii. New York: Oxford University Press, 2005.
———. "Wessex." In Kramer, *Cambridge Companion to Thomas Hardy*, 30.
Gettelman, Debra. "The Psychology of Reading and the Victorian Novel." *Literature Compass* 9, no. 2 (2012): 199–212.
———. "Reading Ahead in George Eliot." *Novel: A Forum on Fiction* 39, no. 1 (2005): 25–47.
Gikandi, Simon. *Maps of Englishness: Writing Identity in the Culture of Colonialism*. New York: Columbia University Press, 1996.

Gilroy, Paul. *Postcolonial Melancholia*. Wellek Lectures. New York: Columbia University Press, 2005.

Glissant, Édouard. *The Poetics of Relation*. Translated by Betsy Wing. Ann Arbor: University of Michigan Press, 1997. Originally published in 1990.

Green, Laura. "'I Recognized Myself in Her': Identifying with the Reader in George Eliot's *The Mill on the Floss* and Simone de Beauvoir's *Memoirs of a Dutiful Daughter*." *Tulsa Studies in Women's Literature* 24, no. 1 (2005): 57–79.

Greenberg, Jay, and Stephen A. Mitchell. *Object Relations in Psychoanalytic Theory*. Cambridge, MA: Harvard University Press, 1983.

Greiner, Rae. *Sympathetic Realism in Nineteenth-Century British Fiction*. Baltimore: Johns Hopkins University Press, 2012.

Griffin, Cristina Richieri. "George Eliot's Feuerbach: Senses, Sympathy, Omniscience, and Secularism." *ELH* 84, no. 2 (2017): 475–502.

Guidotti-Hernández, Nicole M. *Unspeakable Violence: Remapping U.S. and Mexican National Imaginaries*. Durham, NC: Duke University Press, 2011.

Hack, Daniel. "The Last Victorian Novel: II. *The Quest of the Silver Fleece*, by W.E.B. Du Bois." In *The Oxford Handbook of the Victorian Novel*, edited by Lisa Rodensky, 755–64. Oxford: Oxford University Press, 2013.

———. *Reaping Something New: African American Transformations of Victorian Literature*. Princeton, NJ: Princeton University Press, 2017.

Haight, Gordon S., ed. *A Century of George Eliot Criticism*. Boston, MA: Houghton Mifflin, 1965.

Hardy, Florence Emily. *The Early Life of Thomas Hardy, 1840–1891*. Cambridge: Cambridge University Press, 2011.

Hardy, Thomas. *The Dynasts, an Epic-Drama of the War with Napoleon, in Three Parts, Nineteen Acts, & One Hundred & Thirty Scenes, the Time Covered by the Action Being about Ten Years*. The Poetical Works of Thomas Hardy 7. London: Macmillan, 1920.

———. "Embarcation." In *Complete Poems*, 86.

———. "Hap." In *Complete Poems*, 9.

———. "Her Immortality." In *Complete Poems*, 55–56.

———. *Jude the Obscure*. Edited by Dennis Taylor. Penguin Classics. New York: Penguin Books, 1998.

———. *The Life and Work of Thomas Hardy*. Edited by Michael Millgate. Athens: University of Georgia Press, 1985.

———. *Personal Notebooks of Thomas Hardy*. Edited with notes and an introduction by Richard H. Taylor. London: Macmillan, 1979.

———. Preface to *Poems of the Past and the Present*. In *Complete Poems*, 84. Originally published 1901.

———. "The Profitable Reading of Fiction." *Forum* 5 (March 1888): 57–70.

———. *The Return of the Native*. Edited by Tony Slade. Penguin Classics. London: Penguin Books, 1999.

———. "The Sleep-Worker." In *Complete Poems*, 121–22. Originally published 1901.

———. *Tess of the D'Urbervilles*. Edited by Tim Dolin. Penguin Classics. New York: Penguin Books, 2003.

———. "Tess's Lament." In *Complete Poems*, 175–76.

———. *Thomas Hardy: The Complete Poems*. Edited by James Gibson. London: Palgrave, 2001.
Harris, Adrienne. "Gender as Contradiction." *Psychoanalytic Dialogues* 1, no. 2 (1991): 197–224.
Heimann, Paula. *About Children and Children-No-Longer: Collected Papers, 1942–80*. New York: Psychology, 1989.
———. "On Counter-Transference." In *About Children*, 55–59.
Henchman, Anna. "Hardy's Cliffhanger and Narrative Time." *English Language Notes* 46, no. 1 (2008): 127–34.
———. *The Starry Sky Within: Astronomy and the Reach of the Mind in Victorian Literature*. Oxford: Oxford University Press, 2014.
Henry, Nancy. "*Middlemarch*: 1870–2." In *The Life of George Eliot: A Critical Biography*, 181–206. Malden, MA: Wiley-Blackwell, 2012.
Hensley, Nathan K. *Forms of Empire: The Poetics of Victorian Sovereignty*. Oxford: Oxford University Press, 2016.
Hertz, Neil. *George Eliot's Pulse*. Meridian: Crossing Aesthetics. Stanford, CA: Stanford University Press, 2003.
Ho, Elizabeth. "The Neo-Victorian-at-Sea: Towards a Global Memory of the Victorians." In *Neo-Victorian Literature and Culture: Immersions and Revisitations*, edited by Nadine Boehm-Schnitker and Susanne Gruss, 165–78. New York: Routledge, 2014.
———. *Neo-Victorianism and the Memory of Empire*. Continuum Literary Studies 177. London: Continuum, 2012.
Homans, Margaret. "Dinah's Blush, Maggie's Arm: Class, Gender, and Sexuality in George Eliot's Early Novels." *Victorian Studies* 36, no. 2 (1993): 155–78.
hooks, bell. *Yearning: Race, Gender, and Cultural Politics*. New York: Routledge, 2015.
Hopkins, Linda. *False Self: The Life of Masud Khan*. New York: Other Books, 2006.
Hopkins, Philip. "Balint, Michael Maurice [Formerly Mihaly Bergsmann] (1896–1970)." In *Oxford Dictionary of National Biography*. Oxford University Press, 2004. https://doi.org/10.1093/ref:odnb/51076.
Huang, Yu-ting. "Writing Settlement: Locating Asian-Indigenous Relations in the Pacific." *Verge* 4, no. 2 (2018): 25–36.
Imarisha, Walidah, Alexis Gumbs, Leah Lakshmi Piepzna-Samarasinha, adrienne maree brown, and Mia Mingus. "The Fictions and Futures of Transformative Justice." *New Inquiry*, 20 April 2017. https://thenewinquiry.com/the-fictions-and-futures-of-transformative-justice/.
Inlak'ech, Diana Quinn. "Healing Our Ancestors: The Importance of Ancestral Relationships." *Crazy Wisdom Community Journal* 72 (2019): 64–65.
Jacobus, Mary. *First Things: Reading the Maternal Imaginary*. New York: Routledge, 1995.
———. *The Poetics of Psychoanalysis: In the Wake of Klein*. Oxford: Oxford University Press, 2005.
———. *Psychoanalysis and the Scene of Reading*. Clarendon Lectures in English, 1997. Oxford: Oxford University Press, 1999.
———. "The Question of Language: Men of Maxims and *The Mill on the Floss*." *Critical Inquiry* 8, no. 2 (1981): 207–22.
———. *Romantic Things: A Tree, a Rock, a Cloud*. Chicago: University of Chicago Press, 2012.
Jaffe, Audrey. *Vanishing Points: Dickens, Narrative, and the Subject of Omniscience*. Berkeley: University of California Press, 1991.

———. *The Victorian Novel Dreams of the Real: Conventions and Ideology*. Oxford: Oxford University Press, 2016.

James, C. L. R. *The Black Jacobins: Toussaint L'Ouverture and the San Domingo Revolution*. New York: Vintage Books, 1989.

James, David. "Hearing Hardy: Soundscapes and the Profitable Reader." *Journal of Narrative Theory* 40, no. 2 (2010): 131–55.

James, William. *The Principles of Psychology*. Vol. 1 of *The Works of William James*, edited by Frederick Burkhardt, Fredson Bowers, and Ignas K. Skrupskelis. Cambridge, MA: Harvard University Press, 1981.

Johnson, Barbara. *Persons and Things*. Cambridge, MA: Harvard University Press, 2008.

Jordan, John O. *Supposing Bleak House*. Charlottesville: University of Virginia Press, 2011.

Jordan, John O., and Robert L. Patten, eds. *Literature in the Marketplace: Nineteenth-Century British Publishing and Reading Practices*. Cambridge: Cambridge University Press, 1995.

Joseph, Betty. "Here and Now: My Perspective." *International Journal of Psychoanalysis* 94 (2013): 1–5.

———. "Interview with Betty Joseph." By Daniel Pick and Jane Milton. Melanie Klein Trust. 2006. http://www.melanie-klein-trust.org.uk/domains/melanie-klein-trust.org.uk/local/media/downloads/Interview_with_Betty_Joseph.pdf.

———. "On Understanding and Not Understanding: Some Technical Issues." In *Psychic Equilibrium*, 139–52. Originally published 1983.

———. "The Patient Who Is Difficult to Reach." In *Psychic Equilibrium*, 73–86. Originally published 1975.

———. "Psychic Change and the Psychoanalytic Process." In *Psychic Equilibrium*, 193–202. Originally published 1989.

———. *Psychic Equilibrium and Psychic Change: Selected Papers of Betty Joseph*. Edited by Michael Feldman and Elizabeth Bott Spillius. New York: Routledge, 1989.

———. "Towards the Experiencing of Psychic Pain." In *Psychic Equilibrium*, 87–98. Originally published [1981].

———. "Transference: The Total Situation." In *Psychic Equilibrium*, 157–68.

Kahr, Brett. *D. W. Winnicott: A Biographical Portrait*. London: Karnac Books, 1996.

Khan, M. Masud R. "Beyond the Dreaming Experience." In *Hidden Selves*, 42–50. Originally published 1976.

———. "Dream Psychology and the Evolution of the Psychoanalytic Situation [1962]." In *Privacy of the Self*, 27–41.

———. *Hidden Selves: Between Theory and Practice in Psychoanalysis*. London: Maresfield Library, 1983.

———. "On Lying Fallow." In *Hidden Selves*, 183–88.

———. *The Privacy of the Self: Papers on Psychoanalytic Theory and Technique*. Oxford: International Universities Press, 1974.

———. "The Use and Abuse of Dream in Psychic Experience [1972]." In *Privacy of the Self*, 306–15.

King, Pearl. "The Contributions of Ernest Jones to the British Psycho-Analytical Society." *International Journal of Psychoanalysis* 60 (1979): 280–84.

King, Pearl, and Riccardo Steiner, eds. *The Freud-Klein Controversies, 1941–45*. The New Library of Psychoanalysis, edited by David Tuckett, 11. New York: Routledge, 1991.

Klanchner, Jon P. *The Making of English Reading Audiences, 1790–1832*. Madison: University of Wisconsin Press, 1987.

Klein, Melanie. *Envy and Gratitude and Other Works, 1946–1963: The Writings of Melanie Klein*. Vol. 3. edited by Roger Money-Kyrle, in collaboration with Betty Joseph, Edna O'Shaughnessy, and Hanna Segal. New York: Free Press, 1975.

———. "Notes on Some Schizoid Mechanisms." *International Journal of Psychoanalysis* 27 (1946): 99–110.

———. "On the Sense of Loneliness [1963]." In *Envy and Gratitude*, 300–313.

———. "The Origins of Transference [1952]." In *Envy and Gratitude*, 48–56.

Kohon, Gregorio, ed. *The British School of Psychoanalysis: The Independent Tradition*. New Haven, CT: Yale University Press, 1986.

Kornbluh, Anna. *Realizing Capital: Financial and Psychic Economies in Victorian Form*. New York: Fordham University Press, 2014.

Kramer, Dale, ed. *The Cambridge Companion to Thomas Hardy*. Cambridge Companions to Literature. Cambridge: Cambridge University Press, 1999.

Kucich, John. *Imperial Masochism: British Fiction, Fantasy, and Social Class*. Princeton, NJ: Princeton University Press, 2006.

Kuhn, Philip. *Psychoanalysis in Britain, 1893–1913: Histories and Historiographies*. New York: Lexington Books, 2017.

Kurnick, David. "An Erotics of Detachment: *Middlemarch* and Novel-Reading as Critical Practice." *ELH* 74, no. 3 (2007): 583–608.

Lacan, Jacques. "The Function and Field of Language in Psychoanalysis." In *Ecrits: The First Complete Edition in English*, translated by Bruce Fink, 197–268. New York: W. W. Norton, 2007. Originally published 1953.

LaFarge, Lucy. "The Imaginer and the Imagined." *Psychoanalytic Quarterly* 73, no. 3 (2004): 591–625.

———. "Interpretation and Containment." *International Journal of Psychoanalysis* 81, no. 1 (2000): 67–84.

Law, Jules David. "Sleeping Figures: Hardy, History, and the Gendered Body." *ELH* 65, no. 1 (1998): 223–57.

Leavis, F. R. *The Great Tradition: George Eliot, Henry James, Joseph Conrad*. London: Chatto and Windus, 1962. Originally published 1948.

Levine, Caroline. *Forms: Whole, Rhythm, Hierarchy, Network*. Princeton, NJ: Princeton University Press, 2015.

Levine, George. *Realism, Ethics and Secularism: Essays on Victorian Literature and Science*. New York: Cambridge University Press, 2008.

Levinson, Marjorie. "Object-Loss and Object-Bondage: Economies of Representation in Hardy's Poetry." *ELH* 73, no. 2 (2006): 549–80.

Little, Margaret I. *Psychotic Anxieties and Containment: A Personal Record of an Analysis with Winnicott*. Northvale, NJ: Jason Aronson, 1977.

Lorde, Audre. "Uses of the Erotic." In *Sister Outsider: Essays and Speeches*, 53–59. Berkeley, CA: Crossing, 2007. Originally published 1978.

Love, Heather. "Truth and Consequences: On Paranoid Reading and Reparative Reading." *Criticism* 52, no. 2 (2010): 235–41.

Lynch, Deidre. *The Economy of Character: Novels, Market Culture, and the Business of Inner Meaning*. Chicago: University of Chicago Press, 1998.

Main, Alexander. Preface to *Wise, Witty and Tender Sayings in Prose and Verse: Selected from the Works of George Eliot*, ix–xii. Edinburgh: William Blackwood and Sons, 1889.

Markovits, Stefanie. "'That Girl Has Some Drama in Her': George Eliot's Problem with Action." In *The Crisis of Action in Nineteenth-Century English Literature*, 87–128. Columbus: Ohio State University Press, 2006.

Martin, Meredith. *The Rise and Fall of Meter: Poetry and English National Culture, 1860–1930*. Princeton, NJ: Princeton University Press, 2012.

Matache, Margareta. "Dear Gadjo (non-Romani) Scholars . . ." *The White Norm in Gypsy and Romani Studies* (blog). HarvardFXB Center for Health and Human Rights, 19 June 2017. https://fxb.harvard.edu/2017/06/19/dear-gadjo-non-romani-scholars/.

———. "The Legacy of Gypsy Studies in Modern Romani Scholarship." *The White Norm in Gypsy and Romani Studies* (blog). HarvardFXB Center for Health and Human Rights, 14 November 2016, last updated 13 June 2017. https://fxb.harvard.edu/2016/11/14/the-legacy-of-gypsy-studies-in-modern-romani-scholarship/.

———. "Word, Image and Thought: Creating the Romani Other." *The White Norm in Gypsy and Romani Studies* (blog). HarvardFXB Center for Health and Human Rights, 5 October 2016, last updated 13 June 2017. https://fxb.harvard.edu/2016/10/05/word-image-and-thought-creating-the-romani-other/.

Matus, Jill L. *Shock, Memory and the Unconscious in Victorian Fiction*. Cambridge Studies in Nineteenth-Century Literature and Culture 69. New York: Cambridge University Press, 2009.

Matz, Aaron. "Terminal Satire and Jude the Obscure." *ELH* 73, no. 2 (2006): 519–47.

Maxwell, Catherine. "The Brooking of Desire: Dorothea and Deferment in *Middlemarch*." *Yearbook of English Studies* 26 (1996): 116–26.

McClintock, Anne. *Imperial Leather: Race, Gender and Sexuality in the Colonial Contest*. New York: Routledge, 1995.

Meadowsong, Zena. "Thomas Hardy and the Machine: The Mechanical Deformation of Narrative Realism in *Tess of the d'Urbervilles*." *Nineteenth-Century Literature* 64, no. 2 (2009): 225–48.

Meisel, Perry. *The Literary Freud*. New York: Routledge, 2006.

Miller, Andrew H. *The Burdens of Perfection: On Ethics and Reading in Nineteenth-Century British Literature*. Ithaca, NY: Cornell University Press, 2008.

Miller, D. A. *Narrative and Its Discontents: Problems of Closure in the Traditional Novel*. Princeton, NJ: Princeton University Press, 1989.

———. *The Novel and the Police*. Berkeley: University of California Press, 1988.

Miller, J. Hillis. *The Ethics of Reading: Kant, de Man, Eliot, Trollope, James, and Benjamin*. Wellek Library Lectures at the University of California, Irvine. New York: Columbia University Press, 1987.

———. "Optic and Semiotic in *Middlemarch*." In *The Worlds of Victorian Fiction*, edited by Jerome Hamilton Buckley, 125–45. Harvard English Studies 6. Cambridge, MA: Harvard University Press, 1975.

———. "Reading Writing: Eliot." In *Ethics of Reading*, 61–80.
Miller, Nancy K. "Emphasis Added: Plots and Plausibilities in Women's Fiction." *PMLA* 96, no. 1 (1981): 36–48.
Miner, Heather. "Reforming Spaces: The Architectural Imaginary of *Middlemarch*." *Victorian Review* 38 (2012): 193–209.
Mitchell, Stephen A. *Relational Concepts in Psychoanalysis: An Integration*. Cambridge, MA: Harvard University Press, 1988.
Mitchell, Stephen A., and Margaret J. Black. *Freud and Beyond: A History of Modern Psychoanalytic Thought*. New York: Basic Books, 1995.
Moi, Toril. *Simone de Beauvoir: The Making of an Intellectual Woman*. Cambridge, MA: Blackwell, 1994.
Morgan, Benjamin. *The Outward Mind: Materialist Aesthetics in Victorian Science and Literature*. Chicago: University of Chicago Press, 2017.
Mukherjee, Ankhi. "Fissured Skin, Inner-Ear Radio, and a Telepathic Nose: The Senses as Media in Salman Rushdie's *Midnight's Children*." *Paragraph* 29, no. 3 (2006): 55–76.
Munger, Theodore Thornton. *On the Threshold*. Boston, MA: Houghton, Mifflin, 1881.
Muñoz, José Esteban. *Disidentifications: Queers of Color and the Performance of Politics*. Vol. 2. Cultural Studies of the Americas. Minneapolis: University of Minnesota Press, 1999.
———. "Feeling Brown, Feeling Down: Latina Affect, the Performativity of Race, and the Depressive Position." *Signs: Journal of Women in Culture and Society* 31, no. 3 (2006): 675–88.
Nandrea, Lorri G. *Misfit Forms: Paths Not Taken by the British Novel*. New York: Fordham University Press, 2015.
Nebbiosi, Giani, and Romolo Petrini. "The Theoretical and Clinical Significance of the Concept of 'Common Sense' in Bion's Work." In *W. R. Bion: Between Past and Future: Selected Contributions from the International Centennial Conference on the Work of W. R. Bion, Turin, July 1997*, edited by Franco Borgogno, Silvio A. Merciai, and Parthenope Bion Talamo, 164–77. London: Karnac Books, 2000.
Neilson, Brett. "Hardy, Barbarism, and the Transformations of Modernity." In *Thomas Hardy and Contemporary Literary Studies*, edited by Tim Dolin and Peter Widdowson, 65–79. New York: Palgrave Macmillan, 2004.
Nelson, Maggie. *The Argonauts*. Minneapolis: Graywolf, 2015.
Nemesvari, Richard. *Thomas Hardy, Sensationalism, and the Melodramatic Mode*. New York: Palgrave Macmillan, 2011.
Nord, Deborah Epstein. *Gypsies & the British Imagination, 1807–1930*. New York: Columbia University Press, 2006.
Nussbaum, Martha C. *Not for Profit: Why Democracy Needs the Humanities*. Updated ed. Princeton, NJ: Princeton University Press, 2016.
———. *Upheavals of Thought: The Intelligence of Emotions*. New ed. Cambridge: Cambridge University Press, 2003.
———. "Winnicott on the Surprises of the Self." *Massachusetts Review* 47, no. 2 (2006): 375–93.
Ogden, Thomas H. "Analysing Forms of Aliveness and Deadness of the Transference-Countertransference." *International Journal of Psychoanalysis* 76, no. 4 (1995): 695–709.
———. *Creative Readings: Essays on Seminal Analytic Works*. New York: Routledge, 2012.

———. "On Holding and Containing, Being and Dreaming." *International Journal of Psychoanalysis* 85, no. 6 (2004): 1349–64.

———. "On Projective Identification." *International Journal of Psychoanalysis* 60, no. 3 (1979): 357–73.

———. "Reverie and Metaphor: Some Thoughts on How I Work as a Psychoanalyst." *International Journal of Psychoanalysis* 78, no. 4 (1997): 719–32.

O'Hara, Patricia. "Narrating the Native: Victorian Anthropology and Hardy's *The Return of the Native*." *Nineteenth-Century Contexts* 20, no. 2 (1997): 147.

"100 Years of History." Institute of Psychoanalysis: British Psychoanalytical Society. N.d., accessed 13 November 2018. http://www.psychoanalysis.org.uk/who-we-are/100-years-of-history.

O'Shaughnessy, Edna. Review of *Wilfred Bion: His Life and Work, 1897–1979*, by Gérard Bléandonu, translated by Claire Pajaczkowska, with a foreword by R. D. Hinshelwood. *International Journal of Psychoanalysis* 76 (1995): 857–59.

———. "Revisiting Edna O'Shaughnessy's 'The Absent Object.'" *Journal of Child Psychotherapy* 42, no. 2 (2016): 208–16. "The Absent Object" was first published in 1964, in the first volume of the same journal.

Phillips, Adam. *Becoming Freud: The Making of a Psychoanalyst*. New Haven, CT: Yale University Press, 2014.

———. Introduction to *The Electrified Tightrope*, by Michael Eigen, i–xxviii. New York: Karnac Books, 2004.

———. "On Frustration." In *Missing Out: In Praise of the Unlived Life*, 1–33. New York: Picador and Farrar, Strauss and Giroux, 2014.

———. *On Kissing, Tickling, and Being Bored: Psychoanalytic Essays on the Unexamined Life*. Cambridge, MA: Harvard University Press, 1993.

———. "Returning the Dream: In Memoriam Masud Khan." In *On Kissing*, 59–67.

———. *Winnicott*. Cambridge, MA: Harvard University Press, 1989.

Pinch, Adela. "Preserving Attachments." Unpublished paper delivered at the 2017 NAVSA (North American Victorian Studies) conference, Banff, Canada, 13 November 2017.

———. "'A Shape All Light.'" In *Taking Liberties with the Author: Selected Essays from the English Institute*, edited by Meredith L. McGill, paras. 112–55. Cambridge, MA: English Institute, 2013. http://hdl.handle.net/2027/heb.90058.0001.001.

———. *Thinking about Other People in Nineteenth-Century British Fiction*. Cambridge: Cambridge University Press, 2010.

Pinney, Thomas, ed. *Essays of George Eliot*. New York: Columbia University Press, 1963.

Posmentier, Sonya. "A Language for Grieving." *New York Times*, 21 December 2015. https://www.nytimes.com/2015/12/27/books/review/a-language-for-grieving.html.

Price, Leah. *The Anthology and the Rise of the Novel: From Richardson to George Eliot*. New York: Cambridge University Press, 2000.

———. "George Eliot and the Production of Consumers." In *Anthology*, 105–56.

———. "Reading: The State of the Discipline." *Book History* 7 (2004): 303–20.

Quincey, Thomas De. *Confessions of an English Opium-Eater*. Edited by Joel Faflak. Toronto: Broadview, 2009.

Rankine, Claudia. "The Condition of Black Life Is One of Mourning." *New York Times Magazine*, 22 June 2015. https://www.nytimes.com/2015/06/22/magazine/the-condition-of-black-life-is-one-of-mourning.html.
Raven, James, Helen Small, and Naomi Tadmor, eds. *The Practice and Representation of Reading in England*. Cambridge: Cambridge University Press, 1996.
Rayner, Eric. *The Independent Mind in British Psychoanalysis*. London: Free Association Books, 1990.
Richardson, Angelique. "Hardy and Biology." In *Thomas Hardy: Texts and Contexts*, edited by Phillip Mallett, 156–79. New York: Palgrave Macmillan, 2002.
Riviere, Joan. "Those Wrecked by Success." In *The Inner World and Joan Riviere: Collected Papers 1929–1958*, edited by Athol Hughes, 133–54. London: Routledge, 1991. Originally published in 1936.
Rodman, F. Robert. *Winnicott: Life and Work*. Cambridge, MA: Da Capo, 2003.
Rose, Jacqueline. "George Eliot and the Spectacle of Woman." In *Sexuality in the Field of Vision*, 104–22. London: Verso, 2005.
Rose, Nikolas. *Inventing Our Selves: Psychology, Power, and Personhood*. Cambridge Studies in the History of Psychology, edited by Mitchell S. Ash and William R. Woodward. Cambridge: Cambridge University Press, 1998.
———. *The Psychological Complex: Psychology, Politics and Society in England, 1869–1939*. Boston, MA: Routledge and Kegan Paul, 1985.
Rosenberg, Jordy. "Gender Trouble on Mother's Day." *Avidly: A Channel of the Los Angeles Review of Books*, 9 May 2014. http://avidly.lareviewofbooks.org/2014/05/09/gender-trouble-on-mothers-day/.
Rosenfeld, Herbert. "The Psychopathology of Psychotic States." In *Projective Identification: The Fate of a Concept*, edited by Elizabeth Bott Spillius and Edna O'Shaughnessy, 80–81. New Library of Psychoanalysis. Hove, UK: Routledge, 2012.
Rudnytsky, Peter L., ed. *Transitional Objects and Potential Spaces: Literary Uses of D. W. Winnicott*. New York: Columbia University Press, 1994.
Ruskin, John. "Of the Pathetic Fallacy." In *The Broadview Anthology of Victorian Poetry and Poetic Theory*, edited by Thomas J. Collins and Vivienne J. Rundle, 1282–90. Ontario: Broadview, 1999.
Russell, David. *Tact: Aesthetic Liberalism and the Essay Form in Nineteenth-Century Britain*. Princeton, NJ: Princeton University Press, 2017.
Ryan, Vanessa Lyndal. *Thinking without Thinking in the Victorian Novel*. Baltimore: Johns Hopkins University Press, 2012.
Rylance, Rick. *Victorian Psychology and British Culture, 1850–1880*. Oxford: Oxford University Press, 2000.
Sacks, Oliver. "A Summer of Madness: A Review of Hurry Down Sunshine by Michael Greenberg, and Seven Other Books on Mental Illness." *New York Review of Books* 55, no. 14 (2008): 57–61.
Said, Edward W. *Culture and Imperialism*. New York: Vintage Books, 1994.
———. *Orientalism*. New York: Vintage Books, 1979.
———. "Reflections on Exile." In *Reflections on Exile and Other Essays*, 173–86. Cambridge, MA: Harvard University Press, 2000.

Sanborn, Geoffrey. *Plagiarama!: William Wells Brown and the Aesthetic of Attractions*. New York: Columbia University Press, 2016.

Sánchez-Pardo, Esther. *Cultures of the Death Drive: Melanie Klein and Modernist Melancholia*. Durham, NC: Duke University Press, 2003.

Sanders, Lise Shapiro. *Consuming Fantasies: Labor, Leisure, and the London Shopgirl, 1880–1920*. Columbus: Ohio State University Press, 2006.

Scarry, Elaine. "Participial Acts: Working: Work and the Body in Hardy and Other Nineteenth-Century Novelists." In *Resisting Representation*, 49–90.

———. *Resisting Representation*. New York: Oxford University Press, 1994.

Schapiro, Barbara Ann. *Literature and the Relational Self*. New York: New York University Press, 1994.

Schoolcraft, Ralph. "Beckett et le psychanalyste." *SubStance* 22, no. 2/3 (1993): 331–34.

Schwab, Gabriele. "Cultural Texts and Endopsychic Scripts." *SubStance* 30, no. 1/2 (2001): 160–76.

———. "Genesis of the Subject, Imaginary Functions, and Poetic Language." *New Literary History* 15, no. 3 (1984): 453–74.

———. "Words and Moods: The Transference of Literary Knowledge." *SubStance* 26, no. 3 (1997): 107–27.

Sedgwick, Eve Kosofsky. *Between Men: English Literature and Male Homosocial Desire*. New York: Columbia University Press, 2015.

———. "Melanie Klein and the Difference Affect Makes." *South Atlantic Quarterly* 106, no. 3 (2007): 625–42.

———. "Paranoid and Reparative Reading, or, You're So Paranoid You Probably Think This Essay Is About You." In *Touching Feeling*, 123–51.

———. *Tendencies*. Durham, NC: Duke University Press, 1993.

———. *Touching Feeling: Affect, Pedagogy, Performativity*. Series Q. Durham, NC: Duke University Press, 2003.

———. *The Weather in Proust*. Edited by Jonathan Goldberg. Durham, NC: Duke University Press, 2011.

———. "The Weather in Proust." In *Weather in Proust*, 1–41.

Selbin, Jesse Cordes. "'Interpretations are Illimitable': George Eliot and the Challenge of Common Reading." In "The Social Life of Reading: Literary Attention and Mass Culture in Nineteenth-Century Britain," unpublished dissertation, University of California, Berkeley, December 2018.

Shapira, Michal. *The War Inside*. Cambridge: Cambridge University Press, 2013.

Sharpe, James. *Remember, Remember: A Cultural History of Guy Fawkes Day*. Cambridge, MA: Harvard University Press, 2005.

Shires, Linda M. "The Radical Aesthetic of *Tess of the d'Urbervilles*." In Kramer, *Cambridge Companion to Thomas Hardy*, 145–63.

Shuttleworth, Sally. *George Eliot and Nineteenth-Century Science: The Make-Believe of a Beginning*. New York: Cambridge University Press, 1984.

———. *The Mind of the Child: Child Development in Literature, Science, and Medicine, 1840–1900*. Oxford: Oxford University Press, 2010.

Silverman, Kaja. "History, Figuration and Female Subjectivity in *Tess of the d'Urbervilles*." *Novel: A Forum on Fiction* 18, no. 1 (1984): 5–28.

Sklar, Jonathan. *Balint Matters: Psychosomatics and the Art of Assessment*. London: Karnac Books, 2017.

Slade, Tony. "A Note on the History of the Text." In Hardy, *Return of the Native*, xxxix–xxxl.

Smith, Vanessa. "Toy Stories." *Novel* 50, no. 1 (2017): 35–55.

Sperlinger, Tom. "'The Sensitive Author': George Eliot." *Cambridge Quarterly* 36, no. 3 (2007): 250–72.

Spillius, Elizabeth, and Edna O'Shaughnessy, eds. *Projective Identification: The Fate of a Concept*. New Library of Psychoanalysis. Hove, UK: Routledge, 2012.

Spitzer, Jennifer. "On Not Reading Freud: Amateurism, Expertise, and the 'Pristine Unconscious' in D.H. Lawrence." *Modernism/Modernity* 21, no. 1 (2014): 89–105.

———. *Secret Sharers: Modernism and the Debate with Psychoanalysis*. Forthcoming.

Spivak, Gayatri Chakravorty. "Three Women's Texts and a Critique of Imperialism." *Critical Inquiry* 12, no. 1 (1985): 243–61.

Star, Summer J. "Feeling Real in *Middlemarch*." *ELH* 80, no. 3 (2013): 839–69.

Steedman, Carolyn. *Strange Dislocations: Childhood and the Idea of Human Interiority, 1780–1930*. Cambridge, MA: Harvard University Press, 1995.

Stein, Ruth. "The Otherness of Sexuality: Excess." *Journal of the American Psychoanalytic Association* 56, no. 1 (2008): 43–71.

Steiner, Riccardo. "'It Is a New Kind of Diaspora. . . .'" *International Journal of Psychoanalysis* 16 (1989): 35–72.

Stevenson, Lisa. *Life Beside Itself: Imagining Care in the Canadian Arctic*. Oakland: University of California Press, 2014.

Stewart, Garrett. *Dear Reader: The Conscripted Audience in Nineteenth-Century British Fiction*. Baltimore: Johns Hopkins University Press, 1996.

———. *Novel Violence: A Narratography of Victorian Fiction*. Chicago: University of Chicago Press, 2009.

Stoler, Ann Laura. *Race and the Education of Desire: Foucault's "History of Sexuality" and the Colonial Order of Things*. Durham, NC: Duke University Press, 1995.

Stonebridge, Lyndsey. *The Destructive Element: British Psychoanalysis and Modernism*. New York: Routledge, 1998.

Strachey, James. "The Nature of the Therapeutic Action of Psycho-Analysis." *International Journal of Psychoanalysis* 15 (1934): 127–59.

Strachey, James, and Alix Strachey. *Bloomsbury/Freud: The Letters of James and Alix Strachey, 1924–25*. Edited by Perry Meisel and Walter Kendrick. London: Chatto and Windus, 1986.

Tanner, Tony. "Colour and Movement in Hardy's *Tess of the d'Urbervilles*." *Critical Quarterly* 10, no. 3 (1968): 219–39.

Taylor, Clare L. "Heimann [Née Klatzko], Paula Gertrude (1899–1982)." In *Oxford Dictionary of National Biography*. Oxford University Press, 2004. https://doi.org/10.1093/ref:odnb/51066.

Taylor, Jenny Bourne, and Sally Shuttleworth, eds. *Embodied Selves: An Anthology of Psychological Texts, 1830–1890*. Oxford: Clarendon, 1998.

Thomson, Mathew. *Psychological Subjects: Identity, Culture, and Health in Twentieth-Century Britain*. Oxford: Oxford University Press, 2006.

Vermeule, Blakey. *Why Do We Care about Literary Characters?* Baltimore: Johns Hopkins University Press, 2010.

Viswanathan, Gauri. *Masks of Conquest: Literary Study and British Rule in India*. New York: Columbia University Press, 2014.

———. "Raymond Williams and British Colonialism: The Limits of Metropolitan Cultural Theory." In *Views Beyond the Border Country: Raymond Williams and Cultural Politics*, edited by Dennis L. Dworkin and Leslie G. Roman, 217–30. New York: Routledge, 1993.

Watson, Tim. "Caribbean." *Victorian Literature and Culture* 46, no. 3–4 (2018): 601–3.

———. *Caribbean Culture and British Fiction in the Atlantic World, 1780–1870*. Cambridge: Cambridge University Press, 2008.

Weber, Samuel M. *The Legend of Freud*. Expanded ed. Cultural Memory in the Present. Stanford, CA: Stanford University Press, 2000.

Weinstein, Philip. *The Semantics of Desire: Changing Models of Identity from Dickens to Joyce*. Princeton, NJ: Princeton University Press, 1984.

Werning, Kate. "Trauma, Healing, & Collective Power with Generative Somatics, Featuring Spenta Kandawalla, Adrienne Maree Brown, Prentis Hamphill, and Staci K. Hines." Healing Justice, 25 July 2018. Podcast, 49:43. https://www.healingjustice.org/.

Wheatcroft, Andrew. *The Ottomans*. London: Penguin, 1993.

Widdowson, Peter. "Hardy and Critical Theory." In Kramer, *Cambridge Companion to Thomas Hardy*, 73–92.

———. *On Thomas Hardy: Late Essays and Earlier*. New York: St. Martin's, 1998.

Williams, Daniel. "Rumor, Reputation, and Sensation in *Tess of the d'Urbervilles*." *Novel* 46, no. 1 (2013): 93–115.

Williams, Raymond. *The Country and the City*. New York: Oxford University Press, 1973.

Willock, Brent, Lori C. Bohm, and Rebecca C. Curtis, eds. *Loneliness and Longing: Conscious and Unconscious Aspects*. New York: Routledge, 2012.

Winnicott, D. W. "The Capacity to Be Alone." In *Maturational Processes*, 29–35.

———. *Collected Papers: Through Paediatrics to Psycho-Analysis*. New York: Basic Books, 1958.

———. "Communicating and Not Communicating Leading to a Study of Certain Opposites." In *Maturational Processes*, 179–92. Originally published 1963.

———. "Dependence in Infant-Care, in Child-Care, and in the Psychoanalytic Setting." In *Maturational Processes*, 249–60.

———. "Ego Integration in Child Development." In *Maturational Processes*, 56–63. First published 1962.

———. "Fear of Breakdown." *International Journal of Psychoanalysis* 1 (1974): 103–7.

———. *The Maturational Processes and the Facilitating Environment: Studies in the Theory of Emotional Development*. New York: International Universities Press, 1965.

———. *Playing and Reality*. New York: Routledge, 2005.

———. "Playing: Creative Activity and the Search for the Self." In *Playing and Reality*, 53–64.

———. "Primary Maternal Preoccupation." In *Collected Papers*, 300–305. Originally published 1956.

———. "Primitive Emotional Development." *International Journal of Psychoanalysis* 26 (1945): 137–43.

———. "The Theory of the Parent-Infant Relationship." In *Maturational Processes*, 37–55. Originally published 1960.

———. "Transitional Objects and Transitional Phenomena." In *Playing and Reality*, 1–34. Originally published 1951; extended in 1971 edition.

———. "The Use of an Object and Relating through Identifications." In *Playing and Reality*, 115–27.

Woloch, Alex. *The One vs. the Many: Minor Characters and the Space of the Protagonist in the Novel*. Princeton, NJ: Princeton University Press, 2003.

Wood, Michael. "Greatness and Melancholy." *New York Review of Books*, 27 November 1975. http://www.nybooks.com/articles/1975/11/27/greatness-and-melancholy/.

Woolf, Virginia. "George Eliot." *Times Literary Supplement*, 20 November 1919: 657–58.

Wright, Daniel. *Bad Logic: Reasoning about Desire in the Victorian Novel*. Baltimore: Johns Hopkins University Press, 2018.

Wright, Terence R. *Hardy and His Readers*. London: Palgrave Macmillan, 2003.

Wynter, Sylvia. "Unsettling the Coloniality of Being/Power/Truth/Freedom: Towards the Human, after Man, Its Overrepresentation—An Argument." *CR: The New Centennial Review* 3, no. 3 (2003): 257–337.

Young, Robert J. C. *White Mythologies: Writing History and the West*. 2nd ed. New York: Routledge, 2004.

Yousef, Nancy. *Romantic Intimacy*. Stanford, CA: Stanford University Press, 2013.

Zeavin, Lynne. Review of *Bion Today*, by Chris Mawson. Society for Psychoanalysis and Psychoanalytic Psychology, Division 39: American Psychological Association. Book Reviews, Fall 2011. http://www.apadivisions.org/division-39/publications/reviews/bion-today.aspx.

Zieger, Susan. "*Neo-Victorian Literature and Culture: Immersions and Revisitations* ed. by Nadine Boehm-Schnitker, Susanne Gruss, and: *Nineteenth-Century British Literature Then and Now: Reading with Hindsight* by Simon Dentith, and: *Twenty-First Century Perspectives on Victorian Literature* ed. by Laurence W. Mazzeno (review)." *Victorian Studies* 59, no. 1 (2016): 131–34.

Zhang, Dora. "Notes on Atmosphere." *Qui Parle* 27, no. 1 (2018): 121–55.

Zunshine, Lisa. *Why We Read Fiction: Theory of Mind and the Novel*. Theory and Interpretation of Narrative. Columbus: Ohio State University Press, 2006.

INDEX

Abel, Elizabeth, 51
Ablow, Rachel, 17
Abraham, Karl, 11
absence, 30; conintrication with presence, 195; as essential condition for relationships, 192; presence and, 20, 185, 192–96; presence and, the distance between Freud and Winnicott on, 24; recoding in object relations thought, 192–96. *See also* presence
Ahimaaz, 137
Ahmed, Sara, 53, 213n23, 220n91
à Kempis, Thomas, 71, 74–75, 77, 79–83, 106
Albrecht, Thomas, 69
aliveness/ardor, 153–55, 163–64, 185, 190–91
Alix, Lytton, 16
alone/aloneness. *See* solitude
Althusser, Louis, 87, 210n61
Anderson, Amanda, 150–51
Anderson, Robin, 234n37
Anna Freudians, 11–12, 149
Armstrong, Nancy, 72, 221n98
Asghar, Fatimah, 203n34
Auden, W. H., 108
author love, 195

Balibar, Etienne, 210n61
Balint, Alice (née Alice Szekely-Kovacs), 114, 225n13
Balint, Enid Flora (née Albu, later Balint-Edmonds), 225n13
Balint, Michael: air, 118, 120; atmospheres/environment, 109–10, 114–16, 119–21, 151; "basic fault," 13, 111, 145–47, 193; biographical material, 14, 109, 148–49, 224n5; empire, failure to address, 148; "friendly expanses" and "horrid empty spaces," 11, 109–10, 145; "harmonious interpenetrating mix-up," 112, 119–20, 136, 226n21; Joseph, as analyst of, 165; managing distance, 151, 227n21; as a medical doctor, 224n5; object relationships, 114–16, 151; omniscience, 236n72; "primary love," 119–21; "primary substances," 119; psychoanalytic practice/situation, 109–10, 114–16, 120–21, 169, 227n21; reading, feeling of, 113; Sedgwick, 226–27n21; terminology, 227n22; women, collaboration with, 225n13
Barthes, Roland, 162–63
basic fault: Balint's concept of, 13, 111, 145–47, 193; in British object relations psychoanalysis, 148–49; in *The Return of the Native*, 147–48; in Victorian novel studies, 148
Baucom, Ian, 231n62
Bayley, John, 33
Beckett, Samuel, 5
Beer, Gillian: determinism and alternative modes/temporalities, 51–53, 58; on Eliot, 47, 50, 51, 61, 219n82; hap and happiness, 122, 136; on Hardy, 31, 32, 111, 122, 228n24, 229n45; hyperaesthesia, 61; omniscience, 235n66; on women's fiction, 51–52
Benjamin, Jessica, 211n78
Bentham, Jeremy, 33
Berger, John, 211n65

Bion, Wilfred R.: absence, 192, 196; "aliveness" and "deadness," 154; attacks on linking/linking, 15, 54–55, 58, 66, 101, 168; biographical material, 5, 14, 148, 212n3; container/contained, 47, 64, 66–67, 70, 83–85, 89, 219n84; development, 85–86; dreaming, 59–61; empire, 148; epigraph, 46; "F" and "area of faith," 106, 196, 238n3; Freud, 86; frustration, 63; grid used by, 49; hyperspecialized technical vocabulary, 16, 18, 48–49; ideas buried in the future, 46, 100, 102; influential contributions, 47–48; Joseph, 165; Klein, 5, 56, 64–65; matrix of thought, 5, 50, 71, 76, 94, 102; "O," 1, 5, 7, 56, 70, 75–76, 80, 85, 91, 96, 99; Oedipus myth, 54–56, 58, 85, 89; Ogden, 48; paranoid-schizoid and depressive, 60, 101; projective identification, 47, 60, 64–66, 68; psychoanalytic practice/situation, 6, 16, 70, 75; reverie, 61, 64–66, 216n50; "reversible perspective," 57, 76; transformations/"T" and miracles, 75–76; valency, 95; vibratory energy of relational reading, 6; wishes, 82

Black, Clementina, 30, 32

Black Hole of Calcutta, 125–27

Blackwood, John, 173

Blanchot, Maurice, 97, 153, 155, 175–76

Bodenheimer, Rosemarie, 164

Bollas, Christopher: aesthetic theory, 42–44; benign regression, 88–89; gender, 42–44; "genera," 20–21, 220n92; God, self, and personal idiom, 183–85; Heimann, 160–62; movements of voice, 157, 162–63; as a writer, 5

Borges, Jorge Luis, 67

Boumelha, Penny, 41–42, 207n41, 223n4

Bownas, Jane, 229n38

BPAS. *See* British Psycho-Analytical Society

Brantlinger, Patrick, 140

Briefel, Aviva, 132–33

Brinkema, Eugenie, 204n45

British Empire: Black Hole of Calcutta, 125–27; failure to account for, 148–50; Hardy's bonfire-night scene, 131–32; as ongoing, 127–28, 132; Ottoman Empire, 140; Palestine, 137. *See also* empire

British psychoanalysis/psychoanalysts: "aliveness" and "deadness," 154–55; atmospheres, 112–14; "contemporary Kleinians," 165; distinctive insights, 4; empire and geopolitics, 11–15, 110, 148–50 (*see also* British empire); factions of, 11–12; first objects, 7; interests of, 10; object relations theory (*see* object relations psychoanalysis); transference/countertransference (*see* transference/countertransference); Victorian-era novels, 2, 12–17. *See also* Balint, Michael; Bion, Wilfred R.; Bollas, Christopher; Heimann, Paula; Joseph, Betty; Winnicott, Donald W.

British Psycho-Analytical Society (BPAS), 11–12, 202n27

Brocklebank, Lisa, 210n62

Brooks, Peter, 55–56, 58

"Brother and Sister" (Eliot), 104

brown, adrienne maree, 15, 46, 58, 100, 107, 220n90, 222n107

Bulwer-Lytton, Sir Edward, 213n10, 215n44

Butler, Judith, 194

Buzard, James, 222n103

Byatt, A. S., 50, 63

Byrd, Jodi A., 15, 239n16

Carroll, Alicia, 103–4, 106, 222n103

Chatterjee, Partha, 125–26

Cheng, Anne, 194

Chesnutt, Charles W., 53

Clive, Robert, 127

Cohen, William A., 89–90, 119, 218–19n82

Cohn, Elisha, 176, 183, 228n24, 235n66

Cole, Truth Murray, 230n51

Collins, Wilkie, 145

colonialism. *See* British empire; empire

colonial object relations, 110, 116, 141, 148

"contemporary Kleinians," 165
countertransference. *See* transference/countertransference
Curzon, George Nathaniel, 1st Marquess Curzon of Kedleston, 127

Dallas, E. S., 66
Dames, Nicholas, 66, 164–65, 208–9n47, 233n33
Daniel Deronda (Eliot), 178, 215n39, 222n103, 233n33
deadness/weariness, 154–56, 163–64, 173–77, 182, 185–87, 190–91
de Beauvoir, Simone, 53
De Quincey, Thomas, 138
Derrida, Jacques, 182, 188
Descartes, René, 81
determinism, 51–52, 85, 217n66
Dimen, Muriel, 15, 201n14, 211n78
Dimock, Wai Chee, 194
disidentificatory reading/reception, 105–6, 194
Dolin, Tim, 226n19
Doniger, Bryan, 207n28
dreams/dreaming: Bion's emphasis on, 61; Freud's definition of, 58; Kleinian psychoanalysis and, 84; in *The Mill on the Floss*, 58–61; reading and, 66–68; reverie and, 61–62
Dukes, Hunter, 212n5
Duncan, Ian, 145
Dynasts, The (Hardy), 127

Eagleton, Terry, 207n41, 228n35, 236n73
Eckhart, Meister, 70
Eigen, Michael, 3, 76, 106
Eliot, George: the artist as acoustic or optical instrument, 173; "Brother and Sister," 104; *Daniel Deronda*, 178, 215n39, 222n103, 233n33; epigraph, 153; feeling as an enrichment of interpretive abilities, 160; Feurbach translation, 183; hyperesthesia, 61; *Leaves from a Note-Book*, 174–75; *Middlemarch* (*see Middlemarch*

(Eliot)); *The Mill on the Floss* (*see Mill on the Floss, The* (Eliot)); narrative voice, 157–59; "O May I Join the Choir Invisible," 182–83; omniscience, 177–80, 185, 235n66; pen name, 216n64, 218–19n82; "The Spanish Gypsy," 104, 222n103; tiredness of language, 174–75; transmission of feelings, 68–69; vibratory energy in relational reading, 6; Woolf, 217n68. *See also* Evans, Mary Ann
"Embarcation" (Hardy), 127–28, 132, 152, 229n38
empire: British (*see* British Empire); British psychoanalysis and, 148–50; domestic/imperial space, 141; the heath and, 124; Ottoman, 140; racialization of Eustacia, 139–41; space in *The Return of the Native*, 110
Eng, David, 12, 137, 149–50, 224–25n7
Estés, Clarissa Pinkola, 174
Esty, Jed, 85, 217n74, 218n75
Evans, Mary Ann, 72–73, 81, 103, 105–6, 180–81, 216n64, 218n82. *See also* Eliot, George

Fairbairn, W. R. D., 200n8, 206n16
Fanon, Frantz, 105–6, 197
Fawkes, Guy, 130
Feldman, Michael, 233–34n36
Felman, Shoshana, 10, 237n92
Felski, Rita, 201–2n18
feminism: Bildungsroman, 50–53; fault in second-wave, 102; feminist identificatory reading practices, 210n61; futures of, 100; psychoanalytic thinking, 52–53. *See also* gender
Ferenczi, Sándor, 11, 224n5
Ferguson, Trish, 130
Fernández-Savater, Amador, 15, 116, 226n18
Fetterley, Judith, 41
Feurbach, Ludwig, 180, 183–84, 188–89
Foucault, Michel, 139, 150
Frederikse, Julie, 108
Freedgood, Elaine, 34–35, 179–80, 206n12, 221n100, 236n69, 236n72

Freud, Anna, 11, 149, 202n26
Freud, Sigmund: antithetical meanings in single words, 223n4; archaeological excavation comparison, 86; Bion, 71, 196, 238n3; Brooks, 55–56; countertransference, 159; death drive, 149; death of, 11; "discovery" of psychoanalysis, 67; dreams, 58–59; grief/grieving in literary theory, 194; Klein, 3; literary figures, 16; London, 11; Oedipus plot/myth, 52, 54; psychoanalytic technique, 159–60; trauma, 20; Winnicott, 24; wishes, 63
Frost, Robert, 172

Gallagher, Catherine, 32–34, 158
Gattrell, Simon, 225n10
gender: feminist criticism, 52 (*see also* feminism); in *The Mill on the Floss*, 87–91; reading and, 45; in *Tess of the D'Urbervilles*, 39–45
gendered subjectivity, 26
genera, 20–21
Genette, Gérard, 34–35
Gettelman, Debra, 62, 68, 214–15n39
Gikandi, Simon, 231n62
Gilbert, Sandra, 51
Gilroy, Paul, 194
Glissant, Edouard, 197
Green, André, 3
Green, Laura, 53, 210n61, 216n64
Gubar, Susan, 51

Hack, Daniel, 53
Hardy, Thomas: *The Dynasts*, 127; "Embarcation," 127–28, 132, 152, 229n38; epigraph, 108; "harmonious interpenetrating mix-ups," 121; *Jude the Obscure*, 26, 223n4, 228–29n35; late-Victorian life, 228–29n35; literary form, 207–8n41; novels, 8–9, 208n46; "reparative" practice, 38; restlessness, 224n4; *The Return of the Native* (*see Return of the Native, The* (Hardy)); solitude, 22; *Tess of the D'Urbervilles* (*see Tess of the*

D'Urbervilles (Hardy)); "The Sleep-Worker," 232n82; "unrest," 223–24n4; Winnicott and, 24
Hegel, Georg Wilhelm Friedrich, 103
Heimann, Paula: "aliveness" and "deadness," 154; biographical material, 14, 160; Bollas on, 160–62; on countertransference, 157, 159–60, 165–66; on the emotional sensitivity of the analyst, 160; Joseph, analysis of, 165; psychoanalysis, new ideas about, 6, 156–57; relationship as basis of the analytic situation, 157; shifting registers of voice and personality, 160–62, 178; as theoretical grounding for the reading of *Middlemarch*, 19
Henry, Nancy, 182
Hensley, Nathan, 103, 217–18n74
Hertz, Neil, 83
Hirsch, Marianne, 51
Holwell, John Zephania, 125–26
Homans, Margaret, 102, 221n98
hooks, bell, 15, 107, 222–23n107
Hopkins, Linda, 203–4n39
Howard, Richard, 163

imperialism. *See* empire
Independent group, 12, 115, 165, 209n53–54, 224n5, 237n85
Irigaray, Luce, 52, 100

Jacobus, Mary, 4, 18, 52, 100, 201n13, 212n53, 221n98
Jaffe, Audrey, 179–80, 185, 235n65
James, C.L.R., 197
James, Henry, 164, 233n32
James, William, 22
John of the Cross, Saint, 70
Jones, Ernest, 11, 16, 149, 202nn26–27
Joseph, Betty: "aliveness" and "deadness," 154; analytic technique, 156–57; biographical material, 165–66; case history of "C," 167–69; literary interpretation and, 6–7, 19–20, 166, 177; "psychic

change," 167, 189–90, 234n42; transference as "total situation," 165–67
Jude the Obscure (Hardy), 26, 223n4, 228–29n35

Kaplan, Cora, 221n98
Khan, Masud, 3, 14, 148, 203–4n39, 231n68, 235–36n67
King, Pearl, 149, 204n41
Klein, Melanie: absent object turned into bad object, 192; "aliveness" and "deadness," 154; Berlin, 11; Bion, influence on, 5, 56, 64–65; companionship and solitude, 70, 205n1; Eng's reading of, 150; Freud, 3; Heimann, 156; Joseph, 156, 165; London, 11–12; maternal element, 41; paranoid/schizoid and depressive positions, 37; projective identification, 64–65, 215n47; Sedgwick's use of, 150, 209n54; total situations, 166; Winnicott, relationship to and distance from, 38, 151, 205n1
Kleinians, 11–12, 149
Kristeva, Julia, 3
Kurnick, David, 183, 233n30

Lacan, Jacques, 3, 87, 201n13, 237n92
Lacanian psychoanalysis/theory, 16–17, 24, 26, 204n46, 227n21
LaFarge, Lucy, 3, 214n35, 217n71, 219n84
language: "adult," 115, 145–46; Bion's, 60, 85; body, 162; communication going beyond, 4, 115, 146, 177–78; dimensions of, 166; Eliot's narrator's, 158, 162, 164; enactment/statement, 163–65, 167; extralinguistic, 10, 93; of gender binarism, 87, 158–59; global relations, 128; Hardy's, 123, 228n4; as limiting or recuperative force, 153, 175–76; for loss, 193–94; metaphorical, 171, 173, 196 (*see also* metaphor(s)); performative, 69, 96; preverbal, 16–17; race, 139; tiredness of, 173–75
Laplanche, Jean, 3
Leaves from a Note-Book (Eliot), 174–75

Leavis, F. R., 213n10, 218n75
Levine, George, 235n66
Levinson, Marjorie, 39, 206n15, 208n41, 209n58, 210n59
Lewes, George Henry, 66, 216n64, 218–19n82
Lewes, Marian Evans, 73, 216n64. *See also* Eliot, George
literary character: Bollas on "being a character," 43, 184; character love, 196; character to character idealization, 156; discontinuous characterological orders, 142–43; feeling like a, 17, 34, 178; overflowing/fluid connection to other literary figures, 47–48, 52, 61–62, 66, 69, 72, 83, 85, 193; relation to omniscient narrator, 158, 178–80; theory of, 2–3, 5–6, 17–18, 20, 23, 25–27, 29, 32–38, 158, 208n44
literary criticism/studies: author love, 195; belief in rationality, 193; character love, 196; mourning/melancholia, 194; presence/absence, 195; psychoanalytic, 3–4; therapeutic culture in, 150–51; Victorian fiction/novels (*see* Victorian fiction/novels)
London Psycho-Analytic Society, 202n27. *See also* British Psycho-Analytical Society (BPAS)
Lorde, Audre, 15, 100, 220n89, 222n107
Luria, Issac, 70

Macherey, Pierre, 210n61
Magnus, Albertus, 133
Main, Alexander, 157–58
Maxwell, Catherine, 233n29
McClintock, Anne, 13–14, 141, 147
Meadowsong, Zena, 207n41
metalepsis, 34–35
metaphor(s): biological/evolutionary, 87; Casaubon entangled in a concrete, 169–71; Clym as insect, 134; of the color white, 148 (*see also* race/racism); the container as, 82–85; Maggie's appearance as, 102; of the narrative voice in

metaphor(s) (continued)
  Middlemarch, 156–59, 171; Ogden, in psychoanalysis for, 171–73; paternal/maternal of psychoanalysis, 43–44; spatial of British psychoanalysis, 110; think, as a way not to, 169; vibrations as mixed, 94; Winnicott on the connection of the literal to, 38
methodology, relational reading as, 5–11
Middlemarch (Eliot): ardor/aliveness and weariness/deadness, 153–57, 163–64, 173–76, 182, 185–87, 191; as exhausting read, 164–65; idealization, 187–90; language as enactment, 163–65, 167; maturity of, 164, 218n75; metaphors, 156–57, 169–72; mobility/movement, 179–82, 196; narrator/narrative voice, 81, 156–59, 162–63, 177–80, 182, 190, 235n65; omniscience, 177–80, 185, 190, 235n65; recuperation/redemption, 174–77; as romance, 185–87; secularism and faith, 182–85; themes of, 19–20; voice on the page, 160
Miller, D. A., 183
Miller, J. Hillis, 69, 232n4
Miller, Nancy K., 50, 98, 219n86
Mill on the Floss, The (Eliot): Bildungsroman, 50–53, 62, 85, 100; catastrophic development, 85, 87; character love, 196; container metaphor, 83–85; dreaming/reverie, 58–68; the ending, 50–51, 57–58, 62–64, 83, 215n44, 217n74, 218n75; futures embedded in, 53, 100–102; gender conscription/conformity, 87–91; gypsies, 103–5, 107, 221n96, 221n103; Maggie, 95–97, 100–104, 104–7; maturity of, 164, 218n75; maxims, 85, 97–98; moral dilemmas/openness, 96–98; music/romance, 92–95; mysticism of the quiet hand, 70–83; narrator/narrative voice, 61–62, 71–73, 75–81, 90; "O," 91–99; quietism, 80–83; relationality, 69–80, 99; reparative reading, 101; reversible perspective, 57–58; themes explored, 18; vibrations, 1, 6, 94; whiteness, 103, 106; wishfulness, 68, 81–82; wishing and longing, 46–47, 50–51, 58
Moi, Toril, 53
Muñoz, José Esteban, 15, 102, 105–6, 158, 194

narrator/narrative voice: in *Middlemarch*, 81, 156–59, 162–63, 177–80, 182, 190; in *The Mill on the Floss*, 61–62, 71–73, 75–81, 90
Nebbiosi, Giani, 214n28
Nord, Deborah, 103–4, 106, 221–22n103, 221n102
novel, the: capacity of, object relations theory and, 10–11; formal elements of, 17; gender of the narrator in, 41–42
novel reading: atmospheres and, 109; Eliot on, 174; experience *versus* memory of, 112–13, 235n67; Hardy and, 8–9, 35–37; loneliness and, 24; relationality in, 1–2, 193; for relation rather than plot, 55–56; unintegration experienced in, 38–39. *See also* reading; Victorian fiction/novels/studies
novel studies. *See* literary criticism/studies

object relations psychoanalysis/thought: atmospheres, 112; Balint, 114–16; "basic fault," 13, 111, 145–49, 193; Bollas, 160–62; British psychoanalysis-Victorian studies links, 15–17; "capacity," 10–11; colonial object relations and, 148–51 (*see also* colonial object relations); guiding insights, 2–3; literariness, 114; literary criticism and, 151–52; literature on, 3–4; permanent coexistence of presence and absence, 192–94; political sphere and, 12–13 (*see also* colonial object relations); readers, 16; relational reading, 5–7 (*see also* relational reading). *See also* British psychoanalysis/psychoanalysts; psychoanalysis
Oedipus plot/myth, 52, 54–55

Ogden, Thomas: "aliveness"/"deadness," 154–55; Bion, 48, 60–61, 67; metaphor, 171–73; *Middlemarch*, 157; projective identification, 101; as a writer, 5
"O May I Join the Choir Invisible" (Eliot), 182–83
omniscience: in Eliot, 177–80, 185, 235n66; as a literary critical term, 235n65; as a substitute for learning from experience, 98
O'Shaughnessy, Edna, 3, 192, 194, 212n7, 215n49, 238n4
Ottoman Empire, 140

paranoia, 26–27, 37
Petrini, Romolo, 214n28
Phillips, Adam: "bad-enough imperialism," 150; on Bion's frustration/learning from experience, 63, 98–99; British Independents' "negative theology of the self," 237n85; dream-work, 59; on Eigen, 106; "failure of imagination," 63–64, 91; solitude, 24, 37; Winnicott, 203n39; as a writer, 5
Pinch, Adela, 195–96, 212n5, 225–26n13
plot: feminist bildungsroman, 50–53; futurity, 104–7; normative socialization, 91, 163–64; pauses in, 19, 31, 121–22; reading for relation rather than, 54–58; rethinking form and theory of, 18, 55–56, 102, 113
Poe, Edgar Alan, 67
Poovey, Mary, 221n98
presence, 18, 20, 22–24, 27–29, 36–37, 40–41, 138, 185, 192–96. *See also* absence
Price, Leah, 157–58
projective identification: Bion, 47, 60–61, 64–66, 68; British psychoanalysis, 4, 6; Joseph, 166–67; Klein, 64–65, 215n47; multiple purposes and effects, 101
Proust, Marcel, 124, 226n21
psychoanalytic practice/situation: absence, new conception of, 193–95; aloneness, 28; British (*see* British psychoanalysis/psychoanalysts); fault lines in, 13; ideology of determinism, 52; intangibles, 114; literary studies and, 3–4; object relations theory (*see* object relations psychoanalysis); Oedipus myth, 55; presence and absence, permanent coexistence of, 195; reconceptualizing curative mechanism, 6, 40–41 (*see also* Joseph, Betty, "psychic change")

race/racism: empire and, 125–27; Maggie's skin, 102–3; the "racial century," 137; the racial hand, 132–34; racially figured characters, 110–11, 117–18, 132–44; sexuality and, 139–42; whiteness/white mythologies, 103, 106, 110, 118, 133, 139, 142–45, 147–48
reading/reader: British psychoanalysis, as illuminated by, 16; as co-creation, 8–9; feelings of, 17, 20; Hardy on, 8–9; "instruments of research," 162; as never performed alone, 1; novels (*see* novel reading); object relations, 163; Oedipus myth, 54–55; paranoid/reparative, 37–38, 57–58; relational (*see* relational reading); for relation rather than plot, 55–56; reverie, as shared, 66–68; reversible perspective, 57–58
relationality: in anticolonial writing, 197; belief in, 1, 5, 192–93; challenge of, 91, 99 (*see also* relational reading); in the field of Victorian studies, 197; in *The Mill on the Floss*, 69–80, 88, 99; in novel reading, 1–2; temporality, 194; Victorian novels and psychoanalysis, 20
relational reading: concept of, 5–7; Dimock's "resonance" and, 194; Eliot and Bion, 50, 58 (*see also* Bion, Wilfred R.; *Mill on the Floss, The* (Eliot)); Eliot and Heimann/Joseph/Ogden, 156–57, 162–63 (*see also* Heimann, Paula; Joseph, Betty; *Middlemarch* (Eliot); Ogden, Thomas); example of, 7–11; feelings of reading and, 20; geopolitical implications, 13, 197;

relational reading (continued)
  Hardy and Balint, 109–10 (*see also* Balint, Michael; *Return of the Native, The* (Hardy)); Hardy and Winnicott, 23–24 (*see also Tess of the D'Urbervilles* (Hardy); Winnicott, Donald W.); links with other academic fields, 15–17; *Novel Relations*, 17–20; presence/absence, object relations and, 196
relationship(s), 192–93
Rembrandt Harmenszoon van Rijn, 133
Return of the Native, The (Hardy): air, 116–19, 124–25; atmospheres, 109, 111–13, 116–19, 121–24, 136; "basic fault," 147; Black Hole of Calcutta, 125–27; bonfire-night scene, 129–32; class represented by color, 135–37; colonial object relations, 110, 116; empire/geopolitics, 124–28, 131–32, 137, 196; end of, 144–45, 147–48; Eustacia, 138–42; harmonious mix-up, 118–19; hyperlocal and global, 109, 111, 116, 123–24, 128–31; images, 113; landscapes, 119; plot, pauses in, 122; racially figured characters, 110–11, 117–18, 132–44; restlessness, 123–24; setting and backstory, 111; themes explored, 18–19; transitional objects, 9–10; white mythologies/whiteness, 110, 118, 133, 139, 142–45, 147–48
reverie: Bion, 61, 64–66; dreams, 61–62; *The Mill on the Floss*, 47, 59, 61–66; reading, 66–68; *Tess of the D'Urbervilles*, 30, 36, 38
reversible perspective, 57, 76
Rickman, John, 202n27
Riviere, Joan, 3, 19, 154, 156, 204n41
Rodman, F. Robert, 203n39
Rosenberg, Jordy, 15, 151
Rosenfeld, Herbert, 101, 165
Ruskin, John, 25
Ruysbroeck, Blessed John, 70

Sacks, Oliver, 237n88
Schwab, Gabriele, 211n76
Scott, Sir Walter, 102

Sedgwick, Eve Kosofsky: Anderson on, 150–51; on Klein, 150, 209n54; phrases deployed, 226–27n21; psychoanalytic reading, 18; reparative impulse, 149, 152; reparative/paranoid reading, 37–38, 57, 101, 209n49
Segal, Hanna, 57, 165
sexuality, 138–42
Shapira, Michal, 11, 231n70
Shelley Percy Bysshe, 195
Shires, Linda, 207n41
Showalter, Elaine, 51
Shuttleworth, Sally, 214n29
Silverman, Kaja, 26–27, 210–11n65
Siraj-ud-daulah, Nawab, 125–26
Sklar, Jonathan, 224n5
"Sleep-Worker, The" (Hardy), 232n82
Smith, Vanessa, 216n66
solitude: aloneness, paradoxical nature of, 22–24, 39–41 (*see also Tess of the D'Urbervilles* (Hardy)); persecution and expansive release, 32; prescriptive and descriptive, 36–37; reading and, 36–37; of Tess, 24–27; Winnicott, 28–29
"Spanish Gypsy, The" (Eliot), 104, 222n103
Stein, Ruth, 216n51
Steiner, Riccardo, 149, 202n26
Stevenson, Lisa, 15
Stoler, Ann Laura, 139–41
Strachey, James, 16
Strachey, Lytton, 16

Tess of the D'Urbervilles (Hardy): atmosphere, 117; bipolarity and discontinuity, 37–38, 109; gender and maternity, 39–45, 196; literary character, making and unmaking of, 23, 25–27, 29, 32–38; metalepsis and unintegration, 34–39, 44; populated solitude, 22–24, 36–37; solitariness of Tess, 3, 24–27, 39–40; Tess, 22, 24–27, 29–34, 32–34, 224n4; themes explored, 17–18; Winnicottian theory and, 23–24
textuality, dimensions of, 10, 151

transference/countertransference: aliveness and deadness in the workings of, 155; Balint on, 109, 114, 121; Bollas on, 162; as central psychoanalytic insight, 71; Heimann on, 159–60, 165; Joseph on, 165–67; Klein on, 166; as matrix of thought, 71; updating standard conceptions, 4, 6, 156–57
transitional experiences/objects, 8–10
trauma, 20–21
Trent, W. P., 207n32

unintegration, 36, 38–39, 44

Victorian fiction/novels/studies: "basic fault," 148; British object relations thought, 4, 12–17, 151–52; British psychoanalysis, 16; colonial foundations, 110 (see also British empire); colonial object relations, 148; fault lines, 13; genera and trauma, 20–21; geopolitics of, 12–15; relational reading, 5–7 (see also relational reading); resistance of relationality, 2; Winnicott, 39

Watson, Tim, 239n6
weariness. See deadness/weariness
Weber, Samuel, 59
Wheatcroft, Andrew, 140
Williams, Raymond, 108, 111, 130
Winnicott, Donald W.: absence, 193; "aliveness"/"deadness," 154; baby, no such thing as, 7; biographical material, 7, 23; Bollas, 42–43; capacity to be alone/"The Capacity to Be Alone," 10, 18, 23, 28–29, 35–36; companionship, 70; "Controversial Discussions," 149; creative living, 8; dissemination of psychoanalysis, 16; epigraph, 153; Freud, 24; the holding environment, 206n24, 226n21; Klein, 38, 151, 205n1; loneliness, 205n1; maternal element, analysis and, 40–42, 44; maternal gaze, 211n65; "Middle"/"Independent" position, 209n53; Middlemarch, 19; popularity, 150, 201n11; psychoanalysis, new ideas about, 6; relational solitude, 17–18, 23–24; sanity, 209n57; a single word has more than one opposite, 223n4; surveillance, 27; "True Self," 13; "unintegration," 38–39; universalizing claims, 199n2; "unthinkable anxieties"/"agonies," 11; Victorian novel and the work of, 39
wishfulness, 68, 81–82, 100, 107
Woloch, Alex, 35, 208n44
Wood, Michael, 224n4
Woolf, Leonard, 16, 204n41
Woolf, Virginia, 16, 50–52, 82, 164, 217n68
Wright, Daniel, 183

Zeavin, Lynne, 212n4
Zhang, Dora, 15, 116, 223n3, 226n17–18
Zieger, Susan, 239n15

A NOTE ON THE TYPE

This book has been composed in Arno, an Old-style serif typeface in the classic Venetian tradition, designed by Robert Slimbach at Adobe.

CPSIA information can be obtained
at www.ICGtesting.com
Printed in the USA
LVHW032356250322
714338LV00002B/2

9 780691 234598